# WISCONSIN INDIAN LITERATURE

# WISCONSIN INDIAN LITERATURE

## ANTHOLOGY OF NATIVE VOICES

EDITED BY
## Kathleen Tigerman

FOREWORD BY
## Jim Ottery

THE UNIVERSITY OF WISCONSIN PRESS

This book was funded in part by a grant from the Wisconsin Humanities Council, with funds from the National Endowment for the Humanities and the State of Wisconsin. Any views, findings, conclusions, or recommendations expressed in this project do not necessarily represent those of the National Endowment for the Humanities. The Wisconsin Humanities Council supports public programs that engage the people of Wisconsin in the exploration of human cultures, ideas, and values.

wisconsin | humanities | council
*community through conversation*

The University of Wisconsin Press
1930 Monroe Street
Madison, Wisconsin 53711

www.wisc.edu/wisconsinpress/

3 Henrietta Street
London WC2E 8LU, England

Library of Congress Cataloging-in-Publication Data
Wisconsin Indian Litrature:
anthology of native voices / edited by Kathleen Tigerman,
foreword by Jim Ottery.
p.     cm.
Includes bibliographical references and index.
ISBN 0-299-22060-5 (cloth: alk. paper)
ISBN 0-299-22064-8 (pbk.: alk. paper)
1. American literature—Indian authors.
2. Indians of North America—Literary collections.
3. Wisconsin—Literary collections.
4. American literature—Wisconsin.   I. Tigerman, Kathleen.
PS508.I5L58        2006
810.8′098970775—dc22        2006008599

The Indian Nations of Wisconsin
Students and Faculty at the University of Wisconsin–Platteville
Dancing Waters Permaculture Co-op

May whatever merit there is in presenting this book
serve to benefit all sentient beings.

# CONTENTS

### PART 4: LITERATURE OF
### THE POTAWATOMI NATION

# LIST OF ILLUSTRATIONS

# FOREWORD

Kathleen Tigerman's decision to compile American Indian history and literature as *Wisconsin Indian Literature: Anthology of Native Voices* is important for ethical and rhetorical reasons. From an ethical standpoint, Tigerman's work allows the Indian authors included in the anthology to engage in an act of survivance, because, as she writes in the introduction, "instead of reading descriptions of Native people, we read their words." The ethical value of presenting literature about American Indians in this way is confirmed by Malea Powell's discussions of Anishinabe (Chippewa) writer and scholar Gerald Vizenor's concept of "survivance." In "Blood and Scholarship: One Mixed-Blood's Story," Powell, who is of Indiana Miami and Eastern Shawnee ancestry, interprets "survivance" as "survival plus resistance."[1] In "Rhetorics of Survivance: How American Indians *Use* Writing," Powell extends the interpretation by writing that a "critical component of the rhetorics of survivance" is to respond to discourses about being an Indian that were written not by Indians but by whites who were either consciously or unconsciously hostile not only to Indian identity, but to Indians' ways of living.[2]

The rhetorical importance of reading about American Indians in their own words is the value that Indians place on all words. American Indians' respect for language is spiritual, whether the language is used to tell traditional stories and histories or in the poetry and prose of the last centuries and this one. This spirituality of and in language suggests that the academic separation of rhetoric and poetic, which has been imprinted in Euro-Western thought since Aristotle, is not a valid construct in discussions about American Indian stories. Every utterance is part of a story for American Indians— whether the story is a "tale" or the story of how language works in the telling and hearing of the tale. When one speaks of stories this way some white scholars object: *stories* are not "true" or they are not "objective." According to these critics American Indian writers and scholars who believe in an intrinsic value of storytelling beyond Euro-Western traditional categories of content and form are essentialists. American Indian writing and Indian authors and scholars have been criticized as being all of the above when they write in their own words about their own experiences.

In "Blood and Scholarship" Powell describes critics who would make the case for the "objective" approach to the suppression of American Indian stories and scholarship by citing Modoc Indian Michael Dorris's conviction that Euro-Western scholars believe that they "hold a virtual monopoly on 'science,' logic, and clear thinking." This insistence on the superiority of positivistic thinking by Western scholars "marks" the work that American Indian writers and scholars do as "hopelessly subjective and biased," according to Dorris, leading to the dismissal of American Indian writing and scholarship as sentimental and "self-serving."[3]

In *Red on Red: Native American Literary Separatism,* Muskogee Creek-Cherokee writer and teacher Craig Womack writes about another type of critic, the postmodern skeptic who dubs American Indian writing as being essentialist. He cites an experience told to him by Abenaki poet Cheryl Savageau: "I never even encountered the word 'essentialist' before coming to grad school, and then it was thrown at me like a dirty word, mostly because I wrote something about Native writers and the land in a paper. It is just now when we are starting to tell our stories that suddenly there is no truth. It's a big cop out as far as I am concerned, a real political move by the mainstream to protect itself from the stories Native people . . . [and other marginalized people] are telling."[4]

Early in the twentieth century, Yankton Sioux Zitkala-Ša was a well-received writer as long as her stories were about her successfully attaining a white man's education. When she started writing down the traditional stories of her people and doing activist writing such as "Why I am a Pagan," which criticized Christianity as a "superstition" that was used against Indians as a weapon of mass assimilation, it was said that she and her writing were displaying "morbidness."[5] According to Deborah Welch, Richard Pratt, founder of the infamous Carlisle Indian boarding school, called her work "trash" and "worse than pagan."[6]

It is interesting to note that all too often white writers use language in order to do rhetorical violence to a group of people or a body of work that represents their lives and struggles. That fact led Ojibwe-Mdewakanton Dakota rhetorician Scott Lyons to write "Rhetorical Sovereignty: What Do American Indians Want from Writing?" in which he states: "[T]he duplicitous interrelationships between writing, violence, and colonization developed during the nineteenth century—not only in the boarding schools but at the signings of hundreds of treaties, most of which were dishonored by whites—would set into motion a persistent distrust of the written word in English, one that resonates in homes and schools and courts of law still today. If our [American Indians'] respect for the Word remains resolute, our faith in the written word is compromised at best."[7]

But in spite of all that, American Indians do have "respect for the Word" and believe there is something true and essential in language and in American Indian stories. N. Scott Momaday in "The Man Made of Words" writes: "I hope to indicate something about the nature of the relationship between language and experience. It seems to me that in a certain sense we are all made of words; that our most essential being consists in language. It is the element in which we think and dream and act, in which we live our daily lives. There is no way in which we can exist apart from the morality of a verbal dimension."[8]

The Euro-Western separation between poetic and rhetoric is partially explained away by Momaday when he transcribes the oral traditional story of "The Arrowmaker." Momaday remembers his father telling him the story about a Kiowa warrior who defends his wife and home as he is in the process of making arrows. But according to Momaday, the true value of the story beyond the traditional plot is that it is also a story about the importance of language. When he has finished telling the story Momaday explains:

> It is important that the story of the arrowmaker returns in a special way upon itself. It is about language, after all, and it is therefore part and parcel of its own subject. Virtually, there is no difference between the telling and that which is told. The point of the story lies not so much in what the arrowmaker does, but what he says . . . he speaks, and in so doing he places his very life in balance.
>
> It is this aspect of the story which interests me the most, for it is here we are very close to the origin and object of literature; here our sense of the verbal dimension is very keen, and we are aware of something in the nature of language that is at once perilous and compelling. . . . Everything is ventured in . . . [a] simple declaration, which is also a question and a plea.

The story of the arrowmaker is a tale that Western critics would categorize as literary or poetic, and it is that. But it is also rhetorical if one takes the definition of rhetoric beyond Aristotle's "finding the best available means of persuasion." Since the mid-twentieth century, the definition of rhetoric has expanded and includes understanding and making meaning in language and *epistemology*, which according to the *Cambridge Advanced Learner's Dictionary* is "the study of how we know things."[9] Momaday might respond that epistemology, as he wrote of the story of the arrowmaker, "is about language, after all, and it is therefore part and parcel of its own subject." Speaking (and writing) of these things raises "a question" and makes "a plea."

Craig Womack argues, "Native artistry is not pure aesthetics, or art for art's sake: as often as not Indian writers are trying to *invoke* as much as *evoke*." The *invocation* is spiritual, of course. Womack continues, "The idea behind spiritual chant is that language, spoken in the appropriate ritual contexts, will actually cause a change in the physical universe."[10] The invocation is a plea (for) a spiritual response to a question, but such a plea is also an evocation, a similar summoning of essential force. But the intention of storytellers is to evoke a response in an audience, an evocation of truth.

Momaday writes of the truth-value of stories in the preface to *The Man Made of Words:* "Stories are true to our common experience; they are statements which concern the human condition. To the extent that the human condition involves moral considerations, stories have moral implications. Beyond that, stories are true in that they are established squarely upon belief. In the oral tradition stories are not merely to entertain or instruct; they are told to be believed. Stories are not subject to the imposition of such questions as true or false, fact or fiction. Stories are realities lived and believed. They are true."[11]

The stories in *Wisconsin Indian Literature: Anthology of Native Voices* thusly are true. They serve a purpose that is both poetic and rhetorical in nature: they are invocations and evocations of each of us, for as Momaday writes, "The storyteller says in effect: 'On this occasion I am, for I imagine that I am; and on this occasion you are, for I imagine that you are. And this imagining is the burden of the story, and indeed it is the story.'"

In spirit with the deep respect for language felt by American Indians as described above, Kathleen Tigerman has collected to preserve and present the stories of Wisconsin Indians. While Craig Womack was writing his dissertation at the University of Oklahoma, he was concerned that doing the ethnographic work of studying people and their cultures would turn them into objects of study, thus objectifying them. It can be done if the people are allowed to "speak" for themselves. All of the American Indian scholars, even those who are not Indian, cited in this foreword have found ways to represent the depth of humanity of American Indians. As Kathleen Tigerman does the same, my wish for the readers of her *Wisconsin Indian Literature* is that you approach these stories with the respect in which they were first told and with which they have been collected. Consider the humanity that is reflected in the storyteller's cause: "I imagine I am," and in that you, the reader, is "imagined you are." Do not just read these stories, but do as Malea Powell suggests: "*listen* to the texts," listen to the voices in these stories of Indian identity and Indians' ways of living.[12] Consider that "our most essential being consists in language" and experience both writing and reading, the writers' intentions and stories and your attention to both, as acts of survivance for individual American Indian identities and native people's ways of life.

DR. JIM OTTERY

# ACKNOWLEDGMENTS

This work was a collaborative effort by many people and would not exist except for the care, generosity, and knowledge of its many contributors. I chose the excerpts based on a number of criteria: their literary excellence, their historical significance, or their insight into issues of sovereignty as mandated in Act 31. Though I removed some proposed selections by request, I also included others based on individual or collective requests. Overall, I tried to balance historical issues, oral traditions, and early and contemporary fiction and poetry.

I made a concerted effort to obtain permission from each author, but in some cases I was unable to reach him or her. In all cases, I obtained permission from the copyright holder, often the publisher. I consulted with tribal elders and authors from each nation about permission and acceptability. I would like to thank all contributors for allowing me to include their pieces.

My heart-felt appreciation goes first to Dr. Verna Fowler, president of the College of the Menominee Nation, who read the volume in its entirety and wrote letters of support to The University of Wisconsin Press. Her praise and criticisms guided me in the long and challenging process of assembling the pieces presented here. Dr. Cathy Caldwell read the manuscript and contributed her poetic voice to this volume. Wisconsin Poet Laureate and University of Wisconsin-Green Bay Professor Denise Sweet read an early draft of my proposal, sharing her sensitivity to tone and diction in the selection she read.

Dr. Patty Loew, Bad River Ojibwe, was generous with her time and knowledge in looking over the first draft. She deftly influenced me to focus my attention on the current Indian Nations of Wisconsin, rather than including all of the Nations who had once inhabited this territory. She challenged my selections for the section on Ojibwe literature, which enabled me to clarify that I was using a broad definition of literature.

Many other individuals made various contributions. Ada Deer provided input on inclusion in the Menominee section. Her description of her experience as the first Native woman to serve as Assistant Secretary, Bureau of Indian Affairs, opened my eyes to the difficulties of being in such a powerful position.

Of the Ho-Chunk, I am indebted to Susette LaMere-Arentz of the Ho-Chunk Cultural Resources Division, whose wisdom was of personal help to me. Truman Lowe, curator of the National Museum of the American Indian and professor in the art department of the University of Wisconsin at

Madison, graciously allowed me to interview him as he shared his insights into the Gottschall Rockshelter.

Dr. Robert Salzer answered many questions I had about the Gottschall Rockshelter, while Aaron Naumann, tool-kit specialist on this site, tutored me in archaeological concepts and approaches, besides making a well-received visit to my Wisconsin Indian Literature class at the University of Wisconsin–Platteville.

Regarding other archeological material, I am indebted to Nancy Oestreich Lurie, outstanding researcher and emerita head curator of the Milwaukee Public Museum, who critiqued two of my papers and gave me advice and articles pertinent to this text. I am also grateful to Claudia Jacobson of the Milwaukee Public Museum, whose careful scholarship was instrumental in clarifying archival Potawatomi material.

Dr. Danielle Hornett, professor emerita of St. Norbert College, contributed to the development of the Ojibwe section. Dr. Carol Cornelius, director of the Oneida Nation of Wisconsin Cultural Heritage Department, was a wise and knowledgeable consultant on the Oneida section. Dorothy Davids and Dr. Ruth Gudinas were careful, generous, and gracious in their guidance of the Stockbridge-Munsee section. Caroline Andler, Brothertown genealogist, and Dr. Jim Ottery contributed their knowledge and time to develop the very challenging Brothertown section.

A committee composed of members of the Sawyer County Historical Society and the Lac Courte Oreilles Ojibwe Community College in Hayward, Wisconsin, provided maps, advice, photos, personal histories, and books about the flooding of Pahquahwong. I am grateful to all of them.

In response to the generosity of these people and many others, I have established the Ingrid Washinawatok Speakers Fund, to be administrated by the College of the Menominee Nation, to support educators and elders whose voices need to be heard in the classroom. Ingrid Washinawatok, a Menominee activist working with the U'wa Nation in Colombia to develop a school system and to block oil drilling on sacred land, was kidnapped and killed by FARC (Revolutionary Armed Forces of Colombia). In recognition of her spirit, I am dedicating a majority of the royalties from this book to the fund bearing her name.

I acknowledge with gratitude my debt to John Berg, Bob Birmingham, Dave Bissonette, Robert Boszhardt, Alan Caldwell, June Ezold, Carmen Faymonville, Geoffrey Gyrisco, Nick and Char Hockings, Lyle Koehler, Shirley LaFleur, Ric LaMartina, J. P. Leary, Dennis Lenzendorff, Larry Martin, Bobbie Malone, Sue Menzel, Maura Otis, Caryl Pfaff, Saxon St. Germaine, Jerry Smith, Ray Spoto, Theodore Stephenson, James Theler, Andi Wittwer, the Wisconsin Institute on Race and Ethnicity, and the Dean's Fund of the College of Liberal Arts and Education at the University of Wisconsin–Platteville. I am grateful for the unswerving support from the editors and staff of the University of Wisconsin Press, especially Raphael Kadushin, Sheila

Moermond, Adam Mehring, Andrea Christofferson, Benson Gardner, Sheila Leary, and the numerous others who have helped over the years.

I am grateful for my former students: Theresa Schultz, whose energy and assertiveness provoked and stimulated; Amber Lenzendorff, who helped me assemble illustrations; and William Kunst, who guided me through computer problems. I presented much of the material in this book to five successive classes of undergraduates at the University of Wisconsin–Platteville, where I teach in the humanities department. These students contributed fresh outlooks and stimulating questions.

None of this work would have been possible without my experience of living in an intentional community, Dancing Waters Permaculture Cooperative, which taught me the difficulties and rewards of consensus decision-making and collective ownership. To my husband, Carl Arthur Schlecht, and his indefatigable joy, I owe an incalculable debt.

My gratitude goes to all these people and to all the contributors to this volume for their kindness, generosity, and support. It is because of their contributions that this text came into being. All merit belongs to them; the faults are mine alone.

## The Twelve Indian Nations and Bands of Wisconsin, ca. 2000 AD

| NATION/BAND | DESCRIPTION | LINGUISTIC GROUP |
| --- | --- | --- |
| Menominee | Most ancient residents, inheritors of prehistoric Copper Culture | Algonquian |
| Ho-Chunk (Winnebago) | Ancient residents of Wisconsin | Siouan |
| Ojibwe (Chippewa): Lac Courte Oreilles (LCO) [la-coo'-dor-ray] Bad River Red Cliff Lac du Flambeau [lac'-du-flam'-bow] St. Croix [saint-croy] Sokaogon (Mole Lake) [se-CO-gn] | The Anishinabe came from the eastern seaboard. They are the largest Native group in Wisconsin and are organized into six independent bands. | Algonquian |
| Potawatomi | Originally along Lake Michigan shore | Algonquian |
| Oneida | Member of Iroquois Confederacy | Iroquoian |
| Stockbridge-Munsee Band of Mohican | From northeastern US | Algonquian |
| Brothertown | Comprised of seven communities: Mohegan, Mashantucket, Montauk, Algonquian Stonington, Farmington, Niantic, Charlestown | Algonquian |

## Historic Nations That Once Resided in Present-Day Wisconsin, pre-2000 AD

| NATION | DATE | LINGUISTIC GROUP |
| --- | --- | --- |
| Mdewakanton Dakota (Mystic Lake Sioux) | Indigenous in Wisconsin; also called Santee Sioux | Siouan |
| Sauk | Moved from the East in 1600s | Algonquian |
| Mesquakie (Fox) | Moved from the East in 1600s | Algonquian |
| Mascouten | Moved from the East in 1600s | Algonquian |
| Kickapoo | Moved from the East in 1600s | Algonquian |
| Illinois | Moved through Wisconsin in 1600s | Algonquian |
| Miami | Moved from the East in 1600s | Algonquian |
| Ottawa (Odawa) | Entered Wisconsin in 1600s | Algonquian |
| Ioway (Iowa) | Inheritors of prehistoric Oneota tradition | Chiwere-Siouan |
| Tionontati (Tobacco/Petun) | Driven west by Iroquois confederacy | Iroquoian |
| Huron | Fled Iroquois confederacy; in WI in 1650s | Iroquoian |

# Prehistoric Cultures of Wisconsin
## in Reverse Chronological Order

| ERA | CULTURE; ARTIFACT | DESCRIPTION |
| --- | --- | --- |
| AD 1000–historic | **Oneota**<br>Upper Mississippian<br>Pottery:<br>　Orr Phase<br>　Oneota shell-tempered | Fortified Cities and Village Farms<br>Village farming communities sited near<br>　water. Oneotans cultivated corn, beans,<br>　and squash and gathered many wild plants,<br>　besides hunting deer, elk, and bison. Some<br>　villages were large and fortified. Probable<br>　ancestors of the Ho-Chunk & Ioway. |
| AD 1000 – AD 1200 | **Mississippian**<br>Aztalan and Trempeleau<br>　Hopewell Culture<br>Platform Mounds<br>*The Epic of Red Horn*<br>Gottschall Mural<br>Sculpted Head from Gottschall<br>　Rockshelter | Platform Mounds and Astronomical<br>　Observatory<br>Intrusive culture of the hierarchical Hopewell<br>　to the south who built large platform<br>　mounds and astronomical observatories.<br>　Probable artists of the Red Horn Mural<br>　from Gottschall Rockshelter. |
| AD 600–AD 1200 | **Late Woodland**<br>Effigy Mounds | Effigy Mound Culture<br>Earthen mounds built in animal shapes,<br>　effigy mounds had spiritual purposes,<br>　marked territory, and sometimes were used<br>　for burials. |
| AD 500 | Figure with bow painted at<br>　Gottschall Rockshelter earlier<br>　than the Red Horn mural. | Small, corner-notched points indicate<br>　introduction of the bow and arrow, which<br>　replaced the spear. Squash planted and<br>　wild rice gathered. |
| 100 BC–AD 600 | **Middle Woodland**<br>Spearpoints:<br>　McCoy Corner-Notched<br>　Steuben Expanding Stem<br>　Hopewell Platform Pipes | Hopewell: Large Circular Burial Mounds<br>This phase is linked to the Hopewell Culture:<br>　Large burial mounds were circular and<br>　conical, containing multiple burials. People<br>　constructed houses with posts set in holes,<br>　gathered wild rice, and hunted deer. |
| 800 BC–100 BC | **Early Woodland**<br>Spearpoints:<br>　McCoy Corner-Notched<br>　Kramer<br>　Waubesa Contracting | Pottery and Corn Cultivation<br>First use of pottery matched an increase in the<br>　cultivation of plants. Starting with squash,<br>　Early Woodland people also cultivated<br>　sunflower, sumpweed, goosefoot, knotweed,<br>　and corn. |
| 1200 BC–100 BC | **Late Archaic**<br>Spearpoints:<br>　Preston Notched<br>　Monona Stemmed<br>　Durst Stemmed | Red Ocher Burials<br>The appearance of new point styles,<br>　small-stemmed and corner-notched,<br>　coincided with a significant use of native<br>　copper. Regional exchange networks<br>　brought exotic materials into the area.<br>　Sometimes adorned with red powder, the<br>　dead were buried in cemeteries with grave<br>　goods of large ceremonial knives made of<br>　exotic flint. |

| | | |
|---|---|---|
| 4200 BC–1200 BC | **Middle Archaic**<br>Spearpoints:<br>    Matanzas<br>    Raddatz<br>    Osceola<br>    Oconto<br>    Reigh<br>    Madison | Old Copper Complex<br>Large side-notched projectile or knife points appear, along with other technological innovations. One of the oldest metal-working traditions in the world appears in northern Wisconsin: The people of the Copper Culture complex mined and smelted pure copper nuggets left behind by the glacier. A time of warmth and dryness, these conditions favored interspersed woodland and prairies, making rich habitat for deer and elk. The people of the Old Copper Culture were ancestors of the Menominee. |
| 8000 BC–4200 BC | **Early Archaic**<br>Spearpoints:<br>    Hardin Barbed<br>    St. Charles Notched<br>    Thebes Notched<br>    Bifurcate Base | Modern Plants and Animals Appear<br>Subsistence was based on hunting and gathering of modern plants and animals such as elk, deer, and rabbits. The dead were buried in natural knolls. Stemmed and notched projectile points appeared. |
| 8000 BC–5500 BC | **Late Paleo-Indian**<br><br>Spearpoints:<br>    Agate Basin<br>    Hell Gap<br>    Holcombe<br>    Hi-Lo<br>    Cody Complex | Bison Hunters<br>Partly coincides with Early Archaic culture<br>With the mass extinction of very large animals that coincided with the glacier's retreat, big game hunters changed to bison hunting, with unfluted spear points perhaps reflecting this change. The points from this era were stemmed, and adze made their appearance. |
| 10,000 BC–8000 BC | **Early Paleo-Indian**<br>Spearpoints:<br>    Clovis<br>    Folsom<br>    Gainey | Mammoth Hunters<br>The earliest known people followed big game such as mammoths and mastodons on the edge of the retreating glacier in small, mobile hunting groups, using a fluted spearpoint fastened to a short foreshaft and main shaft: the atlatl. Point and foreshaft were designed to separate from the main shaft after a successful strike. The fluting is a longitudinal gouge taken out of the middle of the "flat" surfaces of the points. The Gainey point associated with the Boaz mastodon was made of the prized Hixton orthoquartzite obtained from eighty miles to the NNW of Boaz in southwestern Wisconsin. |

*Editor's note:* The editor respectfully acknowledges that Native people often use a thematic or circular organization in their historical and literary accounts. However, she feels that a chronological outline, as provided in the above three tables, will be useful for some non-Native readers.

# WISCONSIN INDIAN LITERATURE

# Wisconsin Indian Lands Today

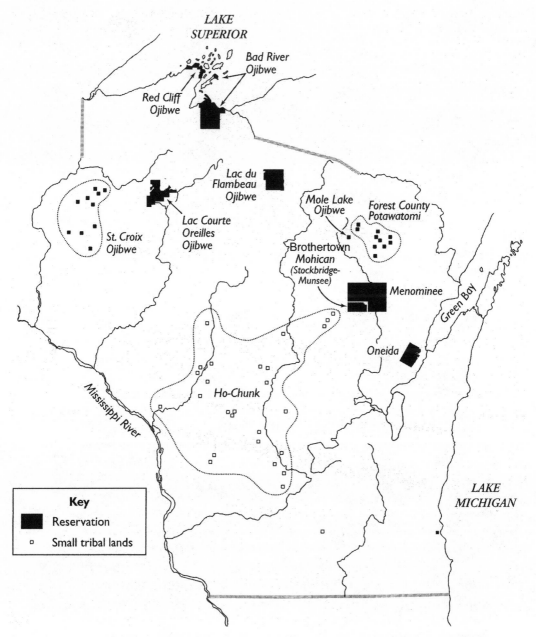

The twelve Indian Nations and independent bands in the state of Wisconsin circa 2006 are the Menominee, Ho-Chunk (Winnebago), Potawatomi, Oneida, Stockbridge-Munsee Band of the Mohican, Brothertown, and the seven independent bands of the Ojibwe (Chippewa): St. Croix, Red Cliff, Bad River, Lac du Flambeau, Lac Courte Oreilles, and Mole Lake (Sokaogon). Reproduced by permission of the Wisconsin Historical Society from Wisconsin Cartographers' Guild and Bobbie Malone, *Mapping Wisconsin History* (Madison: Wisconsin Historical Society Press, 2000), 35.

# Introduction

KATHLEEN TIGERMAN

*Wisconsin Indian Literature: Anthology of Native Voices* presents literature by Wisconsin's Indigenous peoples. Although this collection is the first of its kind, it nonetheless draws from sources that are millennia old and that continue in many forms into the present day. This anthology is rich because Wisconsin has a great number of Indigenous Nations and independent bands: Menominee, Ho-Chunk (formerly Winnebago), Potawatomi, Oneida, Stockbridge-Munsee Band of Mohican Indians, Brothertown, and six independent bands of the Ojibwe or Chippewa Nation: St. Croix, Lac Courte Oreille, Red Cliff, Bad River, Lac du Flambeau, and Sokaogon (Mole Lake). This collection exists because of the cooperation and generosity of the Native people from these Wisconsin Nations.

In contrast to many of the materials on Wisconsin Indians now in print that take a social science or historical approach, this collection presents works of literature, using a broad definition that includes historical narratives, oratory from treaty signings and other historical events, autobiography, creation stories, poetry, short stories, and excerpts from novels. Instead of reading descriptions of Native people, we read their words, although in some cases we are reading their translators' words. While some of our contributors are working in a foreign language—English—others are dealing with an *audience* that is culturally foreign. Compounding the issue of cross-cultural communication is the difficulty of capturing the richness of varied oral traditions and wrestling them into written forms. These difficulties are just some of the issues involved in this attempt at a respectful approach to the Native literature of Wisconsin.

Literature does not exist in a vacuum. It depends upon geography, history, and culture; it is mediated through persons marked by ethnicity, gender, age, and status; and it is edited and read by persons similarly marked by these formative conditions. In spite of or because of these differences, all Wisconsin citizens need to have some knowledge of the historical roots of how Indigenous Nations exist within the borders of the state. My intention in presenting these selections is to respectfully share Native knowledge and discussions on many issues, especially those involving sovereignty and decolonization. I have provided a headnote preceding each literature selection so that readers may understand the excerpt in a general historical context or gain familiarity with an author's background. In some cases, I found that a brief, powerful excerpt may require lengthy framing material but can otherwise stand on its own. For a good overview of Wisconsin's Native history and peoples, I recommend that readers consult Patty Loew's *Indian Nations of Wisconsin* and *Native People of Wisconsin* and Nancy Oestreich Lurie's *Wisconsin Indians*.

The political and social astuteness of the Native people over centuries of colonization, genocide, massacres, forced removals, forced adoptions, assimilation, and other forms of cultural genocide is evident throughout the following pages. This book attempts to redress the general silence in the texts comprising the Americanist canon regarding Native literature, while focusing on ongoing issues identified by Native communities of Wisconsin.

One way these communities have made their voices heard is through the enactment of Wisconsin Senate Act 31, which mandates the teaching of the meaning of Native sovereignty, history, and culture at grade levels in all Wisconsin schools and training in this material by all licensed teachers in the state. Act 31 is only a part of the Native response to the spearfishing controversy in northern Wisconsin occurring during the 1970s, when racist attacks were made on Ojibwe spearers exercising their treaty rights.

Native elders and educators saw the matrix of this crisis as partly owing to the lack of knowledge by most non-Natives of inherent Native sovereignty rights—rights that have not been annihilated by colonialist takings. Although Act 31 was passed into law in 1989, the majority of students taking my course on Wisconsin Indian literature at the University of Wisconsin–Platteville have not been exposed to basic information about the Indian Nations and bands of the state, nor are they aware of the rich body of traditional stories and contemporary writings by members of the Indian Nations of Wisconsin. This text supplies selections from that body of literature.

Some Native stories refer to very ancient times. Over six thousand years ago, the ancestors of the Menominee people, whose territory included over nine million acres from Lake Michigan to the Mississippi River, mined copper from northern Wisconsin, the southern and northern shores of western Lake Superior, and the Keweenaw Peninsula of Upper Michigan. Implements from this Old Copper Culture are spread throughout the state but are concentrated in the state's north and east. At its height, this metalworking tradition was one of the most highly developed in the world. This cultural technology produced, through cold-hammering and annealing, an incredible array of tools and decorations, such as awls, axes, beads, drills, hooks, harpoons, and many other implements made from the pure native copper nuggets and veins left behind by the retreat of the Wisconsin glacier and mined by ancestors of the Menominee.[1] The Menominee creation story tells of the first Menominee man, who was a copper-tailed bear before his transformation.

# From Treaty Lands to Tribal Lands Today

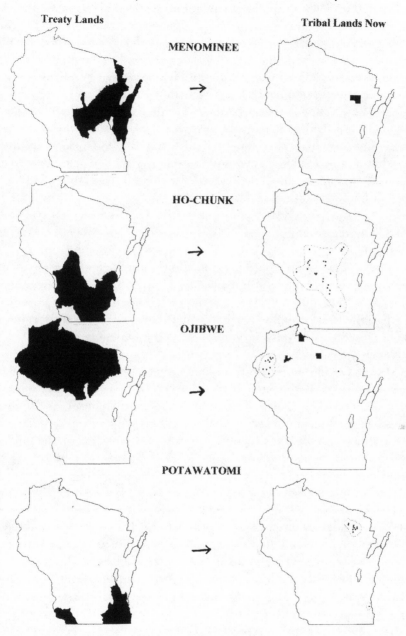

The shrinking of the land base from AD 1800 to AD 2000 for four of the current twelve Wisconsin Indian Nations and independent bands represents significant losses. Many nations were forced out of Wisconsin, such as the Mdewakantonwon Santee Dakota, who had resided in northwest Wisconsin for centuries, but who remain dispossessed of their ancestral land. Adapted from Wisconsin Cartographers' Guild and Bobbie Malone, *Mapping Wisconsin History* (Madison: Wisconsin Historical Society Press, 2000).

Menominee literature has many stories involving a cultural hero who brings gifts but is also a shape-shifting trickster: Manabozho, also called Me'napus, Nanabozho, or Winabojo, meaning Great White Rabbit. Menominee literature is represented here by history and oral traditions told by Verna Fowler, president of the College of the Menominee Nation near Keshena, and other contemporary and classic Menominee storytellers.

The last selection in the Menominee section is by Ingrid Washinawatok, a delegate to the United Nations in 1992. An activist working with the U'wa Nation in Colombia to develop a school system and to block oil drilling on sacred land, she was kidnapped and killed by FARC (Revolutionary Armed Forces of Colombia). In recognition of her spirit, I have established the Ingrid Washinawatok Speakers Fund, administrated by the College of the Menominee Nation, to support educators and elders whose voices need to be heard in the classroom. A majority of the royalties from this book is dedicated to the fund.

A focus of part 1 involves the termination of the Menominee Reservation and the subsequent reestablishment of reservation status. This struggle propelled Ada Deer, now a professor at the University of Wisconsin–Madison, into prominence for organizing work that contributed toward restoration. She became the first Native woman to head the Bureau of Indian Affairs in Washington, D.C.

After the Menominee had been here for millennia, ancestors of the Ho-Chunk (formerly Winnebago) arrived in present-day Wisconsin. They returned again and again to a place in southwestern Wisconsin now known as Gottschall Rockshelter.[2] One thousand years ago, after scraping part of the rock wall and ceiling, they painted a mural that members of the modern-day Ho-Chunk Nation recognize as the story of Red Horn, a hero of the Ho-Chunk, Ioway, Dakota, and other Siouan-speaking peoples. This panel is interpreted as representing a scene from the oral tradition of Red Horn.[3] This rock formation is a premier archaeological site in North America and provides a bridge between the silent artifacts dug from the earth and the living speakers who inhabit that ideological space. Truman Lowe, a Ho-Chunk professor of art at the University of Wisconsin–Madison and contemporary curator of the National Museum of the American Indian in Washington, D.C., described the Red Horn panel and Gottschall Rockshelter as a "library" of Ho-Chunk knowledge.[4]

Ho-Chunk literature is represented here in part 2 by selections from the *Epic of Red Horn*, from the autobiography of a modern-day Ho-Chunk, Mountain Wolf Woman, and from classic trickster tales.

Part 3, the extensive Ojibwe section representing the six independent bands in Wisconsin, includes material about the building of a dam on Pokagama Creek that deliberately flooded the Ojibwe village of Pahquahwong in 1921. The flooding inundated homes and gardens, disturbed graves, and destroyed rice beds to create the artificial Chippewa Flowage and produce electricity for customers in Minnesota.[5] The Ojibwe section addresses many issues, including spearfishing, which was the matrix for the development of Wisconsin Act 31.

The Potawatomi, a member of the Three Fires Confederacy along with the Ojibwe and Odawa (Ottawa), met the Menominee in the sixteenth century as the Potawatomi settled around the southern rim of Lake Michigan. Part 4 on Potawatomi literature stresses the oral tradition and its modern rough equivalent, the Web, with excerpts from the Potawatomi home page offering history, oral tradition, and contemporary poetry.

Three sovereign nations—Oneida, Stockbridge-Munsee Band of Mohican, and Brothertown—joined Menominee, Ho-Chunk, Ojibwe, and Potawatomi in the early 1820s after the state of New York entered into a series of fraudulent leases and treaties that took Native holdings. The Oneida were and are members of the Haudenosaunee, or League of Six Nations, sometimes called the Iroquois Confederacy. This tradition abounds in ancient sources, particularly the oration by the prophet Deganawida, who proclaimed the Great Law of Peace. The Great Law, whose ritual retelling takes over a week, is the foundation "document" of the Haudenosaunee, dating back to the 1300s; excerpts from the Great Law are offered in part 5.

Wisconsin Oneida were delighted when some green notebooks were found in the University of Wisconsin–Madison anthropology building in 1999. A Federal Writers Project of the WPA of the 1930s collected stories by Oneida speakers; these notebooks, translated by contemporary Oneida speakers and historians, yielded several selections presented in this collection.

Although the Oneida helped George Washington's troops survive at Valley Forge by sharing scarce food supplies, the state of New York took Oneida land, forcing them to move to Wisconsin. In a similar situation—landless after they had fought on the American side in the Revolutionary War—the Stockbridge-Munsee band of the Mohican Nation were offered land in Wisconsin by the Oneida.

The literature of the Stockbridge-Munsee Band of Mohican, found in part 6, reflects the early struggles of the indigenous peoples of the Atlantic seaboard with successive waves of invaders: native diplomacy and oratory in the face of colonial onslaughts ring with power, pain, and perseverance. This section is enlivened by a contemporary children's story based on a classic historical text: Kristina Heath Potrykus's text (minus the illustrations) brings the old words to the present. Dorothy W. Davids, chair of the Stockbridge-Munsee Historical Committee, retells their history; an excerpt from contemporary storyteller Eva Jean Bowman celebrates famous warrior Chief Nimham.

The Brothertown Nation of Wisconsin is a community comprising seven Nations from the eastern seaboard: Mohegan, Mashantucket, Stonington, and Farmington from Connecticut, Charlestown and Niantic from Rhode Island, and Montauk from Long Island, along with Pequot influences. Under hostile pressure from Euro-American colonies, they organized under the leadership of Samson Occum and emigrated from their homelands. Besides the fine oratory of these groups discussing issues with the Dutch, British, English, and American colonialists, part 7 also includes a brief history available at the Web site of the Brothertown Nation.

Although the contents of this collection are from different languages and cultures, they all speak of our relationship with each other and with the sentient Earth. These words are gifts—gifts that should be reciprocated by respectful attention. The First People's presence in the Americas predates the European invasion of this continent by twenty-seven millennia. Native people lived in what is now called Wisconsin twelve millennia ago. Their descendants live here still, speaking to all who choose to listen.

1

# Literature of the
# Menominee Nation

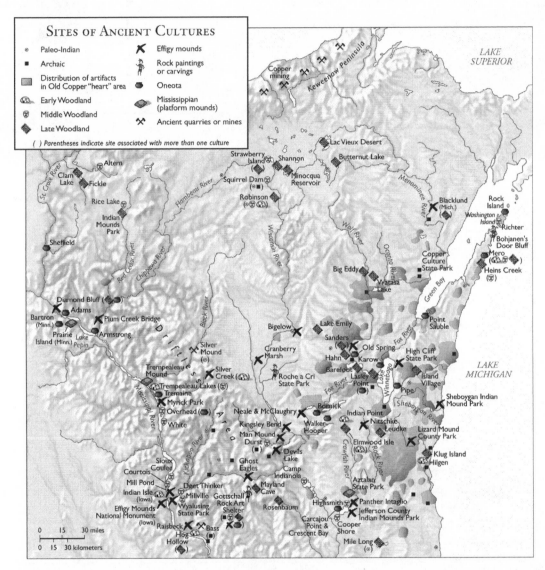

## SITES OF ANCIENT CULTURES

- ⊙ Paleo-Indian
- ■ Archaic
- ▦ Distribution of artifacts in Old Copper "heart" area
- 🐚 Early Woodland
- ◉ Middle Woodland
- ◆ Late Woodland
- ✗ Effigy mounds
- 🏃 Rock paintings or carvings
- 🐚 Oneota
- ◈ Mississippian (platform mounds)
- ⚒ Ancient quarries or mines

( ) Parentheses indicate site associated with more than one culture

*LAKE SUPERIOR*

*LAKE MICHIGAN*

Copper mining — Keweenaw Peninsula

Lac Vieux Desert
Strawberry Island
Shannon
Butternut Lake
Copper
Minocqua Reservoir
Squirrel Dam
Robinson
Blacklund (Mich.)
Rock Island
Washington Island
Richter
Bohjanen's Door Bluff
Mero
Heins Creek
Copper Culture State Park
Big Eddy
Watasa Lake
Point Sauble
Diamond Bluff
Adams
Bartron (Minn.)
Plum Creek Bridge
Prairie Island (Minn.)
Armstrong
Bigelow
Lake Emily
Sanders
Old Spring
High Cliff State Park
Hahn
Karow
Barefoot
Island Village
Silver Mound
Silver Creek
Roche a Cri State Park
Lacley Point
Pipe
Trempealeau Mound
Trempealeau Lakes
Tremaine
Myrick Park
Overhead
White
Neale & McClaughry
Bornick
Indian Point
Sheboygan Indian Mound Park
Kingsley Bend
Walker Hooper
Nitschke
Leudke
Lizard Mound County Park
Man Mound
Durst
Elmwood Isle
Klug Island Hilgen
Sioux Coulee
Ghost Eagles
Devils Lake
Camp Indianola
Aztalan State Park
Courtois
Mill Pond
Indian Isle (Iowa)
Deer Thinker
Mayland Cave
Millville
Gottschall
Rock Art Shelter
Rosenbaum
Highsmith
Panther Intaglio
Jefferson County Indian Mounds Park
Effigy Mounds National Monument (Iowa)
Wyalusing State Park
Raisbeck
Bass
Carcajou Point & Crescent Bay
Cooper Shore
Hog Hollow
Mile Long

St. Croix River
Clam Lake
Altern
Fickle
Rice Lake
Indian Mounds Park
Sheffield
Red Cedar River
Chippewa River
Flambeau River
Wisconsin River
Wolf River
Oconto River
Menominee River
Green Bay
Fox River
Lake Winnebago
Sheboygan River
Black River
Mississippi River
Lake Pepin
Kickapoo River
Crawfish River
Rock River

0    15    30 miles
0    15    30 kilometers

Ten thousand years ago, people lived in what is called Wisconsin today. Ancestors of the Menominee people developed highly skilled metallurgy five thousand years ago. Today this culture is known as the Old Copper Culture. Other ancient inhabitants were ancestors of the Ho-Chunk (Winnebago), who resided in Wisconsin for thousands of years, building effigy mounds from AD 400 through AD 1300. Effigy mounds are large sculptures made of dirt, often in the shape of a bird or animal. A huge Thunderbird with a wingspan of one-quarter mile once graced Muscoda, north of the Wisconsin River. "Ghost Eagle" is the name given to a bird effigy mound that has been destroyed by plowing or plundering. Map by Amelia R. Janes; reproduced by permission from Wisconsin Cartographers' Guild, *Wisconsin's Past and Present* (Madison: University of Wisconsin Press, 1998), 3.

# Creation Story

VERNA FOWLER, MENOMINEE

*The Menominee are the oldest residents of the place now known as Wisconsin, and a possible source of the state's name. "Wis-coo-she," which means "a good place to live" in the Menominee language, eventually became "Wisconsin."[1] Through great effort and cultural integrity, the Menominee have retained a small fraction (¹⁄₃₉) of their original homeland. The ancestors of the present-day Menominee were the first metalworkers in North America, manufacturing copper implements nearly seven thousand years ago. Through the course of millennia, the Old Copper Culture produced a stunning array of tools and decorative pieces: awls, axes, beads, chisels, drills, fishhooks, gaffs, harpoons, and many other items. Native or elemental copper and copper implements were traded all around the Great Lakes region and to the east and south, where some were placed in graves, indicative of their spiritual and material value. One can visit a Copper Culture site: the Old Copper Culture Mounds State Park near Oconto, Wisconsin, where a copper knife dated about six thousand years ago has been found. The site also has the oldest-known cemetery in Wisconsin.[2]*

Maeq-Awaetok (Great Spirit) made the Sun, the stars, and the Earth. Mother Earth gave birth to Keso (the Moon). Then the Moon gave birth to twins, whose work was to finish the creation of the world. Before the people came into the world, the land, rivers, mountains, and lakes were formed. After the plants and animals and other living things had all been made, a great bear with a copper tail arose from the ground beside the Menominee River. As the bear explored the land on which he lived, the Great Spirit changed him into a person. This bear became the first Menominee.

Walking along the river, the bear noticed an eagle flying in the sky. He called out to the eagle, saying, "Come and join me and be my brother." As the bird flew down, the Great Spirit changed him into a Menominee as well.

The two brothers, bear and eagle, continued on their journey. In turn, they came upon the beaver, sturgeon, elk, crane, wolf, dog, and deer. All of them were changed into human beings as well, becoming members of the Menominee tribe.

The bear and eagle were the elder brothers and formed the tribe's major groups, or clans. The earliest Menominee chiefs came from the Bear clan, while the great warriors came out of the Eagle clan.

The Menominee believed that land, like the air, could not be owned. They believed that the land was their mother. She gave them all they needed to live. The land, air, water, plants, and animals were there for them to use. However, they had to use all of those gifts very carefully so that they would be there for the people born in the future.[3]

# The People Who Live with the Seasons

VERNA FOWLER, MENOMINEE

*Verna Fowler recounts how the Menominee came to be known by what another Wisconsin tribe, the Ojibwe, called them. Both the Menominee and Ojibwe languages are part of a large group of related but distinct languages known as Algonquian.[4]*

The Menominee Indians, an Algonquian-speaking woodland tribe, reside on the Menominee Reservation in northeastern Wisconsin. As descendants of Copper Culture people, an ancient indigenous cultural tradition, they are Wisconsin's oldest continuous residents and one of the few tribes east of the Mississippi that inhabit part of their ancestral land. Menominee—the name was conferred on them by the Ojibwe and refers to the *manomin* (wild rice) that (along with sturgeon and maple sugar) was a staple in their diet—referred to themselves as Mamaceqtaw (pronounced ma-ma-CHAY-tua), meaning "the People Who Live with the Seasons."

Menominee land once consisted of 9.5 million acres stretching from Lake Michigan to the Mississippi. The modern 235,000-acre reservation, established in 1934, is home to nearly thirty-five hundred of the tribe's seventy-five hundred enrolled members. The reservation is the largest single tract of timberland in Wisconsin, with an abundance of lakes, streams, and wildlife. The Wolf River, designated for protection in the Wild and Scenic Rivers Act, winds its way through the reservation.

In AD 800 the Winnebago (HoChunk) tribe began its migration from the South onto Menominee lands. Later the Potawatomi and several other tribes arrived from the East. The centuries just prior to European contact saw the arrival of the Sauk and Fox [Mesquakie] Indians. Jean Nicolet, the first European to visit what is now Wisconsin, arrived in 1634 near Green Bay, thus beginning European encroachment into Menominee territory. . . . A structured clan system ensured the tribe's survival amid this influx of newcomers. Five principal clans—Bear, Eagle, Wolf, Crane, and Moose—were divided into various phratries and subphratries, each with specific obligations.[5]

# I.3

# From Native Copper to the Fur Trade

WAIOSKASIT, MENOMINEE

---

*Thinking he had found the Northwest Passage to China, the Frenchman Jean Nicolet disembarked near Green Bay dressed in Chinese robes. The following story describes other misunderstandings. The "sea" mentioned by Waioskasit probably refers to Lake Michigan.*

When the Menominee lived on the shore of the sea, they one day were looking out across the water and observed some large vessels, which were near to them and wonderful to behold. Suddenly there was a terrific explosion, as of thunder, which startled the people greatly.

When the vessels approached the shore, men with light-colored skin landed. Most of them had hair on their faces, and they carried on their shoulders heavy sticks ornamented with shining metal. As the strangers came toward the Indians, the latter believed the leader to be a great manido [spirit], with his companions.

It is customary when offering tobacco to a manido, to throw it into the fire, that the fumes may ascend to him and that he may be inclined to grant their request; but as this light-skin manido came in person, the chief took some tobacco and rubbed it on his forehead. The strangers appeared desirous of making friends with the Indians, and all sat on the ground and smoked. Then some of the strangers brought from the vessel some parcels that contained a liquid, of which they drank, finally offering some to the Menominee. The Indians, however, were afraid to drink such a pungent liquor indiscriminately, fearing it would kill them; therefore four useless old men were selected to drink the liquor, and thus to be experimented on, that it might be found whether the liquid would kill them or not.

The men drank the liquid, and although they had previously been very silent and gloomy, they now began to talk and to grow amused. Their speech flowed more and more freely, while the remainder of the Indians said, "See, now it is beginning to take effect!" Presently the four old men arose, and while walking about seemed very dizzy, when the Indians said, "See, now they are surely dying!" Presently the men dropped down and became unconscious; then the Indians said to one another, "Now they are dead; see what we escaped by not drinking the liquid!" There were sullen looks directed toward the strangers, and murmurings of destroying them for the supposed treachery were heard.

Before things came to a dangerous pass, however, the four old men got up, rubbed their eyes, and approached their kindred, saying, "The liquor is good, and we have felt very happy; you must try it, too." Notwithstanding the rest of the tribe were afraid to drink it then, they recalled the strangers, who were about to return to their boats.

The chief of the strangers next gave the Indians some flour, but they did not know what to do with it. The white chief then showed the Indians some biscuits, and told them how they were baked. When that was over, one of the white men presented to an Indian a gun, after firing it to show how far away anything could be killed. The Indian was afraid to shoot, fearing the gun would knock him over, but the stranger showed the Indian how to hold it and to point it at a mark; then pulling the trigger, it made a terrific noise, but did not harm them. But the kettles were too large and too heavy to carry about, so the Indians asked that they be given small ones—cups as large as a clenched fist, for they believed they would grow to be large ones by and by.

The Indians received some small cups, as they desired, when the strangers took their departure. But the cups never grew to be kettles.[6]

# I.4

# Manabozho and the Wolves

LOUIS PIGEON, MENOMINEE

*A comic character or trickster figure of the Nations of the Great Lakes region has a variety of names, although among the Algonquian languages, these names sound somewhat similar. The Ojibwe call him Nanapush, Nanabush, or Nanabozho, while the Menominee refer to him as Manabus, Me'napus or Manabozho.*

In the spring of the year Manabus was traveling alone by himself and he came to some wolves—an old man and his seven sons. One of them said, "Ha, there is Manabus." The wolves had packs on their backs and they all came and sat down. They were sorry for Manabus, traveling alone, and the oldest said, "Well, Manabus, which way do you go?" Manabus replied, "Everywhere." The wolf asked, "Do you always go alone?" Manabus said, "Yes, there is no one to go with me."

They all sat around and the old wolf looked at the sun. He saw it was about noon and told the oldest boy to go and build a fire. The oldest boy did so, and they made soup of a little game they had with them. Manabus sat waiting patiently to see what they would do.

The old man opened his pack and took out some birch-bark dishes. He had only enough for his family, so he asked one of the boys to look for bark, and he made a dish for Manabus. When everything was ready he dished out the soup and invited Manabus to eat with them. When they had finished he gathered up the dishes, Manabus watched and saw that they packed his dish with theirs, so he supposed that he was to travel with them, but he did not say anything.

The wolves talked among themselves, and when they got ready to go Manabus still sat where he had eaten his soup. He was about to go on his own way, when the old man took his pack on his back and said, "Well, Manabus, you had better come along." Manabus said, "Ho," for he was glad to go with them. He did not know where they were going but followed anyway.

As they were traveling the oldest boy picked up the trail of a deer, ran after the deer and killed it. He came back and told his father he had killed a deer. The old man sharpened a knife and told Manabus to go and skin the deer. Manabus did this, divided the meat, and each had some to carry.

When the sun was getting low the old man said, "We will camp here to-night." All did as they had done at noon. A fire was made and after eating they all smoked around it.

The old man said to one of the boys, "Remove the meat from those bones and grind them fine, for soup," Manabus wondered how the boy could grind bones. The old man was so powerful that he knew what Manabus was thinking, and Manabus was aware of this. Each laughed to himself.

The old man threw a blanket to each and said, "Now cover up your heads." The bones were piled together and the old man did not want them to see how [the bones] were to be prepared. Manabus was curious about this but the old man said very strictly that no one must look out from his blanket. The old man covered his head like the rest, and one of the boys chewed up the bones. Manabus heard the sound, which was terrible; his jaws ached as though he was chewing the bones himself. So he opened his blanket and looked out to see how it was done.

The boy saw Manabus peeking out, and the bone in his hand slipped and struck Manabus in the eye. This caused a sharp pain and the eye turned black. Manabus groaned a little, but did not want to admit that he was hurt. The old man, however, knew at once that something was wrong. The boy stopped chewing the bones and everyone wondered what had happened. They all uncovered their heads and asked why the boy stopped.

Manabus still had his head covered. From under his blanket he said, "My little brothers, what is wrong?"

The old wolf said, "Somebody has peeked, and I think they got hurt because of it." He pulled off the blanket and there was Manabus with his black eye. Manabus began to laugh and said, "Never mind, that was only a joke."

They built a fire, made soup, and had their supper. Then they talked among themselves and went to sleep.

Manabus could not forget how he had been struck in the eye with the bone. All night he thought about it and wondered how he could get his revenge. Finally it occurred to him that he could chew bones as well as the wolf. The next day he told the old wolf that he could chew bones as well as the little wolf.

The old wolf said, "Well, try it."

Manabus told them to cover their heads with their blankets and not peek, but he knew where the wolf sat who had thrown the bone at him. The wolves knew better than to peek. Manabus chewed the bones and after a time he got hold of a knuckle which he threw, hitting a wolf in the eye. This was the wolf who had thrown the bone at him. Manabus said, "The bone slipped."

After a while the wolves got tired of soup made of game. They came to a lake and said, "Now, Manabus, we ask you to get some different meat for our soup."

Manabus said, "I can do it. You wait here and I will get you some ducks."

They waited and Manabus went along the shore. He saw all kinds of ducks out in the middle of the lake. There was red willow growing along the shore and Manabus put a lot of it on his back and walked along the edge of the water. The ducks swam toward him and one shouted, "Manabus, what have you got on your back?"

Manabus replied, "Songs." The duck said, "Sing them." Manabus said, "I must build a brush house first. If you will all come and dance I will sing these songs." The ducks said, "We will come."

Manabus built the brush house in no time at all, and it had only one little opening. Then he said, "All right, friends. If you want to hear the songs you must all walk in here."

After the ducks and all the birds were inside the brush house, Manabus called his friends the wolves to see how he killed his game. They stayed outside the brush house.

Manabus said, "Now, all your little ducks, shut your eyes and I will sing my songs. If you open your eyes you will have little red eyes."

The ducks did as they were told and every little while he would wring a duck's neck and throw it outside to the wolves. The duck said "quack" when he wrung its neck and Manabus would say "That's right, friend. That's the way. You want to quack every little while." A swan was among the ducks and it made more noise than the others. This made the wood duck suspicious, and it opened its eyes a little way. "Manabus is killing us," it cried. Then all the birds tore through the brush house and flew toward the lake. The helldiver was the last, and just as he was going into the water, Manabus put his foot on him, saying, "You will be like a little salt sack after this and have no tail." To the one who peeked, he said, "You will always have red eyes."[7]

# I.5

# Trickster Tales

JOHN V. SATTERLEE, MENOMINEE

*Manabus or Manabozho was the son of a human mother, Wenonah, and a spirit or mani-tou father, the North Wind.*

In the beginning, an old woman lived on an island. Nobody knows where she came from or how she got there, but it is true she dwelt in a wigwam with her only daughter. Wild potatoes were their only food. Every day the old woman took her wooden hoe and went out to gather them. She packed them home and dried them in the sun, for in those old days, fire making was unknown.

One day her daughter begged, "Mother, let me go and help you; between us we can dig more potatoes than you can alone."

"No, my daughter, stay here," said the old woman "Your place is at home caring for the lodge."

"But it's so lonely when you are gone; besides, I could use that old hoe. Please let me go."

At last the old woman agreed. The two armed themselves with their tools and set out. After a little journey they came to a damp ravine. "Here is the place where I always come to gather the potatoes," said the mother; "you can dig here too. But there is one thing that I must warn you about: when you are digging these potatoes, I want you to face the south. Be sure not to forget this. It was because I was afraid that you could not be trusted to remember that I never brought you here before."

"Oh, that's all right, I won't forget," promised the girl.

"Alright then. You stay right here and work; I am going to dig over there."

The girl worked hard, enjoying her task very much. As time passed, the daughter gradually forgot her promise and at last turned round and faced in the opposite direction, to the north, as she dug. Suddenly a great rushing, roaring noise came from the sky, and the wind swept down where she stood and whirled her around. "Oh, mother! Help! Come quick!" she screamed. Her mother dropped everything and rushed to her aid. "Grab me by the back and hold me down!" cried the girl in terror.

The old woman seized her with one hand and steadied herself meanwhile by catching hold of some bushes. "Hold me as tightly as you can!" she gasped. "Now you see why I told you to stay at home! You are being properly punished for your disobedience."

Suddenly the wind stopped. The air was as calm as though nothing had ever happened. The two women hastily gathered up their potatoes and hurried home. But after that the older woman worked alone.

Everything went well for a while, until one day the daughter complained, "I feel very strange and different, mother. There seems to be something within me." Her mother scrutinized the girl, but said nothing, for she knew that her daughter was pregnant by the North Wind. After a while, she gave birth to three children.

The first of these was Manabozho, the second was a little wolf, Muh'wase, and the last was a sharp Flint. When the young woman birthed the stone, it cut her and she bled to death. The old woman deeply mourned her daughter's death. In a fit of rage and grief, she threw away Flint, but Manabozho and Muh'wase she cherished and cared for until they grew up.[8]

# 1.6

# Manabozho Plays Lacrosse

JOHN V. SATTERLEE, MENOMINEE

*Although the birth of Flint killed his mother, Flint is still a gift to humans because it can be used to start a fire. In this story, Manabozho tries to get revenge on the underground manitous who have killed his brother Wolf when he was crossing the ice on a lake, by dragging him underwater. Manabozho is powerful and can transform himself into a tree, or a Great White Rabbit, which is what his name means in the Menominee language.*

The chiefs of the upper world decided to challenge the beings below to a game of lacrosse. The beings below eagerly accepted the challenge and the goals were chosen, one at Detroit and the other at Chicago (Field of Onions). The center of the field was at Ke'sosasit (Where the Sun is Marked on the Rocks) near Sturgeon Bay on Lake Michigan. The above beings called their servants—the thunderers, eagles, geese, ducks, pigeons—and all the birds of the air to play for them, while the great white underground bear called upon the fish, snakes, otters, deer and all the animals of earth to play for the powers below.

As everything was being arranged and the two sides were preparing, Manabozho happened along and heard someone whooping loudly. Running to see who it was, he found a funny little fellow, Nakuti, the sun fish. "What on earth is the matter with you?" Manabozho asked.

"Haven't you heard? Tomorrow we're all playing lacrosse. The fish and animals of the field will be playing for the powers below against the Thunderers and all the birds of the air who are championing the powers above." Nakuti left, whooping with delight.

"I must see this game," thought Manabozho, "even if I wasn't invited."

The next day the underworld chiefs left their homes in the waters and climbed high up on a mountain where they could survey the whole field. Manabozho found their tracks and followed them to their vantage point. Before daybreak he went there and through his magic power changed himself into a tall pine tree, burnt on one side.

At dawn, he heard shouts and derisive voices mocking the enemy. Then the deer, mink, otter, land beings and fish all appeared in human form and

21

took their places on their side of the playing field. All became silent. Suddenly the sky darkened, and the rush of many wings made a thunderous rumbling, above which rose whoops, screams, screeches, cackling, calling, hooting, all in one terrific babble. Then the Thunderers swooped down, the golden eagles, the bald eagles, the buzzards, hawks, owls, pigeons, geese, ducks, and all other birds took the opposite end of the field.

There was silence once more as the sides lined up, the weakest near the goals, the strongest in the center. Someone tossed the ball high in the air and a melee followed, with deafening howling and whooping. Back and forth the players surged, now one side gaining, now the other. At last one side wrested the ball through the other's ranks and sped it toward the Chicago goal. Down the field it went, and Manabozho strained his eyes to follow the ball.

With the ball nearly at the goal, the goalies were rushing to guard it. In the middle of the clubs, legs, arms, and clouds of dust, something was happening that Manabozho could not see. In his excitement, he forgot where and what he was, and he accidentally changed back into a man.

Once he was back in human form, Manabozho came to and noticed that the onlookers had not discovered him. Still wanting revenge on the forces of the underworld because of his brother's death by them, he took his bow which he had kept with him all the time, strung it, and fired twice at each of the underground gods as they sat on their mountain. As his arrows sped to their marks, the gods rushed for the water, falling all over themselves as they rushed downhill. The impact of their diving made great waves roll down the lake towards the Chicago goal. Some of the players saw the huge waves coming, rolling high over the treetops. "Manabozho, Manabozho!" they cried in fright.

At once all the players on both sides rushed back to centerfield to look. "What is the matter?" everyone asked. "This must have been Manabozho's doing. Nobody else would dare to attack the underground gods." But they couldn't find the culprit. "Let's use the power of the water as our guide to find Manabozho," someone cried. All the players waded into the water, and the water rose up and went ahead of them because it knew very well where Manabozho had gone.

In the meantime, Manabozho was running away as fast as he could, frightened at what the consequences might be for his rashness. He looked back and saw the water flowing after him. He ran faster and faster, but still the water was gaining on him.

As he ran he saw a high mountain with a tall pine growing on its summit. Manabozho raced up the mountainside, with the water swiftly rising behind him. "Hey! Nase! Little Brother," Manabozho gasped to the pine tree, "won't you help save me from the water? I am talking to you, pine tree."

"How can I help you?" asked the pine.

"You can let me climb on you, and every time I reach your top, you can grow another length," Manabozho said anxiously.

"But I only have a limited power. I can only grow four lengths."

"Oh, that's fine. I'll take that!" screamed Manabozho in terror, jumping into the pine branches just a few inches ahead of the water. He climbed with all his strength, but the water wet his feet as it rose, and kept rising. He reached the top. "Oh, little brother, stretch yourself," he begged the pine, and the tree shot up one length. Manabozho climbed faster then ever, but the water still wet his moccasins. "Little brother, stretch yourself," he begged again. The tree shot up, Manabozho climbed, and the water followed. When he reached the top, the tree shot up again, and the water still rose.

"Stretch yourself once more, little brother, give me just one more length," prayed Manabozho, "maybe it will save me. If it doesn't, I'll be drowned."

Up shot the pine tree for the fourth and last time. Manabozho climbed to the top, and the water followed. There it stopped. Manabozho clung to the tree, frightened half to death, but the water rose no more.[9]

 I.7

# Me'napus and the Buzzard

JEROME LAWE, MENOMINEE

*Was Manabozho, here called "Me'napus," right to challenge the underground spirits, or was he being rash? In the next Trickster tale, Buzzard tries to trick the Trickster.*

One day when Me'napus was tramping along, he saw some kind of creature flying round aloft. "Well!" he stared at it.

"Oh, I wish I too could go about up there and see the world!" thought Me'napus. So he called to it, "Oh, Little Brother, come here!" and the buzzard came.

"Oh, please, Little Brother, carry me round on your back," he asked.

"Why, that is just your silly way, Me'napus! I couldn't carry your weight. How could we ever do it?" Buzzard asked.

"Oh please, Little Brother! I shall make myself small," Me'napus said. Then he took his seat on top of the buzzard's back. Then the buzzard flew up and flew around.

"Higher, Brother, higher!" Me'napus kept saying.

At last this earth seemed just a surface of yellow vegetation. Then while flying round, the buzzard gave a jerk, like this, with its body, and Me'napus slid off buzzard's back.

As Me'napus fell through space, all kinds of thought went through his mind. "What if I fall into the water?" he worried until he landed, knocked out.

After a while he came to, but there was someone lying with his hind part pointed at him!

"Pew! Just you lie with your hind part pointing some other way!" he said. But it turned out that it must have been his own hindquarter; he must have broken in two in his fall. Poor fellow. When he had fixed himself back straight, he started walking. "Dirty dog of a buzzard. I'll catch you just the same and pay you for what you have done to me!" said Me'napus.

As he was tramping along, suddenly there were some elk grazing about. "Oh, Little Brothers of mine, you are very handsome! Please, do let me too be an elk!" Me'napus said to them.

"Oh, that's just like you, Me'napus! How are we to do it? We were made to be like this," they said.

"Oh please, Little Brothers, please!"

So then, since there was nothing else to do, he was made an elk.

"Come, let me be the biggest one," he said. "Seeing that I am the eldest one. And let my antlers be the biggest."

He must have been a huge elk. He then went with the others. One time they were pursued by wolves. Now, when Me'napus, being the biggest and having large antlers, got caught among the trees, the wolves overtook him and killed him. Then all kinds of creatures ate him, including the crows, who dug out his eyes. When he had been entirely eaten up, only his bones lay there.

That was when Buzzard came. It came and settled a ways off yonder. Of course it was afraid, but nonetheless, it came. There, inside his anus a little lump of fat meat was still sticking, so Buzzard stuck his head in there, pecking at that lump of fat there with its beak. Suddenly Me'napus drew shut his anus and rose up. "What does this fellow amount to?" he said to it.

Then Me'napus started walking around. The Buzzard flapped its wings in the rear of Me'napus for a long time as Me'napus carried it round with him. At last he did let it go from his anus. There sat Buzzard, reeling; its head was entirely bald.

"Now then," said Me'napus to the Buzzard, "this is the way you shall always continue to look, as long as the earth shall endure!" as he started to walk away from there.[10]

# 1.8

# Menominee Medicine Bundle

ANONYMOUS, MENOMINEE

*Me'napus isn't always playing tricks or challenging the underworld. He has been sent by the Great Spirit to help humans, which he does in part by giving humans medicines. The next story is told as part of the ritual surrounding a Medicine Bundle, which is a collection of objects that have power or medicine. These sacred bundles are opened only on ceremonial occasions and are the possession of certain people who guard and protect them and pass each bundle on to the next keeper of the bundle, along with all the ceremonies and rituals that properly accompany it.*

In the beginning, Me'napus was troubled on behalf of his uncles and aunts, the men and women of the world, because sometimes they starved. Wicked medicine men, befriended by the horned owl, plagued the people. These evil old men would circle about in the bushes in the guise of their guardian owls watching the Indians. If any man had good luck in hunting, one of these evil men would steal it away for himself. Out of spite he would drive away the deer and bewitch the traps. Drawing the leaden pellets from the hunter's rifles, he would substitute shadowy spirit bullets of his own so that no matter how truly they were aimed, the hunter's shot had no more effect than if he had not taken aim.

Me'napus was upset because he did not seem to have the power to destroy these evil men. But because he was so sorrowful on behalf of the people, the powers above, the grandfathers and grandmothers of the Indians, took council and decided to give him strong medicine that he might pass on to the people to help and save them.

When the grandfathers prepared to give the bag to Me'napus, a little beaver, a young one, was at the far side of the great water, and though he was so far away he knew by telepathy what was happening. He thought, "I too will help Me'napus and his uncles and aunts." So he swam quickly along the shore toward where the grandfathers were giving the bundle to Me'napus and he came so smoothly and so quietly that he left neither wave nor ripple. As he approached where Me'napus stood, he began to sing:

> Me too, nephew, now I am here,
> Me too, nephew, now I am here;
> If you obey me,
> If you obey me.

"Now," said he, "though I am not a hunting animal to have a right to be in the bundle, yet to show my good will to the people, your uncles and aunts, I will give my skin to be in the bundle to hold medicines."

"All right, my little brother, you can come in the bundle and help the people when they perform this ceremony," cried Me'napus. So he took in the little beaver to hold medicine.

The weasels, who are mighty hunters, who run softly like snakes through the grass in summer, and in winter under the snow, they who are always sure of game when they go hunting, they too came to show their good will towards the people, the aunts and uncles of Me'napus. The weasel came to Me'napus and said, "I shall enter by the deer's mouth and pass out of his rectum; I shall kill him as I pass through his vitals," and he sang a song.

"All right, my little brother, you too shall be in the medicine bundle to help my aunts and uncles, the people, to hunt." So Me'napus put the weasel in the bundle, and weasel's skin may still be found there.

The mink is a mighty hunter, always successful in getting game and returning quickly from the hunt with food. He asked to come in the bundle too that he might hold the tiny bow and arrows and their medicine, which the grandfathers and grandmothers had put there. He also sang a song to Me'napus.

"All right, my little brother," said Me'napus, "you too shall come in the bundle, even as you have asked, to hold the little bow and arrows and their medicine."

Then the bird begged to come in too, and Me'napus permitted him to enter that he might give the people the power to fly from place to place when they hunted as swiftly as he.

Now there were many medicines in the bag that the grandfathers gave Me'napus, and each one had its own song, and the chief of these medicines were: one for the deer, one for the wolf, one for the bear, and one for the skunk. One prevented evil medicine men from harming the possessor of the bundle, and one medicine destroyed the ordinary human enemies of the bundle owner.

So Me'napus took the bundle and learned its uses from the grandfathers. Then he passed it on to his uncles and aunts, the Indian people, that they might outwit evil medicine men and have food to keep them alive. It can only be possessed by a few. No common man may have it; only those who receive it as a reward for their fasting and suffering, or to whom it is given in a vision.[11]

 I.9

# Struggle for Land and Timber

VERNA FOWLER, MENOMINEE

*Perhaps the teachings about Trickster's dual nature as both harmful and helpful enabled the Menominee to deal with demands made by the American government. As the forests of the East Coast were felled, pressure was exerted on the Menominee to sell their lands that contained great stands of virgin timber.*

With the establishment of Fort Howard near Green Bay, Fort Michilimackinac in upper Michigan, and forts at Lake Poygan and Prairie du Chien, the tribe was always aware of the threat of force. From 1817 to 1856, a series of statutes and treaties with the federal government transferred Menominee land to European refugees and immigrant New York Indians. The first treaty, in 1817, was one of friendship; in it the Menominee were promised federal protection. Subsequent treaties involved land cessions at an average of 13.5 cents per acre, while a later agreement established the present reservation "for a home to be held as Indian lands are held." In 1854 a treaty was negotiated for the Menominee by an appointed leader, who cooperated with the Americans but stoutly resisted the government's proposed removal to Crow Wing, Minnesota. A final treaty, in 1856, set aside a portion of the tribe's land for New York's Stockbridge-Munsee Indians. Despite these concessions, however, the demand for Menominee land did not end.

In 1854, Wisconsin lumber barons lobbied for the unilateral purchase of Menominee land. The tribe was able to halt this land sale in 1871, when it obtained permission to harvest "dead and down" timber on the land, thereby using property that whites had wanted to be considered "vacant."[12]

# You Do Not Seem to Know Us

KAUSHKANNANIEW (OR GRIZZLY BEAR), MENOMINEE

*In the 1800s, many Native Nations were being forced from their homelands. Some of these Nations from New York State petitioned the Menominee to allow them to live on their land. But the Menominee were firm about what they had agreed to at the 1831 treaty signing, and their speaker made clear that their decision-making process is collective and consensual.[13]*

You do not seem to know us. We do not change our mind so soon as this. We have already told you that when we have anything to do, we consult together and decide; and when done, so it must be. We have also told you that we do not care . . . whether [the New York Indians] are pleased or not. We will not do anything for them. We would not take all the money our Great Father has, nor all the good things you have offered, to give the N.Y. Indians any more of our Land. You tell us that if we do not agree to do something now by which a settlement will be effected, the Treaty will fall to the ground, and we will lose all the advantages secured to us by it. We say, no matter, let it fall to the ground. We will not do any more. We are willing to do what is right. We will do nothing more.[14]

 I.II

# Resistance to the Timber Barons

NEOPIT, MENOMINEE

*Although legislators in Washington hoped to force the Menominee to sell their best timber, the Menominee were strongly behind their head chief in refusing to sell their land.*

I desire to make the following statement: Shortly after the passage of the great council at Washington (Congress) of the act of February 13, 1971, a general council of the Menominees fully and unanimously disapproved, and in the strongest terms protested against the sale of all our pine and agricultural lands, leaving us for homes and farms four townships of barren sand plains. We want to sell our timber for a fair price, and we will give the purchasers four or five years to take it away in, and then we want our lands allotted to us. But we will not consent to the sale of any more land. We want it for our children and grandchildren. We accepted our present reservation when it was considered of no value by our white friends. And all we ask is to be permitted to keep it as a home.[15]

# Termination and Restoration

VERNA FOWLER, MENOMINEE

*The success of Menominee timbering would soon lead to its reverse. In 1953, termination of reservations became the official U.S. policy, ending federal protection of more than sixty Indian groups, who lost health services and whose lands were now subject to taxation. Many groups sold their land to pay taxes. This loss of land was the explicit intention of Senator Arthur Wilkins of Utah, who wanted to reclaim the lands, particularly those that held exploitable resources, such as Menominee timber.*

*The Menominee Termination Act of 1954 blocked the tribe from receiving an 8.5-million-dollar settlement for earlier takings unless they agreed to termination. Most Menominee who voted to receive the payment were probably unaware that they were also inadvertently voting for termination. Given four years to reestablish their self-governance, the Menominee reorganized into a corporation, the Menominee Enterprises, Incorporated (MEI), but individual Menominee had little control over the board that had a majority of non-Menominee on its board of directors. The federal government no longer awarded Menominee federal contracts for timber; they no longer provided health and education services; there was a slump in house building, plus the new tax burden. To offset these debits, the MEI tried to construct a lake and sell off lakefront property for tourist homes.*

Unable to pay property taxes, the Menominee Enterprises, Inc. (MEI) began to sell the tribe's former holdings. A grassroots movement led by a young Menominee social worker named Ada Deer stopped the land sales and reversed termination. The Menominee Restoration Act, signed by President Nixon on December 22, 1972, re-designated the Menominee a federally recognized tribe. The campaign thrust Deer into the national spotlight and contributed to her eventual appointment as Assistant Secretary of the Interior for Indian Affairs in 1993, by virtue of which she became the first Native American woman to head the Bureau of Indian Affairs.[16]

# 1.13

# The Power Came from the People

ADA DEER, MENOMINEE

*Ada Deer was born in Keshena, Wisconsin, in 1935. She earned her bachelor's degree from the University of Wisconsin–Madison and a master's in social welfare from Columbia University. Since 1977 she has held a faculty position at the University of Wisconsin–Madison in the School of Social Work. The following statement was summarized from an interview with Ada Deer in the 1970s about her social and political education. It is important to note that Ada Deer disputes some of the interpretation of the interview.*

I was born on the Menominee reservation in Wisconsin, and lived there for eighteen years. As a teenager I saw the poverty of the people—poor housing, poor education, poor health. I thought, "This isn't the way it should be. People should have a better life."

I wanted to help the tribe in some way, but I wanted to have something to offer. I decided that going to college and developing my skills was the best way to break out of the bonds of poverty. After college, I entered law school.

In 1961 the tribe was terminated; that is, federal support was withdrawn. Some of us opposed termination from the start, but we were overruled. Only five percent of the people voted; they were lured by the cash payments offered in return for giving up government services. Most of the people were uninformed; they did not protest termination because they did not foresee its drastic implications. The government pushed it through without preparing the people. It was "an experiment."

The years 1961–1973 were a political, economic, and cultural disaster for the Menominee. Formerly, under the tribal system everyone had been equal, with one vote per tribal member. Under the new corporate structure just a few people had the power to make decisions.

We were the state's poorest county, with just one small industry, a lumber mill. We were suddenly faced with massive tax burdens. Our hospital and school were forced to close. The people suffered a great deal. To survive, the tribe had to sell some of its land.

Land is very dear to the Menominee. We have a beautiful reservation— over 234,000 acres of mountains, streams, and lakes. Our reservation is our homeland, guaranteed by a treaty. Our cultural identity is bound to the land.

With termination, many of the people moved to the cities in search of jobs. They lost their connection with their traditional culture and way of life. Then too, termination canceled tribal membership for children born after 1954.

The government had tried for two hundred years to eliminate the Indians. They tried wars, disease, putting us on reservations. They tried acculturation—shipping us off to cities. Termination was the ultimate expression of that . . .

I wanted to get involved. People said I was too young, too naïve—you can't fight the system. I dropped out of law school. That was the price I had to pay to get involved. It was worth it.

In 1970 we started our movement called DRUMS [Determination of Rights and Unity for Menominee Shareholders]. We sought an end to land sales, the restoration of federal support, and full participation of the people in tribal government. To present our goals to our congressman, we staged a march covering one hundred and fifty miles from our reservation to Madison. Our congressman said he didn't think our legislation had much of a chance, but he'd introduce it.

I spent six months in Washington influencing congressmen and mobilizing the support of our people throughout the country. We were able to get our legislation through the House of Representatives 404 to 3—an exciting day. It went through the Senate on a voice vote with no protest and was signed into law on December 1, 1973. The land was restored to trust status; roles in government were opened to young people and to women.

Where did the manpower and womanpower come from to accomplish this? It came from the people. Men and women working together as a total community. Now we Indian people believe we can do anything![17]

# I.14

# Menominee Termination

DETERMINATION OF RIGHTS AND UNITY FOR MENOMINEE
SHAREHOLDERS (DRUMS) COMMITTEE, MENOMINEE

*As the late Senator Watkins phrased it, termination "allowed" the Menominee to assimilate into the dominant culture and "emancipated" them from their Native heritage. House Concurrent Resolution 108, which he sponsored, removed Native lands from their federal trust status. Without federal protection, the greatly sought after old timber stands on the Menominee reservation would be available for exploitation. Verna Fowler writes that "there are some who believe that [Senator Watkins's] motives were much more self serving [than the interpretation offered below]. He had business ties to the lumber industry who desperately wanted the Menominee forest and timber."[18]*

Early in 1953, we Menominee wanted a portion of our 1951 settlement—about $5,000,000—distributed among ourselves on a $1,500 per capita basis. Since congressional approval was required for such disbursement of our assets, Representative Melvin Laird and Senator Joseph McCarthy introduced in Congress on behalf of our Tribe a bill to authorize the payment of our money to us.

This bill passed the House, but in hearings before the Senate Committee on Interior and Insular Affairs, it ran up against an amendment sponsored by the late Senator Arthur V. Watkins (R. Utah) calling for "termination" of federal supervision and assistance to the Menominee. Watkins and the Committee refused to report the bill favorably, calling upon us Menominee to submit a termination plan before we would be given our money! "Termination!" What did that mean? Certainly at that time, none of us Menominee realized what it meant. . . . In June, 1953, we Menominee invited Senator Watkins to visit the Reservation and explain "termination" to us.

Senator Watkins badly wanted our termination. He was firmly convinced that factors such as our status as Reservation Indians, our tribal ownership of land, and our tax exemption were blocking our initiative, our freedom, and our development of private enterprise. He wished to see us rapidly assimilated into the mainstream of American society—as tax paying, hard working, "emancipated" citizens.

On June 20, 1953, Senator Watkins spoke for forty-five minutes to our General Council. He told us that Congress had already decided on terminating us, and that at most we could have three years before our "affairs would be turned over to us"—and that we would not receive our per capitas until after termination.

After he left, our Council had the opportunity to vote on the "principle of termination!" Some opportunity! What little understanding we had of what termination would mean! The vote was 169 to 5 in favor of the "principle of termination." A mere five percent of the 3,200 Menominee people participated in this vote. Most of our people chose to be absent from the meeting in order to express their negative reaction to termination. Many who did vote affirmatively that day believed that termination was coming from Congress whether the Menominee liked it or not. Others thought that they were voting only in favor of receiving their per capitas. . . .

We then set about preparing a termination plan, which the BIA subsequently emasculated, and we received word that Senator Watkins was pressing ahead with his own termination bill. Another general council meeting was called, one which is seldom mentioned, but at which the Menominee voted 197 to zero to oppose and reject termination! But our feelings did not matter—and although the Watkins bill met a temporary defeat on technical grounds in the House in late 1953, Senator Watkins re-introduced it in 1954.

We became convinced that there was no alternative to accepting termination. Therefore, all we pleaded for was adequate time to plan this sudden and revolutionary change in our lives. On June 17, 1954, the Menominee Termination Act was signed into law by President Eisenhower. . . .

Termination represented a gigantic and revolutionary forced change in the traditional Menominee way of life. Congress expected us to replace our Indian way of life with a complicated corporate style of living. Congress expected immediate Menominee assimilation of non-Indian culture, values, and life styles.

The immediate effect of termination on our tribe was the loss of most of our hundred-year-old treaty rights, protections, and services. No amount of explanation or imagination prior to termination could have prepared us for the shock of what these losses meant.

Congress withdrew its trusteeship of our lands, transferring to MEI [Menominee Enterprises, Inc., the corporation which was to supervise Menominee holdings after termination] the responsibility for protecting these lands, our greatest assets. As we shall explain, far from being able to preserve our land, MEI has been forced to sell it. And because our land is now being sold to non-Menominee, termination is doing to us what allotment has done to other Indian tribes.

Congress also extinguished our ancient system of tribal "ownership" of land (under which no individual had separate title to his home) and transferred title to MEI. Consequently, we individual Menominee suddenly discovered that we would be forced to buy from MEI the land that had always been considered our own, and to pay title to our homesites. Thus began the tragic process of our corporation "feeding off" our people.

We Menominee lost our right to tax exemption. Both MEI and individual Menominee found themselves saddled with tax burdens particularly crushing to a small tribe struggling to develop economically.

BIA health, education, and utility services ceased. We lost all medical and dental care within the Reservation. Both our reservation [clinic] and hospital were closed because they failed to meet state standards. Individual Menominee were forced to pay for electricity and water that they [had] previously received at no cost. Our county found it had to renovate at high cost its substandard sewerage system.

Finally, with termination and the closing of our tribal rolls, our children born since 1954 have been legally deprived of their birthright as Menominee Indians. Like all other Menominee, they have lost their entitlement to United States Government benefits and services to Indians. . . . The only major Menominee treaty right which the government has allowed us to retain has been our hunting and fishing right. Wisconsin had tried to deprive us of this right, but in 1968, after costly litigation, the United States Supreme Court ruled that this treaty right had "survived" termination.

We hope you can appreciate the magnitude of these treaty losses to us. Visualize a situation similar to ours happening in one of your home states. Imagine the outrage of the people in one of your own communities if Congress should attempt to terminate their basic property, inheritance, and civil rights.

Today Menominee County is the poorest county in Wisconsin. It has the highest birthrate in the state and ranks at or near the bottom of Wisconsin counties in income, housing, property value, education, employment, sanitation and health. The most recent figures available (1967) show that the annual income of nearly 80 percent of our families falls below the federal poverty level of $3,000. The per capita annual income of our wage earners in 1965 was estimated at $881, the lowest in the state.

This lack of employment opportunities, combined with our high birthrate, forced nearly 50 percent of our county residents to go on welfare in 1968. Welfare costs in the county for 1968 were over $766,000 and our per capita welfare payment was the highest in the state. The majority of Menominee who have left our county to seek work in the cities have become trapped in poverty there also.

With the closing of the BIA hospital, we lost most of our health services, and most Menominee continue to suffer from lack of medical care. There have been no full-time doctors or dentists in Menominee County since termination. Shortly after termination, our people were stricken by a TB epidemic which caused great suffering and hardship because of the lack of local medical facilities.

The loss of the BIA school required that our youth be sent to Shawano County for their high school training. The Shawano school system had assumed that Menominee children possess the same cultural and historical background as [children from the] middle-class white community. . . . Since 1961, our high school dropout rates have increased substantially, absenteeism has soared, and our children apparently are suffering a downward trend in achievement.

We have told a story which is very tragic, yet it is a true story of the Menominee people since termination. We have told how termination has meant the loss of treaty benefits, has pushed our already poor community further into the depths of poverty, forced our sale of assets, and denied us a democratic community.[19]

# 1.15

## Current Resource Extraction

JOHN TELLER, MENOMINEE

*DRUMS and Ada Deer successfully pressured Congress to repeal the Menominee Termination Act and to stop land sales around Legend Lake. Their efforts culminated in 1973 when President Richard Nixon signed the Menominee Restoration Act, which restored the reservation to tribal ownership. But concern about resource extraction is not a thing of the distant past. An issue not resolved until 2003 was Exxon and Rio Algom's Minerals Company (NMC, or Nicolet Minerals Company) proposal to extract iron sulfide from tailings and mine large zinc and copper deposits. Based on NMC's own studies, the Crandon Mine would have released contaminants that violate Wisconsin's groundwater standards. Mine wastes would have destroyed wild rice beds and been toxic for over 200,000 years.[20] In December of 2003, the site of the proposed mine near Crandon, Wisconsin, on the Wolf River, was purchased by the Forest County Potawatomi and the Mole Lake (Sokaogon) Chippewa Band. In this excerpt, former Menominee tribal chairman John Teller makes clear that his opposition to a mine is based on cultural and ecological concerns.*

Crandon Mining Company's proposed construction and operation of a hard-rock metallic sulfide mine at the headwaters of the Wolf River seriously threatens this magnificent river. Water quality and tremendous ecological diversity [are] imperiled, including bald eagle, wild rice, lake sturgeon and trout habitat. The Wolf River is the lifeline of the Menominee people, and central to our existence. We will let no harm come to the river.[21]

# The Power Comes from Within

INGRID WASHINAWATOK, MENOMINEE

*Ingrid Washinawatok was a delegate to the United Nations in 1992, representing Native communities. A filmmaker and writer, she chaired the Committee on the International Decade of the World's Indigenous Peoples and directed the Fund for the Four Directions, which works to promote indigenous languages. While in Colombia working with the U'wa Nation to develop a school system and to block oil drilling on sacred lands, she and two companions were kidnapped and killed by the FARC (Revolutionary Armed Forces of Colombia) in 1999.[22]*

Originally, my people inhabited nine and a half million acres in Wisconsin. We hunted, fished, and harvested wild rice. The name Menominee means "the wild rice people." Parts of our reservation are hilly; we have unusual rock formations, and eighty-two natural lakes. We have one of the best stands of pine in the northern hemisphere. I think people from Germany settled there because it reminded them of the Black Forest. When I was in Switzerland, I remember walking in the woods, and thinking it was a little like home.

Our ancestors understood the value of our resources. The elders told us, "If you harvest the forest from west to east, you'll always have food on the table for your kids." It's no big complicated plan. It's very simple. When we took timber from one area, we replanted, and moved on to the next section. Somehow, through the years, land was sold, or stolen, and we lost much of that resource.

We had a traditional form of government, a general council, with decisions arrived at by consensus. But the Indian Reorganization Act of 1934 changed our government into a corporate structure. In some tribes, dynamic leaders like Wilma Mankiller [Cherokee] are trying to make it work. But the system also produced bureaucrats in tribes all over the country who abuse their authority and take care of their own families exclusively.

Both my parents are Menominee. In the early 1950s, they were living on the Rez where they had grown up. My mom had completed a nursing degree, and worked as an RN at the tribal hospital. I think that in those days our reservation still had a sense of community. You'd take care of Grandma Jones down the street if she didn't have anyone to bring her meat. You'd get a basket, and bring her some food.

In 1954 the federal policy of termination went into effect, ending the federal trust responsibility to certain tribes, so that meant that those of us born after 1954 were no longer eligible to be on the tribal rolls. We no longer had a relationship with the Bureau of Indian Affairs.

Termination was a disaster for the Menominee. We had had our own electric department, our own telephone company, we had schools, we had a hospital. Ours was supposedly a model reservation. But when termination went into effect, they closed down our phone company, our electric department, and a lot of people lost their jobs. The hospital closed—it wasn't up to state codes. When people were sick, they had to go twenty miles or more to the nearest clinic, and few people had cars.

Our kids used to be able to look to adults for safety. There were people who cared enough about a child to look out for him, to say, "Hey, don't do that. You're gonna hurt yourself." But after termination, a lot of people had to go on welfare just to survive. By the 1960s, our annual per capita income on the reservation was down to just around sixteen hundred bucks. So people thought, "How am I gonna feed my kids? I can't pay my bills." When that happens, you stop worrying about the little kid down the street who has no shoes. Your whole existence is wrapped up in survival.

People felt so helpless because they couldn't provide for their families, and that's when a lot of them started drinking. Some of the Menominee were relocated in cities. One of the first lessons they learned is that in order to make it in American society, you have to promote yourself. In order to climb up the corporate ladder, you have to step on everyone. In our culture, and I've seen it in the Black and Hispanic cultures too, that goes against the grain.

We get asked, "Why can't you get a fast-food job and work your way up the way a lot of immigrants have done?" Some Indians have done that, but you have to look at the reality of who we are. This is our land, and we don't have control over it anymore. We feel for those who have come over here from other countries. We can't imagine life being so horrendous that people would leave their homeland and ancestors behind to come here. Ironically, immigrants have a better chance of making it than we have. It's not because we lack industriousness.

It's because historically, we've been herded from one side of the country to the other by the U.S. Army. It's because we see toxic waste being poured into our rivers. We see our land base diminish. Our reservations have been battered. With each trauma that occurs, a piece of your heart is taken away.

My dad didn't finish high school. He was one of twelve children; he couldn't afford to go to college. He joined the navy at seventeen. We have a long tradition of service in the military. The Menominee have fought in every war since the Revolution. My dad only talks about his experience in the service in bits and pieces. He was in the invasion of Normandy. I gather he saw a lot of ugliness in the war. Years later he told me, "You know, they said I was going overseas to fight for my rights. Then after I came home, I became aware of the gross violations of the human rights of Indian people. I realized I was fighting for somebody else's rights."

I think it was in the navy that my dad really started drinking. I've heard from many men how hard it is to deal with the boredom of life in the service, and the killing. If you're Indian, you're brought up to care about all life; it's not okay to bomb towns and blow people to smithereens. But if you question it, then you're told, "You're not a man." You're told, "That person is the enemy; you are there to kill." I think that people drink out of shame—to dull the pain.

It's been very hard for Indian men to discuss this. Some of our communities pride themselves on having kids who have served in the army or the marines. Some of our boys go into the service to get an education. As the mother of a boy, I'm concerned about it, because today if you go into the military, there's a good chance you'll be mobilized to fight in foreign countries where you'll be face-to-face with indigenous peoples, pointing your gun at them.

Also, I heard an estimate that eighty percent of the resources of this country are on Indian land: water, timber, gas, coal, silver, gold, uranium. The mentality hasn't changed since they chased us down at Wounded Knee. In Wisconsin, they throw rocks and beer bottles at Indians spearing on non-reservation lakes. I feel that at any point, if those resources are needed, the guns will be pointed back at us.

My dad went to Michigan State University on the GI Bill, the first in his family to go to college. He got a degree in police administration and political science, but ended up working as an insurance adjuster in Chicago, so that's where I grew up. Compared to a lot of Indians, we had a comfortable "middle-class" life, but it was hard to make ends meet, and my parents struggled.

In school, I was on the outer fringes; nobody wanted to play with me 'cause I didn't look like everybody else. Then I started making friends. I was supposed to know everything about Indians. Well, you get an American education, schools try to turn you into little white kids, but still you're supposed to know everything about Indians. It made me feel dumb. Like "the real Indians" live on the reservation, the real Indians ride horses.

As I got older I found that people expect the Indian woman either to be a backwoods person or a wise woman who knows the secrets of the earth. In old cartoons and movies being shown on cable television, they see an Indian guy with a knife in his teeth swooping down on a poor white family. They don't see real Indian men who come home and laugh and hug their families and say, "I missed you."

My son and I were watching the cartoon "Tom and Jerry." All of a sudden, Jerry has a bow and arrow in his hand, and is shooting arrows at Tom. And my little boy turned to me and said, "Mom, is that supposed to be us?" Last Halloween, on the cover of a parents' magazine, there was a picture of this little kid with flaming red hair—he had three lines of paint on his face, he wore fake buckskin and a fake headdress. For some people, being Indian is comical; they don't see us as human.

So many Indians are really lost. Some don't know they're Indian. I've seen people try to make a better life for themselves. I have friends who have gone to law school; they find out how negotiation has been used to legally swindle Native people out of their land and water rights. Some of them rationalized what they're doing. Some find a balance between their own needs and those of the community. Others go back to ceremony—that's one way of dealing with all the pressures.

What about Indians who go into corporations? I don't know very many who do because when we do, we find there's an emptiness. There's the danger of letting go of who you are as an Indian person, to try to grasp for that American dream which is individualistic, not community-oriented. You might feel sorry for the guy on the corner, you might give him your token quarter, but that's not being a part of your community. And it's an ethical dilemma: how can you be comfortable working for corporations that you know are making a profit by taking our resources and poisoning the earth?

I went to the University of Wisconsin but I left because what I was learning didn't have much to do with the lives of Indian people. I wanted to learn things from the elders. I went to work for the National Federation of Native-Controlled Survival Schools.

In 1984 a group of women active in the Indian rights movement formed the Indigenous Women's Network. There were two hundred women at our first gathering on Janet McCloud's land in 1985. We had sweats, we had talking circles—women talking about battering, about alcoholism, about sexual abuse of children, about feeding your children on food stamps. We asked, "What's the point in working to defend the land if our families and communities are deteriorating?" We formed a board; we started a magazine. Since that time, so much healing has gone on. I have seen women go back to school, become professionals, get Ph.D.s, and the majority of them return to work in Indian communities; they bring their talents home to their people. The changes in the last ten years have been phenomenal.

I moved to New York City to work for the International Indian Treaty Council, translating documents from Spanish to English, and eventually moved to my present job. At first, I missed my reservation. But I was lucky to be welcomed by Shinnecock families who have a reservation on Eastern Long Island. They were there before the first settlers came. Originally, they were a sea people, whalers and clammers. We go out there to visit friends, we go there for powwows.

Everyone thinks there aren't any Indians in New York City, or if there are, they aren't "real Indians." What they don't know is that there's a very long history of Indians in the city. The Mohawk people have worked as ironworkers for generations; they built New York's buildings and bridges, and some of them settled here. I know Indians whose parents originally came to the city with Buffalo Bill's Wild West Show, and stayed on. There are Indian people who come to New York to go to school, to work in banks, the stock market, industry, police administration; some are computer whizzes. So we have a pretty diverse population. Many of us live in Brooklyn.

You can create community wherever you are. I'm on the board of directors of the American Indian Community House in the SoHo district in downtown New York City. We have a whole conglomeration of Indian folks: Hopi, Cree, Winnebago (Ho-Chunk), Mohawk, Lakota, Kunas, Quechuas. There's this one couple that just had a beautiful little baby who's the apple of everyone's eye because it's the new life, the continuation of this beautiful community.

We have an elders' luncheon. People come from Brooklyn, the Bronx, Queens. We can't have them riding trains, so we pick them up. They come and eat, and learn about health issues. We have a day care center. We have a dance group that performs tribal dances, and dance clubs for the kids. Spider Women's Theater performs plays on contemporary issues. Writers come in from all over the country to give readings of their work.

There was a conference a few years ago for Adult Children of Alcoholics. We sat in a circle holding hands, we talked and we listened to each other. I remember sitting next to one of the guys who had recently quit drinking. He was so nervous, he was shaking. All these years, you've flung responsibility to the wind. Then, when you feel responsible for having to maintain your sobriety, it's scary. Recently I met that guy on the street; he told me he has stayed sober for four years, and we just hugged.

I travel a lot, and in communities across the country, I see women in leadership roles. There's recognition that women are powerful, but it's not authority in [W]estern terms. There's a balance between young and old, between men and women. There's a recognition that power comes from within. It comes from having knowledge and vision.

The sun has power. The wind has power. We have the power to bring forth and nurture new life. That's the power Mother Earth has. There's the power of love.

If you raise your children to be good people, then the future is theirs. That's more important than being president of a corporation. How can you not be fulfilled if you teach your children to be loving, honest, thinking people?

I remember how we used to go to Grandfather's house on the Rez. He lived on the Wolf River. I'd sit in the backyard and just look up at the pines and evergreens against the blueness of the August sky. Now, whenever I get homesick for my reservation, I close my eyes and think about that.[23]

# 2

# Literature of the
# Ho-Chunk Nation

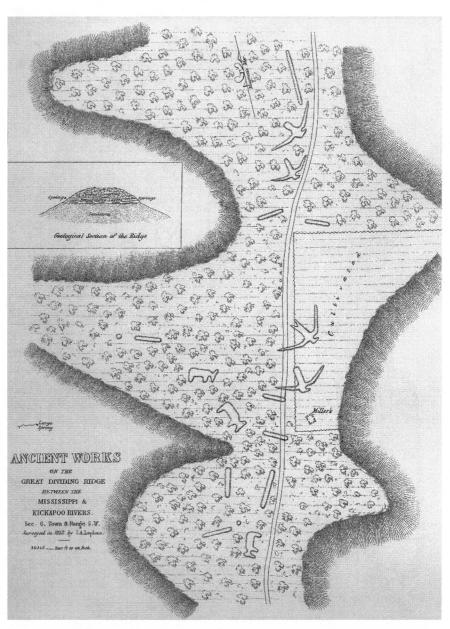

Southern Wisconsin hosts 90 percent of the effigy mounds in the world. This particular site (from among thousands) contains lineal mounds, and Bear and Thunderbird mounds. Plowing or plundering destroyed most mounds in the 1800s. In southwestern Wisconsin, the Kickapoo River meets the Mississippi at Wauzeka, named after a Mesquakie (Fox) chief. The Kickapoo River is named after the Kickapoo tribe, which resided near the river during early French exploration in the 1700s. Reproduced by permission from I. A. Lapham, *The Antiquities of Wisconsin, as Surveyed and Described* (Madison: University of Wisconsin Press, 2001), LI.

# Sovereignty in a Spiritual Landscape

LYLE GREENDEER, HO-CHUNK

*Twelve thousand years ago, a small band hunted the ragged edge of the glaciers. After track-ing mastodon for days, they spotted the curved tusks of a lone mastodon at the side of a glacial stream, his ivories glistening ice. When he scented the hunters, he tried to lift his feet, mired in mud. Raising his massive head, he trumpeted an alarm as many spears entered his mouth and ears. When his hulk thudded down, the earth reverberated underfoot.*

*The hunters selected river stones and quickly shaped tools for butchering the huge carcass. The massive bones could not be transported, although the hunters took a few small ones for tools. When they left, they happened to leave behind a spearpoint at the place now known as Boaz, situated in the rugged driftless or unglaciated region of southwest Wisconsin, a little over an hour's drive west of Madison.*

*The rock from which the spearpoint was made did not come from Boaz, but from an ancient quarry today called Silver Mound in Jackson County, seventy miles northwest of Boaz, where the mastodon had been killed. Even today Silver Mound is known for the beauty and utility of its rock that looks like crystallized maple syrup, a fine-grained silicified sandstone called Hixton orthoquartzite. From this material, the hunters had knapped a "Clovis-like fluted point" that helped to bring down the mastodon. Its skeleton, found by Richland County farm boys in 1897, is on display in Weeks Hall on the University of Wisconsin–Madison campus.[1]*

*Let's fast-forward a couple thousand years to what is now called the Late Paleo-Indian culture of 8000 BC to 5000 BC. The retreating glacier brought drier conditions, which coincided with the eventual extinction of very large mammals, including the mammoth and mastodon. The Late Paleo-Indian era persisted until 5000 BC in northern Wisconsin, and saw the appearance of modern plants and animals, including buffalo.*

*The Early Archaic period's time frame varied from 7800 BC to 4200 BC in southern Wisconsin and 5200 BC to 4200 BC in northern Wisconsin. During the Middle Archaic period from roughly 6000 BC to the Late Archaic, beginning in roughly 1200 BC, the Old Copper cultural complex held sway in the upper Great Lakes region, producing many copper implements that were widely distributed throughout the Great Lakes region.*

*By 800 BC the Woodland period began, where pottery and the cultivation of plants in the southern part of Wisconsin became established.[2] Starting around AD 700, earthen mounds were created having an animal form: an effigy mound. Although northeast Iowa and northwest Illinois (also part of the Driftless Bioregion) have some mounds, Wisconsin has hundreds of effigy mounds, more than any other place in the world. Archaeologists call this period of effigy mound building the Late Woodland period.*[3]

*Members of the modern day Ho-Chunk Nation claim that Ho-Chunk ancestor spirits made these massive constructions in prominent places by waterways.*[4] *Prominent archaeologists also believe that present-day Ho-Chunk are the "likely descendants [via an Oneota stage] of the effigy mound builders."*[5] *The huge Thunderbird mound near Muscoda in the lower Wisconsin River watershed has a wingspan of one-quarter mile. As it is said in ancient stories, the Thunderbirds themselves made the hills and valleys of the Ho-Chunk homeland by denting the Earth with their war clubs. Lyle Greendeer, a Wisconsin Ho-Chunk elder, describes the mounds in the film* Gather Like the Waters, *excerpted here.*

These mounds are made by the spirits of the Indians that fasted within the Indian village. And in order to show the Indians, these spirits, they have to appear on top of the ground, and that's what these are, all of them. They are not made by human beings. It's about time we come forward and claim these places wherever these mounds are, because they're ours. They were given to the Winnebago [Ho-Chunk] people, not anybody else.[6]

# Not an Ordinary Place

TOM HOPINKAH, HO-CHUNK

*Not all mounds contained burials. Mounds were ceremonial sites, celebrating the spirit be-*
*ings and clan totems of the ancient Ho-Chunk tradition. Different types of mounds exist.[7]*
*Their shape could be conical, linear, effigy, or reverse "mounds" called intaglios, that is, a*
*shape dug into the earth, usually in the form of the Underwater Panther. Effigy mounds cor-*
*respond to the organization of the cosmos and society into two parts, the upper world (sky)*
*and the lower realm (Earth, water). Thunderbirds belong to the sky moiety (half); under-*
*water panthers, bears, and hares belong to the lower realm.[8]*

*Sites containing effigy mounds were used for hundreds of years as ceremonial centers by*
*generation after generation. Many mounds were built in the same locale. For example, the*
*twenty miles between present-day Readstown and Gays Mills on the Kickapoo River were*
*once graced with over seventy effigy mounds.[9]*

*In spite of the Ho-Chunk ancestors buried within the mounds, farmers plowed most of*
*them under in the late 1800s. But the "shadow" of the Effigy Mounds—the different color*
*of the disturbed dirt contrasting with the surrounding earth—can still be seen from the air,*
*evidence of both ancestral territorial ownership, and the desecration of the dead. The Ho-*
*Chunk Nation is buying back the ancestral mounds that remain. They welcome contact with*
*landowners who wish to preserve mounds or donate them back to the Ho-Chunk Nation.[10]*

*Effigy mounds are not mere mute shapes. They are part of a symbol system that still*
*speaks to their descendants. To those who can "hear" or interpret their symbolic language, the*
*mounds speak of the clans, territories, and traditions of those who are buried within some of*
*the monumental earthworks.[11] Effigy mounds are visual and sacred language, which speak*
*even after the plow has changed them from actual mounds into ghost mounds.[12]*

Any place where these are built is not an ordinary place. . . . From an Indian
tradition and culture, I think this is, you might say, your pyramid in Egypt,
your Stonehenge—the most significant thing that the Winnebago [Ho-
Chunk] or any Native American retain[s] in what's here on this Earth. It
affects different people different ways, the feeling you have when you walk on
this particular site.

I think this might be in the future a very significant testing ground for our
own Winnebago [Ho-Chunk] to reclaim the things that they have lost. I don't
mean in material things, but I mean the spiritual being of being an Indian.[13]

# 2.3

# Gottschall Rockshelter and
# the Epic of Red Horn

SAM BLOWSNAKE, HO-CHUNK

*The spiritual heritage of the Ho-Chunk is not limited to the monumental artwork of the effigy mounds. Not far from where the Boaz mastodon was found, and about eight miles from the Wisconsin River, Gottschall Rockshelter is an entrance into another consciousness. It is a dictionary that deciphers an archaic tradition that speaks with and to contemporary people. Like the Rosetta Stone of Egypt, which bears the carved glyphs of three languages that unlocked the linguistic code of long-dead speakers, Gottschall Rockshelter gives a voice to the archaeological evidence of pottery, stone, and wood implements. This voice can be heard in the ancient oral tradition as it speaks through its living beneficiaries: contemporary Ho-Chunk of Wisconsin.[14]*

*In her beautifully written history,* Indian Nations of Wisconsin, *Patty Loew describes this rock shelter and its contemporary significance:*

> *Members of the modern Ho-Chunk Nation recognize this composition as the story of Red Horn, an ancient Ho-Chunk hero. This origin epic, told by generations of tribal members and preserved in a cave known today as Gottschall, testifies to the enduring power of the spoken word and the persistence of Native American oral tradition.[15]*

*Besides its significance in Ho-Chunk history, this cave in the rippled hills and deep valleys of unglaciated southwest Wisconsin is a premier archaeological site in North America, with three outstanding features: (1) fabricated and at one time heat-producing sediments; (2) a ten-inch high, carved, incised, and painted sandstone head; and (3) over forty pictographs (paintings) and a smaller number of petroglyphs (incised images), including one panel interpreted as representing a scene from the oral tradition of Red Horn, as recorded by Paul Radin and told by Sam Blowsnake.[16]*

*While Patty Loew cites anthropologist Paul Radin's "Winnebago Hero Cycles" for the Red Horn story, Truman Lowe, a Ho-Chunk who is a University of Wisconsin–Madison artist and professor, calls the rockshelter a virtual "library."[17] He interprets Gottschall Rockshelter according to history as told by his mother. Dr. Robert Salzer, leader of the Gottschall Rockshelter excavation team, describes what Truman Lowe said he learned from his mother:*

Carved head from Gottschall Rockshelter. Painted vertical parallel lines and a chin circle in blue pigment decorate this ten-inch-tall carved sandstone head from Gottschall Rockshelter. Red pigment stains the mouth. Its radiocarbon date is from AD 1000 to AD 1050, placing it in the Late Effigy Mound period. Photo by Chuck Savage. Reproduced by permission from *The Wisconsin Archeologist* 78 (1997).

Gottschall Mural. One of more than forty pictographs at Gottschall Rockshelter in southwestern Wisconsin, this grouping is tied to the oral and written traditions of the Ioway and Ho-Chunk people, specifically the story of Red Horn confronting the Giants. The painting is over one thousand years old. Tracing by Mary Steinhauer. Reproduced by permission of Cultural Landscape Legacies, Inc. Photo by Rick LaMartina.

*She said that in the past the Ho-Chunk had suffered from the devastating effects of warfare and they feared that their traditions might be lost. They carried all of their treasures to a cave for safekeeping. The cave collapsed and sealed these precious items. As a boy, Truman said he had fantasies about just what sorts of "treasure" might be buried in that cave.*

*Truman continues to be a regular visitor to the Gottschall Site. He is enthusiastic about the research and what we are finding. He thinks that it is possible that Gottschall is the cave that his mother talked about, and he now knows that the fabulous "treasures" of the Ho-Chunk are not material items. They are history. They are knowledge. They are heritage. These are, after all, the greatest treasures of all.[18]*

*For millennia, ancestors of the Ho-Chunk and Ioway people returned again and again to this cave now called the Gottschall Rockshelter in the Driftless (unglaciated) Bioregion of southwestern Wisconsin. Starting perhaps as early as 600 BC, users of the cave began to manufacture, from crushed clamshells, limestone, and marsh muck, a heat-producing dirt that released its heat over a period of months. Over an extended period of time, large amounts of this dirt were placed ceremonially in Gottschall Rockshelter—a sandstone cave that faces north and never sees the sun.*

*One section of the Gottschall Rockshelter that had been prepared by scraping has a group of figures that were painted about AD 900 or 1000. This scene is interpreted as representing an episode from the oral tradition of Red Horn and the Giants.[19] The depiction of a scene from the epic of Red Horn on the wall of Gottschall Rockshelter provides evidence of the continuity and vitality of Ho-Chunk cultural and oral traditions. Gottschall Rockshelter is of worldwide significance because it connects ancient rock art with contemporary histories; it creates a continuum between the archaic and contemporary periods with an art that is an entrée into the ideological content that goes with the material artifacts.*

*Gottschall Rockshelter expert Robert Salzer asserts that the Gottschall site artists "were part of the earlier Effigy Mound Culture," and that the "use of anthroseds [manufactured dirt] in Late Archaic times is arguably evidence for continuities in ritual behavior that extend back in time to at least as early as 600 B.C."[20]*

*In 1948, anthropologist Paul Radin recorded Sam Blowsnake's telling of the epic of Red Horn.*

## The Epic of Red Horn

### Kunu Wins the Chief's Daughter in a Race

Long ago, ten brothers shared a lodge where the nine older brothers favored the youngest. While he stayed home, the others hunted bear and deer, returning with their kill at sundown. One morning before the nine had left, a messenger, who had a gourd that rattled as he walked, came to the lodge. He greeted the oldest brother: "Kunu! At last I have found you. I've come to tell you that the chief's daughter will marry whoever wins a race."

"All right!" Kunu exclaimed. When the brothers set off, they told the youngest to stay at home.

As they approached the race site, the people whooped their welcome and the brothers answered. Then someone jeered, "The brother Kunu used to throw deer lungs at is here." Kunu looked behind him. His youngest brother had followed, wearing an untanned deerskin blanket, inside out, the fur on the outside.

"I told you not to come," Kunu said, embarrassed and worried that his little brother's presence would hurt his usual success with women.

"It's all right. He can look after our things," the other brothers said.

When they arrived at the place where the platform was set up, the people said, "Ho! Kunu. It is only for you they are still waiting." The chief's daughter sat up on the platform, surrounded by all those more properly called spirits or powers: the Thunderbirds, the Night Spirits, the Deer, the Bears, and the Winged.

Someone noticed Turtle moving across the valley and shouted: "Hurry! Let's go after Turtle—that troublemaker got a head start." Without ceremony, the race began as the men ran in pursuit. When they came to the top of the first hill, Turtle shook his sacred pipe from the summit of the next. They pursued him to the next hill, just as Turtle crested the next. When they got there, Turtle was going over the third hill, and the same with the fourth. One of the people said, "Turtle is very tricky. Someone should stop him." When they found a small red turtle hiding in their trap, they stomped him, buried him, and went back to watching the race.

"He Who Gets Hit With Deer Lungs is trying to win the race—look at him," the spectators laughed, but Kunu's brother kept running, eventually passing him. "Youngest Brother," Kunu gasped, "I can't make it. Try with all your strength to win." The youngest passed all of his brothers one by one, each urging him on as they raced west on the racetrack around the rim of the world to their goal, the place of the setting sun.

As Youngest Brother ran, he spotted another group of runners ahead: Black Hawk, Hummingbird, Eagle, and two other Winged Ones. When he saw he could never get any closer to them by running, he turned himself into an arrow and shot himself in their direction, alighting beside them. With his brothers shouting encouragement, Youngest Brother shot another arrow and flew past all the Winged Ones. Then he ran as hard as he could, leaving them way behind.

As he came within sight of the goal, he saw Turtle walking in the middle of the valley. The people said, "He Who Gets Hit With Deer Lungs is coming," as Youngest Brother passed Turtle and the last group of runners.

"Who won the race?" someone asked.

"The winner has just come in."

Turtle said, "Kunu's little brother followed me in pretty close. I must be getting old."

"Hey Turtle, you are always making trouble. Kunu's little brother won the race," the people said.

Turtle ignored them. "Bring down your sister-in-law," he told his brother, Oval Turtle, who climbed the platform, but the chief's daughter refused to leave. Then Turtle himself climbed the platform, grabbed her by the wrist, dragged her down, and took her to his home. Although the chief's wife's sister cried out, no one stopped Turtle. When Kunu returned from the race around the world's edge, the people told him, "Kunu, your youngest brother won the race, but Turtle has taken the chief's daughter home."

"All right!" Kunu said as he grabbed his bald-headed war club. "I've always wanted to get a hold of him. Where does he live?"

When Kunu arrived, Turtle was still holding the crying chief's daughter by the wrist.

"Turtle," Kunu said, "my little brother won the race, but you took his prize, the chief's daughter. I have come for her."

"It is true that your brother followed me in real close," Turtle replied.

Kunu grabbed the woman by her free wrist but Turtle wouldn't let go.

Kunu struck Turtle with his war club, making a tremendous sound. Turtle stood on his four legs, wheezing, "I am going to make friends with your brother who won the race and that is why I am giving you this woman, not because I am afraid of you."

Kunu returned home with the chief's daughter, but the Youngest Brother said he was not old enough to marry. "You should marry her," he said to the second youngest brother. But this brother said he was not old enough to marry either, and offered her to the next oldest. All the other brothers also declined and offered her to the next until she was offered to Kunu. "All right!" he said. He thanked his brothers and married the chief's daughter.

### Red Horn's Power

The next morning the nine older brothers went hunting. Kunu returned first, carrying a deer. Putting his bow and arrows next to the lodge, he laid a de-haired skin in the middle of the lodge where he dressed the deer carcass, setting the lungs to one side. His wife picked up the deer lungs and threw them at Youngest Brother, hitting him in the chest. She laughed.

"Why did you do that?" Kunu asked angrily.

"I've heard you always do that to him, and that's why he's called He Who Gets Hit With Deer Lungs," she explained.

"No one ever did that to him before. Once I told him to fast and he refused, so I threw a deer lung at him. That's why they call him by that name, but no one ever hit him with a deer lung."

When the other brothers returned, the youngest told them, "Our sister-in-law hit me with a deer lung."

"How did that happen? Didn't you see him?"

"No, I didn't see him," she lied.

The youngest brother said, "Those in the heavens who created me didn't call me He Who Is Hit With Deer Lungs; they call me He Who Wears Human Heads As Earrings." He spit into his hands and fingered his earlobes, and as he did this, little faces appeared on them, laughing, winking, and sticking out their tongues. He said, "Those on earth, when they speak of me, call me Red Horn." He spat again. As he drew his hands over his head, his hair became very long and red.

His brothers were delighted. "What power you have," said the next youngest brother. Red Horn spat into his hands again. As he passed his hands over his brother's head, his hair became yellow on one side. When another brother admired this, Red Horn spat into his hands, passed then over the brother's head, and his hair became very long. The Red Horn said, "This is no ordinary power. I will do no more of this."

### Red Horn Marries She Who Wears White Beaver Skin

On the village outskirts, a young woman who wore a white beaver skin as a wrap lived with her old grandmother who wanted her to court Red Horn.

The granddaughter refused, but her grandmother insisted that Red Horn liked her. Finally, the young woman teased Red Horn and he turned and smiled at her. The other women started being mean to her, but the grandmother comforted her, saying, "They are jealous. He will be your husband so stop your crying."

For the fourth time, the men went on the warpath. The first night when they camped outside the village, many young women visited the camp to offer Red Horn a pair of moccasins as a marriage proposal. He refused them all, except for the pair offered by the woman who wore the white beaver skin. Jealously, the other young women shoved her around.

The war party camped ten nights, took ten scalps, and this time Turtle won war honors. When they returned, they sent a messenger ahead who announced: "Storms As He Walks was killed first; Red Horn was killed second." Grandmother told She Who Wears White Beaver Skin that her husband had been killed. "I will cut your hair in mourning." The young woman cried bitterly and protested. Then they heard the victorious whoop. Red Horn was first in the line of returning warriors. "Oh!" said the old woman, "I have spoiled my granddaughter's hair!"

They danced for four days. Many of the young men were friendly with Red Horn, encouraging him to court their sisters, but he refused. Instead he asked, "Where does that girl who wears the white beaver skin as a wrap live?"

"We tell you about some fine women and you refuse. What do you want with her? She lives by the dump pile," some said.

"Why do you say that? Maybe he likes her," others said, and told him where she actually lived.

Before he got there, Grandmother knew that Red Horn would be coming. She encouraged her granddaughter to accept him as a husband. When someone with a lighted brand showed Red Horn to their place, Grandmother rose from her bed. She covered the couple with a fur robe, saying to Red Horn, "I am afraid this orphan will not keep you very warm." Red Horn married the woman of his choice.

## Gaming with the Giants

One day, some men came to the village carrying a sacred pipe, asking for the chief's lodge, which was in the middle of the village. The villagers pointed out Turtle as one of the chief's friends. The men then offered him the pipe, and requested assistance in a ball game with the Giants. Turtle made a drum and drummed all night. His friends waited for him to call them, but Turtle never did. Instead, when he left in the morning, very few followed him. These few could do little against the Giants, and the people were defeated again.

Some evenings later, the newcomers returned. The villagers told them to go to the chief's lodge. Ignoring Turtle, they offered the pipe to Red Horn, but he said to Turtle, "My friend, you smoked the pipe with them before, you may smoke it now."

"Ho," said Turtle, and stuck the pipe in his mouth. Turtle drummed that night and in the morning the chiefs and many others went to encounter the Giants. Their best player was a Giantess with red hair. Turtle said to Red Horn, "My friend, the Giantess has hair just like yours. She is a very fast runner and is winning the game for them. You know, Coyote and Martin are married to Giantesses and that helps them immensely."

Turtle went to talk to Wolf, suggesting that they go and match up the lacrosse sticks. They put Red Horn's with the Giantess' stick so they would be playing against each other. They matched Storms As He Walks against a Giant, Wolf's stick against Coyote's, and Otter's against Martin's.

"When are we going to play ball? I am eager to get started," said the Red Haired Giant Chieftainess.

"Just as soon as my friend comes we'll start," Turtle replied.

"Why does your friend take so long?"

"Wait till he comes. You'll laugh when you see him."

"What is so funny about him that I would laugh?" she asked.

"Just wait until you see him," Turtle said.

When Red Horn was ready, he and Turtle went to look at the sticks. The Giant Chieftainess saw Red Horn and laughed; she bowed her head.

"There you go," Turtle teased, "I thought you said you wouldn't laugh."

"Well, yes, but I didn't laugh at him," she said.

"Look again," Turtle told her. As she looked, the small heads Red Horn wore in his ears stuck their tongues out at her. She laughed again and looked down. Turtle made fun of her.

The people clamored for the game to begin. Turtle said to Red Horn, "Let's the two of us start the game." Giving a war whoop, they tossed the ball to the Giants. Turtle told Red Horn to hit the Giants' sticks when the ball came close.

With Red Horn keeping the Giants away, Turtle caught the ball, swung his stick, called them cowards, and threatened them. He threw the ball to Wolf and Coyote, who caught it and started running. Turtle yelled to Wolf, "Friend, do something." Wolf watched Coyote carefully and sent him flying by shouldering him in the side. Turtle retrieved the ball, scored a goal, and won the first point.

"Come on, come on, this is great!" Turtle shouted.

They played again, this time with Otter and Martin guarding the goal. Turtle got the ball toss and whirled around in the middle of the Giants. Getting clear, he threw the ball just beyond Otter and Martin, who caught it and ran while Turtle shouted, "My friend is going to do something." Otter headed Martin off and shoved him, sending him into the air. "Oh! Our son-in-law!" wailed the Giants as Otter scored the second goal.

Martin got up slowly, using his lacrosse stick as a cane. "Come on, let's play ball!" some shouted and the game resumed. Storms As He Walks and the Giant Chieftainess guarded the goal. Turtle caught the ball and whirled it into the midst of the Giants. "You cowards, stand back or I will knock you down," he goaded. Getting clear, he threw the ball to where the Chieftainess and Storms As He Walks stood. He retrieved the ball and ran, with the Chieftainess after him. When she caught up, he ran harder, which made the sky thunder. Frightened, she jumped aside. Turtle, now on the sidelines, gave a whoop and taunted her. The Chieftainess' mother yelled, "You good-for-nothing woman, hit him!" The Chieftainess ran closer, but Storms As He Walks ran all the harder and thundered more. She screamed and jumped away. Turtle kept shouting insults at her while Storms As He Walks ran through the goal, winning the third point.

"Come on! Come on! This is great. Let's start again!" exclaimed Turtle.

They gave a whoop and started a fourth time. While Kunu and Turtle waited for the toss-in, Turtle said, "My friend usually swings his stick pretty wide." Sure enough, Kunu swung wide, blocking the Giant's stick, and giving Turtle a chance to catch the ball. Getting clear of the Giants, Turtle threw it to where Red Horn and the Giant Chieftainess stood. Red Horn ran with it, with the Giantess after him. Turtle shouted and laughed at her. Just as she caught up with Red Horn, he turned and the little faces in his earlobes stuck out their tongue and winked at her. She had been running with her stick up, but she laughed at the faces and let her stick down. Turtle whooped and shouted, "My friend, look back at her, look back at her!" Her mother muttered, "That good-for-nothing woman, she is smitten with him! She will make the whole village suffer!" Red Horn ran through the goal, winning the fourth point against the Giants. The Giant Chieftainess' people punished her for losing the game.

The Giants wanted another try and the Chieftainess said, "I will match myself against Red Horn no matter what happens to me." Red Horn's friends, the chiefs, matched themselves with the Giant chiefs. Excepting some of the very old people, the whole village of Giants played. Red Horn and his friends won; the Giants lost all four points.

Then Turtle said, "My friends, something just occurred to me. The Giantess has the same color hair as my friend Red Horn. I think we should spare her life and let Red Horn marry her." All agreed.[21]

# Origin Story of Lake Winnebago, Wisconsin

WAUKON G. SMITH, HO-CHUNK

*The storyteller here is Waukon G. Smith, of the Thunder Clan. In a footnote by the editor of the collection, David Lee Smith states: "This origin story dates back to when the Winnebagos first moved to Wisconsin. Ma-ona sent Wak'djunk'aga to earth to help humans and he could not leave until orderly life was established. Wak'djunk'aga was not ready to travel to the Spiritland. For this reason, he could not visit the Creator."*[22]

One day in the woods, Wak'djunk'aga, the Winnebago trickster, was talking to Brother Bear. "Brother Bear," he said, "do you think I can see Ma-ona the Creator?'

"Sure," said Brother Bear, "but you have to die first."

So Wak'djunk'aga went to a village where the warriors were shooting arrows. He cried out, "Shoot me! Shoot me! I bet you can't hit me!"

They shot him full of holes, but he could not die. Wak'djunk'aga now felt especially sad because he could not see Ma-ona. So he went to the top of a cliff and cried and cried until his tears formed a large lake. Lake Winnebago is the creation of Wak'djunk'aga's tears.[23]

# 2·5

# Frenchmen Arrive

ANONYMOUS, HO-CHUNK

*A Ho-Chunk hunting party encountered their first European man on the eastern edge of Lake Superior in 1614.[24] Twenty years later, Jean Nicolet, believing he had found a water route to China, arrived at Red Banks, on Green Bay, Wisconsin, with guns blazing and wearing a Chinese robe. The clan chiefs feasted with him and his party.*

Once something appeared in the middle of the lake (Green Bay). They were the French; they were the first to come to the Winnebago. The ship came nearer and the Winnebago went to the edge of the lake with offerings of tobacco and white deerskins. There they stood. When the French were about to come ashore, they fired their guns off in the air as a salute to the Indians. The Indians said, "They are Thunderbirds." They had never heard the report of a gun before that time and that is why they thought they were Thunderbirds.

Then the French landed their boats and came ashore and extended their hands to the Winnebago, and the Indians put tobacco in their hands. The French, of course, wanted to shake hands with the Indians. They did not know what tobacco was, and did not know what to do with it. Some of the Winnebago poured tobacco on their heads, asking them for victory in war. The French tried to speak to them, but they could not make themselves understood. . . . Then the French taught the Indians how to use guns, but they held aloof for a long time through fear, thinking that all these things were holy.

Suddenly a Frenchman saw an old man smoking and poured water on him. They knew nothing about smoking or tobacco. After a while they got more accustomed to one another. The Indians learned how to shoot the guns and began trading objects for axes. They would give furs and things of that nature for the guns, knives, and axes of the whites. They still considered them holy, however. Finally they learned how to handle guns quite well and they liked them very much. They would even build fires at nights so that they might try their guns, for they could not wait for the day, they were so impatient. When they were out of ammunition they would go to the traders and tell their people that they would soon return. By this time they had learned to make themselves understood by various signs.

The second time they went to visit the French, they took with them all the various articles they possessed. . . . Then the leader of the whites took a liking to a Winnebago girl, the daughter of the chief, and he asked her parents for permission to marry her. They told him that her two brothers had the right to give her away in marriage. So he asked them and they consented. Then he married her. He lived there and worked for the Indians and stayed with them for many years. He went home every once in a while and his wife went with him, but he always came back again. After a while a son was born to him, and then another. When the boys were somewhat grown up, he decided to take his oldest son with him to his country and bring him up in such a way that he would not be in danger, as was the case here in the woods. The Indians consented to it, and they agreed that the mother was to bring up the youngest child.

So he took his oldest boy home with him. When he got home, he went to live with his parents, as he had not been married in his own country. He was a leader of men. The boy was with him all the time and everyone took a great liking to him. People would come to see him and bring him presents. They gave him many toys. However, in spite of all, he got homesick and he would cry every night until he fell asleep. He cried all the time and would not eat. After a while the people thought it best to bring him back to his home, as they were afraid that he would get sick and die. Before long they brought him back. The father said, "My sons are men and they can remain here and grow up among you. You are to bring them up in your own way and they are to live just as you do."

The Indians made them fast. One morning the oldest one got up very early and did not go out fasting. His older uncle, seeing him try to eat some corn, took it away from him and, taking a piece of charcoal, mashed it, rubbed it over his face, and threw him out of doors. He went out into the wilderness and hid himself in a secret place. Afterwards the people searched for him everywhere, but they could not find him. Then the people told the uncle that he had done wrong in throwing the boy out. The uncle was sorry, but there was nothing to be done anymore. In reality the uncle was afraid of the boy's father. They looked everywhere but could not find him.

After a full month the boy came home and brought with him a circle of wood, that is, a drum. He told the people that this is what he had received in a dream, and that it was not to be used in war; that it was something with which to obtain life. He said that if a feast was made to it, this feast would be one to Earthmaker, as Earthmaker had blessed him and told him to put his life in the service of the Winnebago.[25]

# 2.6

## It Was Not a Sale; It Was a Loan

FOUR LEGS, HO-CHUNK

*After Americans replaced the French as the colonial power, corporate interests pursued the timber wealth of the Menominee Nation. In a January 1825 treaty at Butte Des Morts, the New York Indians sold land "they had supposedly purchased from the Menominee and Ho-Chunk to the Brothertown, another displaced tribe from the east."[26] A Ho-Chunk leader at the 1827 treaty meeting with Governor Cass of the Michigan territory, which at the time included Wisconsin, spoke in defense of the Menominee contention that they had not sold land to the New York Indians, but had loaned it to them out of pity.*

I will tell you what has passed between our brothers from the East and us. I will tell you the truth. What I say, I say before the Great Spirit who is the Father of Life, as well as the Heaven above us, as the Earth upon which we stand.

They said, "Our Brother! It was at the request of our Great Father that we have come here to meet you. We are here on your lands. Our Brothers! Winnebago [Ho-Chunk] and Menominee! We are poor. We ask you to take pity on us. We are not master of our own land; neither of the waters within it nor of the trees on it. We ask of you, therefore, the charity to let us sit upon your land here!"

Father! When they first came, they asked for a small piece of land, sufficient for them to put their children on, that they might live. They and the Menominee were assembled at the first visit, and that Menominee Chief who has spoken to you was hesitating for two days—so much, that he did not know what answer to make.

They said, "Menominee, our Brothers! We hope you will give us what we ask. We ask you to lend, and not sell us, a small piece of land. Do this, in charity to our impoverished situation."

Father: It was long before the Menominee would consent; but we, the Winnebago, interfered and said, "What harm can it do, to grant their request, since they only want to borrow the land, and not to buy it." It was not a sale, nor a gift, but it was a loan. We had too little ourselves to be willing to sell it. The New York Indians told us that we should not regret the loan, nor the charity we had yielded them. If they had sugar camps, our children should occupy them in common.[27]

# 2.7

# Theft of the Lead Mining District

NAWKAW CARAMANI, HO-CHUNK

*In the Treaty of Prairie du Chien in 1825, the Americans had promised that no more whites would settle on Ho-Chunk lands or work the lead (galena) mines without permission. Yet in the lead rush of the 1820s, over ten thousand miners violated this law and poured onto Ho-Chunk lands, driving them out of their quarries.*

*The Ho-Chunk were angry about this and other wrongs. But it was a lie that tricked the peaceful and respected Ho-Chunk Chief Red Bird, leader of the Prairie La Crosse band, into "taking meat." This revenge killing, understood by Ho-Chunk to be correct, triggered an over-reaction by the Americans and a marshalling of many American troops. Because he wished to prevent injury to his people, Red Bird surrendered himself to American troops at Fort Winnebago (Portage) in September of 1827. Chief Nawkaw Caramani (also spelled Caramaunee) led a one-hundred-person entourage escorting Red Bird to the Americans where Caramani expressed his people's understanding of the event.*

They are here. We know of no wrong they have done; they have but fulfilled the tribal law; to us they are heroes. We ask only this: treat them as braves; do not put them in irons.[28]

 2.8

# Red Bird Surrenders

RED BIRD, HO-CHUNK

*After solemn assurances that Red Bird "would not be put in irons," he surrendered with great dignity. Indian agent Joseph Street wrote: "This manly, chivalric act, his open, free, and high-bearing at the time, has something more than ordinary in it."[29] Red Bird was put in irons and died in prison in February of 1828.[30]*

I do not know that I have done wrong. I come now to sacrifice myself to the white man because it is my duty to save my people from the scourge of war. If I have done wrong, I will pay for it either with horses or with my life.

I do not understand the white man's law, which has one set of words for the white man and another for the red. The white men promised us that the lead mines would be ours, but they did nothing to put the men who came to take possession away from them. If an Indian took possession of something belonging to a white man, the soldiers would come quickly enough.

We have been patient. We have seen all this. We have seen the ancient burial grounds plowed over. We have seen our braves shot down like dogs for stealing corn. We have seen our women mocked and raped. We have seen the white men steal our lands, our quarries, our forests, our waterways, by lying to us and cheating us and making us drunk enough to put marks on papers without knowing what we were doing. When first the Long Knives came, the prophets told us they would never be honest with us. We did not believe them. We do now.

When word came to us that Wamangoosgaraha was slain, I went forth and took meat. I did not know the report was false; so I did no wrong. I fulfilled the law of the Winnebago. I am not ashamed. I would not be ashamed. I have come because the white men are too strong, and I do not wish my people to suffer. Now I am ready. Take me.[31]

# The Treaty of 1829

## WAUKON DECORA, HO-CHUNK

*Put in irons, Red Bird sickened and died in prison while awaiting trial and before a presidential pardon arrived. Meanwhile, thousands of miners and settlers poured into the lead-mining region of southwest Wisconsin and northwest Illinois, while the young Henry Dodge, soon to be the first governor of the Wisconsin Territory, refused to budge from his stolen lead diggings. In the face of unrelenting pressure, Ho-Chunk signed the papers that ceded the Lead District lands at a council in Green Bay in 1828, forcing them to vacate the southern side of the lower Wisconsin River.*

*When commissioners arrived in Prairie du Chien in July 1829, they made it clear that they wanted to take Ho-Chunk land.*

I speak not for myself, but for my chiefs and young men. You know I am not a full-blooded Indian, like my chief there [probably pointing to Nawkaw], but they place me here to speak for them. It is not the way of our nation to talk about our land; we think it a great crime. But as others have done so, I now speak. It is not the first time we have heard you talk about our land. We have heard our Great Father [President Adams] speak of it also. . . .

When we first saw you here you told us our Great Father wanted to see the size of our country. We are always glad to hear from him—we know him to be a man who does not speak with two tongues.

Fathers, when we first assembled around the great council fire at this place [in 1825 at Prairie du Chien], our Great Father had then together six or seven nations of his red children to make peace between them; he then saw and knew the size of our country. Then we heard at Green Bay [in 1828] from our father [Governor Cass], that our Great Father wished to see us—fifteen of us went to see him. Before we left Green Bay our father told us his young men should not work over the line between us in the mineral country. We gave them nine months to smelt up the mineral they had dug. We have heard that we were to be paid for the damages done on our land [on] the other side of the line. We think we ought to be paid for the damages committed by you.[32]

# Do You Want Our Wigwams?
# You Live in Palaces!

LITTLE ELK CARAMANI, HO-CHUNK

---

*The treaty negotiators never offered to pay for the damages done to Ho-Chunk land, although the miners destroyed vast tracts. Here the Ho-Chunk responded to the 1829 commissioners by pointing out their greed.*

The first white man we knew was a Frenchman—he lived among us as we did. He painted himself, he smoked his pipe with us, sang and danced with us, and married one of our [women], but he wanted to buy no land of us!

The Redcoat came next. He gave us fine coats, knives, and guns and traps, blankets and jewels. He seated our chiefs and warriors at his table with himself, fixed epaulets on their shoulders, put commissions in their pockets, and suspended medals on their breasts, but never asked us to sell our country to him!

Next came the Bluecoat, and no sooner had he seen a small portion of our country than he wished to see a map of the whole of it, and having seen it, he wished us to sell it all to him. Governor Cass, last year, at Green Bay, urged us to sell all our country to him, and now, you fathers, repeat the request. Why do you wish to add our small country to yours, already so large?

You ask us to sell all our country and wander off into the boundless regions of the west. We do not own that country, and the deer, the elk, the beaver, the buffalo, and the otter, now there, belong not to us . . . we have no right to kill them.

Our wives and our children now seated behind us are dear to us, and so is our country where rest in peace the bones of our ancestors. Fathers, pity a people, few in number, who are poor and helpless. Do you want our country? Yours is larger than ours! Do you want our wigwams? You live in palaces! Do you want our horses? Yours are larger and better than ours! Do you want our women? Yours now sitting behind you are handsomer and dressed better than ours! Look at them yonder! Why, fathers, what can be your motive?[33]

# Where in the Name of God
# Shall We Live?

LITTLE ELK CARAMANI, HO-CHUNK

*Recognizing that their pleas meant nothing to the commissioners, the Ho-Chunk decided that they must part with some of their land. They were informed that the formerly proposed boundary lines were not enough: they had to give up not only the mineral lands of northeast Illinois, but also all of the country north to the Wisconsin River.*

My fathers, we expected the piece offered was large enough. Where in the name of God shall we and our families live if we give more [land]? I am a man who comes out of the earth, and am one of the land holders [a member of an earth clan], and we agreed to give more than we first marked off, and thought it was enough. We and our chiefs agreed to give more and thought we were parting with a large tract—although I suppose you think it small. When our fathers here said it was too small, we agreed to move the line to Sugar Creek; to move the line a third time, we cannot.

My fathers, I am going to say a few words to you and they are the truth. I speak with no forked tongue. Last year we had a council with our father [Governor Cass] and we went to see our Great Father, the president. When I saw him, I was naked and he shook my hand hard and took pity on us. He told us only once what you have told us. He said we had that in our land which shone bright, and laid deep, and what his people wanted. He told us how much he wanted, and that was not as much as you do. We have marked a large piece; it is a good piece from where this chief [Henry Dodge] here lives. Our Great Father only expected the line to be where it was last year.[34]

# 2.12

# The Black Hawk War

## LITTLE ELK CARAMANI, HO-CHUNK

*After the Sauk had been driven out of their land and had their cornfields plowed under, their chief, Black Hawk, led one thousand men, women, and children back east across the Mississippi River to plant in their traditional territory. This was perceived as an act of war, and the American militia was called up. The Sauk party sent white truce flags to the Americans but was fired upon three times. At the confluence of the Bad Axe and the Mississippi, at what today is called "Victory," Wisconsin, American troops fired on Black Hawk's truce flag. His people, attempting to swim across the Mississippi, were slaughtered. Accounts tell of how the river ran red with blood.[35]*

*The Ho-Chunk, who were largely neutral during the Black Hawk War, nonetheless were forced to give up all of their lands in Wisconsin. Because the war had disrupted their ability to plant corn, they were in danger of starvation. They presented their case to George Porter, territorial governor of Michigan.*

Since the Sacs [Sauk] and Foxes [Mesquakie] have been destroyed, we examined into the conduct of all our young men. They all showed us a clean hand, and a clear heart. I hope therefore that the conduct of the tribes I represent may be made known to our father, the president [Andrew Jackson] that he may take pity upon us, his red children, and alleviate our miserable conditions. We want assistance in the way of provisions. All our corn has been destroyed during the past summer. Our only hope for the present is the chase—game is scarce, but I hope we will be able to make out to live till our Great Father can render us his aid. Had it not been for Black Hawk and the prophet, the Rock River band would not have been engaged in staining our land with the blood of the whites. It was some of their young men, who were related to the Sacs, that have caused all this trouble to our nation. . . .

This spring, when the snow went off, the Sacs and Foxes came to us and said they were going to raise the war club against the whites, and wished to persuade us to join them. We said we could not, because we considered ourselves Americans. I soon after went down the Rock River, and we got to the American war chief's camp [General Henry Atkinson's camp] and he told us to drive the Sacs back. But we could not—they wanted to bloody our land.

Black Hawk, a Sauk chief, sought allies among the Ho-Chunk. His people were massacred at the confluence of the Bad Axe and Mississippi Rivers as they tried to flee to the western shore of the Mississippi. This site is called Victory, Wisconsin. Reproduced by permission of the Wisconsin Historical Society. WHi-25690.

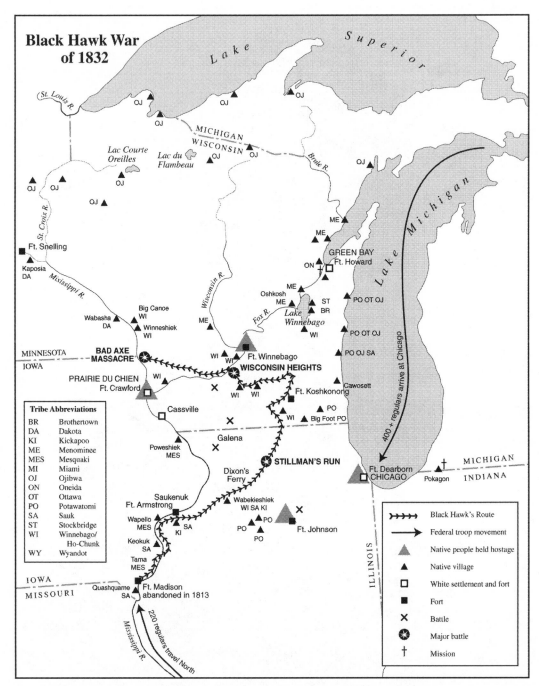

**Black Hawk War of 1832**

*Lake Superior*

*St. Louis R.*

OJ

OJ

OJ

OJ

OJ

MICHIGAN
WISCONSIN

*Brule R.*

OJ

*Lac Courte Oreilles*

*Lac du Flambeau*

OJ

OJ

*Lake Michigan*

OJ

OJ

OJ

OJ

ME

ME

GREEN BAY
Ft. Howard

ON

Ft. Snelling

Kaposia
DA

*Mississippi R.*

*St. Croix R.*

*Wisconsin R.*

ME

PO OT OJ

Big Canoe
WI

Oshkosh
ME

ME

ST
BR

PO OT OJ

Wabasha
DA

Winneshiek
WI

ME

*Fox R.*

*Lake Winnebago*

WI

PO OJ SA

MINNESOTA
IOWA

**BAD AXE MASSACRE**

WI

WI

WI

Ft. Winnebago

**WISCONSIN HEIGHTS**

400 + regulars arrive at Chicago

PRAIRIE DU CHIEN
Ft. Crawford

WI

×

WI

WI

Ft. Koshkonong

Cawosett

Cassville

×

Galena

WI

PO

Big Foot PO

Poweshiek
MES

×

Dixon's Ferry

**STILLMAN'S RUN**

Ft. Dearborn
CHICAGO

MICHIGAN

Pokagon

INDIANA

Saukenuk
Ft. Armstrong

Wabekieshiek
WI SA KI

×

Wapello
MES

PO

PO

Ft. Johnson

SA
KI

PO

PO

Keokuk
SA

Tama
MES

ILLINOIS

IOWA
MISSOURI

Quashquame
SA

Ft. Madison
abandoned in 1813

*Mississippi R.*

220 regulars travel North

**Tribe Abbreviations**

| | |
|---|---|
| BR | Brothertown |
| DA | Dakota |
| KI | Kickapoo |
| ME | Menominee |
| MES | Mesquaki |
| MI | Miami |
| OJ | Ojibwa |
| ON | Oneida |
| OT | Ottawa |
| PO | Potawatomi |
| SA | Sauk |
| ST | Stockbridge |
| WI | Winnebago/ Ho-Chunk |
| WY | Wyandot |

Black Hawk's Route

Federal troop movement

Native people held hostage

Native village

White settlement and fort

Fort

Battle

Major battle

Mission

On three separate occasions, Black Hawk's people were fired upon when they were under a truce flag, and they were massacred at Victory, Wisconsin. Black Hawk's account of his life is an early Native autobiography. Although few Ho-Chunk joined Black Hawk, the Ho-Chunk were nonetheless forced to leave their ancestral lands in southern Wisconsin because of Black Hawk's defeat. The Black Hawk War of 1832 ended large-scale Indian resistance east of the Mississippi. Map adapted from Helen Hornbeck Tanner, *Atlas of Great Lakes Indian History* (Norman: University of Oklahoma Press, 1987), 152.

When he [Atkinson] saw we could not get them off our land, he advised us to leave our land, to go away from our country, and to keep out of his way. We said we could not do that as we had nothing to eat. He then said we should eat whatever we found in our country in the way of cattle, hogs, etc., but we told him we could not do so, as there would be claims enough presented against us by the whites at our payment.

We thought it was only us that were foolish—that could tell lies, but I find that some of your whites are as good at it as many of our young men. . . . They took all our corn and many articles as they passed our villages, and have even taken up the dead that were buried, and took off the blankets, etc. in which they were wrapped. . . .

I have been told by some of the white chiefs that as soon as the fuss would be over, we should be recompensed for our losses. I am looking for something to eat hereafter from our Great Father. If we should not get something, we shall certainly lose half of our nation.[36]

# 2.13

# If They Did Not Sign,
# He Would Kill Them

DANDY, HO-CHUNK

*In 1837 the Ho-Chunk sent to Washington, D.C., a young, low-ranking delegation that had no status to conduct business in the name of the tribe. This delegation was told they would not be allowed to return home without signing the treaty. Although they were forced to sign, their signatures could not be binding because the group had few members from the Thunder clan and none from the Bear clan, the two clans empowered to deal with external and internal politics dealing with land issues.*

*In order to defeat the fraudulently obtained treaty, Dandy, Caramani, and Yellow Thunder met with Governor Henry Dodge, who supervised Indian affairs in the Wisconsin territory.[37]*

Father, you see this pipe; after you have smoked, we will all smoke it. Father, they call me Dandy, and when I go to council, I take this pipe, and though I am very small, whatever I undertake I succeed in. I believe the Great Spirit likes me, because whatever I try, I succeed in. Father I love that pipe, and now as all your children have smoked it, I will present it to you. Father, I have spoken to you with no forked tongue . . .

Our agent [Thomas Boyd] told the Indians when he took them to Washington, that he would make but one road for them; that flour, pork, tobacco, and salt was due them from former payments, and that he was going to get it for them; that if they would go with him, they should have these articles and a double handful of money besides . . . and that they should not be talked to about a sale of their country.

The Indians did not wish to go to Washington, but their agent forced them to go, and when they did go, they thought Gov. Cass, or Clark, or Dodge, would be with them to take care of them. But they passed on without either of these.

[I] learned from the [Little] Soldier that he alone spoke against the treaty at Washington, all the others of the delegation being in favor . . . that their agent, on the way, kept company only with the Blind Dekori, and that he

[Decora] and their agent made all the arrangements about the treaty . . . that their agent told them at Washington if they did not sign the treaty, he would put them into a house, or on board of a boat, and kill them. This was the reason why the Soldier signed the treaty—that he was unwilling to do so, but was threatened with death; that he did refuse for a long time, saying their Great Father did not want to purchase the land, but that their agent did. To induce the Soldier to sign, he [Soldier] was told their annuity should be paid to them for four years at the Portage as formerly, and he then agreed.[38]

# 2.14

## Forced Removals: The Ho-Chunk Trail of Tears

WINNESHIEK, SHAKING EARTH CARAMANI, BIG HAWK, AND BLACK HAWK; HO-CHUNK

*Because of the fraudulent Treaty of 1837, the Ho-Chunk lost all their homelands east of the Mississippi. Soldiers rounded up the people and burned what they had to leave behind. This began the many "trails of tears" where the Ho-Chunk suffered forced removals to territories held by other Nations. The treaty-abiding faction was moved in 1840 to the misnamed "neutral ground" near Turkey River in Iowa, an area being fought over by the Sauk and Dakota (Sioux). In 1846 Ho-Chunk were then moved to northern Minnesota on the Long Prairie River, where Ho-Chunk people were used as a human buffer zone between Dakota and Ojibwe. Ho-Chunk were forced to move again in 1855 to the Blue Earth reservation in southern Minnesota, when the Dakota Uprising of 1862 was used as an excuse to again seize Ho-Chunk lands. Although the Ho-Chunk had not participated in the uprising, settlers grabbed the land that the Ho-Chunk had so laboriously cleared and cultivated. In the harsh winter of 1863, Ho-Chunk were forced west to the Crow Creek Reserve, South Dakota, and "settled" among their Dakota enemies. Over six hundred Ho-Chunk died on this forced march. Fearing for their lives, Ho-Chunk sold Crow Creek and bought land from the Omaha, to form the Nebraska Winnebago Reservation, "but the Winnebagos' [Ho-Chunk's] enthusiasm for owning farms was irrevocably diminished by the injustice of their removal from Minnesota." Those who stayed in Nebraska were called "dwellers on the muddy" or the ni'sojaci.[39]*

*But some resisted removal. While some made dugout canoes to get to their purchased land in Nebraska, others continued down the Missouri River to the Mississippi, where they turned upstream to the Wisconsin River, rejoining the Ho-Chunk who had successfully evaded the four removals by armed troops. The Wisconsin Ho-Chunk were called "dwellers among the pine" or wa'zijaci.[40] Makaja Zi or Chief Yellow Thunder led some of these holdouts. Even though he had been made to sign the Treaty of 1837, when the chief found out after the signing that the treaty forced his people out of the state, he refused to leave. But under the pretext of inviting him to a meeting at Fort Winnebago, the military abducted him and sent him out of state. He soon led a band of exiles back to Baraboo, where he bought back his land. In 1874 he died in his Wisconsin homeland.[41]*

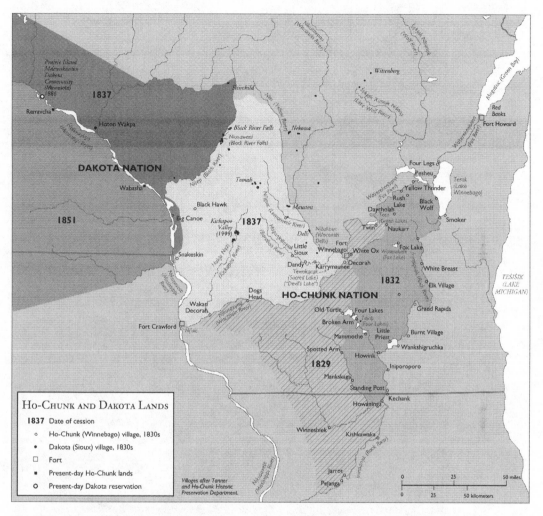

The following labels appear on the map:

**HO-CHUNK AND DAKOTA LANDS**

1837  Date of cession
- ○  Ho-Chunk (Winnebago) village, 1830s
- •  Dakota (Sioux) village, 1830s
- ▢  Fort
- ■  Present-day Ho-Chunk lands
- ⦾  Present-day Dakota reservation

Villages after Tanner and Ho-Chunk Historic Preservation Department.

DAKOTA NATION

HO-CHUNK NATION

1837 · 1851 · 1837 · 1832 · 1829

Prairie Island Mdewakanton Dakota Community (Minnesota) 1865 · Remnicha · Hoton Wakpa · Wabasha · Big Canoe · Snakeskin · Fort Crawford · Wakan Decorah · Dogs Head · Black Hawk · Kickapoo Valley (1999) · Tamah · Mauston · Little Sioux · Dells · Fort Winnebago · Dandy · Tewakacak (Sacred Lake) (Devil's Lake) · Karrymaunee · Decorah · White Ox · Fox Lake · Nissawara (Black River Falls) · Black River Falls · Nekoosa · Rainchild · Wittenberg · Red Banks · Fort Howard · Four Legs · Pesheu · Yellow Thunder · Rush Lake · Black Wolf · Daycholah · Twin · Naukarr · Smoker · White Breast · Elk Village · Grand Rapids · Old Turtle · Four Lakes · Broken Arm · Burnt Village · Mammothe · Little Priest · Wankshigruchka · Spotted Arm · Howink · Iniporoporo · Manskaiga · Standing Post · Kechank · Howaning · Winneshiek · Kishkawaka · Jarrot · Pejanga · Tesisik (Lake Michigan)

The Mdewakanton Dakota or Mystic Lake (Santee) Sioux once inhabited northern Wisconsin. From 1736 to 1854 they were often at war with the Ojibwe over the wild rice lakes in northwestern Wisconsin. In the 1800s many Dakota moved west of the Mississippi River to Prairie Island Reservation in Minnesota. At present, some Dakota are trying to reestablish a site on the Wisconsin side of the Mississippi River in their ceded territory. Already suffering from European-introduced diseases, the Ho-Chunk, formerly known as Winnebago, met the Frenchman Jean Nicolet at their village of Red Banks on Green Bay. Moving south along their ancestral territory around the important Fox River–lower Wisconsin River trade route, they had a strong presence in southwestern Wisconsin until the lead rush in the 1820s when 10,000 miners defied U.S. law, illegally taking Ho-Chunk land. The Ho-Chunk suffered four forced removals, the last to the Crow Creek Reserve in Dakota Territory. The Ho-Chunk who remained hidden in Wisconsin were called Wazijaci ("Dwellers among the Pines") and faced repeated military removals until 1874. Map by Zoltan Grossman; reproduced by permission from Wisconsin Cartographers' Guild, *Wisconsin's Past and Present* (Madison: University of Wisconsin Press, 1998), 9.

Ho-Chunk women pose in a Black River Falls photographer's studio in the 1910s. Reproduced by permission of the Wisconsin Historical Society. WHi-10151.

*Also in 1874, the chiefs wrote to President Ulysses S. Grant, outlining the terrible conditions among the Wisconsin Ho-Chunk in Nebraska and their desire to return to Wisconsin.*

We respectfully show to your excellency that there are now on their reservation nine hundred of our people, and we are poor and in need of help. Very many of our people are dying from want and exposure. Thirty of them have been buried within the past nine days. The agent here has given us very little to eat, only five pounds of flour and five pounds of beef per head every week.

We had deer, ducks, rats, and fish . . . also pork, tea, coffee, and sugar, and lived like white people back in Wisconsin. The commissioner, Mr. C. A. Hunt, told us that if we would come here we should have $40.00 and three blankets each, and that each man should have a farm and wagon and horses, plow, and white men to teach us to be farmers like white men, with good houses to live, and that we should have churches and schoolhouses.

We have been here a long time now, and have none of the things that the commissioner promised us. The Mankato (or Blue Earth) Indians will not allow our people to cut wood to keep us from freezing. We have no farms, and the Mankatos say that the land all belongs to them, and if any of our people put their tents up, then the Mankatos will drive them off.

Now we want you to send a good man to us to show us where our farms are, and to give us some tea, coffee, and sugar. Winneshiek is sick and cannot get well on such food. We want the money and the blankets promised us by the commissioner. We cannot live here in this way and unless you do something for us, we shall go back to Wisconsin where we can hunt and fish. We cannot hunt and fish here as there is no game and no fish to be caught. We want you to write to Winneshiek and tell him what you will do for us at once.[42]

# 2.15

# Mountain Wolf Woman:
# The Autobiography of
# a Winnebago Indian

MOUNTAIN WOLF WOMAN, HO-CHUNK

*The year 1874 marked the last of four attempts to force the Ho-Chunk from their homeland. In her autobiography, Mountain Wolf Woman mentions the last removal and her relatives' return to Wisconsin in a dugout canoe from Nebraska. Of all the "composite compositions" that were published as a result of Indian/Euro-American collaboration,[43]* Mountain Wolf Woman, Sister of Crashing Thunder: The Autobiography of a Winne-bago Indian *has one of the highest claims to authenticity because it was told to Nancy Oestreich Lurie due to her kinship with Mountain Wolf Woman. Lurie had been adopted as a daughter by Mitchell Redcloud Sr. "I thus acquired a Winnebago name, a clan affiliation, and a host of relatives upon whom I could rely in continuing the task Redcloud and I had begun," Nancy Lurie writes in her preface to* Mountain Wolf Woman *(xii). When Mountain Wolf Woman first met Nancy Lurie in 1945, she greeted Lurie as a niece. "My aunt," Lurie writes, "soon proved to be not only a valuable informant, but a good friend as well. . . . Mountain Wolf Woman readily agreed to my request for her story" (xii–xiii), viewing it as part of a relative's honored duty. Lurie writes, "During the course of our work she thought of herself as a visiting relative. . . . When my teaching schedule interrupted our work, she found ways to occupy her time, and even between daily recording sessions she was never idle. Indeed, she is incapable of idleness and equates personal contentment with useful activity. She sewed clothing for herself, and even split wood for the fireplace" (xv). This was in 1957, when Mountain Wolf Woman was seventy-three years old.*

## Earliest Recollections

Mother said she had me at our grandfather's home—at East Fork River. We lived there in the spring, April, at the time they were making maple sugar. She said that after a while the weather became pleasant, everything was nice and green and we moved from this place back to where we usually lived—at Levis Creek, near Black River Falls. There father built a log house. I suppose it took

Mountain Wolf Woman, a Ho-Chunk of Wisconsin, tells her story of seventy-five years of living through monumental cultural changes. Born in 1884, she tells her adopted niece, anthropologist Nancy Oestreich Lurie, about her childhood as part of a family making seasonal rounds, her stay in a mission school, and her marriages, children, and religious experiences. Reproduced by permission from Nancy Oestrich Lurie, *Mountain Wolf Woman, Sister of Crashing Thunder* (Ann Arbor: University of Michigan Press, 1961), xxii.

a long time to build it because mother said the log house was newly finished when I walked there for the first time. There, where we regularly lived, mother and father planted their garden.

In the summer that followed the second spring—after my first birthday— we went to Black River Falls. Mother, oldest sister White Thunder and I went to town. We were returning and mother carried me on her back. I was restless and she had taken me off the cradleboard. I remember being there on mother's back. We crossed a creek and I saw the water swirling swiftly. Mother said, "Ahead is your older sister." A woman was walking in front of us carrying an empty cradleboard. I saw that she held up her skirt just high enough to wade through the water. After that I forgot. Once I asked mother if that ever happened. I told her what I had seen. "Oh," mother said, "I remember, that was your oldest sister White Thunder who carried your empty cradle on her back—Do you remember that?"

"Yes," I said.

"You were probably frightened," she said, "and perhaps that is why you remember."

White Thunder was the oldest child in our family and Crashing Thunder was second. Then followed [the] second older sister, Wihanga, Bald Eagle. Next was Henaga, the second son; he was called Strikes Standing. Then came the third son, Hagaga, and he was called Big Winnebago; Haksigaga, the third daughter died when she was still quite small. They did not know how this death came about. However, there was an old lady who was related to my mother, and any time that my father brought home deer from hunting, summer, winter, anytime my father killed deer, this old lady got some. Yet, the old lady was envious of my mother about her share of the meat. Mother used to say that she poisoned Haksigaga. She killed her because of jealousy about meat. Next was the fourth daughter, Kinakega. She was called Distant Flashes Standing. And then I was the last child—"Poor quality" they used to say of that one.

It was about the time that my older sister Bald Eagle was born that they went to Nebraska. Mother used to say they were taken to Nebraska that winter; they were moved from one land to another. Many Winnebago were moved to Nebraska and there mother took her three children. Grandmother had relatives in Nebraska. Grandmother was the oldest daughter in her family. In Nebraska she saw her sisters, the second and third daughters. They were very eager to see their relatives. But, mother said, some of the Wisconsin Winnebago did not like the removal. Some even cried because they were taken there. However, mother used to say, "The fact that we would see my relatives made me happy that we were going. And when we reached the Missouri River, our uncles came to meet us. When they heard we were coming, Squeaking Wing and Captures The Lodge and a third uncle Hagaga came to meet us."

As their uncle Squeaking Wing came through the train he called out, "Bends The Boughs [Mountain Wolf Woman's mother], where is she? Bends The Boughs, where is she?" At last he found them and there was much rejoicing when they saw one another. Brother Crashing Thunder was dressed in a fringed buckskin outfit, and when my uncles saw him they lifted him up in the air and they said, "Oh, how cute our nephew is!" Eventually they arrived at the reservation.

It was winter. Everyone had his own camping outfit, and they all made their homes here and there. They built wigwams. Then spring came and mother said that the Winnebago died in great numbers. Deaths occurred almost every day. When someone died, the Winnebago carried away their dead, crying as they walked. All those who had a death in the family cried as they walked along. They were going to the graveyard, and there was much weeping.

Mother was frightened. "Why do we stay here?" she said. "I am afraid because all the people are all dying. Why do we not go back home?" They were with some uncles at the time. The first was called Good Village, the next was called Big Naqiga and the third was called Little Naqiga. In the spring they moved to the Missouri River where they cut down some big willow trees and made dugout canoes big enough for two, mother said. She must have been talking about fairly big boats that they made. There in the spring when the weather is very pleasant, mother used to say, a large group went down the Missouri River. Thus she returned home with some of her relatives. They went down the Missouri to River's Mouth Place, as they used to call St. Louis. From there they traveled back on the Mississippi River; they traveled upstream on the Mississippi.

Eventually they stopped at a certain place where they saw some white people. Nobody knew how to speak English, so they said, "Where is Henaga? Where is Henaga? He is the only one who knows the name of that place." They meant Captures The Lodge, who was just a little boy. When they brought him they said to him "Say it! Say it!" He was the only one who knew that one word, and he said, "Prarsheen? Prarsheen?" I guess he was saying "Prairie du Chien." Then the white people understood him, and said it was Prairie du Chien. They stopped there for a while and eventually they left and arrived at La Crosse. They lived there for a time and then they moved out towards Black River Falls.

It seems that many Winnebago came back to Wisconsin. My family was evidently not the only ones who returned. Also, some of the Winnebago in Wisconsin lived way out in the country a great distance from any town. These people said that they had not been found so they did not go to Nebraska, mother said. Thus, not all of the Winnebago left in the removal.

It must have been at this time that my parents took up land, that is, a homestead. Some of them acquired homesteads there at Black River Falls. However, father was not interested in such things. Even when they were in Nebraska his brother said, "Register, older brother, claim some land for yourself and claim some for your children." But father did not do it, so they did not have any land in Nebraska. Mother and her uncles did not take any land, but some of the Winnebago took land in Nebraska so they had property, but eventually they sold it. However, my parents did not realize what they were doing and that is why they acted as they did. Some of the Indians took homesteads but father did not understand so he did not take a homestead. That was when my mother took a homestead. There was an old man who was a grandfather to us who took land. His name was Many Trails. I used to see him; he was a little old man. He said to my mother, "Granddaughter, why do you not claim some land? I claimed some and if you take a homestead right next to me, then we can live beside each other." So mother took forty acres.

Indians did not look ahead to affairs of this sort. They never looked to the future. They only looked to the present insofar as they had enough to sustain themselves. This is the way the Indians used to live. The fact that my father did not care to obtain any land was because he was a member of the Thunder Clan. "I do not belong to the Earth." He said, "I do not belong to the Earth and I have no concern with land." This is why he was not interested in having any land. But mother was also one—one of the bird clan people; she belonged to the Eagle Clan. She said, "By this means we will have some place to live," and so she took forty acres. Here my father built the log house where we usually lived.

Once when I recalled that we camped at a place where the country was very beautiful, Mother said, "You were then about two years old." I remember there was a fish there. That beautiful country where we were camping was at Black River Falls at the old depot in back of what is now G.W.'s general store. There was not a house around. We lived there in the spring of the year and my father fished. I suppose all of the Indians fished. There my father speared a big fish, an enormous fish, a sturgeon. When my father brought it home, carrying it over his shoulder, the tail dragged on the ground. He brought it back to where we were living. There I saw this big fish that looked like a man with a big fat belly, lying on his side with his belly protruding. I remembered that and then I forgot.

We must have been camped at the Black River where the bank is very steep. There they lost me and everybody helped my mother look for me. They were afraid I fell in the water there, over that high bank. There was an old lady and my mother brought her tobacco. Anything they asked of her, the old lady always knew the answer. They brought her tobacco because she was able to do this. Before she was able to say anything, somebody came back from town. They all said, "Sigaxunuga is lost! Sigaxunuga is lost!" Then the person who returned from town said, "Oh, her father is in town with his daughter, leading her by the hand." It seemed that father was going toward town. On the way there was a cow that was probably tethered there and I was frightened by that cow. Father did not know that I was following along behind him. Evidently, in fear of that cow, I began to cry. Then father led me by the hand. He went to town taking me with him. In time we returned, and so they brought me back alive.

We probably went back to our home again that spring, as it must have been at that time that I was sick. I was very sick and my mother wanted me to live. She hoped that I would not die, but she did not know what to do. At that place there was an old lady whose name was Wolf Woman and mother had them bring her. Mother took me and let the old lady hold me. "I want my little girl to live," mother said, "I give her to you. Whatever way you can make her live, she will be yours." That is where they gave me away.

That old lady wept. "You have made me think of myself. You gave me this dear little child. You have indeed made me think of myself. Let it be thus. My life, let her use it. My grandchild, let her use my existence. I will give my name to my own child. The name that I am going to give her is a holy name. She will reach an old age." There they named me with a Wolf Clan name; Xehaciwinga they called me. It means to make a home in a bluff or a mountain, as the wolf does, but in English I just say my name is Mountain Wolf Woman.

I do not know if they were jealous of me and that is why they never called me by that name. Just once in a while they called me by that name.[44]

# 2.16

# A Ho-Chunk Autobiography

SAM BLOWSNAKE (A.K.A. CRASHING THUNDER), HO-CHUNK

*Sam Blowsnake, the narrator of* The Epic of Red Horn, *also produced an autobiographical account of his life. Paul Radin, the anthropologist who asked him for his story, thought his Ho-Chunk name Ha'gaga, in English "Big Winnebago," sounded silly, so Radin took Sam's brother's Indian name, Crashing Thunder, and used that name to present Sam Blowsnake's autobiography. In any case, Sam and his brother Jasper Blowsnake are Mountain Wolf Woman's brothers. One critic has argued that Sam Blowsnake was consciously emulating the Ho-Chunk trickster and was not reliable,[45] but Nancy Oestreich Lurie, emeritus director of the Milwaukee Public Museum, argues that Blowsnake was not positioning himself as a Trickster, but was trying to come clean about his dissolute life before he converted to the Peyote way.[46]*

It was at this time that I desired to court women and I tried it. However, I did not know the proper thing to say. The young men always went around at night courting. I used to mix with the women in the daytime, but when I went to them at night I did not know what to say. A brother of mine, the oldest, seemed to know how to do it. He was a handsome man and he offered to show me how. Then I went with him at night. We went to a girl who was having her menses at that time. She was a young girl. When girls get their menses they always have to live apart. It was to such a one that we went. We were very cautious about the matter for the girls were always carefully watched as their relatives knew that it was customary to court them at such a time. (One of the precautions they used) was to pile sticks and branches about the lodge so that it would be difficult to enter. If a person tried to enter he was likely to make a noise moving the branches and this would awaken the people living in the larger lodge nearby and they might run out to see what was the matter.

It was to such a place that we went. After working at the obstacles placed near the entrance for some time, my brother entered the lodge. I went as close as possible and lay down to listen. He spoke in an audible whisper so that I might hear him. Sure enough I heard him. However after lying there for some time I fell asleep. When I snored my brother would wake me up. Afterwards the girl found out and she sent us both away. Thus we acted every now and then.

After a while I entered the lodges myself. We always had blankets wrapped around us and we took care to have our heads well covered (on such occasions).

Sometimes a girl was acquainted with quite a large number of men and then these would gather around her lodge at night and annoy her parents a good deal. We would keep them awake all night. Some of these people owned vicious dogs.

There was one old woman who had a daughter and when this daughter had her menses, she stayed in an oblong lodge with just room enough for two persons. She watched her daughter very carefully. Finally she slept with her. We nevertheless bothered her all the time just out of meanness. One night we went there and kept her awake almost all night. However, just about dawn she fell asleep, so we—there were several of us—pulled up the whole lodge, poles and everything, and threw the poles in the thicket. The next morning the two were found sleeping in the open, it was rumored, and the mother was criticized for being overcareful.

The reason why some of the (older) people were so careful at that time was because it had been reported that some young men had forced themselves into lodges where they had not been received willingly.

Once I went to see a young girl and arrived there before the people had retired, so I waited near the lodge until they would go to sleep. As I lay there waiting, listening to them, I fell asleep. When I woke up it was morning and as the people got up they found me sleeping there. I felt very much ashamed of myself and they laughed at me. I was not long in getting away.

We always did these things secretly for it was considered a disgrace to be caught or discovered.

On another occasion, in another place, I was crawling into a lodge when someone woke up as I was about halfway in. I immediately stopped and remained quiet and waited for the people to fall asleep again. However in waiting I, myself, fell asleep. When they woke me up in the morning I was lying halfway inside the lodge, asleep. After waking me up they asked me whether I would not stay for breakfast, but I immediately ran away.

After a while I began going around with some particular girl and I liked it so much that I would never go to sleep at night. My older brothers were very much the same. We used to sleep during the day.

While we were acting in this manner, our parents saw to it that we had food to eat and clothes to wear. We never helped, for we did nothing but court girls. In the fall the Indians used to pick berries after they all came together. We used to help on such occasions. However, we were generally out all night and were not able to do much in the morning. I used to go out courting and be among the lodges all night, and yet, most of the time, I did not succeed in speaking to any of the girls. However, I did not mind that for I was doing it in order to be among the girls and I enjoyed it. I would even go around telling people that I was really keeping company with some of the girls. I used to say this to some of my men associates. In reality, however, I did not get much more than a smile from one or two of the girls, but even that I prized as a great thing.[47]

## 2.17

# Trickster Tales

WAUKON G. SMITH, HO-CHUNK

*The ancestors knew many sacred stories, but there were other kinds of stories, too, ones that could be told at anytime and to anyone. They especially liked to tell tales about Wak'djunk'aga—the name of the Ho-Chunk Trickster. The following tale is from a member of the Thunder clan.*

One day as Wak'djunk'aga, the Winnebago trickster, was walking in the woods, he called his friends to join him. He called to Brother Rabbit, Brother Coyote, and Brother Squirrel, and they all came running to their friend. He told them, "Let us go to that high cliff and look at the beautiful country."

As they traveled along, Rabbit ran and hopped high off the ground. Coyote sneaked slowly along. Squirrel climbed up and down the trees. Seeing his friends enjoying themselves, Wak'djunk'aga commented, "Brother Coyote, how I wish I could sneak along the ground like you!"

"You can sneak as I, if you only try," replied Brother Coyote.

As the friends continued on their journey, Wak'djunk'aga spoke to Brother Squirrel, "Brother Squirrel, how I wish I could climb up and down trees like you!"

Answered Brother Squirrel, "You can! You can! If only you try!"

Looking at the sky, Wak'djunk'aga saw an eagle flying around a high cliff, and he noticed young eagles learning to fly and sail as well. He screamed to Sister Eagle, "How I wish I could fly and sail as you can!"

"You can and I will teach you," replied Sister Eagle.

As Sister Eagle and Wak'djunk'aga approached the top of the cliff, she explained to the Trickster how he could fly, "Wak'djunk'aga, jump off the cliff. As you do so, wave your arms very quickly, and then hold them out as I showed you earlier."

So, raising his arms, Wak'djunk'aga the Trickster jumped, but he fell straight down, wildly flapping his arms, and hit the ground with a smashing blow.

Sister Eagle lit next to him on the ground and said, "If Earthmaker wanted you to fly, he would have given you feathers, wings, and a tail."[48]

# Wak'djunk'aga and the Car

DAWN MAKES STRONG MOVE, HO-CHUNK

*Trickster stories are not confined to the past. Here, from a contemporary Ho-Chunk story-teller, is a clearly modern tale.*

One snowy day, Wak'djunk'aga was driving along a road as fast as he could. As he drove along, he came upon Brother Rabbit walking. He said to himself, "I bet Brother Rabbit is cold walking in the snow." So he stopped and picked up Brother Rabbit.

When Brother Rabbit got into the car, he immediately put on his seat belt after closing the door. "Thank you," said Brother Rabbit, "it sure is cold walking out in the wind and the blowing snow."

Once again Wak'djunk'aga started driving down the road as fast as he could. Not long thereafter, Wak'djunk'aga and Brother Rabbit met Brother Bear driving toward them. Brother Bear passed them and turned around; he then followed Wak'djunk'aga and Brother Rabbit. Wak'djunk'aga rolled down his window and called over to Brother Bear, who seemed to be pointing at the car, and asked, "Brother Bear, what seems to be the problem?"

Brother Bear answered, "Pull over to the side of the road. I want to talk to you."

"All right, Brother Bear," said Wak'djunk'aga. But he turned the wheel too sharply and slid off the road, down the ditch, up into a fence, and then crashed into a telephone pole.

Wak'djunk'aga went flying through the windshield and cracked his head open on the telephone pole. Wak'djunk'aga got up and held his head together with his hands. He turned and watched Brother Rabbit get out of the car and laughed at himself, and said, "it is for these things that people call me crazy."[49]

2.19

# How It Is Today

JIM FUNMAKER, HO-CHUNK

*In 1994, the Winnebago changed their name back to Ho-Chunk, their traditional name. They are involved in buying back traditional homeland in Wisconsin, where they now own about ten thousand acres—a good deal less than the ten million acres of their heritage, but this amount is still growing.*

*Because some Ho-Chunk lived in scattered and hidden settlements during the series of forced removals, they were able to avoid some of the assimilation that took place in other tribes, and they have retained much of their culture. Tribal headquarters and the Ho-Chunk Historic Preservation Office in Black River Falls run the Wazijaci [Dwellers among the Pine] Language and Culture Program, along with other projects.*

*Today, Wisconsin Ho-Chunk own a 640-acre buffalo farm at Muscoda (pronounced MUS-ka-day after the Ho-Chunk chief) on the Wisconsin River. This farm is part of the Inter-Tribal Bison Cooperative headquartered in South Dakota, which encourages spiritual and cultural kinship with the buffalo. Although the woodland buffalo, indigenous to Wisconsin and a smaller cousin of the plains buffalo, was hunted to extinction by 1850, its larger relative now lives in Wisconsin.*

*When the federal government abandoned the Kickapoo Dam Project in southwestern Wisconsin, Ho-Chunk entered in an agreement with the State of Wisconsin to co-manage land in the Kickapoo Valley Reserve. This 1999 agreement is part of a larger effort to identify sites and artifacts and protect them from vandalism. Another initiative, which came after Congress passed the 1988 Indian Gaming Regulatory Act, was the establishment of the Ho-Chunk Casino in Lake Delton, which soon became the largest employer in Sauk County.*

*These and other initiatives hold the promise of a self-sustaining base on ancestral land and living in ways that are traditional, innovative, and Ho-Chunk.*

I like this place and this is sacred to me.[50]

# 3

# Literature of the
# Ojibwe Nation

# 3.1

# The Anishinabe

PATTY LOEW, BAD RIVER OJIBWE

*Anishinabe or Ne shna bek, which means "original man," is the name of an alliance of the Ottawa, Potawatomi, and Ojibwe, which is also known as the Three Fires Confederacy. These three nations share the central Algonquian linguistic tradition that extends from the Atlantic Ocean through the Great Lakes into the western plains of the United States, and the Canadian provinces of Quebec, Ontario, Manitoba, and Saskatchewan. The Anishinabe people have the widest geographic range of any Native group in the United States.*

The Anishinabe remember a time when they lived "on the shore of the Great Salt Water in the East." In the words of Ojibwe medicine man Edward Benton-Banai, their numbers were so great, "if one was to climb the highest mountain and look in all directions, they would not be able to see the end of the nation." This eastern domain, however, had not always been their home. According to oral tradition, their original homes were in the Great Lakes region, where long ago the Creator, Gichi-Manidoo [Great Spirit], had placed them on the last of the Four Worlds he created. He taught them everything they needed to know and gave them medicines to keep them healthy.

Over time, however, the people lost their way and began to quarrel among themselves, so Gichi-Manidoo told them to leave. They migrated east and were gone so long they forgot the way home. Sometime later, speaking through a prophet, Gichi-Manidoo told them it was time to return. They were to follow a Sacred Shell that would lead them to seven stopping places and, ultimately, to the "Food that Grows on Water."[1]

# 3.2

# The Great Flood

EDWARD BENTON-BANAI,
LAC COURTE OREILLE OJIBWE

*Before the Anishinabe could return to the land where food grows on water, a great flood covered the earth. Edward Benton-Banai, Fish Clan of the Lac Courte Oreille Band, is a full-blood Ojibwe Anishinabe and a spiritual teacher and educator who lives on Madeline Island. He has written and illustrated a book for the young reader,* The Mishomis Book: The Voice of the Ojibway, *which honors and teaches the traditional ways of the Anishinabe.*

There are many Ojibway teachings that refer to a man named "Way-na-boo'-zhoo." Some people have actually referred to Anishinabe or Original Man as Waynaboozhoo. Most of the elders agree that Waynaboozhoo was not really a man but was a spirit who had many adventures during the early years of the Earth. Some people say that Waynaboozhoo provided the link through which human form was gradually given to the spiritual beings of the Earth. Everyone agrees that Waynaboozhoo had many human-like characteristics. He made mistakes at times just like we do. But he also learned from his mistakes so that he could accomplish things and become better at living in harmony with the Earth. These things that Waynaboozhoo learned were later to become very useful to Indian people. He has been looked upon as kind of a hero by the Ojibway. These "Waynaboozhoo Stories" have been told for many years to children to help them grow in a balanced way. In our teachings from now on, we will use the name "Waynaboozhoo" to refer to the spirit of Anishinabe or Original Man.

The teaching about how a new Earth was created after the Great Flood is one of the classic Waynaboozhoo Stories. It tells of how Waynaboozhoo managed to save himself by resting on a chi-mi-tig' (huge log) that was floating on the vast expanse of water that covered Mother Earth. As he floated along on this log, some of the animals that were able to keep swimming came to rest on the log. They would rest for a while and then let another swimming animal take their place. It was the same way with the winged creatures. They would take turns resting on the log and flying. It was through this kind of sacrifice and concern for one another that Waynaboozhoo and a large groups of birds and four-leggeds were able to save themselves on the giant log.

They floated for a long time but could gain no sight of land. Finally, Waynaboozhoo spoke to the animals.

"I am going to do something," he said. "I am going to swim to the bottom of this water and grab a handful of Earth. With this small bit of Earth, I believe we can create a new land for us to live on with the help of the Four Winds and Gitchie Manito."

So Waynaboozhoo dived into the water. He was gone a long time. Some of the animals began to cry for they thought that Waynaboozhoo must have drowned trying to reach the bottom.

At last, the animals caught sight of some bubbles of air, and finally, Waynaboozhoo came to the top of the water. Some of the animals helped him onto the log. Waynaboozhoo was so out of breath that he could not speak at first. When he regained his strength, he spoke to the animals.

The water is too deep . . . I never reached the bottom . . . I cannot swim fast enough or hold my breath long enough to make it to the bottom."

All the animals on the log were silent for a long time. Mahng (the loon), who was swimming alongside the log, was the first to speak.

"I can dive under the water for a long ways, for that is how I catch my food. I will try to dive to the bottom and get some of the Earth in my beak."

The loon dived out of sight and was gone a long time. The animals felt sure he had drowned, but the loon floated to the top of the water. He was very weak and out of breath.

"I couldn't make it," he gasped. "There appears to be no bottom to this water."

Next, Zhing-gi-biss' (the helldiver) came forth.

"I will try to swim to the bottom," he said. "I am known for diving to great depths."

The helldiver was gone for a very long time. When the animals and Waynaboozhoo were about to give up hope, they saw the helldiver's body come floating to the top. He was unconscious and Waynaboozhoo had to pull him onto the log and help him regain his breath. When the helldiver came to, he spoke to all the animals on the log.

"I am sorry my brothers and sisters. I, too, could not reach the bottom although I swam for a long ways straight down."

Many of the animals offered themselves to do the task that was so important to the future of all life on Earth. Zhon-gwayzh' (the mink) tried but could not make it to the bottom. Ni-gig' (the otter) tried but was unsuccessful.

All seemed hopeless. It appeared that the water was so deep that no living thing could reach its bottom. Then a soft, muffled voice was heard.

"I'll try," it said softly.

At first, no one could see who it was that spoke. The little Wa-zhushk' (muskrat) stepped forth.

"Ill try," he said again.

Some of the animals laughed and poked each other. The helldiver jeered, "If I couldn't make it how can he expect to do any better?"

Waynaboozhoo spoke, "Hold it everyone! It is not our place to judge the merits of another; that task belongs to the Creator. If little muskrat wants to try, I feel we should let him."

The muskrat dived down and disappeared from view. He was gone for such a long time that Waynaboozhoo and all the animals on the log were certain that muskrat had given up his life in trying to reach the bottom.

The muskrat was able to make it to the bottom of the water. He was already very weak from lack of air. He grabbed some Earth in his paw and with every last bit of strength he could muster, muskrat pushed away from the bottom.

One of the animals on the log caught sight of muskrat as he floated to the water's surface. They pulled his body onto the log. Waynaboozhoo examined the muskrat.

"Brothers and sisters," Waynaboozhoo said. "Our little brother tried to go without air for too long. He is dead." A song of mourning and praise was heard over all the water as Wa-zhushk's spirit passed to the next world.

Waynaboozhoo spoke again. "Look! Muskrat has something in his paw. It is closed tight around something." Waynaboozhoo carefully pried open muskrat's tiny paw. All the animals gathered around trying to see. Muskrat's paw opened and there, in a little ball, was a piece of Earth. All the animals cheered! Muskrat had sacrificed his life so that life could begin anew on the Earth.

Waynaboozhoo took the piece of Earth from the muskrat's paw. At that moment, Mi-zhee-kay' (the turtle) swam forward and said, "Use my back to bear the weight of this piece of Earth. With the help of the Creator, we can make a new Earth."

Waynaboozhoo put the piece of Earth on the turtle's back. All of a sudden the noo-di-noon' (winds) began to blow. The wind blew from each of the Four Directions. The tiny piece of Earth on the turtle's back began to grow. Larger and larger it became, until it formed a mi-ni-si' (island) in the water. Still the Earth grew but still the turtle bore its weight on his back.

Waynaboozhoo began to sing a song. All the animals began to dance in a circle on the growing island. As he sang, they danced in an ever-widening circle. Finally, the winds ceased to blow and the waters became still. A huge island sat in the middle of the great water.

Today, traditional Indian people sing special songs and dance in a circle in memory of this event. Indian people also give special honor to our brother, the turtle. He bore the weight of the new Earth on his back and made life possible for the Earth's second people.

To this day, the ancestors of our brother, the muskrat, have been given a good life. No matter that marshes have been drained and their homes destroyed in the name of progress, the muskrats continue to multiply and grow. The Creator has made it so that muskrats will always be with us because of the sacrifice that our little brother made for all of us many years ago when the Earth was covered with water. The muskrats do their part today in remembering the Great Flood; they build their homes in the shape of the little ball of Earth and the island that was formed from it.[2]

# 3·3

## Where Food Grows on Water

PATTY LOEW, BAD RIVER OJIBWE

*Madeline Island is one of the islands along the southern shore of Lake Superior, part of the Apostle Islands of Wisconsin.*

Perhaps as early as 1500 B.P. [before the present], the Anishinabe, an alliance that includes the Ojibwe, Potawatomi, and Ottawa, left their homes along the Atlantic Seaboard and traveled west. Among the stopping places were Kicki-ka-be-kong—a powerful place of "water and thunder" known today as Niagara Falls—and Baw-wa-ting, an excellent fishing area, which the French later renamed Sault Ste. Marie. The Anishinabe continued on to the site of present-day Duluth to a place known as "Spirit Island" and explored the south shore of Lake Superior. There, according to oral tradition, they found Manoomin, meaning wild rice, the "Food that Grows on Water." They also found their final resting stop: an island they called Mo-ning-wun-a-kawn-ing, translated as either "the place that was dug" or "the place of the gold-breasted woodpecker." In 1792, the eldest daughter of White Crane, the hereditary chief of the Crane Clan, married French fur trader Michel Cadotte and took the Christian name Madeleine. The Ojibwe renamed the island in her honor.

According to a copper plate belonging to Chief Tagwagane of the Crane Clan, the Ojibwe had arrived on Madeline Island well before Columbus encountered the New World. Tagwagane's ancestors had carved a notch with each passing generation. By 1844, nine indentations had been incised on the copper plate. Using a conservative life expectancy figure of forty years, approximately 360 years had passed since the Ojibwe had established a village on Madeline Island. According to this same medallion, the Ojibwe had encountered—or at least heard about—whites at least a decade before Jean Nicolet arrived in present-day Green Bay in 1634. Near the third notch, someone from that generation had etched the figure of a man in a large hat. The figure may have been Étienne Brûlé, who is believed to have explored Lake Superior in 1622. . . .

Madeline Island, with its major trading post at La Pointe, was not only the economic headquarters of the Ojibwe nation, but also its spiritual center.

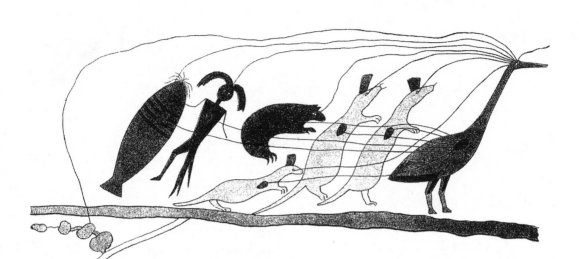

Symbolic petition of the Chippewa Chiefs, 1849. Many Ojibwe in the migration of one thousand to five hundred years ago settled in the lake country of northern Wisconsin where food grew on water: wild rice. When Euro-Americans coveted the trees and minerals of this region, they attempted to remove the Ojibwe (Chippewa). In 1849 a delegation traveled to Washington, D.C., to petition for permanent homelands in Wisconsin. The figures represent the totem animal of the tribal leaders making the petition; the four circles to the left represent ricing lakes, and the lines joining hearts and minds symbolize the unity of the petitioners. Originally rendered by the Chippewa on birch bark and redrawn by Seth Eastman in Henry Rowe Schoolcraft, *Historical and Statistical Information Respecting the History, Condition, and Prospects of the Indian Tribes of the United States* (1851). Reproduced by permission of the Wisconsin Historical Society. WHi-1871.

The "Three Fires," as the Anishinabe referred to their religious alliance, re-turned to the island at various times of the year to conduct Midéwiwin, or Great Medicine Lodge ceremonies. The Midéwiwin, through its songs, stories, and rituals, embodies the spiritual heritage of the Anishinabe and offered a code of conduct to keep them culturally rooted and physically and spiritually healthy.[3]

# The Indian Always Talks to the Spirit

3·4

ARCHIE MOSAY (OR NIIBAA-GIIZHIG),
ST. CROIX OJIBWE

*Anton Treuer, of the Leech Lake, Minnesota, band of Ojibwe, has collected stories of the elders and presented them in Ojibwe with an English translation in his anthology,* Living Our Language: Ojibwe Tales and Oral Histories. *His introduction to Archie Mosay, hereditary chief of the St. Croix Ojibwe, honors and teaches about Archie, but it also discusses spiritual integrity and perseverance in maintaining and advocating cultural and social practices that ensure the enhancement of the Ojibwe people.*

*"Born in a* wiigiwaam *[wigwam] on August 20, 1901, near Balsam Lake, Wisconsin," Treuer writes, "Archie was raised in a traditional Indian community."[4] When he died in 1996, over a thousand people attended his funeral, testimony to his wide and beneficent influence.*

And the Indian does this when he talks to the spirit, when he wants the head spirit to think of us. That's what they did in the medicine dance. That's why the Indian participated in it, why he started [his life], why he lived. That's why he was involved.

And this Drum the Indian uses here today, it was placed among the Indian people there at Mille Lacs as it is called, placed there for him so that the Indian could start [his life] as it was before. That's why that Drum started there. They all went out there toward the east; they were told this of the Drums. Today the Indian still keeps this in mind, how the spirit gave him this to start [his life]. That's why it was given to him.

And when the Indian sweats, a certain [person] was given this so that the Indian could do so. And while it will be the warm season, at that time the Indian was told to sweat. And when it's fall already or when it's winter, the Indian was told to sweat at that time too. When the Indian was afflicted with something, that's when the Indian was told to do this.

And that is what the Indian did long ago when he sweated and again when he fasted in his youth—boys, girls. Now long ago they fasted so the spirits would want them to be considered [for pity]. That is why they did that. And that is why the Indian came to know names there to be given to the Indian people. That is why they knew them there, knowing the animals and the birds.

And every one of the animals running about here on earth, they were blessed for a reason—the bear as he is called, and also the bald eagle. And they pitied the Indian for a reason, giving him things to improve his condition, appeasing the Indian when he talked. That is why the spirit gave things to him.

And the girls, they were spoken to by the old ladies and told how the Indian lived before. When they were talked to by their parents, that is how the Indian knew what to do. I hope he will come to know this by the way I lived myself, when he thinks about it.

And when the Indians went hunting long ago as well, when a young man first killed an animal, whatever kind of animal was first killed, he smoked to the spirit. He offered tobacco for killing this animal first. Again tobacco was offered to the spirit when he ate that which he killed. He talked to the spirit first.

And this here rice, the Indian could not eat it when he finished making it. After they offer tobacco to the spirit, at that time they ate the rice. And now already when he knocks [gathers] it, at that time too he speaks to the spirit, offering him tobacco when he will take this from the waterways so that the spirit gives permission for the Indian to have a traditional diet.

And this here medicine the spirit gave us to use, when the Indian wants to pick it, he offers tobacco first. That is how the Indian used medicine long ago. Thus he could not use it, the spirit told him, tobacco was to be put down first when he wanted to pick medicine or already the spirit will change its condition on this earth. That is what he was told by the spirit.

This too, this water where the fish live, for them too one thinks of them respectfully first of all. He offered the spirit tobacco first when he wanted to eat those fish.

In this way the Indian was put [here] long ago.[5]

# Creation Story

EDWARD BENTON-BANAI,
LAC COURTE OREILLE OJIBWE

*Spiritual teacher and Mide leader Edward Benton-Banai lives on Madeline Island in Lake Superior. Here he tells how humans came to be on the Earth.*

This teaching was handed down by word of mouth from generation to generation by my ancestors. Sometimes the details of teachings like this were recorded on scrolls made from Wee'-gwas (birchbark). I am fortunate to be the keeper of several of these scrolls. They will help me remember some of the details of what I give to you.

When Aki (the Earth) was young, it was said that the Earth had a family. Nee-ga-gee'-sis (the Moon) is called Grandmother, and Gee'-sis (the Sun) is called Grandfather. The Creator of this family is called Gi'-tchie Man-i-to' (Great Mystery, or Creator).

The Earth is said to be a woman. In this way it is understood that woman preceded man on the Earth. She is called Mother Earth because from her come all living things. Water is her lifeblood. It flows through her, nourishes her, and purifies her.

On the surface of the Earth, all is given Four Sacred Directions—North, South, East, and West. Each of these directions contributes a vital part to the wholeness of the Earth. Each has physical powers as well as spiritual powers, as do all things.

When she was young, the Earth was filled with beauty.

The Creator sent his singers in the form of birds to the Earth to carry the seeds of life to all of the Four Directions. In this way life was spread across the Earth. On the Earth the Creator placed the swimming creatures of the water. He gave life to all the plant and insect world. He placed the crawling things and the four-leggeds on the land. All of these parts of life lived in harmony with each other.

Gitchie Manito then took four parts of Mother Earth and blew into them using a Sacred Shell. From the union of the Four Sacred Elements and his breath, man was created. It is said the Gitchie Manito then lowered man to the Earth. Thus, man was the last form of life to be placed on the Earth. From this Original Man came the A-nish-i-ná-be people.[6]

# 3.6

# Spearfishing

WALT BRESETTE, RED CLIFF CHIPPEWA

*With the establishment of reservations, Wisconsin Ojibwe continued their subsistence hunting and fishing both on and off reservation, but around the beginning of the twentieth century the State of Wisconsin began harassing off-reservation subsistence activities in the ceded territories. In the early years of the 1900s, sport fishing and tourism became popular, and in 1908 the Wisconsin Supreme Court outlawed spearfishing.*

*Although there were many skirmishes, the issue of spearfishing came to a head in 1974 when the Tribble brothers of the Lac Courte Oreilles (LCO) Band were arrested for spearfishing on Chief Lake, south of Hayward, in off-reservation waters. Federal District Judge James Doyle ruled against the LCO, which filed suit against the Department of Natural Resources. The U.S. Seventh Circuit Court reversed Doyle's decision, which the U.S. Supreme Court then upheld in 1983 by refusing to review the case. With this decision, the other signatories of the 1837 and 1842 treaties, the Red Cliff, Sokaogon Mole Lake, St. Croix Chippewa [Ojibwe], and Lac du Flambeau bands joined the LCO in subsequent lawsuits. After Judge Doyle died, Judge Barbara Crabb took over the case and in large part reaffirmed the legal basis for usufructuary rights by the Ojibwe spearfishers. The six Wisconsin Ojibwe bands joined with Minnesota and Michigan tribes to form the Great Lakes Indian Fish and Wildlife Commission (GLIFWC), which established mechanisms for conservation, habitat protection, stocking, and related issues.*

*The conflict was far from over. Many anti-spearing groups sprang up: PARR (Protect Americans' Rights and Resources), ERFE (Equal Rights for Everyone), and STA (Stop Treaty Abuse). Dean Crist, leader of STA, marketed "Treaty Beer," which protested spearfishing on its label. Many racist signs sprang up in northern Wisconsin, one of the most infamous saying "Save Two Walleye, Kill a Pregnant Squaw." Demonstrators at the boat landings shouted, threatened, and shot at spearers.*

*Walt Bresette and Rick Whaley co-founded Witness for Non-Violence and the Midwest Treaty Network to deal with the issues involved with spearfishing. They are also the authors of* Walleye Warriors: An Effective Alliance against Racism and for the Earth.

When two brothers from one Chippewa [Ojibwe] village in northern Wisconsin acted to assert their rights, they unwittingly led the others of us on a journey of identity and of historical place. However, their act of sovereignty in 1974 was not isolated. They were expressing a renewed sense of Chippewa identity traceable to a legacy that emerges out of the mist of human history. In order to understand the significance of the acts of these two Chippewa brothers, we must meet their ancestors and the paths from which they came.

The Tribble brothers are from Lac Courte Oreilles (LCO) Reservation in the northern part of what is now called Wisconsin — one of the fifty states that make up the United States of America. LCO is one of the small areas (about 70,000 acres) that remains of the once vast territory of a people called the Chippewa [Ojibwe]. The Chippewa once controlled lands from Niagara Falls to the northern Great Plains and on both sides of the upper Great Lakes. In Wisconsin alone there were almost 20 million acres of Chippewa territory.

Today six Chippewa villages in northern Wisconsin make up this part of the story. In addition to LCO, they include Red Cliff and Bad River Reservations, across the bay from each other on the southwestern shores of Lake Superior, both within sight of Madeline Island. Near the Michigan border in northeastern Wisconsin sits the Sokaogon or Mole Lake Chippewa Reservation. Fifty miles west of Mole Lake and about one hundred miles inland is the Lac du Flambeau (LdF) Reservation. To their west about one hundred miles is LCO, and sixty miles southwest of LCO is the St. Croix Chippewa, not a contiguous reservation but scattered parcels of land in northwest Wisconsin.

These six villages are part of the group called the Lake Superior Chippewa, a band of Chippewa that signed treaties with the United States throughout the nineteenth century. This band is comprised of additional villages in Michigan's Upper Peninsula and in the northern portion of Minnesota. These different villages, whose leaders signed the respective treaties, today inherit the band-wide identity of Lake Superior Chippewa. However, since those earlier days, especially since statehood, village autonomy and state (Wisconsin) identity have undermined the political value of the Lake Superior Band as a whole. . . .

Despite the colonial taking of our homeland through warfare or coerced treaties, small patches of land remain, usually called "reservations." However, large land areas within the former homeland remain under partial jurisdiction of our tribal governments. These land areas of the Lake Superior Chippewa and some other tribes are called "ceded territory," or lands that were sold in treaties. With the Lake Superior Chippewa, a return to recognition of this partial jurisdiction resulted from the Tribble brothers' actions in testing off-reservation harvesting rights in 1974. The federal court upheld the hunting, fishing, and gathering rights reserved in our cession treaties. The court said that, since the treaties were signed, there has been no intervening action that gave the state jurisdiction over the Chippewa. Because the courts are set up by district, this case dealt only with the Wisconsin villages of the Lake Superior Chippewa. But the legal and political ramifications have touched all the Anishinabe and forced us to revive the concept of unity among the bands. . . .[7]

I was talking to Sierra [a Witness spokesperson] on the phone about a week ago, right after the Minnesota Chippewa tribes signed an agreement to give up their rights [like] the Chippewa rights in northern Wisconsin. We were talking about this upcoming meeting and I was emotionally distraught when she called. I don't know if she realized that. I didn't know what to do, that signing was like a death knell to what's going to happen here in Wisconsin. And as we were talking I did a flash-forward, like one of those things you do in novels or the movies. I did that, right on the phone. I mean it was incredible and there I was an old man. And there was a young man there next to me, and he was my grandson. I don't have any grandchildren, yet. And he looked at me and said, "Grandpa, do you remember when you had treaty rights?" and I nodded. And he said, "How come they sold them? Who sold them? And what's left for me?" and I cried on the phone. Because I tried to imagine what kind of an explanation I could give this child. I reached inside of my heart, inside of my mind, and couldn't find an answer.

It's as though Martin Luther King [Jr.] went to the mountain, saw the vista out there and went back and negotiated with the goddamn racists in the south and said, "Yes, you can call us niggers. It'll only cost you a million dollars. No, we won't sit in the front of the bus, but you gotta pay us $500,000. No, we won't sit at the lunch counter, but that will cost you two and a half million dollars." That's what happened in Minnesota. That's what's going to happen and that's what's being negotiated right now in Wisconsin [at Mole Lake]. It is illegal. It is immoral. It is an abrogation of treaty rights through intimidation. It is de facto abrogation of treaty rights. . . .

We used to have buffalo here in Wisconsin. I remember I traveled to the southwest and I had this yearning in my heart when I was there. There's something there that was missing here. . . . Our buffalo, which is the pine, are gone. Our identity, which is a woodland identity, was slaughtered, is slaughtered. All of the spirits associated with a woodland culture were devastated. A holocaust occurred in the Great Lakes that was part of our identity. And so, we've never mourned, we've never mourned the loss of our identity. Instead, we look at the books on Wisconsin and we see the big piles of wood and the big people standing on the pile of wood celebrating the building of Milwaukee and Chicago, all over the loss of our identity of our homeland. The pine was our buffalo. And that's what's missing. And we need to yet mourn that. And we need to stop mourning things we shouldn't be losing in the future.[8]

# 3·7

# It Gives Me a Strong Feeling

NICK HOCKINGS, LAC DU FLAMBEAU OJIBWE

---

*With the implementation of Judge Crabb's ruling in favor of treaty rights to fish and harvest, an important aspect of Ojibwe culture was affirmed. Nick Hockings was one of the founders of Wa-Swa-Gon, which means "spearfishing" in the Anishinabe language.*

Walleyes range from minnow size all the way, some of them get to be up to twenty pounds. Walleye is a member of the perch family.

The unique thing about a walleye, aside from the fact that they're very good eating fish, the unique thing about them that sets them apart from all the other fish in the lake is that their eyes shine. The easiest way I could say it is if you look at a star, you can see the brightness of the star in the blackness of the sky. When you shine light in the water and there's a walleye there, oftentimes their eyes will be shining that bright. They have a real sparkle to them, a real shine. . . .

Sometimes when you're going along the lake shore, it's very dark and you're standing up in the bow of the boat shining your light off into the distance and it's calm enough you can see the walleyes moving. You can see all these little eyes just swarming around.

They're relatively easy to find. Even if you're going to a new lake, all you have to do is keep going along the shoreline until you see those eyes sparkle. They're usually right up in the shoreline all the way to the deepest part of the lake. But that time of year [two or three weeks of spring spearing], they're up in the shallows. When you see these eyes, you get ready. Often times, they're moving . . . all different stages of movements. Some are just [lying] there, some are moving toward you, some are very fast. But you see the eyes, you can get an idea of where the rest of the body is.

It feels real good to be out there. Some of these lakes, after one hundred years, one hundred fifty years, we're just beginning to go back and spear lakes that probably our ancestors speared on. It gives me a strong feeling.[9]

# The Flooding of Pahquahwong

WILLIAM WOLF, LAC COURTE OREILLE OJIBWE

*Some Indian people feel that social problems can stem from disturbed graves. Many Native graves and cemeteries have been pillaged and looted for the grave goods buried with the deceased or for the bones themselves, which have been shipped off to many institutions. After long struggles by Indian activists, in 1990 Congress passed the Native American Graves Protection and Repatriation Act (NAGPRA), which required that those museums and universities receiving federal funding must return human remains and cultural objects. But respect for the dead was not in evidence when the Ojibwe village of Pahquahwong was flooded.*

*Although the Treaty of 1854 guaranteed the Ojibwe a small remnant of their land "in perpetuity," land at the southern end of their reservation was taken against the unanimous opposition of the Lac Courte Oreilles (LCO) Band. The dam on the Chippewa River near Winter, Wisconsin, completed in 1923, flooded the old settlement of Pahquahwong (pronounced "pah QUA ah wong"), submerging five hundred acres; it destroyed cranberry and rice beds and inundated a two-centuries-old cemetery. Although the Wisconsin-Minnesota Light and Power Company had agreed to disinter and rebury the Native remains before flooding the sacred site, they reneged on their promise. For years, Indian remains were exposed above water when the dam operators lowered water levels.*

*William Wolf, who was interpreting for the band, read the following statement expressing the feelings of the LCO people.*

To put under water our sacred bones of our noble forefathers is outrageous. The prayer and desire of this band is to be in the same bosom that shields the remains of our fathers, whenever the time comes. This has been the home of the Ojibways from time [im]memorial and at present there are several Indians in this village, those who are absent are not visiting, but laid beneath the sod which we call or claim as our home. We have in this village one of the beautiful spots in the reservation and the land is covered by a large tract of small pine, which some day the children of the present reservation will enjoy. And further, I the Indian, trusted the Government, which is plain in our treaties, to be our guardian, and [even] if our guardian consents to the flowage, I will not; I will still hold to my treaty.[10]

# 3·9

# Abrogating the Treaty

PIMOSEGEJIG, LAC COURTE OREILLE OJIBWE

*The Wisconsin State Legislature had passed a 1911 law that allowed for "a system of storage reservoirs on the headwaters of the Chippewa River." In 1914, the Wisconsin-Minnesota Light and Power Company bought rights to develop a dam on the Pahquahwong Creek of the Chippewa River watershed to generate electricity for Eau Claire and for Minneapolis and St. Paul. "Surveyors estimated that approximately 5,600 acres of reservation land would be flooded, submerging maple groves, wild rice and cranberry beds, hunting lands, and the village of Post itself."[11] Flooding would also cover the gravesites of ancestors.*

I am speaking for all and we all say, no, we don't propose to have this land overflowed. The government told us the land would be ours forever and forever.

In regard to our people whom we have buried along the banks of the river from the mouth of the Chief River down to the reservation line, we cannot think of having their graves covered by the overflow.[12]

# 3.10

# Cultural Genocide

PATTY LOEW, BAD RIVER OJIBWE

*The high water destroyed the established rice beds; even though the Wisconsin-Minnesota Light and Power Company had agreed to provide wild rice to the people, they reneged on their promise.*

By late summer of 1923, twenty-five feet of water covered the village of Pah-quahwong and the resources that had sustained it for nearly two centuries. The company had broken its promises. When the remains of hundreds of deceased Ojibwe began washing ashore, a horrified community learned that seven hundred Indian graves were left behind. Further, the water level in the newly created impoundment fluctuated dramatically, making it impossible to sustain new rice beds. The Ojibwe learned a sad truth about the reservoir that became known as the Chippewa Flowage: "The Food that Grows on Water" could not grow on this water.[13]

 3.11

# Elders Refuse to Move

EDWARD BENTON-BANAI,
LAC COURTE OREILLE OJIBWE

*As the dam was closed and the floodwaters moved closer to the old village, now called Post, some residents would not leave. Edwin Tainter, a resident of Post said, "Some weren't even moved out yet, because they really didn't believe this was going to happen to them. I saw the men trying to get people moved out of the homes, you could just see the heads of the horses sticking out of the water."[14] The story of this cultural genocide, which cut the reservation in half and destroyed the rice beds that were central to cultural integrity, was told to the young.*

Many times when elders would stand and talk about the flooding, tears would come to their eyes. Grandmothers, tears, bones of our relatives floating upon the water. There were actually times when people would just wail. And there would be an attempt to comfort them. But in that early time, I didn't fully understand. That went on for a long time, and I watched and I listened because somehow I was always drawn to it. I remember once or twice, people putting together ceremonial wrappings of food and tobacco, and someone getting in a boat and taking it out into the water, and letting it down into the water. So little by little, I began to get a fuller picture.[15]

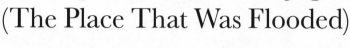

# Dealing with Mooskadoojiigan
# (The Place That Was Flooded)

GAIASHKIBOS, LAC COURTE OREILLE OJIBWE

*The Federal Power Act of 1920 abrogated the treaties of 1837 and 1854 and ordered Wisconsin-Minnesota Light and Power to pay an annual lease of $1,200 for the dam at Winter, Wisconsin. In 1971, when the fifty-year lease was up, LCO Indians and members of the American Indian Movement (AIM) protested the lease's renewal, initiated a lawsuit against Northern States Power, the reorganized Wisconsin-Minnesota Light and Power Company, and won. LCO took over operation of the dam. As James Oberly, an "expert witness on behalf of Wisconsin Ojibwa bands in treaty-rights litigation," comments: "Nearly seven decades later, there is a strong feeling among the LCO Ojibwas that what took place in 1921 and after was truly the crime of the century. For more than half a century the people of LCO had lost control over the land within their reservation."[16]*

Incredibly, it took forty years and an act of Congress for electricity generated for cities and towns downstream to reach the village of New Post. Today, when you boat across the water that covers the wild rice beds, the village of Post, and the graves of our People, listen, maybe you can hear the voices of the People, the sound of the Drum.[17]

# 3·13

# Drum of the People

### GAIASHKIBOS, LAC COURTE OREILLE OJIBWE

---

*Northern States Power was ordered to pay past damages and legal expenses and to give back "4,500 acres of company-owned land to the band, including 2,300 acres situated within the 1854 treaty boundary of the reservation." LCO built their own power-generating plant and agreed to work with the Department of Natural Resources to adjust water levels to promote fish populations and control downstream flooding."[18]*

DRUM OF THE PEOPLE

I hear the Drum of the People,
The spirits of our People.
I hear the echo of the loon,
The son of the bullfrog.
A fish swirls, an eagle soars,
The wind whispers through the trees.
I hear the Drum of the People.
I hear the cries of the Grandmothers,
The Grandfathers reluctant to move,
The children fearful,
Surveyors determine the high water mark.
I hear the Drum of the People.[19]

# 3.14

## Mole Lake Sokaogon Chippewa

FRED ACKLY, SOKAOGON CHIPPEWA

*Al Gedicks argues in his book* Resource Rebels: Native Challenges to Mining and Oil Corporations:

> *For the past 25 years, one of the smallest and poorest native nations in the United States has successfully prevented some of the most powerful multinational mining corporations in the world from constructing a large mine next to its tiny, 1,800-acre reservation at the headwaters of the Wolf River in northeastern Wisconsin. The determination of the Sokaogon Chippewa, one of the six bands of the Lake Superior Chippewa Nation, to resist unwanted mining has developed into a multiracial anti-mining movement. . . .*
>
> *On March 29, 1995, the U.S. Army Corp of Engineers held a public hearing on the Mole Lake Sokaogon Chippewa Reservation to take comments on Exxon-Rio-Argom's proposed underground zinc–copper sulfide mine next to the reservation near Crandon, Wisconsin. Tribal members testified about the historical origins of their present reservation and the significance of the wild rice they harvest from Rice Lake on the reservation. Fred Ackly, a tribal judge, recalled the history of the creation of the reservation at the hearing.[20]*

*This issue was resolved when the site of the proposed mine was purchased by the Forest County Potawatomi and the Mole Lake Sokaogon Chippewa Band in 2003.*

The government asked our chief why he wanted this reservation on this spot. Our chief walked over and gave him a handful of wild rice, and he said, "This is the food of Indian people. This is why I want my reservation here on this lake. There are six or seven other lakes in this area where my people have been harvesting food for a long time." So he wanted his reservation right here on this lake for the wild rice.

Through the hard times that we've had to live as Indian people here in Mole Lake, we realized that money and everything else that the white people had didn't count. Because what the Great Spirit gave us was the food for our people—subsistence to go on another year, to have another offspring, to bury another elder. Also, he taught us how to pray for that every year. We've been doing that every year. Here in Mole Lake we still pray for everything we get. We do it our way.[21]

# 3·15

## From Aboard the Night Train

KIMBERLY BLAESER, WHITE EARTH OJIBWE

*While it took nearly three generations to make partial recompense for past wrongs, another issue has presented an opportunity or a disaster: gambling. Putting one's fate to one's medicine power has its place within Native North America. Since times always require one to be able to respond to difficulties, gambling is a way to test one's powers—one's ability to make the best of things, to take hardships in stride, to meet what one has been given—or lost— with wit and patience. These cultural traits underlie the general support of gambling, even from some traditionals. Although some express ambivalence and unease about casinos, others think casinos are a perfect means for righting centuries-old injustices: For once, greed operates in favor of the Indians. Since the eleven federally recognized Nations and bands in Wisconsin have sovereignty negotiated by their ancestors, casinos have, at the moment, a fragile protection. In this short story, Kimberly Blaeser, an Ojibwe, and professor at the University of Wisconsin–Milwaukee, writes about how tribal sovereignty and gambling intersect in contemporary times.*

The moon gives some light and I can make out the contours of the land, see the faint reflection in the lakes and ponds we pass. Several times I see or imagine I see glowing eyes staring back at me from a patch of woods beside the track. When we pass through the tiny towns, I try to read their signs, catch their names from their water towers or grain elevators. Occasionally the train stops at . . . Portage . . . Winona . . . Red Wing.

Once, traveling on the Fourth of July, I sat aboard the Amtrak and watched one Mississippi river town at its annual fireworks. Balls of light burst over the water, illuminating the bank, the families gathered together on blankets, the lovers sitting with hands, arms, or legs entwined, the jubilant children exploding in motion like the rockets overhead. I knew I had the best seat in the house—and the loneliest.

Watching that scene, I remembered one summer in France. By chance I had landed at a lovely village called Anncey during a local festival. I checked in to a hotel just across the street from the festival grounds and went to enjoy the activities. But it was all happening in another language. I didn't even know what they were celebrating. Wandering into a carnival area, I stood

112

back and tried to figure out the games they were playing. Everywhere I went, I could have been behind the glass of an Amtrak train, I was just a gawker. I walked two miles that night in order to have dinner at a hotel away from the festivities. Then, back in my own lodgings, I tried to block out the sounds from the crowded street below. Although the next night I returned to the festivities with some locals and had as fine a time as anyone there, I never forgot that first night, when the whole world was happening without me.

In my sleeping compartment, watching the night countryside, I feel that same way now. So much world rolls by my window. Like a voyeur I watch the various reunion scenes. The little dark-haired boy in a leather jacket sits, legs dangling, on the hood of a car waiting for someone to arrive, scoop him up, and give him a present from the trip. I imagine myself stepping off the train onto the depot platform and reaching out to tousle his pollen-soft hair. I'd like to hear him sing the songs they teach in his school. But instead I watch the woman in the terrible plaid pants take his hand and I can't help but imagine that someday that little boy will be a golfer with ugly plaid pants of his own. The night continues on that way scene after scene. Vast opportunities. My great distance from them. And yet I feel these scenes add up to something, some meaning or lesson about all life, and I try to put it into words for myself but find I can't. I finally give up, roll over, go to sleep, and dream.

At first, I am back in France sitting on a stone wall, holding an open bottle of wine and watching my companions do the cancan in slow motion. Then the director of my dream abruptly cuts that scene and begins to loudly berate the camera crew. The scene goes dark, I jump off the wall and land in another dream I know very well: I am lost in urban America.

The basic plot of the recurring nightmare has remained the same for years. Sometimes I am the wrong color in some neighborhood or another, trying not to draw attention to myself. Sometimes I have taken a walk on a lovely day and suddenly realize, in Hansel-and-Gretel fashion, that the markers to my safe haven have all disappeared and night is descending. Always I am without the resources I need to find a way out, to escape, to return to my friends or family who are somewhere at a picnic, or gathered for a holiday celebration, or fast asleep (early to bed, early to rise), I don't know where I am—except in the wrong, wrong place. I have no map. I'm dressed differently than everyone around me and they are beginning to stare at me or point or mumble loudly about the intruder. Either public transportation in not available or I don't know how to use it. Either it's after bus and train hours, or I have somehow been stranded without any money. In one dream I actually had a friend with me and we had a car, but all the streets were one way going the wrong way, in the direction where something dreadful was about to erupt. We abandoned the car and ran on and on through streets we didn't recognize, feeling ourselves pursued and about to become the victim of someone's violent behavior. The closest I ever came to escaping was in that dream when we jumped aboard a boat that would take us away, we didn't know to where, but away from that particular urban nightmare. I awoke from that dream just as I was reaching into my pocket for the forty dollars we would need to pay our way. I don't know if I found it, but at least we had a chance that time. Most of the nightmares end when I thrash myself awake and lay sweating and re-assuring myself that I am safe and vowing that never, never will I venture into the heart of any city alone.

Tonight, as usual, I struggle violently to escape. I cry out as I wake and then sit up, listening, wondering if anyone has heard. Finally I relax, lie back, feel the rhythmic rocking of the train beneath me, and turn on my side to be comforted by the farm fields and woodlands we pass.

Through the years I've gotten used to these nightmares, I understand why noisy crowded streets—whether indifferent or threatening or simultaneously both—should frighten me. The daily Chicago news is of gang violence, ran-dom beatings, and drive-by killings. Over the years I've read hundreds of re-membrances of families whose child or mother or sibling has been abducted and presumed or found dead. I've read of the families' usually belated real-ization that someone is missing and their futile searches for the lost or stolen member. And at night I dream the part of the abducted, the innocent who wanders into the wrong neighborhood, who asks direction from the wrong silver-haired gentleman, who gets into the wrong cab. It makes sense that I should have these nightmares, I who come from a five-block-main-street kind of midwestern town.

But now I am awake, keeping my vigil over the Midwest's pastoral king-dom. Chicago, even Minneapolis seems a long way away. A few hours later, still in the deep night hours, the train arrives at my stop, Detroit Lakes, the closest I can get to my destination.

Suddenly, as I descend the two steps from the train, the porter hands me into one of the reunion scenes. "Hi, honey, how was the trip? Did you get any sleep?" "A little. Been waiting long? How are the roads?" "Long enough to beat your dad in two games of cribbage . . ." Hugging and kissing, we carry on the usual end-of-the-trip conversation. Glancing back at the train win-dows, I get an uneasy feeling. I imagine I am looking into eyes hidden behind mirrored sunglasses.

Rumors about the coupons surface in nearly every conversation about town. The paper will carry coupons for five dollars in free chips. The shopper will have the coupons. People have been wearing disguises in order to cash in more than one coupon a day. Folks set their alarms for two, three or four A.M. and arrive bleary-eyed to cash in the midnight-to-five A.M. coupons. They skip lunch and run out on their noon hours to cash in the day coupons. This week the *Fargo Forum* will have coupons. Someone ordered forty papers. The papers last week were all sold out. Someone has been following behind the stopped truck when it makes its night deliveries stealing the papers from the mailboxes.

We decide to stay up late just to see. We sit in the porch with the lights out. Night scenes begin to unfold again. I think of how we used to sleep in the porch in the summer and then slip out in our pajamas to run about the yard and sometimes all the way to the other end of town. Giggling, sshssshing and sneaking our way through the alleys, we waked dogs, dropped to the ground at the first sight of car lights, and swiped carrots to nibble along the way.

I remember the winter night that big dog came and ran off with our car's extension cord and we all watched thinking it must be mad and the summer night that skunk wandered into town and, barefooted, we followed it around the neighborhood—at a safe distance—trying to figure out what it was doing there. And I remember that night the tornado hit Bejou and we all stood at the dining-room window watching the storm and never realizing the danger and terror a few miles away. And the time that stranger was around town in the blue car and we were all wary of him but afraid to tell our parents because they might want us to stay in when we wanted to play chase or walk down to the park and swing in the dark.

Tonight, watching out the window with a lone mosquito buzzing about my ear, I feel my past alive on the other side of the screen, hiding in the shadows of the bushes, about to jump out. With that hope or expectation pressing against all my organs, pressing against my very skin, I reenter the present night.

Not much happens now as we watch. Two people go by on bikes. We spot a couple of cats. We haven't seen a car for ten minutes, just the lights when they U-turn in the filling station on Main Street. One by one everyone wanders back into the house, forgetting about the intrigue of the shopper thefts. We go back to the real world of cut-throat and widow whist. After an hour of card play, I no longer watch us as from the window.

I have gone out for my first look at the casino. It's not at all like Las Vegas or Reno and yet it is. I mean, there are a bunch of shinabes [Anishinaabe] dressed in white shirts and bow ties! These are people whose first name is always placed in quotation marks in print as if to say "Honest, this is the real name." Now they all wear these pins bearing names like "Frogman" Joe Brown, "K-Girl" Wanda Clark, or "Blackduck" Frances Wadena. I wonder if the casino management complained at all about the extra expense. I mean, these pins have to be really big to accommodate some of the names, like "Catbird" Sylvester Littlewolf or "Sailor" Rodney LaDue Be-She-Ke. There are all kinds of people I know whizzing about looking like dressed-up paper-doll images of themselves. Remember using the fold-over tabs to attach a new hairstyle to the dolls and it always looked a little like George Washington's wig? Or how a tab would slip and the hair would assume some wild angle? I keep waiting for someone's tab to slip, the transformation seems just too unreal.

In Las Vegas or Reno there are a bunch of strangers whizzing about and lots of lights blinking and noise everywhere and smoke and you don't expect it to make sense or be familiar. But here I see people I've known my whole life, looking like little mechanical parts in one of those machines where you put the coin in and everything moves until the money runs out or the time or however they count it. I want it to stop for a minute so I can get my bearings, but someone keeps putting money in. My former high school psychology teacher wanders by carrying a notebook. I see my old 4-H leader having breakfast in the dining area and I swear I see her checking the muffins for tunnels like she used to each year at the county fair. The town's best piano teacher is playing nickel slot machines, one with each hand. I get stamped and collect my tokens and begin feeding the poker machines. I'm laughing and talking to my machine and I feed almost all my money but then I hit a straight flush and win fifty dollars. I cash in my money and walk around to see the other machines. I notice something happening at the blackjack tables and I wander over. I'm standing back a little and it's a good thing because I gasp when I get a good look at the dealer. He's probably in his late forties, a good-looking man, very Indian with prominent cheekbones and long graying braids wound with colored cloth. Not that unusual, but I recognize him. Only I remember him as a young man with black, black hair, a great laugh, and eyes I could never meet straight on. He was an apprentice medicine man.

Before the full absurdity of it can sink in, I take in the rest of the scene. A crowd has gathered round because one player is on a winning streak. She too is Indian. Seventy years old, I guess, a slight woman, yellow-gray hair, some age spots on her face. Nothing physically striking about her. Her voice is unpleasantly shrill, the sound of a killdeer. I've watched craps players before for the sheer joy of hearing their chanting and romancing of the dice, but her call and response is too nervous, too thin to bring pleasure. Yet she speaks constantly to the dealer or to her audience. "Come on, deal. Deal me blackjack." "Okay, dealer, let's go, I need an ace." "Call for your card, call for your card." "Okay, bust dealer, bust." And she gets her blackjack. Or the dealer busts. I watch several hands, inching my way forward, and then I see what I knew I would see and yet what surprises me just the same because it's here in a casino at a blackjack table. Sage, cedar, twigs of a kind I do not recognize, spirit stones, feathers, a beaded leather pouch—the entire space in front and to the right of her playing space is covered with Indian charms and, I imagine, love medicines. But there's more, a whole menagerie of dime-store variety good luck charms: rabbit's foot, horseshoe, four-leaf clover in a key ring, flowers, little statues, everything but a chia pet! Piled among these charms, piled high in twenty or more stacks are her winnings, stacks of one-, five-, ten-, and twenty-dollar chips.

I watch until there's a change in the dealer and the apprentice medicine man goes off on break. I watch while the new dealer comes under her spell and she continues to pile up chips. Then I feel someone at my elbow and turn. It's another old friend who is another employee here who tells me the charm lady was in yesterday too and did the same thing then. We shake our heads and laugh together in a companionable little gesture but I leave feeling uncertain of what either of us meant by it.

But I have won myself and I go off thinking about how the first computer was funded partly by gambling, by the horse racing industry (the better to figure the odds, my dear), which had, as it turned out, a more farsighted vision than many people in the federal government, who didn't think the idea of the computer would ever amount to much. This is the same government, of course, that worked so diligently to wipe out the "savage" Indian.

I think about progress a lot in the next few days and about what passes for progress. We drive out into the country to look at some land and find lots of roads I think would make wonderful access roads in the winter because a person could easily get stranded with any reasonable snowfall. I think of Aldo Leopold and how he loved to be stranded by high water in the spring. I think of the story of my cousin's birth at the grade school where his mother got stranded when a blizzard blew in while she was hemming towels with the ladies' aid and the story of the baby's first appearance at their farm: wrapped in swaddling towels (neatly hemmed), he arrived by horse and sleigh because the access road was impassable by car.

Nightly we walk about town, talk marriages and funerals and DWI tickets, then sit on the newly installed benches on Main Street. Together we assemble from our memories the town as it was twenty or twenty-five years ago. We remember the little Model meat market and the old Pioneer office. We rebuild the Landmark Hotel, take down the vinyl fronts from the grocery store, bring back the old Red Owl, change the light posts, the awnings, the names of the current businesses. I put back the old depot, you the corner funeral home. But soon we are distracted and leave things half constructed when we begin to add the people, what's-his-name, the square dance caller; Ed, the fire chief; and Lydia, the town's best gossip. On the walk back home, we have begun to list very specific things, which is the closest we get to the intangibles: the rental meat lockers, the four-digit telephone numbers, the free ice cream during dairy month.

Late at night in my old bed, I listen to the night sounds of the house and fall asleep counting the changes that have come to my little hometown: The park is off limits after dark now, the football field is fenced in, one-hour photo has come to town along with a tanning salon and a pizza parlor. The dry goods store is gone, the dairy, long gone. People lock their houses now more than the once a year when the carnival comes to town. But all of these changes pale in comparison to what has replaced the bait shop, the used car lot, and Mr. Morton's small farm, what has sprung up on Highway 59 at the edge of town: Las Vegas–style gambling.

When the weekend comes, the casino parking lot is packed and cars line the adjacent street and highway. We go there one more time before I leave and lose some money and time. I think about the jobs and see lots of people working who have never held a steady job before and who I imagine look very proud in their uniforms. I see Elvis having lunch and the rumor is he's going to sing later. Everybody really knows it's not him, but just here and now it's as easy to believe it as not. So he signs autographs and eats a Northern Lights special. A few people in suits get a tour. One lady, who according to rumors didn't want to come and play, wins a progressive jackpot of $32,812.43. I wonder if they give her the pennies too. I ask a few people about the protesters and if that was all settled, but nobody here wants to talk much about that. They also either don't want to talk about or don't know anything about how the profits will be spent. "Big payments . . . spendoolicks every month!" jokes one of the cocktail servers. "Maybe they're gonna educate us again," another says with a laugh. I ask one of the ladies at the change booth, one of the money changers, about handling all that cash and she says after a while it just seems like Monopoly money. I say I think I know what she means. I cash in my few remaining chips, wave at Elvis on my way out, and reenter the sunlit world.

Around town, everyone admits to eating at the casino because they have good specials, but not too many folks admit to spending any money there. Even those I ran into in the casino itself were all there, they said, for the first time and just came to cash their coupons, but they all knew of other people who were there all the time and had lost a lot of money and . . . hadn't I seen the Gamblers' Anonymous meeting notice in the *Mahnomen Pioneer*?

Taking the train back, I decide to put on pajamas and crawl under the sheets, hoping to trick myself into a good night's sleep. It seems to work. I have slept soundly for several hours, but then the dreams start. I fall in and out of them. But they are not the usual nightmares. I am in a place where folks know you ten, fifteen, twenty years after you've left and still see in your face that of your grandfather or aunt or cousin. I know I am home and I feel safe.

But soon strange, strange things begin to happen. I arrive to find all the quiet of my little town gone. People are very busy, too busy to notice my return. They have a schedule that can't be disrupted for conversation over the alley hedge or coffee at the local café. I feel a little like the returning-from-the-dead Emily in *Our Town*, who can't get anyone's real attention. Something has happened here to wind these folks up too tight, to make them over like some kind of diseased Stepford wives who have seen the error of their midwestern ways.

I wander around trying to discover someone or someplace that hasn't been transformed; instead I find a drive-up bank, a health club, and a thirty-minute oil change. Still these seem such small tokens of the yuppie life that I don't believe they could transform an entire town. Then while I stand there in front of the Ben Franklin store, everything begins spinning around me. Cars battle for the angle parking spots on Main Street, drivers honk and shout angrily at one another, shoppers push and shove and toss sale merchandise carelessly about, people line up to buy newspapers and then begin madly clipping coupons. Just as quickly as it began, the action is over. The store clerks are clucking their tongues about the silliness of all the people. I feel implicated but I don't know why. I wonder what plague has descended on my hometown and if somehow I am responsible. I take my vague sense of guilt home only to find my own parents buzzing about getting ready to go out for spinach quiche. Through the remainder of the night, these lost-pastoral dreams return in different variations. People sitting around watching the 200 stations they can get with their satellite TV, eating microwave dinners in dim artificial light, staying out of the sun because they don't want to freckle or burn. I come in from ice fishing and see dainty little shoes with heels lined up on rugs by people's entryway doors. When I sit down to play cards everyone is dealing bridge instead of whist or poker. I have faithfully dieted before coming, but no one offers me homemade pie or real mashed potatoes made with butter. I have a flat tire on Highway 59. Cars slow down, but no one stops to help me. Instead, they click their door locks or call out to me to get a nametag. Just before first light, I abandon hope of restful sleep, dress, and then watch the sun rise over all the lakes and towns we pass.

I have an early breakfast with a would-be journalist and some ski vacationers who want to talk about election prospects and the politicians who have written bad checks. Although I too believe the bad checks phenomenon makes a wonderful metaphor for the state of the world, I merely feign attention. I nod or laugh on cue, while I try to read upside-down a story in the would-be journalist's newspaper that has caught my eye. It is about the Russian space station and the cosmonaut who has been up in orbit during the takeover attempt and ultimate dissolution of the Soviet Union. After sixteen long months, they are bringing the capsule back. While the train carries me back to my current home and away from my former, I keep thinking about that poor cosmonaut coming back to find his whole world changed, to find himself a man without a country—at least without the country he left behind.

I watch the ten o'clock national news broadcast. I see him emerge from the capsule. I see him try to stand and have his knees buckle. I know they said it was because he hadn't been able to exercise for such a long time, but I wonder if his weak-kneed feeling might not have more to do with what he saw out the window of the space station and with how the world was happening around without him.[22]

# 3.16

# Avian Messiah and Mistress Media

ANDREW CONNORS, BAD RIVER OJIBWE

*Andrew Connors, born in Ashland, Wisconsin, is of the Bad River Band. Active in theater, he heads the Woodland Nations Troupe. This short story, set in Milwaukee, shows the cultural tensions negotiated by a man named Cloud.*

Janice Sebline scribbled lazy notes in a minute notebook while Reginald Throckmorton, rising young executive, rambled on about the company's success, his success, and the grand illusions of their future combined successes.

"Yes"—he beamed—"our projected urban development projects will not only be an economic boon for the city, state, and a national American blueprint for better tomorrows, but we at the Laurel Robins Corporation tower above our competitors. Our Human Services Division, for example, greatly benefits every man, woman, and child, regardless of their racial, ethnic, political, and religious background, here in this great country of ours."

Which made little sense to Janice, who popped chewing gum, reread her notes, noted Throckmorton's politically correct behavior—contrary to the Laurel Robins' record—and responded with "In other words you stand to make some money."

"I can't complain," Throckmorton tacitly acknowledged, leaning back in his leather chair. "But of course that's off the record."

Janice nodded. "Yeah, yeah," she said. "We're going to need stills, Mr. Throckmorton."

"Just call me Reggie," Reggie said.

She ignored his overture, looked past him and out the window. "Maybe we can get a picture of you and this view?"

Reggie imperiously smiled. "Oh yes, you can see the whole city. We call it our regal view. I can see the marina from here. In fact, I can see my boat. Have you ever been on a sailboat before, Miss Sebline? Thirty footer?"

She walked to the window and looked down. The view from thirty stories up in the First National Wisconsin Building was breathtaking. Particularly when one had a fear of heights. She stepped back. "I've been in a sailboat, Mr. Throckmorton . . ."

120

"Reggie . . ."

" . . . and I'd prefer things with motors. Sailboats bore me, take too long. We'll film your interview tomorrow morning."

"Sure, whatever you say," Reggie agreed. "This is just a public interest piece, right?"

"A dirty job, but somebody's got to do it," Janice replied, not too thrilled about this assignment. But that was the card she drew. Being cub reporter on an Old Boy station, she took whatever assignments they gave her.

"Perhaps lunch," Reggie offered, his choppers gleaming, brown eyes beading.

"Maybe another time," Janice smoothly rebuffed. She flipped the notebook into a backpack, a collegiate holdover, and headed toward the door.

"Maybe dinner," Reginald Throckmorton, young exec on the go, quickly suggested.

She rolled her eyes, cursed Fate, and turned stonily around. "Maybe not," she said malignantly.

Just then she spotted something from the corner of her eye and heard a dull *thump* bump against the window. She jumped somewhat, exclaiming "What was that?"

Throckmorton didn't notice, "What was what?'

"Something hit the window."

"Oh, that." He glanced outside. "Who knows, could be anything. Maybe the window cleaner dropped a rag? Maybe a bird hit the window? Up here, could be anything. Why, I remember that big hailstorm awhile back. The hail was slamming off the windows something fierce. Thought for sure we'd lose a window. Did I mention I own a Jaguar XKE?"

"Whatever," she remarked over an exiting shoulder. "We'll be here ten-thirty tomorrow morning to finish your interview segment."

"The public relations one, right?"

"Of course, public relations," Janice answered, slipping out the door. She sallied past his secretary, thinking perhaps the window cleaner would make a better interview. Probably had many interesting stories dangling forty stories up, overlooking beautiful downtown Milwaukee. She also knew Reginald Throckmorton, thwarted young VIP, had but one thing on his mind. And there'd be none of that, no sir and thank you.

Janice Sebline had a fledgling career to think of, one she worked hard for. Now it was all for one and that one is me. She shared once too often. Yet she had this effect on men, men in high places getting higher. Ah, a sigh, an unfulfilled moan, adieu; but love could come later, much later—considering what *he* did to her.

She waited for the elevator wondering if that big breaking assignment would ever come her way.

Meanwhile . . .

He didn't mean to say what he said; oh hell, he meant exactly what he said. Let's face it, he had enough of their bull—my food is undercooked, overcooked, and how do you cook this; and concluded food service was no longer what he wanted to do. Been doing food service for almost fifteen years. Much too long for any sane person.

So he went off on a customer: I'd like to speak to the manager; yeah, what do you want; you should do something about that rude employee over the phone; you want me to call a rude employee over the phone; no, the one that answered the phone was rude; did he do it with tact, though: What? Look, I'd like to register a complaint; will that be one room or two; what?

And that's what he said, going on and on with a customer, toying with his complaint, belittling his reasons, mocking hyperboles. He shouldn't of . . . but that's the restaurant biz. Sometimes a customer will go so far. Those of you who've worked in restaurants would know what I'm talking about. The rest of you are the cause of the restaurant worker's misery. Which is neither here nor there, unless you're Cloud, former pizza restaurant manager and bellicose busboy.

So Cloud walked away from his job feeling he'd had enough. Never occurred to him that he didn't have money socked away. Such was the whimsical price of split decisions.

Whenever Cloud needed a major life decision—like now, for example—he rode public transportation round and round the city. This put things in tactile perspective; particularly his lot, which at that moment was in low-wattage overload. This bothered him sometimes, like I suppose it'd bother most of us, yet he often used this as a brain cleaning: get the brains in order, move off and get on with life. Cloud, unlike most of us, gets away with irrational moves because he has no one to answer to. Which may or may not be why he's riding this particular bus on this particular day.

Maybe he likes bus people? Bus People gave him different life perspectives.

Bus People rode the bus because they had to. That was it, just it, and all it would ever be. Bus People had ends to meet, bills to pay, mouths to feed, and people depending on them for clothes, roofs, scraped knees, missed meals, and pure survival: survival without guilt. Bus People dealt with tight schedules, indifferent drivers, inclement weather, loud-mouthed children with blaring boom boxes blasting in confined spaces, standing room only, and missed stops, not because they wanted to. Egad no; no one in their right mind rode the bus when they didn't have to. Bus People rode the bus because they had to, there was no other way. Real people.

While Cloud, rarely in a right mind, used bus riding to mellow mesmerizing life panoramas.

He took the 30 from Hampton to Sherman, Sherman to 43rd, 43rd around the bend to 35th, 35th to Wisconsin, and down the avenue. Which was about the farthest he'd normally travel to get his fill of real people. Route 30 took him through Milwaukee's heart, where all the real people lived. And once through the heart, you were on the East Side, where no one had any idea what was going on. A good place to raise money for any given cause. But not very conducive to real-world values, survival without guilt.

Cloud watched a toothless woman haul cart and all on the bus. She took her sweet time, and no one complained. That was bus riding in Milwaukee. Some kids cracked jokes about the woman, while other riders averted meandering attentions into space. Urban indifference, the bus rider's code. The toothless woman gummed verbal exchanges with silent wraiths, while spying everyone and thing around her, looking for the high ground. She pushed her stolid presence solidly into a side seat, shopping cart blocking the narrow aisle, and the driver rolls his eyes, closes the door, and moves on.

Yes, Cloud thought, she represents real-world values, survival without guilt. So I had a bad night with some bozo customers. Is that as bad as this woman's life?

The toothless woman spied him spying her and flipped him the middle-fingered salute, the silent bird of serious business. Truly, survival without guilt. That woman definitely came to terms with life. No problems.

She also showed him. Imagine, transferring our problem on another, hoping their problem is worse than yours. For what purpose? What is your means? She showed you with her salute, didn't she? Now Cloud's problem was twofold, a reluctant survivor struggling with guilt. He sat smirking, enjoying the joke played on him.

He told a customer off, so what, big deal. This woman told him. And so it goes. He stared out the window and realized he passed his usual stop. What the hell? Today he'd take a different stop.

Today is a good day to walk.

He got off at the next stop, 16th and Wisconsin, and strolled down the avenue, people watching. Some watched back from recessed doorways and porno shops, while others, Marquette students and total world survivors, watched themselves watching traffic. Traffic watched no one and proceeded willy nilly to and fro, prepositional wanderers along the straight and narrow byways of urban sentences.

Before long Cloud found himself standing before the First National Wisconsin Building. From 16th and Wisconsin to Jackson and Wisconsin. Where did the time go? Human patterns swirled around him. He didn't notice. Cloud was drawn to the building and its height. The next best thing to flying, way up there. Up there he could look out over the sprawling metropolis, see the world's problems in all their grimy splendor, and weigh them against his own.

He rooted to that spot, lost in thought, staring at the forty-story icon. Two policemen across the street, however, took keen interest in Cloud.

"Whadda ya think?" Officer Krantz queried his partner.

His partner, Officer Matthews, munched doughnuts and slurped coffee. "I think we should form our own response to the League of Cultural Sensitivity," he said between bites.

Krantz whirled his eyes and sighed. "No, I'm talking about that guy standing across the street."

Matthews followed Krantz's directions. There was indeed a man standing across the street. But he didn't seem to be bothering anyone. He looked average, blue jeans, blue jeans jacket, red T-shirt, dirty tennis shoes, long black hair tied in a lazy ponytail, glasses, just an average-looking guy looking at a tall building. Matthews looked up at tall buildings from time to time. Nothing odd about that.

"Looks like an average guy to me," Matthews said.

Krantz studied the man across the street. "Hmm, I don't know . . . looks suspicious to me."

"You'd know," Matthews agreed.

"Damn right, I'd know, rookie." Krantz was pleased with himself and his nineteen years of experience. He'd get his rookie on the straight and narrow. "Ah-ha," he exclaimed knowingly. "Look at that, the security guard's going over to him. Observe, Officer Matthews."

"Whatever you say, George," Matthews acknowledged. "You're the boss."

Cloud felt the presence next to him. He continued studying the gleaming glass obelisk stretching above him. What was this building's purpose? Then he noticed little bodies littering the sidewalk alongside the building.

"Say, buddy, what do you think you're doing here?"

Cloud turned and faced a stocky man in pseudopoliceman blue nervously caressing his holster. The man's face was an acne-scarred paradise marooned on a flat head bobbing on a thick neck. Cloud couldn't help it. He smirked. The guard misinterpreted.

"I asked you what do you think you're doing here," the man repeated forcibly.

"Just standing, looking at the magnificent monument to man's technocratic achievements," Cloud replied pleasantly.

Immediately creating dubious notions in our friendly security guard. A troublemaker. "Well, I'm afraid you're going to have to move on," he returned, firmly pleasant.

"Why?" Cloud asked, turning back to the small bodies littering the sidewalk. They were minute avian ghosts attesting to mankind's preoccupation with itself. He looked for problems greater than his and found them lifeless on a sidewalk.

Meanwhile the guard quickly thought of a reason why Cloud should vacate this spot. "People are complaining. Move on."

Cloud surveyed the perimeter for complaining people. He saw people around a hot dog stand, probably complaining about ketchup and onions; more things restaurant people had to contend with. He empathized with the hot dog vendor. Others walked to and fro, watching themselves watching traffic—the same old line in a new setting. No one gathered around the security portal to watch him.

"What people?"

The guard searched for support. He was dealing with a live one: *Now how did that manual say?* "Look, pal, you've been standing here for quite a while. Now maybe you're not up to nothing in particular, but you just can't stand here all day."

"Why?"

"Look," the flustered guard pleaded, "if you don't get moving I may have to run you in for vagrancy."

Cloud chuckled, "So that's it. Run me in for vagrancy? Is it because I have a ponytail?" The guard stood motionless. "Is it because I'm wearing blue jeans and dirty sneakers? You'd better watch out, you'll never know who snuck up on you."

"What seems to be the problem?" Officer Krantz asked officially, magically appearing beside his comrade in security.

"This man refused to leave the premises after I've asked him to leave." The guard replied, breathing easier now that official help was on the scene.

Cloud beamed at the policemen.

Janice Sebline strolled out the front door steaming about this assignment. Interview Laurel Robins Corporate officials about their upcoming real estate developments in the Milwaukee area. How interesting. How thought-provoking. Such human interest. So far she laid out the groundwork with three high Laurel Robins VIPs. They all said the same things, and they all tried to pick her up—including a female. Yuck. Surely Janice Sebline was meant for better things than this.

She walked straight through the crowd towards Jackson and Wisconsin, hoping a parking ticket wasn't mocking her troubles. A modest knot of people standing off to the side attracted her attention, cueing the reporter's instinct screaming to erupt. She moved through the throng toward the rapidly expanding crowd. She noticed two police officers and a security guard questioning an average-looking man wearing blue jeans and a ponytail. Great, something humanly interesting going on here.

"I don't understand what all the fuss is about," Cloud said, somewhat amused. "I'm not bothering anyone."

"You're refusing an official order to remove yourself from a public premise," Officer Krantz explained.

Cloud looked puzzled. "I don't understand, I've only been standing here for ten minutes. Could I help it that I was attracted to this building? Do you realize this place is obscene from all over the city?"

"Do you have any identification?" Officer Krantz asked.

Cloud nodded. "Of course I do. Who in their right mind would walk around this place without proper identification?" He reached into a back pocket. "What if a person got hit by a bus or something?" His hand came away empty. "You know, sometimes a person leaves home with many things on his mind, and he forgets things."

Officer Krantz looked knowingly at his partner, "You mean you don't have any identification?"

Cloud looked knowingly at Krantz's partner. "Well, at least I know who I am."

"And just who is that?" Krantz asked.

"I am Aanakwad," Cloud proudly announced. "In your language that would mean Cloud."

"Cloud? That's it?" Officer Matthews asked.

Cloud nodded. "It's an old family tribal name, passed on to me from my granduncle Clyde Cloud, who got the name from Clinton Cloud. Seven generations that name travels. That name's worn many shoes. You see, my father, Cliff Cloud, couldn't come up with any more 'cl' beginnings, so he opted for just Cloud. Or that's the way I heard it."

Sebline latched on to the tribalness of the name: Aanakwad, Cloud. Now here is a human interest tale, one she'd been seeking since the degree arrived in the mail, five years too late. Her storytime instincts noticed the security guard slipping away. Something more was afoot than the mere hassling of "a person of color," a true tribal man. Funny, though, his skin didn't look tribal. She edged closer to the trio. The crowd surged around them.

Krantz thought troublemaker, "Roy, run a make on that name, see if there's anything on Mr. Cloud."

"I've had that name made once before," Cloud rambled on, dismissing the officers. He had nothing to be guilty about, therefore nothing to worry about. He thought about an Abbott and Costello movie: *I fear nothing when I am in the right; whoever pushes me around will find me full of fight.* Odd how these things crop up at the strangest times.

He thought about the birds flying free and then smacking into this eclipsing monolith to progressive patterns and induced dreams. Now that was indeed a problem, a problem far greater than any problem Cloud-Without-a-Job had. Not even the toothless woman on the bus came close to this problem. The security guard returned and whispered something to the policeman. Officer Krantz nodded, staring victoriously at Cloud. Janice Sebline stepped between the foursome and into the light.

"What seems to be the problem, Officers?" she inquired affably.

"I was just standing here mourning lost avian dreams," Cloud offered in an offhand manner.

"Just who in the hell are you?" Office Krantz inquired in return.

Janice snapped open her wallet. "Janice Sebline, WMTJ News."

"Christ, a reporter," Krantz mumbled.

"Oh, yeah, where's your camera?' Officer Matthews added, for no apparent reason.

Cloud smiled while wild-eyed dreams danced within his mind. Real-world survival didn't exist on this dead square. Survival lay sprawled on a city sidewalk, and a lone man in khaki workclothes strolled nonchalantly among tiny corpses, quietly spearing and hiding them in a canvas bag.

"Our cameras are our eyes," Cloud announced, facing the crowd swelling around them.

Krantz moved to block Cloud, but Janice slipped between, asking, "And what exactly did you do, sir?"

"I wondered how I could save myself from this," Cloud began, his hands animated motions of purpose and design. "But they drove me here." His eyes fell on the dead birds disappearing in a workman's bag. "Oh yes, what good is flight when demands keep pulling you back? Like take your extra cheese and feed it to the birds. That's all it's good for."

"What the hell," Krantz moaned. He saw Matthews dodging traffic, heading back.

Janice believed she was on to something big. "Exactly what do you mean, they drove you here?" she asked. "Who drove you here? The birds?"

"Will you please get out of here?" Krantz asked Janice through politely clenched teeth.

"I'm only doing my job," she said. The crowd began stirring. A few clapped and whistled.

Cloud stared at the sky. "I remember a Hitchcock movie. Oh, could their revenge be so sweet. And we think we've got it bad."

Neither Janice nor anyone else quite knew what to make of this. So Janice interpreted it according to her knowledge and dreams. "Are you saying that one day nature will rise up against humankind and put us back in our place?"

Cloud paid no mind to the gathering crowd, Janice's questions, or the policemen. He was thinking about next month's rent. Shouldn't have quit the job, he scolded himself. He shook his head: rash move, always with the rash moves. But those customers. He hated dealing with those customers. I want this, I didn't get that; Christ help me, those customers are getting to me. And then the cooler going out—rising dough everywhere.

"We've got to get them out of this place before they rise completely," Cloud said absentmindedly. "Or else everything we've worked for will be destroyed."

Krantz's orbs rolled with disgust just as Matthews joined the crowd, which by now had swelled to some fifty people. Many were dressed in business uniforms, while many were street people doing such things as street people do. The Streets had Security twitching.

"What kept you so long? Why didn't you call from here?" Krantz stared coolly at his partner, who stuffed a doughnut crumb into his mouth. "Well, did you get anything on this Cloud?"

"You won't believe this, but there is a Cloud," Matthews said. "I mean, just like that, Cloud. No first name."

"Did you cross-check?"

"Of course I cross-checked," Matthews said. "I found a lot of Clouds, but only one Cloud with no first name."

"An address?"

"Yup." Matthews wiped his mouth and studied the situation. "What's going on?"

"Nothing I can't handle," Krantz replied. "Did you find anything else on our Mr. Cloud? Parking tickets?"

To which Cloud responded, to no one in particular, "For thirty-five years, yea and verily, I have wrestled with the problem. Like sovereign birds blowing free, riding currents and waves, avian dreamers in urban lands. And then this . . . this eclipsing monolith of progressive patterns and induced dreams steals those dreams. Buries them away in canvas sacks, poof, gone," Cloud shook his head sadly.

A tear rolled down Janice's face. "O God, that was beautiful," she said. Some in the crowd sighed along with her, others engaged in conservative laughter.

Krantz motioned for his partner to stand ready. "Are you on some kind of drugs?"

Cloud shook his head. "Always demanding, give me this, give me that— how much, how much, how much, how much? Can't they read? Everything they need to see is right there in front of them. Oh, how they tie up phone lines with questions and petty complaints."

Janice furiously jotted all this down, wishing they had sent a television crew along with her. Oh, well, she'd write an article for the *Journal*, and for further developments she'd get a television crew.

Krantz noticed that the crowd was half Suits and half Streets. It wouldn't be long before the Streets outnumbered the Suits. There was bound to be an occurrence. Especially with this lunatic babbling nonsense; not to mention the guy spouting off about dead birds and unruly customers. Krantz decided to diffuse the situation before it became an incident.

"All right, Cloud, if that's your name," Krantz said officially, "I think you'd better come down to the station with us."

"But why?" Janice asked indignantly.

Cloud watched as the last bird was stuffed into the workman's bag. He scanned the forty floors searching for other tiny birds. "You know, those birds wouldn't have to suffer so much if we'd only take the time to really notice them. But who notices anything anymore? The only thing people notice nowadays is if they get sausage and wanted pepperoni. Oh, boy, they notice that, all right."

Krantz nodded to his partner. Matthews grabbed Cloud's arm. "C'mon, buddy," he said. "We're going to take you downtown for questioning."

Cloud said nothing. He smiled, looked up, looked around, shrugged his shoulders, and said, "Sure, why not," because he had nothing better to do.

Janice turned on Krantz. "Exactly what has this man done, Officer?"

"Look, lady," Krantz said, prepared to politely squash this so-called reporter before things went any further. "It's just routine. Our friend here has no identification."

"But according to Cloud . . ."

"That's Mr. Cloud," Mr. Cloud added.

She continued without skipping a beat. " . . . Mr. Cloud was just standing here ten minutes," Janice persisted. "Now, I've been here for nearly six minutes, and from what I've heard, and I'm sure these people have also, he hasn't really said anything that warrants this type of action." The kid was on a roll.

"This isn't really any of your business," Officer Krantz said. Another squad car pulled alongside the curb. Krantz gave them the sign.

"Did it occur to you that maybe he was waiting for the bus?" Janice asked pointedly.

"I just got off the bus," Cloud offered. "Buses are little worlds unto themselves. They roll through this aimless urban universe like meandering starships through birdseed intersections climbing the walls."

Janice halted and asked him to repeat that. Cloud shrugged and smiled. "It's that extra cheese that really gets me," Cloud offered in explanation. "It's hardening their arteries like this building obstructs avian dreams. One day a dream bird will fly into their hearts, but that cheese, like this building, will stop that dream, dead, plop, into the workman's bag."

"Amen," some people in the crowd shouted.

"Jesus H.," Krantz swore. Now he had to get this nut case off the streets before some unsavory character took advantage of him. "All right, let's break it up. C'mon now, let's get a move on." Krantz and the squad officers began dispersing the crowd.

Matthews led Cloud across the street. "Having a bad day?" Matthews casually asked.

"Bad month," Cloud answered. "Sometimes it's like that. Tomorrow it'll be better. Come to think of it, I don't have any money to get home."

"In the wallet, huh?" Matthews opened the door for Cloud.

"Maybe the transfer's still good?" Cloud checked his pockets. "This will probably take awhile, right?"

Matthews nodded, patting Cloud down and ushering him into the backseat. "We have to verify your identity. You know, routine."

"Yeah," Cloud agreed. "Didn't have anything better to do today."

"Officer," Janice demanded, standing defiantly before Krantz. Now she knew what her mother was talking about. Dear old mom, a protest marcher from the sixties. "You just can't take a man in for questioning simply because he has no identification. What is this, the Soviet Union?"

"Yeah," people in the crowd chanted. "What is this, the Soviet Union?"

"Lady . . ."

"That's Miss Sebline," Janice corrected.

Krantz rolled his eyes heavenward, trying to keep his temper under control. Nineteen years of service, still the same old thing. "Look, Miss Sebline," he said, "this Cloud was asked to leave. He refused, and he also doesn't have any identification. We have to take him in—it's for his own good. You heard him . . . did any of that make any sense to you? And besides that, there isn't a Soviet Union anymore. What kind of reporter are you, anyway?"

Janice, though miffed at the last sentence, thought hard on the previous one. What exactly did Cloud say? "From what I understand, he only stopped here to say a prayer for the birds that were killed in front of this building." Janice offered.

"Bird killers," someone in the crowd shouted.

"They kill the birds, they kill us," someone else added.

At that moment, strange as it may seem, a WMTJ television van happened to drive by. "Hey, Joe, isn't that that new reporter?"

Joe looked out the window. "Yeah, that Sebline kid. Say, she ain't bad."

"I wonder what's going on? Cops here and everything." So the van stopped, which in turn stopped traffic on Wisconsin Avenue.

Two more squad cars appeared on the scene. Cloud greeted the officers with a smile when they stepped over to question Matthews.

Krantz rested his hands on his hips, taking a firm stance. "All right, all right, that's enough of this. C'mon, let's break this up. There's nothing happening here." Krantz and the officers moved through the crowd. The crowd decided it was time to party. You know how crowds get.

Joe and Fred, and the WMTJ camera crew, walked up to Janice and Officer Krantz, camera shooting, and asked, "Say, what's going on here?" Which wouldn't have been all that bad, except at that moment a crosstown rival, WJTM TV, happened to be driving by. The same conversation as before ensued, and soon their cameras were in on the fray.

Camera lights flashed on the crowd. The crowd responded with a hearty "Bird killers, bird killers!" and put on a scene. The Streets loved it, while the Suits began backing out of the picture. Wasn't good for the image. Of course a few liberal Suits stayed behind to watch. And many then discovered that their watches, among other things, were missing. One Suit turned just as a Street sneaked away. "Hey," he shouted, "that man stole my wallet!" The Suit chased the Street, two policemen joined the pursuit, and all collided with a little old lady on her way to pay her home mortgage under threat of eviction.

Meanwhile, another Suit broke away from the crowd, dropping a crisp new empty leather wallet in a black kid's hands.

The cameras caught it all.

Later that evening . . .

Cloud sat across from Officers Krantz and Matthews wondering if it would be raining when he left. He didn't mind the rain, it was walking west along Wisconsin Avenue that bothered him. Riding the bus and watching *real* people was one thing. But traveling among them, late at night . . . no sir, he'd have to find a way home.

Krantz glowered at Cloud, standing over him like a red bear in blue. "We should arrest you for inciting a riot," he growled.

Cloud looked at Matthews. "Do you think you could lend me a quarter to make a phone call? Someone I know must be home."

Krantz snarled. "That's what you said an hour ago. It seems nobody you know is at home. What, did they all know you were calling?"

"I'll pay you back," Cloud said. "If not, maybe I can use your phone. Have the city send me a bill."

The station sergeant, Murphy, strolled over to the desk. "Well, Krantz, we really have nothing to hold him on."

"What about that incident at the First National Wisconsin?"

"He was in the car when all that happened," Murphy said. "We don't have anything to hold him on. Why don't you let him go?"

Krantz couldn't let him go. Krantz had to have him because Cloud was responsible for that melee with the crowd. Splattered all over the local news, and Krantz with a torn pocket, gotten while avoiding the little old lady who belted him for running her over. In glorious living color on the Six O'Clock News.

At that moment a harried young lieutenant rushed into the office. "Good Lord, it's that reporter again. She's got an ACLU lawyer with her and they're clamoring for his release."

Krantz chuckled, "Where did you get a word like clamoring, Chris?"

"I read, I read," the lieutenant shot back. "Look, Krantz, we have nothing to hold him on. We're letting him go."

"Don't bother me," Matthews agreed.

"I suppose," Krantz relented. "But I'm going to be watching you, Mr. Cloud. No identification, no job . . . Christ, just what in the hell kind of city are we running anymore?"

"Does anyone know if it's raining?" Cloud asked.

"Not yet," Matthews said. Krantz slapped his shoulder.

"I suppose a walk would be okay. I'll take the long way around. No, that wouldn't be good, that's a long way." And Cloud rambled on as Officer Matthews led him into the lobby.

"You know, I get off in a half hour," Matthews said, "I'm heading toward the Northside, maybe I can give you a lift?"

"That would be cool," Cloud readily agreed.

"Besides, I'd like to hear more about that powwow you were talkin' about."

"You wouldn't believe the energy," Cloud said, pushing through a door, "Very high positive energies. I like them.

"Sounds like it'd be a good time," Matthews said.

The high-wattage television lights blinded Cloud, Officer Matthews, and anyone else unfortunate enough to be standing behind door number one. Fortunately for Cloud, his right hand managed to shield the glare and save his front teeth as Janice Sebline, WMTJ TV's newly created Video Crusader, thrust a microphone in his face.

"How have they treated you, Mr. Cloud? How were your conditions? We've been talking with some of your supporters and they're behind you one hundred percent." Janice Sebline didn't pause for breath.

"Supporters?" Cloud and Matthews asked.

At that moment, large hand-painted signs filled the lobby. A MAN HAS A RIGHT TO PRAY, HONOR THE WORLD, SAVE THE AVIAN DREAMERS.

Twelve more microphones snaked around Miss Sebline, and she presented her best profile.

Cloud stepped back when he discovered that his supporters consisted of the Sorority Sisters of Misguided Multiculturalism; various American Indian college student organizations bearing names like the Native American Student Movement, the American Indian Student Association, and the American Indian Native Student Coalition; local conservation groups—college and radical fringe; a multitude of bird-watching societies; the curious with nothing better to do; and people milling around in the police lobby waiting to pay fines and other police-related events.

"Supporters?" Cloud asked once again.

"Oh yes, Mr. Cloud . . ."

"Cloud would be fine," Cloud said.

"These people have heard your message," Janice rapidly continued. "It's the message you people have been trying to tell us for so long."

The crowd cheered.

"Tell me, Mr. Cloud," a reporter began before Janice could, "what was it that drew you to the First National Wisconsin?"

Cloud gazed at the man, trying to figure out what was going on. He barely remembered what he had said. That was hours ago. Cloud recalled going there because he had nothing better to do. Which is why he easily agreed to coming down to the station. All he wanted to do was go home and think about asking for his job back. After seeing the birds sprawled along the sidewalk, he knew he could deal with extra cheese no pepperoni for a while longer.

"Did the First National Wisconsin have you arrested because of some alleged involvement in the Indian bingo fiasco?" the same reported asked.

"Well," Cloud began, figuring out a way to get these people off his back. "I no longer had a job and I wanted my job back . . ."

"So," another reporter interjected, "then you were one of the displaced tribal workers."

"I displaced myself," Cloud answered.

His answer was drowned out by a host of shouted questions that, somehow or another, were answered before a word slipped from Cloud's mouth. Questions like did he approve or disapprove of the Columbus Highway? Or some large corporation's involvement in Indian gambling interests? Or humankind's disrespectful treatment of the natural world, as evidenced by the monolithic First National Wisconsin building? Even one on personal karma was asked and answered. Each question built on the other, and the reporters and supporters were confusing themselves more than Cloud confused himself.

What to do, what to do?

Cloud wanted to go home. The police officers wanted Cloud to go home so things could resume their normal chaos. But no one else seemed to want to go home. Maybe they didn't have any homes? Who knows? It was clear, however, that one thing was getting accomplished, and that was a protest rally against the Avian Dream–stealing (as it was now called), First National Wisconsin building and all that it represented. And Cloud would be the spokesman.

Lights, camera, action.

Cloud tossed a few Grouchoisms at the reporters and managed to slip away. The reporters noted every word and slipped off to make their copy. The show must go on. The college students and various social organizations slipped off to plan tomorrow's rally. The station captains slipped off to try to figure out where in the budget was the money to police this rally.

Unnoticed to everyone, one lone old man sat in the lobby corner, watching everything. His face was masked by a wide-brimmed hat. He was furniture quietly surveying the madness around him.

That night, Cloud's face was flashed across the local media and into everyone's home. Raymond Felician, his wife and daughters were sitting lazily before the television, not paying much attention. Ray's wife looked up and tapped his shoulder. "Say, isn't that Cloud?"

Ray shifted his glasses, marked his place in a book and looked up. "Well, I'll be damned, what has the boy gone and done now?"

His daughter listened closely, "I think he said he was thinking about asking for his job back."

Ray chuckled. "Had to go on television to do that? Of course he can have his job back."

In another living room another couple watched the evening news. "Say," Man said, "that's the jerk that told me to take my extra cheese and stuff it."

Woman glanced at the television. "Sounds like he was preoccupied with something else when he yelled at you."

Man listened to Cloud's interview. "You know, honey, he has a point there."

Honey snuggled next to Man. "Maybe we should go to that rally tomorrow?"

Man caressed Honey. "I think we should do something about those birds. Imagine, flying all that way only to smash against that building."

Cloud walked into his apartment and flopped into a chair. "I don't need another day like this," he told a large Groucho Marx poster.

The phone rang. It was Sebline. "Hello, Cloud," she began cheerily. "I just wanted to tell you that we're all behind you. You did disappear rather quickly. Did you watch the news tonight? You looked great. I just got word that CNN is sending a crew up here to cover tomorrow's rally. That's at two o'clock, just in time for the Six O'Clock News. You will be there, you're the main speaker. We're all behind you one hundred percent. If you'd like, I'll come by and pick you up?"

"Er," Cloud said.

"Fine, I'll see you tomorrow at one-thirty. Have a good night, Mr. Cloud, We won't let you down." *Click.*

Cloud shrugged, replaced the phone, popped *Duck Soup* into the VCR, and fell asleep happily.

The next day Cloud was on the phone talking to Raymond about a possible vacation when there came a resolute ringing of his apartment doorbell. Cloud excused himself and answered the door.

"Good afternoon, Cloud," Janice greeted cheerily. She looked stunning, and quite overdressed.

Cloud wore blue jeans, one sock, and nothing else—he too was dressed for the occasion. "What do you want?"

"Surely you haven't forgotten," Janice answered, barging into the apartment. "You're not even ready. Cloud, it's almost one-thirty."

Cloud looked for a working clock. The VCR flashed 12:00, 12:00, 12:00. "What's going on at one-thirty?"

"You must be looking for my brother," Cloud said, hanging up the phone.

"I'm sorry? Were you talking on the phone?"

Shit, I hung up on Raymond, Cloud thought. Oh, well, "Yeah, I forgot about the rally," Cloud answered. "I thought I was just dreaming yesterday."

"No, sir," Janice said. "CNN, ABC, NBC, WMTJ, WJMT, WITV, and 92 'LIP will be covering the rally."

"All them, huh?" Cloud found a shoe. "I have just one question." Cloud found yesterday's T-shirt. He put on what he found so far. "What exactly is this rally all about?"

Janice hesitated, then smiled broadly exposing gleaming white teeth. "You are such a kidder." She tapped him on the shoulder. Cloud smiled. "Do you know you don't have a sock on that foot?" She pointed to his foot wearing a shoe and no sock.

"I'm making a fashion statement," Cloud said. "And you're going to drive me there?" He found his other shoe.

"Are you going dressed like that?"

Cloud looked himself over in the mirror. "I suppose I should throw on a jacket. It might rain, you know."

The drive to the First National Wisconsin building was uneventful. Janice chirped all the way. Cloud watched the people. They didn't appear concerned about the great rally, if they even knew about it. They went about their business and Cloud wanted to join them.

It would be good to get back to work.

The west wall of the First National Wisconsin was jammed with people. Surrounding the people were police officers, and surrounding the police officers were news cameras. Banners proclaiming avian dream rights and denouncing Laurel Robin's alleged misdeeds flowed on the left. Banners decrying the liberal banners and sprouting Pro-American locations and promoting progressive anti-everything causes flapped on the right. The media were having a field day as slogans were belted back and forth like a rampaging porcupine in a nudist colony. The crowd cheered and jeered when Janice Sebline, the Video Crusader, and Cloud stepped from the car.

"Save the birds, down with Laurel Robins," one side shouted.

"USA, USA, USA," the other side screamed, for lack of anything better to say.

Petty arguments erupted around the fringe, neither side making much sense, and the newscams gleefully recorded it all for posterity and a possible jump in the ratings. Reporters stood on the perimeters babbling incoherent nonsense and hot dog vendors closed their stands, having sold their supply in less than one hour.

A police escort guided Janice and Cloud through the crowd. Janice loved it all. She smiled and waved, shook hands and showed her best profile. Cloud wondered where his other sock was.

A pole of a man with red hair, a large nose, oversized glasses, and casually dressed in a tweed sport coat and gray corduroys stepped up to the podium when Cloud reached the makeshift stage. "As mayor of the City of Milwaukee, I would like to acknowledge your cause, Mr. Cloud," he salutated (if there is such a word?). The crowd roared. The mayor stretched out his arms looking like a windswept clothesline pole and continued. "As our fair city suffers through these trying times, times of racial discord and mutual suspicions, of economic crisis and environmental distress, of the homeless and downtrodden, of the . . ."

"Enough already," someone shouted.

". . . inclement weather and depressing headlines," the mayor, who wasn't doing well in the opinion polls, rolled on. "You, Mr. Cloud, have presented our city with a simple message, one that we, as citizens, have been seeking for a long time."

"Save the birds, save ourselves," the avian dreamers sang.

"USA, USA, USA," the Pro-American progressive conservatives hooted.

Cloud studied the dais. He recognized various "people of color" leaders who stood by politely clapping. He glanced out at the faces, a lively sea of clashing hues, waiting expectantly for him to say something wise and enlightening, or vicious and slandering, depending on your political stance. The college students looked adoringly at him and flashed their banners. Cloud stepped up to the mayor, shook his hand, and stood before microphones, video cameras, scribbling reporters, and what looked like a million eyes, friendly and otherwise. He cleared his throat.

"Tell it to the world," the Reverend Curtis R. Porter, of the Northside League of Urban Justice, belted out.

Cloud smiled at the man wondering what he was talking about. The mayor hesitated, then said, "We know how overwhelming this must be, Mr. Cloud." Once again he thrust out his long arms, looking as before. "The fine citizens of Milwaukee are waiting for your words. We support your cause."

"Words," Cloud said, puzzled.

"Save the birds, save the birds."

"USA, USA, USA."

An austere-looking woman leaned over the podium and said, "We are with the avian dreamers. For too long we have asked how much, how much, how much? Do we really need the extra cheese?"

"You sure don't," someone called out. The crowd laughed.

"And we've forgotten our purpose," the woman continued, unruffled. "We have forgotten about the simple things. Must the birds pay for our arrogance?" She was on a roll. "What you said was true, Mr. Cloud, we are all tribal sisters and brothers, despite our differences in color."

The crowd was silent, trying to decipher what Lady Gregory Denise Hill-Quickdraw was saying this time.

The reporters chuckled. "Thank you, Alderperson Hill-Quickdraw," the mayor said.

"Tribal brothers and sisters?" Cloud asked the mayor.

The crowd erupted in a cacophony of cheers and jeers. One rather large man wearing a pronounced American flag pin and girlie tattoos bulled through the crowd. "Der ain't nothing tribal about me," he shouted, shaking a hamfist at Cloud. "Why don't youse go back wre you came from and leave the bingo to da churches?"

"Bingo?" Cloud inquired. Bits and pieces of yesterday's folly were beginning to filter back to him. He remembered some things he said, but this?

"Oh, why don't you chicks go back home and let the man speak?" a small, wiry African-American man shouted back.

"You can't stop us from talking anymore," a burly Latina woman added.

"Why don't you people get jobs and quit bitchin'?" a handsomely chiseled Adonis in a Khan's three-piece said.

"Dream stealers, dream stealers," one side of the crowd erupted.

"USA, USA, USA," you know who added.

The cameras whirled merrily along.

A wordball formed in Cloud's throat. If he could only remember what he said. Yesterday he had nothing to do and was in a very snide mood. A mood brought on by self-pity and rash decisions. A guilty mood, actually.

Guilt. There was an answer. He scanned the crowd. The crowd looked for a cause, any cause, because they had nothing better to do. Their world was guilt, thriving and dying with it. He remembered the bus ride. He looked up suddenly.

There, standing ten feet in front and protecting a shopping cart loaded with refuse, was the toothless woman. She spied him spying her and flipped him the bird.

Cloud erupted in laughter. The crowd paused.

"Guilt, that's what's been bothering me" Cloud said, his words echoing between buildings. The crowd waited expectantly, waiting to pounce in either direction.

"How do we survive without guilt?" Cloud asked.

"Learn from the birds," Alderperson Hill-Quickdraw shouted.

"Go back to the Southside," someone shouted.

"Tell the world about the sins committed against us tribal people of color," Reverend Porter wailed.

"Reverend, could you tell us about the alleged mishandling of League funds?" a reporter loudly asked.

The reverend shook his head. "There it is," he hollered, standing up and looking defenseless. "They always attack us with lies and heresy. They don't want us coming together. They're suppressing us and denying my rights."

Cloud shook his head, saying to himself, "And what have I done?"

"You have given us a voice," a man shouted.

Cloud continued talking to himself. "I suppose I can deal with the extra cheese—that's the way it is. But they always want so much."

"How much?" a heckler queried.

"Why don't you let the man speak?" a woman retorted briskly. "He has come from the Indian lands, ready to tell us what the Indians have to say about this."

"Wait a minute," Cloud began, realizing his voice was carrying.

"Tell us what the Indians know," the crowd chorused. One side anyway.

"Indians?" Cloud stared at the crowd. "I just don't know," he said softly.

"That's an Indian for you," someone screamed. The crowd hissed and cheered the man.

The mayor smiled, waving for cooler heads to prevail. The police readied themselves. The newscams whirred and clicked. Cloud stepped back and looked up at the First National Wisconsin building. He looked back at the crowd.

A tall old man wearing a floppy-brimmed hat stood across the street, watching everything around him and, yet, looking directly at Cloud. Cloud heard a small thump-bump against something far away. He faced the sound just as a tiny body hit the sidewalk behind him.

The crowd had long ago decided to carry out its own agenda. Both sides stood toe to toe, accusing each other of every social and environmental ill in history. Some pushed, some shoved, and a long line of blue wearing white helmets and dark visors moved through the crowd. The cameras whirled. Janice Sebline twitched excitedly, speaking to a camera. "This is Janice Sebline, the Video Crusader, reporting on the spot for WMTJ News. As you can clearly see, the city is divided over the issue of saving the poor birds that have no place to call home . . ."

Barry Martin, WJTM reporter, talked with a Laurel Robins corporate official. "I don't know what all the fuss is about," the official officially said. "After all, we here at Laurel Robins Corporation helped support the peregrine nestings on the top floors of the First National Wisconsin building. We at Laurel Robins support any and all causes that benefit mankind."

Barry Martin smirked knowingly. "Yes, Mr. Talltale, but isn't it true the peregrine is a bird of prey, and isn't it true that the Laurel Robins Corporation is preying on the socioeconomic depressive state of the near Northside?"

The Laurel Robins official officially excused himself.

Cloud stood over the sparrow watching it twitch. He stooped down and studied the bird. Its eyes moved slowly back and forth, its beak hung open, its little bird tongue lolled listlessly, and it flopped weakly about, struggling to maintain a hold on life. Cloud picked the bird up gently. He cupped it in his hands and faced the crowd.

"All you want to do is survive without guilt," he said softly. "This isn't your fault. He looked out over the crowd, which had begun a shouting match that drowned out a low-flying jet passing overhead. No one was paying any attention to the dais. The mayor slipped away. The reverend got into a shoving match with the nosy reporter. Alderperson Hill-Quickdraw and her women's rights supporters got into a free-for-all with antitreaty rights protestors—who showed up anywhere the word Indian was mentioned. News crews got into fistfights with other news crews for the best angles. Officer Krantz got into a procedural argument with a liberal station captain.

And the lone man standing across the street stared at Cloud, nodding his head.

Cloud floated through the crowd like a passing cloud, gently carrying the bird to the lone man. No one noted his passing. The lone man was a vision, a face Cloud had seen in his past. He stood before the man, holding the bird out.

"Can we save it?"

The lone man smiled and led Cloud away.

And the cameras whirred and clicked, flashed and popped, catching nothing and missing it all.

"This is Janice Sebline, reporting from the scene." [23]

# My Mother and I Had a Discussion One Day

DENISE SWEET, WHITE EARTH OJIBWE

*Denise Sweet, a White Earth Anishinabe, is a professor and former chair of the American Indians Studies Program at the University of Wisconsin–Green Bay. In 2004 she was the poet laureate of Wisconsin. This poem is from the book* Songs for Discharming, *which was the winner of the North American Native Authors First Book Award: The Diane Decorah Award for Poetry.*

## MY MOTHER AND I HAD A DISCUSSION ONE DAY

and she said I was quite fortunate
to have two sons
and I said how is that? and she said
with daughters you worry for them
birth control, childrearing,
you worry for them, the threat of rape,
and then there is the wedding expense.
I looked into her tired eyes
and clouded face and saw
that she was quite serious.
Yes, but, I said,
boys eat more.

My mother and I had a discussion one day
and she said why do they call it
women's music?
and I said because they sing it,
take from it, feel good and strong
when they walk away from it
while we sit here this is going on.
Are you telling me, my mother said

up until now, I have been listening
and no women have been singing?
and I said that is right
and she said that was ridiculous
and hummed a tune
of her own.

My mother and I had a discussion one day
and she said why do you want to leave
this house, it is a fine house?
and I said I didn't think there was much of a market
for a nosewiper, a kitchen keeper,
an under the bed sweeper
and she said my smart mouth
would get me in trouble one day
and I looked at her scarred knuckles
and quivering chin and realized
that I had spit in the face
of a thousand thousand women and I wept
with my mother. [24]

# 3.18

# Sage Dreams

DANIELLE M. HORNETT, BAD RIVER OJIBWE

*A writer and educator, Dr. Danielle M. Hornett was formerly the associate dean of cultural diversity at St. Norbert College in DePere, Wisconsin. The following selection is an excerpt from her novel* Sage Dreams, Eagle Visions.

The tired, rusty bell over the door clunked her arrival. The reservation's only mini-mart was empty except for the two elder cribbage buddies huddled over a beat-up card table at the back of the long room. Amanda's uncle glanced at her and waved.

"Saving on electricity?" she asked Winky, "or is that game so exciting you hadn't noticed it was getting dark?" She found the light switch. The fluorescent hummed and blinked a few times before catching. Taking a Coke from the pop machine and grabbing a chair that had seen better days, Amanda joined the men.

"Turn them on," Winky grumbled pointing his lips toward the lights, "and folks'll think I want their good business. Can't ya see we're busy?" He scratched the stubble of his day-old beard and studied his cards.

"Howdy gal," Uncle Dan said. "What'cha been up to? I called earlier but ya musta been bumming." He peered at her over his glasses. "Ya ain't been out slippin' a around with your new admirer now, have ya?" He turned to his sidekick. "Don't know if I mentioned it, Winky, but Punky Jakes was droolin' over my niece here like a love sick puppy over at church last Sunday." He chuckled.

"Ya mean a St. Bernard puppy, don't ya?" Winky came back. "Remember what a string bean that young-un was. Wouldn't know it to look at him now, would ya?"

"You guys are disgusting!" Amanda scolded. "I came by 'cuz I wanted some company, but now I'm not so sure." The old men hooted. "As a matter of fact," she continued, "I've been at Annie's, but knowing the rez hot line, you already knew that." Dan and Winky snorted confirmation. "Noah is doing a healing tomorrow night at her place and wants to know if you two'd like to come. He wants Ben and Yemmy to come too."

"Lord, help me," Winky wheezed a laugh. "Been a long time since I been to one of them things. 'Course we'll go. If Noah needs us, we'll be there . . . right, Dan?"

Dan grunted his surprise. "How'd that happen?" he asked. "Can't imagine Annie agreeing to anythin' like that. She never was one for Indian ways."

"JR talked her into it. I saw him and Winnie last night. They're worried sick and so am I. JR said that his ma's been going downhill even after the doctor assured her they got all the cancer. I almost didn't recognize her the first time I stopped by." She took a long sip of Coke.

"Good for JR," her uncle said. "Annie never could say no to that boy. Guess 'cuz he's always been the man of the family. His pa's been drunk and not worth a shit since day one." Amanda winced. Her uncle usually didn't talk about people, even if they were Neil Butler. "That man could make babies," he grumbled, "but not take care of 'em. I always felt sorry for that Annie girl."

Both Winky and Amanda waited for Dan to continue. When he didn't, Amanda told the old men about the spirit at Annie's and what she knew of Noah's plans to send it away.

"He said you shouldn't fast because of your diabetes," she told her uncle.

"I know, I know." Dan folded his hands, any interest in the game lost for the evening. "Winky, why don't you donate some corn and I'll fix manomin. I still got enough to feed a hungry dozen or so."

"I got fruit too," Winky said. "Dang, if this ain't the most excitin' thing that's happened to me for a long time." He smiled his lopsided jack-o-lantern smile and leaned back in his chair and lit a cigarette. She doubted they even knew she was gone.

Miss-Never-Late had spent more time than she should have looking for cloth for the tobacco ties Noah wanted. Finally she ran into WalMart for remnants and arrived at his cabin by seven-thirty. As she stepped into the small porch, Niijii opened his eyes, then closed them again without barking. Amada guessed she'd been accepted by the shaggy no-breed guarding the door.

In an uncommonly serious mood, Noah smudged each of them, the cloth, and finally the tobacco before they began working on the ties. After tying up her fingers a few times, Amanda learned to twist her wrist just so, in order to secure the tobacco solidly into the cloth squares. While they worked, Noah told her what she needed to know to help him at sunrise and in the afternoon. When they finished he insisted they rest, saying she could sleep in his room and he'd take the couch.

"I'll wake you just before sun-up," he said between yawns.

Amanda's body was ready for sleep, but her mind raced with thoughts about the ceremony and her place on the reservation after fifteen years in Milwaukee. The sage smoke smell in her hair reminded her of Great-uncle Hobo, and her grandma, . . . and of the first time she'd visited Noah. He'd walked her to her car and his braids had slipped into the open window—was that really just a few weeks ago? She could still hear Niijii snoring softly out-side the bedroom door. He'd adopted her this evening after Noah let him back in.

*"Is this it, Gramma?" the little girl asked as she picked up a piece of sage. She studied its wooly, greenish-blue leaves before handing it to the old lady in the red flowered dress and faded blue shawl.*

*Her grandmother took the sage with one hand and reclaimed the hand of the five-year-old Amanda with the other. They continued down the rutted path behind the cabin.*

*"Yes, Manda, that's it. Isn't it beautiful?"*

*"It don't smell so boo-tiful," the little girl said. Because she loved these times when Gramma and Hobo would take her to the woods with them, and they always smelled of burnt sage, it made her feel safe. Sometimes the sage was used for smudging or medicine, she knew. But often her grandmother would tie it in small bundles with red string and put them on the windowsills in the house—for protection, she'd say. Gathering new sage was an im-portant chore and Amanda was proud to be part of it.*

*Slipping her free hand easily into her Uncle Hobo's crinkled, dry one, Amanda squinted up at Gram's brother. He was the oldest person she knew—probably even as old as God, she thought. Hobo never made her feel like a bother like some grown-ups did. And he had such a wonderful face—all wrinkled like Gramma's prunes. Amanda scrunched up her face, won-dering if she'd look like that some day.*

*The two elders spoke only in Ojibwe. That was okay even if Amanda didn't understand what they were saying. She knew it was hard for Hobo to speak English. He'd try, but his words got all mixed up with Indian. When she couldn't understand, he'd smile his toothless smile and make hand gestures that sometimes helped.*

*Hobo was very thin, stood ramrod straight, and always walked as though he was on his way to someplace special. Amanda tried to walk like him, stretching her little legs as far as she could. His long white hair was tied at the back of his neck in a ponytail and held by a brown leather strip. As he walked, she watched the tail bounce with a life of its own. Amanda tossed her head from side to side, feeling her braids hit the side of her shoulders. Sometimes she could talk Mom into a ponytail like Uncle Hobo's but not too often. Her hair liked to slip out of the tail and look "lazy," as Mom called it. Better to have braids so it would behave.*

*Sometimes just she and Gramma would gather sage, then Gram would tell stories of "the old days" as they walked slowly over the dirt road that led from the back of the pond to the place where the sage grew. As hard as she tried, Amanda couldn't imagine her old grand-mother as a young girl and Uncle Hobo as a young boy riding horses through these woods. What her mind saw were child bodies with the heads of her Gramma and Uncle Hobo as she knew them now. Even at her age, Amanda recognized this as a silly picture, and stifling a giggle, she'd struggle to act grown up, knowing that's what Gramma'd want. At times like this Gram would look down at her and smile, like she was reading her mind. Hobo could do that too. Amanda thought that probably was something all old people could do.*

She woke to rapping on the door. "Amanda? Time to get up." She struggled to respond, the dream world and the real world confused in her half-sleep state.

Noah tapped his knuckles against the door again and waited until she grunted. "Dress warm, it's icy out there." He paused, "Are you awake?"

"Yeah . . . be right there." The faint smell of sage filled Amanda with longing for her grandmother and great uncle. It didn't feel like thirty years since she'd seen them or twenty since she'd left the rez for college. Jumping out of bed, she threw on jeans and a sweatshirt. As she ran her fingers through her hair, the screen door slammed. Noah was already back outside.

She brushed her teeth with her finger and gulped down a glass of orange juice, then grabbed her jacket and followed Noah. A fire flickered in the small pit he'd dug in the back yard. He was warming his hands over the flames. Amanda tripped, nearly falling over pieces of sod he'd removed to make the hole.

"Careful," he said, not looking at her. "I'll put that back when I'm finished. You'll never know we dug here. That way we won't scar mother earth. The sun will be up in fifteen minutes," he said, looking at the still-dark sky in the east.

Amanda watched the sky begin to lighten, remembering how Hobo had explained that the space between the spirit world and the human world was thinnest now—the best time to communicate with the spirits.

"Pray with me," Noah said.

He pulled a pipe from his bag. "My tools," he grinned at her. "This bag holds everything I need." He handed her the pipe while he dug in the bag again. "Got special tools for special jobs," he grunted and squinted into the bag. "I can't always find what I need right away . . . but . . . everything is in here . . . someplace." He finished digging and sat back on his heels, "ah, asemaa, special-made red willow for ceremonies." He held some out to her. "Hobo taught me how to make it. Someday I'll teach you."

Amanda was filled with wonder at the connection between her and Hobo, and Hobo and Noah; that Noah's teacher had been her great uncle and in turn, Noah was teaching her. The circle continued.

He put the other things away and took the pipe from her. He held it sky-ward and prayed in Ojibwe. He gave the pipe back. "I want you to fill it."

"I don't know how." She shivered; sweat peppered her forehead despite the cold.

"Then it's time you learn," he said in that old-time voice that went with all important instruction.

The sky began to lighten behind the pines as he led her through each step. She repeated what he told her to say in English while he prayed in Ojibwe; their breath pierced the cool, predawn air with ghostly puffs of punctuation.

First they thanked the Creator for their lives and the new day. Then they prayed for clear minds and good thoughts to help them face the duties ahead. They asked for their spirits' helpers to come. They explained, each in their own language, what was happening at Annie's and what they planned to do. They prayed for help to send the lost spirit home. Noah pulled the other tools out of his bag and asked blessings for each of them. By the time they finished the prayers, red streams of morning sun filtered through the trees.

"Can you feel the spirits?" he asked. "They're all around us."

"I felt the air pressure change," she whispered. "Did the spirits do that?"

An eagle called from overhead. Noah smiled. "Migizi just answered you," he said. They watched the Grandfather's messenger circle twice before moving out of sight behind the tall pines. Amanda saluted the Grandfather's sign—his messenger.

"You're gonna do okay," Noah told her.

Amanda added a silent prayer for courage—and hoped she looked more sure of herself than she felt.

Noah added wood to the fire. "We'll keep this going all day and take the coals to Annie's. Fire's an important part of the ceremony."

Amanda looked around, took a deep breath and choked on the morning-crisp air. "I don't remember if I was ever up this early," she laughed and cleared her throat. "We almost beat the birds up," she nodded toward a red-winged blackbird watching them from his perch on a thin reed at the edge of the trees. Its new-day whistle filled the air.

"You'll be happy to know I saw a couple of robins in the yard last week," he said. "They looked like scouts to me." She returned his grin. His humor was returning; this was the Noah she knew.

By noon Amanda was exhausted. She sat by the fire resting her head on her up-drawn knees.

"Go take a nap," Noah said, "I'll get you up in an hour or so."

Too tired to argue with him, she went inside, kicked off her shoes and threw herself across the bed. Niijii stood next to her, his head on the covers, eyes begging. She fell into a dreamless sleep before she could put her hand out to pet him.

Amanda woke three hours later and looked outside. Noah still squatted near the pit. The fire was almost out. He looked up when she pushed the screen door open.

"Get that bucket near the door there," he directed with his chin, "that's how we'll carry the fire to Annie's."

She did as she was told, ignoring the concern that nagged at her. Noah should know what he was doing, she hoped, as he shoveled the hot coals into the bucket.

"Here." He gave her the keys to the Bronco. "Go open up the back for me."

"Won't that start a fire?" she asked.

"I hope so, that's why we're taking it," he said, "or do you think the Bronc needs a heater?'

"Noooooo. I mean in the car. The bucket's hot, won't it start the carpet on fire?"

"Run grab that piece of plastic from under the stoop. That should take care of any problem."

Amanda dug under the small porch and found a broken piece of carpet protector, the kind she used under her chair at the office. She put it on the floor in the back of the Bronco and eyed it warily as Noah put the bucket on it. Even with its wide bottom, she was sure the bucket would tip when they went around the corners. Noah shook his head and grinned.

"Don't worry," he said, "the spirits are with us."

"Maybe so, but . . . do they want us taking foolish chances?" she asked.

He laughed at her and went to the unused garage out back, returning with an old washtub. "This won't tip," he said. Carefully, he poured the coals from the bucket into the tub. She shook the edge of the tub—it sat solidly in place. "Satisfied?" he asked.

"Satisfied," she told him.

They arrived at Annie's just as Dan and Winky were walking up the rickety steps, each loaded down with a large box. The Vincents' and JR's cars were already there. Dan walked by the door to give Amanda a hug.

"I'm proud of you," her uncle said. "And Hobo would be too," he added, as though he were reading her concern about her place in the ceremony.

Amanda blushed and hugged him back. "And I'm proud of you."

"Hey, what about me?" Winky cried.

"I'm proud of you too," she said and smiled at him.

"No, I don't care about that," he groused. "Where's my hug, gal?"

She hugged the old man. The tic in his eye was worse this afternoon; it was one long, continuous wink.

JR met them at the door. The kitchen smelled of meat, pies, and fry bread. Annie was sitting at the table staring out the window. Butts smoked down to the nubs overflowed the stained glass ashtray in front of her. She was dressed; no torn chenille robe and blue plastic beach thongs today. Annie's hair had been brushed but still hung dull and stringy around her thin face. Dark circles emphasized her green eyes and classic cheekbones. Her fingers worried the top button of the oversized denim shirt she wore.

"Might as well get started," Noah said. "Sundown in about twenty minutes and we better be ready. I'll get the coals for the fire. Come on, Amanda. JR?" JR nodded. "We'll meet you out back," Noah said.

As she came around the corner of the hours, Amanda stopped. A replica of Noah's pit was dug into Annie's yard—same shape, same size. JR walked next to it.

"How did he know to do that?" she asked Noah. "Did you call him?"

Noah shook his head. "Didn't have to. He was told what he needed to do when he prayed at sun-up. Our spirit helpers tell us everything we need to know if we just listen and believe. JR's a listener, and a believer."

In a few minutes Noah and JR had the fire blazing and the three went back inside.

"Amanda will smudge everyone here and then do the house while I set up my altar in Annie's bedroom," Noah said. "Amanda," he turned to her. "Do that room first." He pointed with his lips to the back room. "Then do them," he tipped his head toward those in the kitchen. "When you finish, join me."

Amanda nodded and took the shell he held out. She recognized this ritual for protection; Gramma had done it often. She lit the rolled ball of sage with the wooden match Ben came up with, and blew lightly to help it catch. Noah took the shell and smudged her. Following his example, she smudged him. He motioned with his chin for her to go. She went to the bedroom alone.

She directed the sage smoke into each corner, around the windows and doors, under the bed that was made today, and in the closet, leaving the door open. The presence hung heavily in the room and stirred the air as she smudged. The hair raised on Amanda's arms and the back of her neck. She was glad to return to the kitchen. Without a word, Noah took his bag and went to Annie's bedroom.

The four elders, Annie, JR, and his wife, Winnie, stood in a circle around Amanda, waiting. She smudged them one by one, starting with Annie.

"I'm so glad you're here, my friend. Thank you. I've missed you so." Annie's voice broke.

Amanda put her arms around her frail cousin. "Please help her," she prayed silently as she brushed sage smoke over Annie's head, and up and down her body with miigwan, her feather.

That done, Amanda smudged every nook and corner of the house, coming back to the kitchen once for more sage. Finished, she went to the bedroom where Noah had already begun. The room smelled of bear medicine and cedar. Unseen hands slipped an invisible shawl lightly around her shoulders as she entered the room. Noah ignored her so she knelt on the worn linoleum, slightly behind his left shoulder, resting her weight on her heels, waiting for a sign or a word. White and blue spirit lights zipped and danced around his head.

"There's more than one," he whispered. "Can you feel them?"

Amanda nodded. A male presence was strong, and there was at least one, softer, female presence. Her eyes were drawn to the left up into the farthest corner near the ceiling. She frowned.

"Yep, that's where he is," Noah said. "The others are afraid of that one. They're hiding. They're willing to go, I think, but he won't let them." Noah continued praying, first in Ojibwe, then in English. Using Annie's Indian name, he told the spirits to leave her house; told them they didn't belong here, told them they couldn't stay. He repeated this four times.

The air began moving, so slowly at first Amanda barely felt it, but it rapidly got stronger. She looked at Noah who didn't seem to notice. She felt, rather than heard, a high-pitched buzzing coming from somewhere inside the house.

"Go open the back door," Noah said, "then stand aside. Keep the others away from the door too."

She moved to do as she was told. Halfway to her feet, she heard Noah laugh. "No, she can't go with you. She has to stay here . . . *you* go!"

Amanda looked at him, confused. She was still half standing.

"That male spirit insists you go with him," Noah told her, chuckling. "Wanna take a trip?"

"You're kidding me, right?" she whispered.

He turned away from her and spoke to the spirit in the corner. This time the laughter had left his voice. It was stern, almost unrecognizable. *"Because she's alive,"* Noah said, "She still had many things to do in this world. She belongs here. You don't! You're not alive . . . you can't stay. It's time for you to move one! She stays . . . you go! She stays, you go."

Amanda's cramping legs began to shake. She knelt again. "What's happening?" Her constricted windpipe allowed only a squeak to escape. She wasn't sure he'd even heard her. Amanda gulped, cleared her throat, and tried again. "Noah, what the hell is going on?"

Again, Noah didn't answer. He repeated his earlier words to the spirit, then spoke, for what felt like a long time to Amanda, in Ojibwe, "Okay," he finally said. "Do as I told you. Go open the back door and stand back—way back. Tell the others to stay back too. But *you* especially. This guy still wants you. . . . Go!" he ordered when she hesitated.

She did what she was told, glancing backward as she limped from the bedroom babying muscles strained by her crouch. In a few minutes Noah followed, urging something forward, something invisible . . . guiding it toward the door with his eagle fan. He was praying in Ojibwe. A gust of wind ruffled Amanda's pant legs as he passed. He indicated he wanted the others to help. The four elders joined Noah's prayers.

On the back porch, Noah motioned to Amanda to stand beside him. They watched as JR stepped back quickly as the cold wind whirled past him and pushed tongues of flames out in several directions from the center of the fire.

"That should do it," Noah said. His voice was tired but his black eyes twinkled. JR looked at them for a second, then raised his fist in a silent gesture of triumph. He joined them on the steps. Together they went in to the kitchen where everybody was hugging everybody else and laughing, wiping away tears.

"Can't ya feel the difference already, Ma?" Winnie asked. "I can! What a relief. Thank you Noah, thanks, Amanda. You don't know what Annie means to me." Suddenly the big woman's shoulders shook. She turned her back and sobbed into the crook of her elbow

Yemmy put her arthritic arms around her. "We all feel it, Winnie. Annie will get better now, I just know it. You're gonna have her for a while yet."

JR hugged his wife. Together they went and sat next to his ma. Both of Annie's hands clamped on to her son's good one, unshed tears making her eyes shine. She smiled crookedly at her daughter-in-law.

Dan and Winky slapped each other on the back. "Well. When we gonna eat?" Winky asked. His tic had slowed considerably.

"Right now!" Dan answered. The two old men began setting the table with the paper plates Winky'd brought. Still sniffling, Winnie pulled venison out of the oven. JR grabbed a brown, grease-stained bag of fry bread off the top of the refrigerator. With Winky's vegetables and fruit and Dan's wild rice, the feast was ready in five minutes. Ben offered thanks for the meal and ceremony, then Annie filled a dish of food as an offering for the spirits who'd come to help.

Noah took it to the other room. "Don't want to put this outside. . . . that guy might see this as an invitation and decide to come back," he said. Amanda threw him a look he chose to ignore.

The celebrants ate like they'd been fasting forever. Even Annie. Noah livened up the already jubilant atmosphere in the kitchen with his story about Amanda's spirit admirer. As much as Amanda wanted to enjoy the story with the others, she was too busy nervously watching the door, unaware that she was chewing on her thumbnail.

By nine-thirty the meal was finished and Annie's kitchen cleaned. Amanda's whole body screamed for sleep. The elders took turns yawning loudly; no one objected when Noah said, "Time to rest, we all earned it."

Noah and Amanda waved at Dan and Winky as they drove off in Winky's noisy pickup. Amanda noticed that he still hadn't fixed his taillight. Noah turned to Amanda. "I'll call you Thursday morning and we'll talk about a movie. Right now I'm too tired to even think," he told her at her car. "You'll sleep tomorrow, and so will I."

"I won't sleep all day!" she said.

"Sure you will," he laughed. "It's okay. I will too." He hugged her quickly. "Sweet dreams."

"You too," Amanda said. She yawned, then smiled at him. "Well, maybe you're right."

Amanda couldn't help herself. As he walked to his Bronco she called to him. "Noah?"

He turned.

"You were kidding about that spirit, weren't you? I mean, that really didn't happen did it?"

"Yeah, it did. Probably I shouldn't have said nothing. I didn't think it would scare you so bad."

"Why wouldn't it?" she hadn't meant to sound so nasty. "I mean, well, couldn't he follow me home?"

Noah walked back to her. "No, he's gone. Look," he put his hand on her shoulder. "I'm sorry I told you. It's just that when you came into the room, he wanted to negotiate, to delay, but he liked you too. I thought you'd enjoy that. Not everyone can turn a spirit's head." He laughed and brushed a stray lock of hair from her face. "But remember, a spirit can't take a living being any place that human doesn't want to go. So stop worrying." He watched her face. "You gonna be all right?"

"Yeah, I guess. It was just a shock, is all." The night eagle, an owl, hooted—a sound that had scared a young Amanda until Hobo assured her that owls were simply the Creator's night messengers and their cry was just to let people know they were around. The unseen hand tugged at the invisible shawl reminding her of the protection that was still around her. She felt Hobo's presence in the night and smiled.

"I'm okay," she said. Suddenly she knew she was.[25]

# The Importance of Madeline Island

WILLIAM WHIPPLE WARREN,
MADELINE ISLAND OJIBWE

*Returning to the place where this chapter began, this selection emphasizes the importance of Madeline Island to the Ojibwe Nation. Son of Marcus Warren and Mary Cadotte, William Whipple Warren attended mission schools on Madeline Island. He was a legislator in the Minnesota House of Representatives, 1851–1853, and was an early historian of the Ojibwe. This selection, from his* History of the Ojibways, Based upon Traditions and Oral Statements, *records the answers given to him by one of the four Mide priests who were conducting a Midewiwin ceremony.*

While our forefathers were living on the great salt water toward the rising sun, the great Megis (sea-shell) showed itself above the surface of the great water, and the rays of the sun for a long period were reflected from its glossy back. It gave warmth and light to the Ani–ish-in-aub-ag (red race). All at once it sank into the deep, and for a time our ancestors were not blessed with its light. It rose to the surface and appeared again on the great river which drains the waters of the Great Lakes, and again for a long time it gave life to our forefathers, and reflected back the rays of the sun. Again it disappeared from sight and it rose not, till it appeared to the eyes of the Ani–ish-in-aub-ag on the shores of the first great lake. Again it sank from sight, and death daily visited the wigwams of our forefathers, till it showed its back, and reflected the rays of the sun once more at Bow-e-ting (Sault Ste. Marie). Here it remained for a long time, but once more, and for the last time, it disappeared, and the An-ish-in-aub-ag was left in darkness and misery, till it floated and once more showed its bright back at Mo-ning-wun-akuan-ing (La Pointe, Madeline Island), where it has ever since reflected back the rays of the sun, and blessed our ancestors with life, light, and wisdom . . .

"For the last time the Me-da-we lodge was erected on the Island of La Pointe, and here, long before the pale face appeared among them, it was practiced in its purest and most original form. Many of our fathers lived the full term of life granted to mankind by the Great Spirit, and the forms of

Indian sugar camp. Besides wild rice, another cherished food source among the woodlands was maple syrup. The sap of maple trees was gathered in late winter or early spring and then boiled down into syrup and sugar cakes. Drawing by Seth Eastman. Reproduced by permission of the Wisconsin Historical Society. WHi-9829.

many old people were mingled with each rising generation." . . . Mo-ning-wuna-kaun-ing is the spot on which the Ojibway tribe first grew, and like a tree it has spread its branches in every direction, in the bands that now occupy the vast extent of the Ojibway earth. . . . It is the root from which all the far scattered villages of the tribe have sprung.[26]

# 4

# Literature of the
# Potawatomi Nation

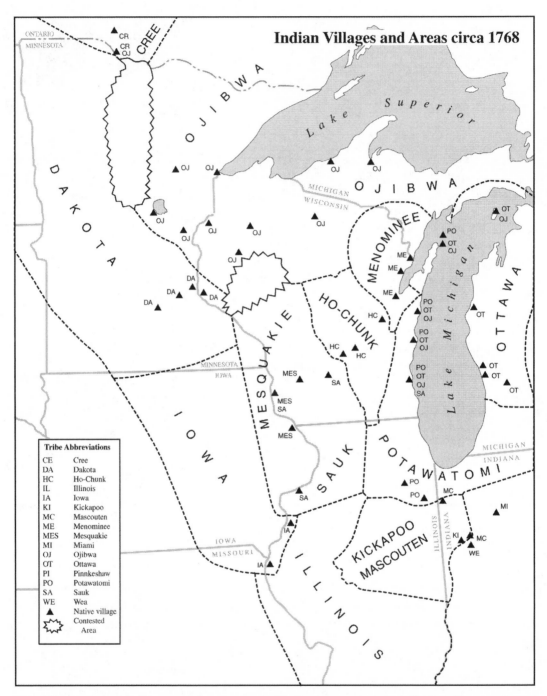

Dotted lines on the map indicate approximate territory of Indigenous peoples, with individual villages marked by a triangle. Toothed areas represent contested regions. Map adapted from Helen Hornbeck Tanner, *Atlas of Great Lakes Indian History* (Norman: University of Oklahoma Press, 1987), 58.

# The Creation of the World

### WAPUKA, POTAWATOMI

*The Potawatomi or "Keepers of the Fire" are related to the Ojibwe and Ottawa, but speak a distinct Algonquian language. The Potawatomi, Ojibwe, and Ottawa nations make up the Three Fires alliance. Fleeing the complex intertribal strife unleashed by European pressures on the Atlantic coast, particularly the warriors of the Iroquois or Five Nations Confederacy, the Potawatomi began leaving their territory in lower Michigan after 1640. From the eastern shore of Lake Michigan, they moved to the Door County peninsula of Wisconsin around 1665. Developing favorable trading partnerships with the French, by 1820 the Potawatomi extended their influence into a large area around the southern shore of Lake Michigan including Milwaukee and Chicago and along Lake Michigan's eastern shoreline, but many forced treaty signings and removals dispersed their numbers. The Forest County Potawatomi, residing in northeastern Wisconsin, are descendents, in part, of people who resisted removal to Iowa Territory. This story from the oral tradition shows the generosity of the animals in helping the Potawatomi.[1]*

In the beginning there was nothing but water everywhere. No land could be seen. On the waves there floated a canoe, and a man sat in it and wept for he had no idea what his fate would be. At length a muskrat clambered up on the canoe and said, "Hau, grandfather! What are you crying for?"

"Oh!" answered the man, "I have been here a long time, and I cannot find any land."

"But there is earth under all this water," replied the muskrat.

"Can you get me some?" asked the man.

"Yes," replied the animal, and he dove down and came up again with both paws full of mud. He dived again and brought up a ball of earth in his mouth.

"Are you all alone?" asked the man.

"No," answered the muskrat, and he called up to the canoe several aquatic animal chiefs. The first to come was a white muskrat.

"I hear that you want to see us," he said to the man.

"Yes, I want you to bring me some earth so I can make the world, and I will also create on it a good place for you to stay."

"Hau," replied the animals, "We will start at once."

So they all began to dive, and the beaver came and helped them also. They saw their grandfather kneading the mud that they brought to him and molding it into a long column that reached from the surface to the bottom of the water. It projected above the waves, and he kept adding to it. They kept on day after day, until it was finally solid. At last there was considerable space there. It was big enough to walk on. Then the man planted a great tree there. He still added to his island.

As the man worked on the north end of the island, he noticed in traveling back and forth that the ground grew dry and dusty. He asked his animals helpers how they liked what he had made, and they told him it was a good place to sun themselves. He told them to persevere in bringing him earth, and he would make it still better. Thus he kept on, until the world was completed. Then he told his animal friends that it would be covered with green grass and trees. He took a stick and marked out where he wanted the rivers to run, and then he had the muskrats dig out the channels.

At last the man built a wigwam. When he had it ready the muskrats were close by in a lake, so he went over and planted rushes along the shore for their benefit. Then he got into his canoe and paddled out into the ocean, and called on the muskrats to help him again while he built another world. He built it up until it met the first one.

"Now," he said, "I have it the way that I want it."

One day he walked up to the north end of his island and found some people there. He approached them and inquired of them where they came from and when. They were the Potawatomi, and they asked in their turn who he was.

"I am Wi'saka," he replied.

"Well, we have heard of you; you must have come from above, as we did."

"No," answered Wi'saka, "I have always been here, and I made this earth and all that you can see on it."

"Well," said one, "This must be the Great Spirit."

"Yes," answered Wi'saka, "That is who I am. Who can do any more than I have?"

"But, if you are the Great Spirit, why didn't you put us here?"

"You came too soon, there were others to precede you," he said to them, and they believed, and asked him what he ate. Wi'saka told them that he lived upon muskrats and he ordered the muskrats to dive into the lake and fetch him yakepin roots. When he had plenty he told them to stop, and then he gave the roots to the Indians. They camped beside his lodge and he lent them his cooking utensils. He showed them how to make clay kettles and how to cook their food.

Wi'saka likewise showed the people the forest he had made, and in the woods he showed them how to peel bark and make household utensils. He showed them how to make string to tie their lodge poles together. He instructed them how to gather and prepare reeds to weave mats, and how to make rush-mat wigwams. The next day he told them that there would be animals in the world, and at his command deer, buffalo, and other game appeared.[2]

# 4.2

# We All Sing

ANONYMOUS, POTAWATOMI

*Respect among animals, humans, and the Great Spirit seem to underlie the "profoundly egalitarian" relationships within and between villages.[3] This joyous celebration of harmony with all creatures and the creation is from the* Chants of the Man Bundle *of the Potawatomi.*

### WE ALL SING

Everybody sings, everybody sings, everybody sings!
Sing with this world, sings with the wind, sings with the water.
You can hear the water roar.
I sing in the wind, sing to be heard.
I strike my drum, my drum is singing in this world.
I shake my gourd, and it sings also.

So we are all singing and dancing
Dancing in thanksgiving that we have lived so long.
So I am singing in the water, I am singing in the air,
I am singing with my drum, I am singing with my gourd.
So are we all singing in this roaring water,
As we hear it roar, roar, roar!

I know that the Great Spirit will help us
While we are singing, singing,
Singing in this world.[4]

# 4·3

# Now We All Move

ANONYMOUS, POTAWATOMI

*In the following chant from the* Man Bundle *ritual, all of creation moves as one. The merging with the world seems an essential element in an ecstatic song.*

### NOW WE ALL MOVE

Now we all move, moving with this earth.
The earth is moving along, the water is moving along.
The grass moves, the trees are moving, the whole earth is moving.
So we all move along with the earth, keeping time with the earth.
That is the way the Great Spirit gave us,
To move with this world.
So we are moving along.
Now I am moving, moving, moving with the world.
As the water moves, as the trees move
Everything is moving
Even the grass, and we are moving,
So we ask you to give us the right way,
That we may move with the Great Spirit,
Where the Great Spirit wants us to move.
So everybody, move, moving, moving,
The way of the world is moving.[5]

# 4·4

# The Trail of Death:
# Potawatomi Diaspora

SUSAN CAMPBELL, CITIZEN POTAWATOMI NATION

*Potawatomi were forced to relinquish their lands in Wisconsin at the Treaty of Chicago. Instead of heading west of the Mississippi River, some bands returned to their villages along Lake Michigan, until the Dakota (Sioux) Uprising in Minnesota provided another excuse to force Natives west of the Mississippi. Some groups hid in forested areas in northern Wisconsin and became known as the Strolling Band of Potawatomi. Some moved to Menominee land and became known as the Forest County Potawatomi. Of the Potawatomi who were forced west of the Mississippi, the removal in 1838 from Twin Lakes, Indiana, to Kansas was known as the Trail of Death.*

*In the following selection, Susan Campbell, Citizen Potawatomi, renders the anguish of the Trail of Death in poetry. First she supplies her family history.*

> Susan Campbell's ancestor, Jacques Vieau, was considered by some to be a founding father of the state of Wisconsin, establishing trading posts in many locations from Green Bay to Milwaukee before his retirement to Green Bay. He and his half-Menominee wife Angelique Roi, a daughter of Joseph Roi and a descendant of Chief Ahkenepoweh, had eleven children. One of their sons, Louis, worked with his father in the family business, beginning at an early age. Louis married a Potawatomi woman, Sha-Note, and they first lived in Skunk Grove [Wisconsin], now Franksville, running a post with Louis' brother, Jacques, Jr. In the 1833 Treaty of Chicago, it was decreed that all Potawatomi in the area were to be removed west of the Mississippi River. They were given three years to sell their property and leave. Louis and Jacques, Jr. sold their post in 1836 and removed, with their families and other Potawatomi, to land provided for them outside Council Bluffs, Iowa, a location called "Half-Breed Farms." There they lived until 1846, when they were moved again, joining Potawatomi who had been removed from Indiana on the infamous 1838 Trail of Death to Kansas (Sha-Note's father and other family members had been a part of this group.) They were ultimately established on a reservation north of what is now Topeka, Kansas, where Louis farmed and ran a toll bridge across the Vermillion River on the Oregon Trail. In the mid-1860s there was one final move when the Kansas group split and forty families took allotment land in Oklahoma, the result of a division between the traditional Prairie Band, who wanted to live on the reservation and maintain their language and customs, and the non-traditional

*Citizen Band who wanted individual allotments. Those who stayed in Kansas became known as the Prairie Band Potawatomi while those who moved to Oklahoma were called the Citizen Band Potawatomi, now the Citizen Potawatomi Nation.[6]*

*Susan Campbell says her poetry comes from many years spent researching her Potawatomi roots, and it is her way of telling their story. Here she describes the context for her poem.*

*Between September 3 and November 4, 1838, approximately 859 Potawatomi Indians were removed from their homes at [Potawatomi] Chief Menominee's village near Twin Lakes, Indiana, and transported under guard to Sugar Creek Mission, Linn County, Kansas. Of these, approximately 40 died along the way; the exact number has been lost to history. Untold others disappeared, going north into Wisconsin and eventually Canada where they settled to begin again. The following poem is dedicated to the memory of my 4th Great-Grandfather Cheshawgen who, with his family, was removed to Kansas on the Potawatomi Trail of Death.*

### CAGE NOKMISEN
**For my grandmothers**

Quiet whispers,
the clicking of beads,
echoed our Spirit prayers
as we knelt at the altar.
Called together by the promise-breakers
we prayed for peace
until rude shouts,
thundering boots
broke the silence.
Before our eyes
the altar was stripped bare
as careless hands
brushed candles and communion plates
into clanging piles on the floor,
wine staining blood-red
the purity of the communion wafer.
Bayonets drawn
the soldiers forced us from our mission church.
With tears in our eyes
we watched it burn.
Allowed only a few moments
to gather together a lifetime
and bid farewell to the Ancestors,
we wept aloud
to see it all go up in flames.
Dejected, defeated, following our chiefs

chained in white prison wagons,
we shouldered our present,
held the hands of our future,
and began the longest walk of our lives—
from the land of our freedom
to the emptiness of our captivity.

And we died.
We ran and we hid—
some escaped north—
but mostly we died.
A few physically—
we laid them gently in the earth,
covering them from intrusion
before hoisting our bundles to move on.
Emotional death kept our feet moving
our minds numb to the shock of removal.
Of our removal.
But the sounds of night—
the mourning for what was
and would never again be.
Muffled sobs, groans.
With swollen eyes we rose each morning
to face a bleak new dawn
and move on.

Sometimes our path
took us through townships.
People came out to stare at us,
curiosity bright in their faces.
Some reflected our sufferings.
Their hands bore food—
warm clothes, blankets—
gestures of concern.
A young child ran after us,
eager to join our strange caravan,
until his worried mother
took him by the hand
and led him home.
Some people jeered us,
calling us "those dirty Redskins."
They threw stones
until ordered to stop.
Then they glared at us, hatred in their eyes.

Others thought to lighten our spirits
by providing us with music,
a music foreign to our ears
for whom the drum, the chant,
and birdsong had been our only chorus.
But we recognized their kindliness
and listened as we ate their bread.

Some days we marched near water.
we could hear it before freeze-time.
In a strange land,
too distant to retrace our steps,
we were allowed to stop—
to enjoy the luxury of bathing.
Clean hair.
Clean clothes. Water for cooking.
Enough to drink.
There were too many dry days.
We didn't see water,
couldn't hear its laughter.
Our stores grew rancid
and sickened us.
We smelled
and were ashamed.

From forests of hardwood
creaking in the wind
we entered treeless plains
where the wind roared at us unmercifully.
The last of summer's heat beat down on us by day unimpeded
while the nights grew increasingly chill.
Fall became winter with keen swiftness that year.
Whom the soldiers hadn't killed,
whom the sickness hadn't struck down,
the cold found a way to strike.
It blew through us unimpaired,
becoming our constant companion.
We all suffered.
But our elders
our children
theirs was the hardest to bear.
More of us died
and we stopped for burial.
Our eyes ran red from tears,

from sun and cold.
Yet we walked on.

Bereft of our priest
we conducted what ceremonies we could
to mark a passing.
But illness and grief
eventually take their toll
and we were permitted the Black Robe
for our comfort, our survival.
He loved us.
He encouraged us.
When our spirits plummeted
he was able to lift them up.
He guided and directed our worship.
He conducted our ceremonies of passing.
And then he died with us.
"What greater love has a man . . . ?"
We walked on.

And then we were there.
Where, we had no idea,
but the dogs barked,
children ran.
Men and women in black robes,
beads clicking from their belts,
smiles of warmth on their faces, in their eyes,
took our hands in theirs in greeting.
They bade the soldiers to lay down their guns
and to take up hammer and saw.
They led us to food,
to beds in makeshift lean-tos,
to new opportunity, new life.
While they set about destroying our spirits
and the way of our Ancestors.

In our confusion
we felt relief at journey's end.
In our tiredness
we felt thankfulness at a chance to rest.
In our emptiness and our grief
we felt restored by the compassion in understanding eyes.
In our bodies we stopped to sit awhile.

But somewhere in our deepest selves
where the remembering,
the whispers of our Ancestors,
lay in wait,
we picked up our bundles and walked on.[7]

# 4·5

# Chief Menominee's Petition

CHIEF MENOMINEE, POTAWATOMI

*Menominee, a Potawatomi chief who was forcibly removed from his land, wrote three letters to the American government, protesting their treatment. In the following letter to Lewis Cass, the secretary of war, Chief Menominee decries the illegal taking of their land and requests proper treatment. In spite of their just grievances, Menominee and his people were removed by order of President Andrew Jackson.*

We do beg you Honorable Sir to inform out Great Father and Senate that it is a false treaty that neither we Menominee, Parkartahmowah, Pepenowar, and Wesheke, the son of Notarkah (deceased), who are recognized chiefs by the Treaty of Tippecanoe, and neither any of our bands but two excepted, consented or signed anything like a treaty or sale of our reserve.

And consequently, we do by this object and protest against any sale of our reservation. Our mind is now as it was last winter, to remain upon our lands to cultivate them. To become subjects of the laws of the state and live like white people. We wish to state further that we were very ill treated by the same Col. Pepper last payment. Most all our money was given to the whites and none of us was allowed to speak.

Fearing to be cheated further, we chiefs left the payment without taking our annuity or giving our names or signing any paper. This is now two years that we have not received any money. Consequently, if our names are seen in any paper, they have been put there without our knowledge, and are false signers for this reason. We do by this object and protest against them. Our wish is further to be delivered from the agency of that Col. Pepper because without any provocation he treated us too bad. And as we are sure that the mind of our Great Father is not to treat his red children that way, we do confidently apply to him for justice and remedy in our sorrows.

Wherefore we sign and send this in village this 15th day of Nov. 1836.[8]

# I Am Not Going to Leave My Lands

CHIEF MENOMINEE, POTAWATOMI

*Many Potawatomi who had been rendered landless had settled in Menominee's village. Although other Potawatomi chiefs had agreed to leave by August 6, 1838, Menominee refused to leave, chiding Col. Pepper for his underhanded treatment.[9] He diplomatically does not blame President Jackson in this second protest letter. The Potawatomi, nonetheless, were forced westward, although some escaped the removal to become the present-day Forest County Potawatomi.*

The president does not know the truth. He, like me, has been imposed upon. He does not know that you made my young chiefs drunk and got their consent and pretended to get mine. . . . He would not drive me from my home and the graves of my tribe, and my children, who have gone to the Great Spirit, nor allow you to tell me that your braves will take me, tied like a dog . . . The President is just, but he listens to the words of young chiefs who have lied; and when he knows the truth, he will leave me to my own. I have not sold my lands. I will not sell them. I have not signed any treaty, and will not sign any. I am not going to leave my lands.[10]

# 4·7

# The Story of a Faithful Wife

JOHN NUWI, WISCONSIN POTAWATOMI

*This story celebrates the courage of a Potawatomi woman who was the first "to earn the title of Watasa'kawao, or Brave-Woman."*

A Potawatomi named One-Noise was once captured by the Kiowa and taken off to the west. Although his horse wandered back, no one could find his body, so the Indians all gave him up as dead. His wife, however, told the men that they were no warriors, and that she would go and hunt for him herself. She followed the trail to the battleground, and found the path of the victorious Kiowa. She followed that until she heard the noise of a drum. She kept on all night and the next day, coming, late in the afternoon, to a creek bottom; she staked her horse and dried her blanket about three miles from the camp of the enemy. There she rested until late in the evening, when she heard the drum once more. Then she mounted her horse and went as close to the camp as she dared.

At the Kiowa camp she saw a great fire with a crowd dancing around it. As she was wrapped close in her blanket like many of the enemy she approached and joined them. She saw her man spread-eagled, that is, tied by the outstretched hands and feet to a post. She could hardly restrain herself from rushing in, but she held back and managed to raise her blanket while the men were gathering wood, so that her husband saw and recognized her. He said nothing, but bowed his head so that she knew he was aware of her presence. Then she went to one side and lay down. Little by little the dance slackened, for the Kiowa, very tired from all their fighting and dancing, broke up early and went to bed. The woman was resolved either to save her husband or to die with him, so she made a prayer to the Great Spirit, begging him to help her by causing the Kiowa to fall asleep.

Eight men were left to guard the captive Potawatomi, and in a little while the fire died down and they slept also. The woman now walked up to the stake and cut her husband's bonds, but he was too stiff and sore to walk, so she took him on her back and carried him, stepping over the guards. She went to a horse, cut its picket rope, tied that on the horse's nose for a bridle, and setting her man on its back, she led it to her own horse. They got to a creek about dawn, and by this time the man was able to dismount and bathe, though still scarcely able to walk. The woman made a saddle of her blanket by cutting it up, and stuffing it with buffalo grass. This she tied on the captured horse, and placing her husband on her own horse, rode the other.

They fled as fast as they could, but at dawn, when they approached some mountains, they could see the Kiowa pursuing them. They swam a great river, and when night overtook them, camped at an unexpected hollow, where other Indians were encamped not far away. Early in the morning, they set out for home again, having had no food. Soon they saw two men approaching on horseback who had bridles that were mounted in silver like those of the Potawatomi. They woman waved to them and when they came over and dismounted, she found that one of them was her uncle who was mourning for her. He gave his horse to her husband to ride, and they all went back together. When they reached the village, they first of all told the people they had been pursued by the Kiowa, and a war party went out to meet the enemy. They found that the Kiowa had discovered another of their village sites where there were at the time only old men, women and children, and were attacking it. The Potawatomi charged at the same time as the Kiowa and succeeded in killing many and chased the rest away.

This woman was the first Potawatomi woman to earn the title of Wata-sa'kawao, or Brave-Woman. Thereafter she always went to war with the men.[11]

# 4.8

# How Mko Lost His Tail

LEE WHITE, FOREST COUNTY POTAWATOMI

*Lee White retells the following traditional story, appropriate for lower-grade-level students. In the prologue, the author says that according to his tradition, the bear once had a long tail; he writes that the word* bear *in Potawatomi spelling is* mko *and is pronounced "mu-kow." His booklet gives the page numbers in Arabic numerals and in Potawatomi.*

One day Mko was walking through the forest in search of a meal. In his search he came upon a sight that looked too good to believe. In the distance there was a fox on a frozen pond, with at least a half a dozen fish lying on the area around him.

Mko told the fox he was hungry and that he wanted the fox's fish to eat. The fox, being sly and quick-witted, told Mko, "Why as big as you are these fish would only be a snack. If you wanted a real meal, I will tell you how to catch many more fish than I have." The fox told Mko to dig a hole in the ice, only large enough to pull the fish through. "Then put your tail in the hole and into the water. When a fish bites on your tail, pull up, and you will have a fish caught."

Mko went to work eagerly and rapidly. He made the hole and put his tail in the hole. After a short time Mko felt a bite on his tail and thought, "I'll wait until I get a tail full of fish then pull them up." Mko waited, and just as he expected, he began to get more bites on his tail. Finally, Mko felt he had enough fish. So with a mighty pull he jumped up about four feet, up in the air. But when he turned around to get his fish, there were none, and his tail was frozen into the pond. The fox had left already, and all that was left behind was the skeleton of the fish. And that is how Mko lost his tail.[12]

4·9

# Now I Raise My Hand

ANONYMOUS, POTAWATOMI

*In this, the fourth chant from the* Man Bundle *ritual, the celebrants petition the Great Spirit and express their gratitude.*

### NOW I RAISE MY HAND
Now I raise my hand. I raise my head,
I raise my head up to the skies.
That is all that I can do.
I will raise my hand,
I will raise my head up to the skies.
That is all that I can do.
I can call as loud as I please,
I can call up to the skies as loud as I please
But I never get an answer.
So I am calling for help from our Father.
Our Father, Help us!
Help the people, help them all.
So I am raising my hand and head to the sky.
That shows that He is above,
And he will help us. All we do is to raise our hands
And thank the Great Spirit.
We hope that He will help us all.[13]

# 4.10

## Dance with Our Mother Earth

ANONYMOUS, POTAWATOMI

*In this dance song from the* Chants of the Human or Man Clan, *the participants are instructed to dance with the Earth.*

### DANCE WITH OUR MOTHER EARTH

Now we dance, dance earnestly!
Now we dance, dance earnestly!
Dance with our Mother Earth.
She is moving and dances with us.
Hold up your hands when I blow the whistle.
Turn your faces towards the east.
Turn your hands towards the east and pass them over your face.
Turn to the west, where the light goes down.
The Great Spirit is bound to see us.
The Great Spirit is bound to bless us.
So dance, dance with our Mother Earth.
She is the one who increases our kind,
She is the one who helps us in this world.
Dance with this earth.
Dance with her earnestly in your minds.
She is the one who was put here to help us.
To provide for us,
So I am dancing, dancing earnestly to the Great Spirit
And dance and dance till I can dance no more.[14]

# One People: The Ojibwe, Ottawa, and Potawatomi

4.11

*Although many authorities say that the Ojibwe, Ottawa, and Potawatomi Nations were once one people who evolved into three distinct but closely aligned Nations, this story from the oral tradition tells it the other way around but nonetheless makes the point of the closeness of the three Nations.*

In old times three tribes, the Chippewas [Ojibwe], Potawatomi, and Ottawa were enemies and used to war a great deal against each other for a long time. One Chippewa had ten children, all boys, and he used to go with the warriors. At last all of his ten sons were killed. Also an Ottawa went with the warriors, and he had ten children, and they all got killed. A Potawatomi had ten children and all his sons were killed. So the three fathers were left without children. The Chippewa mourned so for his sons that he wept long, and, at last, determined to wander far off away from all his kin and tribe, and die by himself. The Ottawa felt the same way. He wandered off and hunted a place to die. The Potawatomi did the same.

The Chippewa, when he left his home, traveled until he was completely exhausted. As he came to a resting place, he saw a tree standing. He came from the East and was going toward the West, and the tree had a root that ran to the East. It was at least the length of the tallest tree, a hundred feet or more, and very large around. When he came to this root he laid down and rested awhile, and then looked towards the South. There he saw a root running towards the south and it was just the length of the East root. He went to the West and there was another, and to the North, there was another. The grass between these roots was as green and as light as feathers. He followed the roots around and came to the East root again, and then followed it till he came to the tree. It was a very beautiful tree, and he thought that it would be a nice place to lie down and die. As he stood at the tree, he looked at the roots and saw that from the tree, the four roots ran directly to the four directions.

As he stood there, he looked up at the top of the tree, and he saw there were four great branches, going one to the East, one to the West, one to the South, and one to the North. On the branches were beautiful leaves, and there were only these four branches, and they extended out as far as the roots. As he stood examining the tree, he saw that a great root ran straight down into the earth. While he looked up into the air he saw that the tree sent up a great branch from the center, and there were no leaves on it till the very top, and then there were only a few. All around the tree he could see the blue sky, and it was perfectly still with no wind.

The Chippewa man walked around and felt happy, forgetting all his troubles and sorrow, and no longer remembered the past. He sat down and saw how lovely this place was and thought how, in all his many travels, he had never seen so beautiful a place. While he sat there, he heard a noise, like the cry of a human being. He looked around, but could see no one although he still heard the cry. At last he saw a person coming and this man was weeping and mourning as he came, in the same way as the Chippewa had approached the country. Then he saw the newcomer was an old man, as old as he was, and he approached from the South and came to the South root. As he came to this spot, he saw how blue and lovely the grass was, and he stopped mourning and looked around at the root and grass.

The first man was sitting at the base of the tree and watched the second man. As he watched, the man approached wiping his eyes and looking happier. As he got to the tree he noticed the center root. Then he looked up and saw the branch extending to the sky, as the first man had done. The second man then noticed the first man, and the first asked why he was mourning.

The second person was the Ottawa. The Ottawa asked the Chippewa why he had come. The Chippewa said, "I will tell you. I had ten children and I lost them all in war. So I decided to die and I wandered till I came to this beautiful place."

The Ottawa said, "I did the same as you. I had ten children and they were all killed and I did not wish to live. I wandered off to die and came to this place."

They talked over the past, and while talking they forgot their sorrow and felt happy and in good cheer. While they talked, they heard a noise and listened, and heard a person crying. Far off they saw a man approaching, mourning and crying. It was some time before the man came into sight after they first heard the crying. It was an old man, apparently about the age of the other two, and as he walked along wearily, he mourned and cried. They watched him as he came from the West and approached the West root. There he stopped and examined the root, and noticed how lovely the place was. They saw him wipe away his tears. As he came up to the tree, the Chippewa and Ottawa asked him who he was, and why he was mourning. He answered that he was a Potawatomi and he mourned because in war he had lost his ten sons and not wishing to live longer, he had wandered off to die. He had come with a sad heart till he came to the wonderful root.

The Chippewa then told the Potawatomi that he had come in the same way, mourning, and the Ottawa said that he had come that way, too, "Now we are all together, and all childless."

The Chippewa said, "Probably it is the will of the Great Spirit that we all meet here together."

They all believed this. They began to examine the place together, looking up at the top of the tree, and they saw that the air was very still and not a leaf moved. It seemed to them that every word they spoke would enter into all the spirits and would be heard by them. It was so still.

It was near midday, and they all seemed to feel alike. Their spirits seemed to be alike, and as if the three were in mind but one. They said, "Probably the spirits have sent us here to council. There has been much fighting in our lives and perhaps they think we have been too cruel."

The Chippewa said, "I think I had better go back to my people."

The Ottawa said, "Yes, I think it has been wrong for us to fight all the time. We have suffered much by it, neglecting our children. It is best for us to go home."

The Potawatomi also said, "This is true. I think it is wrong to kill our women and children in this way. I think it best for us to go home, and stop war and live in peace."

They lit their pipes and smoked, and passed them to one another. How long they talked they did not know. Perhaps they slept there. As they smoked and talked and planned, the Chippewa, having been the first to get to the tree, thought he had a right to speak first. "Now I will be the eldest brother. And the Ottawa will be our second brother. And you, Potawatomi, will be the youngest brother, and we will unite as one."

After the Chippewa was through talking, they consented to his plan. The Chippewa said, "Now my brothers, I will make a pipe and then I will make a stem. I will put tobacco in the pipe and then I will make an offering of food, and when I get home I will present it to my people. I will say to them that I had ten children and they were killed in war; but I will wash that away, and I will take this pipe stem and paint it blue, as the sky is blue, and this pipe will be used when we make peace with other nations."

The Ottawa said, "It is good. I will also do the same. I will remind my people of my songs, and I will have them quit war."

The Potawatomi said, "I am in favor of this. I will make a pipe of peace and furnish provisions. I will call a council of our people and tell them of our resolution, and explain the folly of causing our old people and women and children to suffer and be killed."

The Chippewa said again, "It is good. Our spirits have brought us together at this point, and influenced us to all agree and think the same."

The Ottawa and Potawatomi left it to the Chippewa and said, "As you will, we will do. We will follow your rules and yours laws."

The Chippewa said, "It is well." This first thing I will do is to make a pipe, get provisions, tobacco and call my people together. And say to them, "This is the pipe of peace. We will smoke it and give up fighting and live in quiet and happiness."

The three old men made rules, and represented them as a path that their people must follow. They must keep it clean and sweep it with the turkey feather, and they must all go on this path in peace and all be as true brothers and visit each other. They must live always in peace and friendship after meeting together at this lone tree. From this time they kept their rules and the tree tribes lived in peace and intermarried and came to be almost as one people.[15]

# The Origin of Tobacco

### ORAL TRADITION, POTAWATOMI

*The use of tobacco for sacred and solemn purposes has an ancient history that intersects with other Nations' histories. This story, from the oral tradition, points to Potawatomi history on the Atlantic seaboard.*

Long ago, when the Potawatomi still lived on the ocean in the east and close to their grandfathers the Delaware [Lenni-Lenape], a man had a dream that something extraordinary would grow in his garden that was in a clearing he had made in a nearby river bottom. In his vision, he was warned never to let any women approach his farm, so he lopped down trees that fell partly over from the upright stumps, thus making a fence. The people of his village grew to suspect that something was going on, but when they peeped, they could see nothing. So it came about that his uncles and nephews who had the right to jest with him, teased him about his garden, and asked him how he expected a crop of anything when he had planted no seed. They teased him so much that he became angry, and when everyone else went on the summer hunt in July, the old man stayed at home to tend to his field.

At length, a broad-leafed herb began to spring up, unseeded. The old man did not know what to call the plant, but he hoed it well, and it prospered and grew thick. At last a neighboring Delaware came to visit him, and he showed his friend what he had and explained that it had come as the result of a vision sent by the Great Spirit.

"Why," said the Delaware, "my people have this sacred herb also. One of us also dreamed of it, the same as you did."

"How do you use it?' asked the Potawatomi.

"My grandson, if this was a gift to you from the Great Spirit, you ought to know. Certainly it will be made manifest to you. Still, if that doesn't happen by Fall, come to me and I will show you in what way we use ours."

The old man was more puzzled than ever, so he decided to fast and see if the Great Spirit would tell him what he wanted to know. When he had gone without food for two days, the Great Spirit appeared to him and told him to gather the leaves and dry them for sacrifices when at prayer, to burn in the fire as incense, and to smoke in his pipe. He was told that at every feast and sacrifice, tobacco was to be the principle thing.

When he had had this revelation, the old man went to a place near the sea where there was a hill of soft black stone. He broke off a long rectangular piece and blocked out a pipe. It was very hard to make and, especially to bore, so at last he went to his Delaware friend for help. This man had a long copper tool like an awl, which worked very well. Then they made a pipe stem out of pithy wood. By this time the Delaware saw that his Potawatomi friend had learned the use of tobacco, so he took out his own pipe, filled it from his pouch, lighted it and passed it to his Potawatomi friend. The latter laughed and said, "I intend to smoke, but I certainly did not understand before."

The two men made the pipe stem out of dry ash wood, and the Potawatomi had his wife sew a buckskin wrapper around the stem and make him a tobacco pouch of the same material. Then he harvested and dried his tobacco.

When the hunters returned from the hunt, the people all went over to see what had grown in the mysterious garden. They were surprised at the peculiar appearance and the strong taste of the broad leaves. No one knew what to call it. The old man soon saw that the people had been taking the leaves from the garden, and he asked the chief to keep them out. So the chief walked all around the village himself, announcing that the people must keep out of that garden and respect its owner on account of his age. "Wait until he is ready to tell us about it," he counseled.

One day the old man gave a feast and seated the chief on his left. He said, "I am glad that you all have been quiet about my garden, and have listened to my wishes. You all know that it was impossible for me to make this herb, or to start it growing spontaneously. You are aware that I did not find it anywhere, and none of us have ever seen it growing before. We are all equal, every man here. I know no more than any of you. We have eyes in our heads, but we may never be sure of what we see. Yet, the way anyone sees anything, that is the way that he thinks about it. Now we have rules in our religion that we all follow. There are those among you who never have fasted, but revelations were made you in dreams, and your fortunes came to you for nothing you believe and follow what you have learned in your vision.

Now here I am. I dreamed that something was going to grow where I had burned and cleared the earth for a garden, so I fenced it off as though a sacred bundle hung there. That was to keep the women away from it. I knew I was right, and that is why I stayed away from the hunt. I was anxious to protect what I had, and to see what it might be. Then came one of our Grandfathers (a Delaware), from his home on the salt water, and I took him down to see, as he was older than I. He knew at once what it was, and he told me to find out, as that was the best way. So I fasted, although I didn't build a fasting lodge. I am old, my wife has passed the change of life, she is no girl to be sick, so I fasted there with her in my own wigwam, while she slept outside on a scaffold. Everyone understood, and no one entered my lodge. Then the Great

Spirit Himself appeared and told me how to use this herb in sacrifices, and to place it in the fire and smoke it, and whatever I asked for, he would give me.

"Now, he told me that the name of this herb is to be sa'mau, or nin sa'mau, and I give this feast in honor of the new blessing that is to be with us now for all our lives."[16]

# 4.13

## The Adventure of a Poor Man

ORAL TRADITION, POTAWATOMI

*Although the Potawatomi had encountered French Jesuits at their mission at Chequamegon in northern Wisconsin in 1668 and "accommodated this new religion," it wasn't until the 1800s that numbers of Potawatomi became Christians or incorporated Christian beliefs. Others who followed the traditions of the Midéwiwin or the Drum society settled at the McCord Indian Village in Oneida County, Wisconsin.[17] Changing times did not change traditional attitudes toward the spirit world. Respect for and honoring of the dead figure prominently in this story from the oral tradition.*

Once a poor orphan, who was not well brought up and who was respected by no one, and never invited to feasts or ceremonies, managed to get married, and went hunting on foot or with his canoe. He found but little game, but once when he was out in the forest for an all night stay, he killed a deer. He built a rude shelter, hung the venison around the fire, and sat down to rest with his dog beside him. He smoked and dozed, and after a while he opened his eyes and saw a person standing there.

On his second glace, the person vanished, and what made it seem all the stranger, his dog took no notice. The man turned his meat and, looking up again, saw two men there. They seemed pitiful and unable to speak. "Hau," said the man, "My friends, you frightened me. For all I know one of you may be the Woods-elf, and the other the brother of Wisaka. I am poor. No one brought me up to know what to do under these circumstances. I should like to know who you are, but I do not know how to ask." The two smiled and nodded to him in a friendly manner, so he went on: "Well, I shall feed you, and do what I can for your comfort." They nodded again. "Are you ghosts?" the hunter inquired. Again they smiled and bowed, so he began to broil meat on the coals, as one does for the souls of the dead.

Now it happened that this man was camped right in the middle of an ancient and forgotten cemetery and, guessing something of the sort, he offered prayers to the dead in his own behalf, and for his wife and child. He offered to make a feast for the dead, and always to mention the names of the two visitors, or at least to speak of them.

The very next day he killed four bucks right in the trail and luck went with him wherever he traveled. When he got home, he told his wife what had happened, and how he had been frightened when these two naked, soundless men stood there. He told her to help him prepare a feast for them, although he did not know their names, for he hoped that these ghosts would help them to become accepted by society. He made a scaffold and invited one of the honorable men of the tribe, and told him of the strange adventure that had befallen him. He explained that he did not know how to go about giving a feast of the dead, and he turned it over to the elder.

The old man said that the poor man had done the right thing, and that the appearance of these ghosts was a good omen. So the feast was held.

A long time passed, and the poor man became a very great hunter, but he never forgot to sacrifice holy tobacco to the two spirits. He could even find and kill bears in wintertime, something that no one else even thought of doing, but he could locate their dens at will. At length he even became one of the leaders of the tribe, and held the office of the man who was supposed to apprise the people of the arrival of visitors. He was the first to give presents to visiting strangers, and his name was Nwakto, or Keeps-on-even-with-everything.[18]

# 4.14

## They Will Sometime Find Their Mistakes

SHAWEQUET, POTAWATOMI

*After the forced removals to Indian Territory (now Oklahoma), the Potawatomi worked to preserve and promote their culture. An old warrior, who was called Shawequet as a young man, talked with Jeremiah Curtin in the summer of 1883.*

This is told from the good feeling in my heart. This is the way I understand the Great Spirit and the spirit of all the animals. It is well for me to relate these things, that they may be given to the rising generation. You must not think that because there were no books and writings that my parents and grandparents gave me nothing. They taught me many things and I have always kept them in my heart, and I feel that I am doing right in giving them to you. I think it is the will of all the spirits, and it is easy for me to relate them to you for they came to me easily. And it is not hard for me to relate them.

I never gambled in my life. It is a very mean thing and it would cause me much trouble and my mind would have become troubled. I never have had bad feelings now against my enemies, though I've always had some enemies and I don't wish evil on them. I have been examining the world since I was middle aged and I found it was wrong to go with the wicked. And I decided as I realized that but a short life remained to me, and it was best to do right.

I had been tempted to steal but I have never yielded to the desire. This is why I told you the other day that our lives are running low and we have to look to the Great Spirits to give us life. You may think that we red men are weak. We are, of course, ignorant. Therefore, it is the will of God that gives you wisdom and intelligence. We know that there are good and bad spirits, and that if we do good, it is well, and if we do wrong the bad spirits will shorten our lives. . . . It has been said by some white men that the red men came from brutes, that they knew nothing. They must not think so. It is wrong. And they will sometime find their mistakes.[19]

# 4.15

## Queen of the Woods

SIMON POKAGON, POTAWATOMI

*When most Potawatomi were forced westward, Chief Simon Pokagon, of the St. Joseph's Band of Potawatomi in Michigan, resisted removal. He and his band were staunch Catholics, and he abhorred alcohol. He is known for a fictionalized semi-autobiographical novel called* O-Gi-Maw-Kwe Mit-I-Gwa-Ki, *or* Queen of the Woods. *One critic asserts that this novel was ghost written and "bore no relationship to traditional Potawatomi literary style, form, or content."[20] However, a central theme of the novel is its vehement denunciation of alcohol, a theme expounded upon in a diatribe after the novel proper in the odd compendium that C. H. Engle published posthumously in 1899 as* Queen of the Woods. *This novel romanticizes and stereotypes the non-alcohol-drinking Indian as noble when in a natural state. The narrator, Simon, falls in love with Lonidaw, who speaks and understands the languages of birds and animals. Her companion is a pet albino deer. This story provided the inspiration for the Disney cartoon* Bambi.

Near the summer's close, while living there, a little maiden, every now and then, appeared across the stream, with waist of red and skirt of brown, with raven tresses floating in the breeze, following up, but never down the stream. She was always singing, as she gaily tripped along, in mimicry of the music of the birds. Sometimes in her songs, in fancy I could hear and see close by, in bush or brake, the bobolink tuning his voice to cheer his nesting mate. At other times I would look up, *almost* convinced that I could see him dancing in the air, on wing, rising and falling with time and tune, then at the close alighting on the bush from whence he rose. Then, changing time and tune, in fancy I could see some robin perched on topmost bough of tree above, pouring forth his song in tones of richest melody. At times, a snow-white deer about the maiden played in circles, like the lamb; and again, after she had passed along and out of sight, like a dog hunting for his master, he would follow on her track. At first I felt impressed that she must be from the happy hunting ground beyond; and how it was that she could mimic woodland birds, and throw her voice across the stream, and so deceive my ears, was to be a hidden mystery.

While I was fishing along the river's bank for several days, each morning she so appeared while I was all alone, awakening such sacred feelings in my soul that I held it as a vital secret from my mother.

One morning just before the rising sun, I stood upon the river's shore watching the maid in admiration of her warbling song, when a gentle footstep reached my ears, and looking up, there stood "nin-gaw" (my mother) close beside me. Quietly she said, "Ne-gwis-esh (my son), why are you here at such an early hour as this?" Hiding the real feelings of my heart, I pointed out to her the maid beyond the stream, and said, "To hear her sing, and see that deer of white around her play." She replied, "Ne-gwis-esh (my son), ne-wob-quay-zans (I see the girl), but hear no song except the songs of pe-nay-shen-wog (birds)." I then said, "O-gaw-shi-maw (mother), she has the time, tune, and song of all the feathered warblers of the woods. Come, sit down upon this log, and listen." She complied with my request, and as she harkened most intently, gazing in all directions, finally said, "Gwai-ak (surely) it must be nin-bi-ba-giwin (her voice) I hear, and in nin-ga-mon (her song) she brings before me me-no-ma (the bobolink), ope-tchi (the robin), and kik-biko-meshi (lark); and what seems so strange and droll to me is, it really sounds as if they were on this side of se-bin (the river) near by us; but when I look for them, none can be seen. It must be she is from Man-i-to Au-ke (the spirit world) beyond." During the remainder of that day, my anxiety greatly increased to learn all I could about the woodland maid and the deer of white, and so I concluded to cross the stream, as soon as I could construct a boat for that purpose.

On the following day I went to work with a will, made a small bark canoe large enough to carry one, and launched it at close of day in a bay close by. The next morning before the break of day, I dressed myself with moccasins and pants, all of deerskin made, wearing a birch-bark cap with quills and feathers trimmed. Thus attired in native style, with bow and arrows armed, I went forth, and in my new-made "tchi-man," crossed the river deep and broad. As I neared the other shore, all was still. No breeze disturbed the glass-like surface of the stream; every leaf was motionless, and quiet as the morning air. No artist hand could paint the beauty of the inverted shore as in the water it appeared, fringed with trees, brush, grass, flags, and flowers, with sky below deep down as heaven is high. Carefully I rowed my frail bark under some over hanging willow brush that fringed the shore, and there, almost concealed, with deep anxiety watched and listened, that I might catch with eye or ear the little maiden's first approach. Nor waited long, for soon I heard the bobolink, dancing on the wing, rising and falling with its tune of flute-like notes that seldom fail to reach the lover's heart. It ceased, and then the robin poured forth its thrilling roundelay of love just above me. Hark! I faintly hear some muffled footsteps near, and peering through the leaves of green I see a pair of moccasins trimmed with colored quills, moving with gentle tread toward me; and now a skirt of brown, and next a waist of red, half covered with tresses long and black that almost touch the ground. Another step, and now before me stands the maid, so close that I can see her bosom swell at every breath. A single rose with opening buds along adorns her hair. Perfect she appears in make and mold of body and of limb. Her ruby lips stand just apart, exposing teeth of perfect make and white as snow.

Her dark eyes full of soul beam forth surprise. She sees the newly made birch canoe—the boatman sees. Softly, on tiptoe, she turns about, moving noiselessly away. With struggling heart pressed in my throat, I step from out the boat upon the open shore, saying, "Boo-zhoo?" (How do you do?). Then I said, with trembling voice, "Nic-con" (My friend). With modest smile, almost suppressed from her dark eyes, she greeted back, "Nic-con," with voice so winning and so bland my heartstrings vibrated with her tones. I now felt more at ease, for well I knew that she was flesh and blood, and understood the language of my tribe. Quietly and slowly I stepped toward her, when backward she withdrew, saying by look and deed, "Please, sir, no nearer come." I stayed my steps, and she again stood still, but watched me with suspicious eyes. Backward a space I stepped, as if to take the boat, and asked "Kwaw-notch qua-zayns au-nish?" (Fair girl, who art thou?) Reluctantly and low, with downcast eyes, she said, "Lo-ni-daw." I then asked, "Au-ne-zhaw-kin?" (Where dost thou live?) "A-wass we-di" (Beyond the hill) she replied, pointing to an abrupt headland toward the rising sun. I then asked, "We-ni-aw ne-os-see-maw?" (Who is thy father?) Soberly she replied, "Ne-bou" (He is dead). "Do-dan ki bi-ma-dis ni-ji-ke?" (Dost thou live alone?) I asked. Shaking her head, she said, "Kaw" (No)[.] "Nin-bi-ma-dis-nind o-gaw-she-maw" (I live with my mother). I then asked, "Nin-de- a-i-an ni-mot-og kema a-we-mog?" (Have you any brothers or sisters?) Shaking her head, she replied, "Kaw." She then started off, walking faster and faster until she gained a run, passing out of sight among the trees.

All now seemed like a dream, and as I reflected upon her presence, I well knew in my "o-daw" (heart) I never, never saw before so fair, so fair a one. Just as I stepped into "tchi-man" to cross se-bin, I glimpsed the snow-white deer coming up the stream, bounding toward me through bush and brake, through goldenrod, flags, and rushes tall. I now could hear and feel each pulsation of my heart. Nor will you think it strange when I tell you that the white deer, or albino deer, as white men call them, are very rare, and when seen in the forests among those of the natural color (red), the contrast is indeed striking. They have been called by our people, for time out of mind, "Mon-i-to-esh waw-be-waw-mawsh-kay-she" (The sacred deer of white); and we are taught from early childhood that if we should shoot at one, we would be sick, and if we should kill one, we would surely soon die.

On came the sacred deer, to the very place where the maid had stood. Here he stopped; and facing about, stood still, with head erect. His antlers were triple-pronged and shaped alike, perfect in make, and white as snow. He stood so near that I could see his flashing eyes, see him wink, and hear him breathe. About his neck a wreath of flowers of red, white, and blue he wore.

With nose upturned, and nostrils expanded wide, he snuffed to find what scented the morning air; then, with a piercing, whistling snort, he wheeled about, going like the wind on the maiden's track.

Returning home, I told "nin-gaw" (my mother). I opened wide the door of "non-o-daw" (my heart), telling her she "kwaw-notch au-quay" (was the prettiest maid) I ever saw, and that she had awakened a strange admiration in my soul. She listened with marked attention, in wonder and surprise, asking me many strange questions, and most solemnly advising me to make no further attempts to solve the mystery of the mocking "ik-we" (maid) and the sacred deer of white, as she greatly feared some evil might befall me thereby.

However on the following day again I crossed the river, climbing the headland beyond which the maiden said her mother lived. Coming to an ancient trail, that plainly showed it had been lately used, I [lay] down near it, among the "anag-an-ask" (tall ferns), and there concealed myself, hoping the maid and deer might pass that way. Soon her voice I heard; but it sounded now more like the soft and tender notes of the mourning dove in the distance, and again more like the jay in imitation of the hawk, and again like the squirrel's sneezing, scolding bark, awakening the solitude with her varied chants and broken songs. Soon she came in sight, with hasty steps passing along the winding trail. But now, to my surprise, she wore a skirt of green and waist of white, holding in her hands some stalks of bloody cardinal in full bloom, which cast a halo of livelier green upon the foliage around. As she approached,—and I was intently gazing upon her slender form and steps so light and free,—she paused, and standing still near by me, backward looked along the trail. I said to my throbbing heart, "Be still!" then held my breath to drink her native beauty in. I faintly heard a rustling sound, as when the wind sweeps through the tall prairie grass, and soon saw, coming along the trail, the sacred deer of white, with bundles of rushes held between his spiky horns. Both passed by, leaving me unobserved.

Squirrels red, black, and gray came following on the trail, as though they sought the woodland maid to see. Meditating there awhile, I arose, recalling to mind the advice of "nin-gaw" (my mother) not to pursue the mocking "ik-we" (maid). With grave misgivings in "nin-o-daw" (my heart), I followed down the trail until I reached a valley deep below, where underbrush almost concealed a wigwam tent of colored rushes made, that glistened like the rainbow among the trees; while all about hung mats of different shades, shapes, and sizes, adorned with various colored quills and feathers.

Nearing, on tiptoe, the secluded spot, all was silent as the grave. No sound I heard, except the babbling brook close by. But all at once there burst upon my listening ears a whistling snort that made the welkin ring. I shuddered like a child that hears a panther scream. Quickly I turned around, and there before me stood the sacred deer of white, stamping his feet to frighten me away. Cautiously I stepped up to the rainbow-colored tent, and there listening awhile, heard someone in a whisper say "Pe-naw! Pe-naw!" (Hark! Hark!) No other sound I heard within. Cautiously as the mousing cat I walked around the tent, but found no place to enter in. At length with trembling hand I pulled a cord that I thought might be the latchstring of some matting door, when lo! To my surprise, all sides of the wigwam rolled up in a scroll! And there, in open, broad daylight, before me sat the maiden and her mother!

They laid aside their braid, and gazed at me as though I had no business there; and so I felt, but as pleasantly as possible for an intruder in such a fix, "Boo-zhoo-nic-con-og?" (How do you do, my friends?) Both timidly responded, with speech suppressed, "Boo-zhoo-nic-con." Rising to her feet, the mother said, "Pin-di-gayn" (Come in). I stepped inside; so did the deer, and stood beside the maid, with his nose upon her shoulder laid. The mother picked up a fancy mat, placing it upon the ground beside me. I said, "Ne-gwetch" (Thanks), and reclined upon it. She then reached above her head and pulled a cord; the matting scrolls unrolled, and down they came, enclosing us on every side. At first it seemed as if the shades of night were coming on; but soon, more like the dawn of day, the light came on apace, till all within the room was plainly to be seen.

The mother had a queenly step and royal mien, but the many furrows in her cheeks most plainly told they had been deepened by many a flood of tears. At length the maid, with modest smile almost concealed, spoke out, and said, "Ne-ge-wob ke-waw-waw pe-tchi-maw-go se-be" (I saw you at the river yesterday). I replied, "Ka-ge-te" (Truly so). The mother, with a curious smile, almost suppressed, now asked, "We-I-ke?" (Who art thou?) "Pokagon," I replied. She then asked, "Waw kaw-in Ogi-maw Pokagon Pottawattamie?" (What! Not old chief Pokagon of the Pottawattamie?) I replied, "Kaw o-daw-en-guis" (No, I am his son). "Au-nish! (What!) Not young Simaw?" I answered, "Ne-ween" (I am he). Then [I] said, "Did you know Ne-os-see-maw" (my father)? Anxiously she inquired "Au-nish! Po-ka-gon au-ke-wa-she Leopold smo-ke-mon?" (What! Not the son of Chief Pokagon—Leopold, as white men called him?) "Ae" (Yes), I said. She then replied, "Ke-au-yaw kitch-ti-wa-wis au-nish-naw-be—o-gi-maw" (He was a noble man and chief). "Win-sa-gi-i-we—man-i-tan ba-ta-do-dan" (He loved right and hated wrong). "Nin wid-i-ge-ma-gan (my husband) was chief under him many, many years; they went together to see the great white chief at Washington." She then advanced a step toward me, saying "Nind an-am-i-et-a-waw ki sa-nagise kwi-wi-sens (Bless you, my dear boy), Simaw! I have swung you in tik-in-a-gan (hammock), and carried you on nin-pik-wan (my back) time and time again. Bless you! I lived with your o-gaw-she-maw when you were born. And you are my boy, Simaw. The Great Spirit bless you. Does ke-o-gaw-she-maw (your mother) yet live?" "Ae, nan-ge-kaw" (Yes, certainly), I replied. "Au-ne-zhaw?" (Where?) she asked. "Just across the great Sebe," I replied.

The maiden now drew near, followed by the deer, and stood beside her mother. She gave me the most winsome smile I ever saw. The mother saw it, too, and said, "Ma-bamki-da-nis Lo-ni-daw" (This is my daughter Lonidaw).

Again she smiled, more winsome than before. A strange feeling came over me. I felt a sacred thrill of joy, unknown before, rush through my frame, reaching my very soul, to which my heart responding said, "The maid is surely mine."

The mother again asked: "And do you really mean to say your o-gaw-she-maw still lives?" I replied. "Ka-ge-ta maw-got!" (It is surely so!) "Au-nish! (What!) Ka-law-na Po-ka-gon?" "Ae; that's my mother's name by Christian rule and law." Statue-like she stood, finally saying, "Neen-ke-no-bo shong-we ne-go-twos-we! (I was sure she died fifteen years ago!) And yet she lives? Au-to-yaw? (Is it possible?) I was left nin-gi-wis (an orphan) at my birth; your mother's mother brought me up. Ae, your o-gaw-she-maw and I nursed and played with your no-ko-miss (grandmother) together. We slept [in] oni-ka-mag (her arms) together; were carried on odi-niman-gan (her shoulders) to-gether; swung from wa-nak'-ong (tree top) in her hammock together; ba-pine-nim gaie maw-win mam-awi (rejoiced and wept together). And you do say she is still alive, and ni-be-win (camping) just across the Sebe?" "Ae," I said, "but we may leave for home wa-bang (tomorrow)." She then exclaimed, "Ne-dge-bawn! (my soul!) ne-gaw-wob-yaw ne-gon-ke-sus (I must see her be-fore the sun goes down). Ke-na-wind-ke-win ne-go-ting (We will go home with you at once)." "All right," I said, "but ne-tche-maw-nes-on (my boat is small), and will float pa-zhig (but one)."

"Well, then," said she, with a smile, "Lo-da-haw-yea-ne (Loda and I) will bim-a-daga a-jaw-aona (swim across)." She then said, "Lo-da, get ne-waw-bo-yon (my blanket) and a ball of twine." The blanket was brought, and ten-derly thrown over her head and shoulders. I started homeward, followed by the mother and the maid, and the deer brought up the rear.[21]

# Literature of the
# Oneida Nation

# The Thanksgiving Address

## THE ONEIDA NATION

*According to Dr. Carol Cornelius, director of the Oneida Nation of Wisconsin Cultural Heritage Department, the Thanksgiving Address of the Haudenosaunee (Iroquois or Six Nations League) "has its origins in Haudenosaunee Creation. It is reinforced in the Great Law of Peace, which provided a system of government, and in the Code of Handsome Lake, which outlines a way to continue the old ways and adapt to the realities of the year 1800. The Thanksgiving Address was spoken at the opening and closing of all ceremonial and governmental gatherings, and this practice continues to the present day."[1]*

### THE THANKSGIVING ADDRESS

The People were very strong in their beliefs and their ways.
Let's put our minds together. So be it in our minds.

Our mother earth takes care of all lives.
Let's put our minds together. So be it in our minds.

Grass carpets the earth.
Let's put our minds together. So be it in our minds.

Strawberries are good medicine that help all the people.
Let's put our minds together. So be it in our minds.

Tobacco is the head of all the medicines here on earth.
Let's put our minds together. So be it in our minds.

Three sisters are the leaders of all foods here on earth.
Let's put our minds together. So be it in our minds.

Medicines here on earth were left for all Oneidas and
    other Indian benefits.
Let's put our minds together. So be it in our minds.

Deer here were left, they are the head of all animals and
    also the reason they stay to help the Oneidas.
Let's put our minds together. So be it in our minds.

Maple they gave us for syrup and medicine in the spring
    to give thanks to all the trees.
Let's put our minds together. So be it in our minds.

Water they give us strength also a good life. Water gives
    us strength to live.
Let's put our minds together. So be it in our minds.

The winds bring the changing of the seasons.
Let's put our minds together. So be it in our minds.

Birds, their songs they use to lift our minds when we are sad.
Let's put our minds together. So be it in our minds.

The thunders wake us up, here on earth, it brings the warm
    winds for all things to grow.
Let's put our minds together. So be it in our minds.

Our grandmother, the moon has charge of women's needs.
Let's put our minds together. So be it in our minds.

Our eldest brother the sun helps us for all things to grow
    whatever our foods for our survival. He gives us light to
    be able then to work every day.
Let's put our minds together. So be it in our minds.

Stars give us light so that we don't get lost, also tell us when it's
    that time to give thanks to the winter.
Let's put our minds together. So be it in our minds.

Four messengers they give us guidance, how that all became of
    one same mind.
Let's put our minds together. So be it in our minds.

The one who made all things that we are thankful for here on earth.
Let's put our minds together. So be it in our minds.[2]

# 5.2

# The Oneida Creation Story

DEMUS ELM AND HARVEY ANTONE,
ONEIDA

---

*The Oneida Creation Story by Demus Elm was recorded on tape by Dr. Floyd Louns-bury. Some portions of this tape were lost before they were transcribed, but twenty-five years after the original recording, Dr. Lounsbury and Dr. Bryan Gick met a living relative of Mr. Elm, Harvey Antone, who remembered hearing the creation story from Mr. Elm. Antone agreed to record the missing sections and translate the original tapes. As this story appears in the University of Nebraska Press edition, the English translation is given side-by-side with the Oneida language.*

When I was a child, I used to hear the old people tell stories about how it came to pass that people began to live on the Earth.

Once there lived people in a certain place, among whom there was a very rich man. They had everything that they needed there; nothing was ever lacking; they were so happy that there was no sickness, and no one ever died.

It is said that this rich man had a lot of servants who always kept him entertained. They were playing lacrosse. The man and his wife were sitting and watching them play ball. He sent her off, saying "Would you go and get some water, I want a drink."

So she went to the spring. She went to get water, and one of the ball players came along. He was very sweaty, that ball player, and he said, "Couldn't I have a drink?" So then she gave him something to drink, enough that he drank his fill. Then she refilled the water and took it back to where her husband was sitting.

He said, "Why did you put another before me? I sent you to get water."

It is said that she replied, "He was so sweaty, I took pity on him. That is why I gave the water to him, because he was playing ball."

He said, "I told you before that you should never let another man come between us. But now, you have broken your promise to me. Now we will have to fulfill what we agreed upon. For if ever our minds become separated, then we will truly go our different ways."

193

*Sky Woman.* In the Oneida Creation Story, a woman is thrown from the heavens and descends to Earth, where she is met by birds who break her fall. She then rests upon the back of Turtle. *Sky Woman* painting by Ernest Smith, 1936, reproduced by permission from the collections of the Rochester Museum & Science Center, Rochester, NY.

Then, it is said, he called to some strong men, saying, "that tree over there, the one with the long root—the white pine—uproot it. Throw her down there, because now we are divided."

At that, they uprooted the tree. He sat her down on the hole and pushed her. Then she reached out to her right side. There she grabbed onto a strawberry plant, and carried it along with her, and with the other hand, it is said, a tobacco plant, and so these are the things she brought with her when she fell into the hole.

Down and down she falls, and as she is enveloped by darkness, she keeps falling down and down. Then, at last, a light suddenly appears in the direction towards which she is falling. There were already creatures living down there, different kinds of creatures living in the water. There was no earth, just muddy water.

Then one of these, a muskrat they say, was looking up. He said, "What's that way up there, flying this way?"

So then they were all looking up there, the different creatures were all looking up, and finally they saw something flying down, and they kept looking and looking up there. There were also birds living there, and they went flying up. The one in front said, "It's a human coming down, it's a human coming down!"

It was then that one of them called out, one of the animals that live in the water. (I am not able to say what kind of animal it was, but that's what happened.) This one called out, saying, "Come close together, all of you who live in the water." Then, when they had come together, he asked who might be able to hold up this woman who is falling through the air from above. Some animal that was floating on the water said, "I can hold her up." He replied, "No, you're not able to do it." Then another one of them, another kind of animal that was also floating there said, "I can support the human." But he said, "No, you're not able to do it."

Then it was the turtle that was floating there, who had a big enough back, who said, "I would be able to support the woman; I would be able to do it, she could stand on my back."

So he said, "Yes, indeed, you will be able to do it." The next thing he said was, "Who is there that would be able to go and meet the woman as she comes down from above?"

Then, it is said, one of the loons that sat there said, "I would be able to go and meet the woman; as we fly together, she could stand on us, and we will slowly come back down."

He said, "Yes, truly you will be able to do it."

"Now then, the woman that is coming down from above, let's go and meet her." Thereupon, they flew up, going around and around in circles, screaming as they flew. They went up so high that their voices could no longer be heard, and nothing could be seen of them. Thus it was for some time that their voices did not become audible again, and then once more their voices could be heard. Then they were coming back down. Thus they came, with the woman standing on them as they flew.

Very slowly, they left her on the back of the turtle that was floating there. There she stood; the back of the turtle was only big enough for her to stand there with her feet together. So it was, for some time there was daylight, and then darkness fell upon her. By that time, the Earth was of such a size that it was possible for her to lie down on it. Her feet were at one end of the Earth, and in the opposite direction, her head was resting on the other end of the Earth. That is how big the Earth was, it was possible for her to lie down on it. So it was until dawn came upon her, and then the Earth was of such a size that it was possible for her to walk around. And so it was until darkness fell again, and then at this time, the Earth was large. Now this time it was comfortable in the place where she lay down to sleep. Then another dawn came upon her, at which time the Earth was still bigger. That is the way the Earth kept getting bigger and bigger. And now she was no longer able to walk over all of it, so big was the Earth.[3]

# 5·3

# People of the Standing Stone

THELMA CORNELIUS MCLESTER, ONEIDA

*Oneida is one of the Nations of the Haudenosaunee or Iroquois Confederacy, which refers to a still-vital alliance that dates back to long before European invasion of the American continent.*

The Oneida people (Onyote'a:ka, "People of the Standing Stone") are members of the Six Nations of the Iroquois or Ho'de'sho'ne (People of the Long House). Even before European invasion of the North American continent, these people were living in distinct territories in the northeastern section of the country. The Oneida territory was in what is now New York State, with the Mohawk Nation east of this land and the Onondaga, Cayuga, and Seneca territories to the west.

Today the Oneidas of Wisconsin have the largest population of the three remaining Oneida communities. The tribal enrollment in Wisconsin is 12,623, compared with approximately 1,100 in Oneida, New York, and 4,000 in Southwold, Ontario, Canada. In Wisconsin, about 4,500 enrolled members reside on the Oneida Reservation, with the remaining members living throughout the United States.

The Revolutionary War brought about significant changes in the lives of the Oneidas. . . . They not only fought alongside the colonists, but also served as lead guides and scouts for the American cause. In the winter of 1777, the Oneidas and Tuscaroras [sixth member of the Iroquois Confederacy] provided bags of corn for George Washington's starving army at Valley Forge even though they themselves did not have enough food. . . .

In 1784 the Treaty of Fort Stanwix was to have guaranteed the Oneidas and Tuscaroras territorial lands in New York in exchange for their help in the Revolutionary War. This guarantee came from the Continental Congress, but the state of New York later ignored this treaty and worked actively to remove all Indians from its borders. As a consequence, the Oneidas steadily lost their lands in New York. The loss of lands was one of the most significant factors that led to the Oneida people moving out of New York. Some Oneidas remained, but most moved to Wisconsin Territory or migrated north to Ontario, Canada, where the Mohawks and other Iroquois groups had located after the war.[4]

# 5·4

# Jigonsaseh, Mother of Nations

JOHN C. MOHAWK, SENECA

*By the late 1700s, New York State had taken over five million acres of Oneida land. Between 1820 and 1830 the Oneida, along with other Nations, migrated from New York to Wisconsin.*

*For centuries, the Oneida had been one Nation in the League of Five Nations: the Cayuga, Mohawk, Oneida, Onondaga, and Seneca. But when Carolina colonists sold four hundred Tuscarora into slavery, the survivors petitioned to join the League of Nations in 1714. In 1723, the Haudenosaunee accepted them as relatives, linked by the Great Law of Peace (Kianerakowa or Gayaneshakgowa), and this confederacy became the League of Six Nations, more commonly known as the Iroquois Confederacy. Jigonsaseh, "the Peace Queen, . . . was the first woman to accept the Great Law of Peace."[5] In the following essay, John C. Mohawk, of the State University of New York at Buffalo, describes this history. Professor Mohawk is a Seneca, one of the Nations of the Haudenosaunee.*

The oral tradition recounting the founding of the league is called the Gayaneshakgowa, or Great Law of Peace. This tradition identifies a Huron individual, Deganawida [also spelled Tekanawita] (known in Iroquois tradition as the Peacemaker), as a prophet who was inspired with a plan to end human beings' abuses of other human beings. This mission began at a time of great confusion and blood feuding, when assassinations and murder were common and when war parties were often dispatched to distant lands to avenge an act of violence, which then escalated into warfare between clans, villages, and whole nations.

The Peacemaker enlisted the assistance of a former Onondaga chief, Hiawatha, to carry his message to the nations. The message they brought was complex, and the tradition that relates it requires over a week in the telling. The Peacemaker proposed that the leaders of the communities organize for the purpose of creating a forum at which "thinking will replace violence." This assembly of leaders became the Grand Council, and eventually there were fifty sachems, or chiefs, from the various nations: nine Mohawks, nine Oneidas, fourteen Onondagas, ten Cayugas, and eight Senecas. They would assemble at Onondaga, at the geographical center of the country of the Five Nations. And would gather under what the Peacemaker called the Great Tree of Peace. There, reason would prevail. . . .

198

The women of the clans would meet under the leadership of a clan mother and select the men who would assemble as chiefs in the Grand Council. . . .

There was initial opposition to the plan of unity from a powerful Onondaga war chief whose name was Tadodaho. He was said to be the embodiment of evil, an individual who had woven snakes into his hair to intimidate all in his presence, and he had no interest in supporting a league dedicated to peace. The Peacemaker and Hayanwatah (Hiawatha) despaired of ever converting him until they voiced their concerns to Jikohnsaseh [Jigonsaseh] a woman chief of the Cat (or Neutral) Nation. She suggested that he could be won over by being offered the chairmanship of the Great League. When the nations assembled to make their offer, Tadodaho accepted. Jikohnsaseh, who came to be described as the Mother of Nations or the Peace Queen, seized the horns of authority and placed them on Tadodaho's head in a gesture symbolic of the power of women in Iroquois polity.[6]

# 5·5

# The Peacemaker

MOHAWK PEOPLE,
HAUDENOSAUNEE ORAL TRADITION

*The Peacemaker brought the vision that established the Haudenosaunee, or the Iroquois Confederacy. In this effort, he was joined by Hiawatha, who brought the Great Law of Peace to the Onondoga Nation.*

## The Birth of the Peacemaker

It happened at a place called Kanienkeh a long time ago. A boy was born in a Huron Village near the Bay of Quinte, on the shores of Lake Ontario. This baby was born with a name, but our people today know him only as the "Peacemaker," as his name is held in high esteem. His coming had been announced to a young virgin woman in a dream. In this dream, a spirit messenger from the Creator told her that she would bear a son who would be named Deganawida. "He will be a messenger of the Creator and will bring peace and harmony to the people on earth. When he has grown to manhood and desires to leave home to spread the good message of the Creator among the Nations, see that no obstacle is placed in his way."

The young girl's mother felt much shame when learning that her daughter was with child and vowed to avoid disgrace. The woman's mother would not accept answers regarding a dream or a Spirit Messenger. She demanded to know who[m] the young woman was sleeping with and wished to resolve her daughter's pregnancy with marriage, to avoid shame and embarrassment. The daughter could not tell her who the father was, for she didn't know. She ultimately convinced her mother that it was impossible for her to have slept with a man, for she and her mother were always together. The mother realized that she had never let her daughter out of her sight and began to suspect that this might be the work of an evil sorcerer. She decided to take her daughter farther away from the village until the baby was born, then end the life of the child at birth and return to the village.

One day after the birth of the child, the Grandmother took the boy while his mother slept and went to an ice-covered river to cut a hole in which to drown the baby boy. The Grandmother put the baby in the hole, and the current swept him away. Upon returning to the lodge, she discovered the baby back in the arms of her daughter. The next day, the Grandmother again stole the baby, and went to the woods to build a fire. When the fire was built, she threw the baby into it and returned to the village, only to find the baby back again.

The Grandmother was now convinced that this was the work of a sorcerer, and decided that the next day she would cut the baby up with a hatchet. During the night, as the Grandmother slept, a Spirit spoke to her in a dream advising that the baby was sent to this world to do work on behalf of the Creator, and not to interfere. Realizing that, the Grandmother helped her daughter raise the child.

Everything seemed normal for the mother and her child, until he was seven years old. Then, he announced that he knew he had a great mission on earth and that he needed to be alone to receive his instructions.

During the time he was growing into manhood, the boy demonstrated many unique powers that gave proof of his ability. When the Peacemaker became a man, he said one day to his mother and Grandmother, "I shall now build my canoe from this white stone, for the time has come for me to start my mission in this world. I know I must travel afar on lakes and rivers to seek out the council smoke of Nations beyond this lake, holding my course toward the sunrise. It is now time for me to go and stop the shedding of blood among human beings." When he finished his canoe of white stone, he bade farewell to this mother and Grandmother. "Do not look for me to return," he said, "for I shall not come this way again." He reminded them of his purpose in life and began his journey.

## The Messenger of Peace

The Peacemaker crossed Lake Ontario and approached the land of the Hotinonshonni [Haudenosaunee]. He looked for signs of ascending smoke from any villages, but saw none, for all the villages were back among the hills. Those were evil days, for the Hotinoshonni were all at war with one another.

When the Peacemaker came near the land, he saw the figures of men, small in the distance, running along the shore, for some hunters had seen a sparkle of light from the white stone canoe and ran to see what it could be. When he approached, he asked them where they were headed. They explained that they were hunters and were running away from their village, for there was much bloodshed among their people. "Go back to your people," instructed the Peacemaker, "and tell them that goods news of peace, power, and righteousness has come to your nation." The hunters asked the Peacemaker who he was, and he answered that he was sent by the Creator to establish peace in this world. They saw his canoe of white stone and realized that he had special powers, so they at once agreed to take this message back to their village. As soon as the hunters left for this village, the Peacemaker continued on his journey toward the sunrise. He came across a house of a certain woman who lived by the warriors' path that passed between the east and west. This woman was very evil, for she would entice the warriors and hunters who passed by her house to come in, rest, and enjoy a home-cooked meal. Instead, she would poison them. The Peacemaker sensed that this would happen to him.

Upon entering her lodge, she bade him welcome and offered some food to the handsome traveler, thinking that she had another victim. Instead, the Peacemaker spoke to her saying, "I know what you have been doing to other men who pass by your lodge. You shall stop this wicked practice and accept the good message that I bring from my father who sent me here to offer it to all human beings of this world." Realizing that he was on to her scheme, she fearfully asked him the words of his message. He told her, "The message I bring is that all people shall love one another and live together in peace. This message has three parts: peace, righteousness and power, and each part has two branches. Health means soundness of mind and body. It also means peace, for that is what comes when minds are sane and bodies cared for. Righteousness means justice practiced between men and between Nations. It means a desire to see justice prevail. It also means religion, for justice enforced is the will of the Creator and has his sanction."

The wicked woman said, "Your words are true, and I will accept your message of peace, righteousness, and power and enforce it. I vow never to return to my evil practices of bringing harm to humans who come to my lodge." The Peacemaker said, "Since you are the first to accept the Law of Peace, I will declare that it shall be the women who shall possess the title of Chieftainship. They shall name the Chiefs."

The woman was thankful, but warned that unless all men and Nations accept peace, there will be no end to killing. She asked, "Where will you take the good message first?" He answered, "I shall continue on my journey toward the sunrise." The woman cautioned, "That way is dangerous, for in that direction stands the house of a man who eats humans." The Peacemaker replied, "Then that is where I must go first, for these are the people I must confront to bring such evils to an end, so that all men may go about this earth without fear."

## The Peacemaker Meets Tekarihoken

As the Peacemaker continued on his journey toward the Flint (Mohawk Nation), he came upon the lodge of the man who eats humans. There he waited until the man came home, carrying a human body, which he put in a big kettle on the fire. The Peacemaker had climbed the roof and lay flat on his chest, peering through the smoke hole.

At that moment, the man bent over the kettle and saw a reflection of the Peacemaker's face, which he immediately interpreted as his own. Why would a man whose face was so kind and wise and possessed such strong characteristics have to resort to eating humans? He took the kettle out of the house and emptied the contents into a hole that he dug. Seeing the Peacemaker's face had obviously affected the evil mind of Tekarihoken. "Now I have changed my habits," he stated. "I will no longer kill humans and eat their flesh, but I have not changed enough. I cannot forget the suffering I have caused, and my mind is not at peace." When he returned to his lodge, he met the Peacemaker who had climbed down from the roof. They entered the lodge and sat across the fire from each other. "I am the Peacemaker. I am the one who has caused this change to take place in your mind. I am the messenger of the Creator, and the message is that all men should live together in peace, and live in unity based on a Law of Righteousness, Peace and Power. I will now hunt for your meal. I will bring to you what the Creator wishes you to eat from now on." With those words, the Peacemaker left, and not long after, returned with a deer. The Peacemaker told Tekarihoken that it was the Creator's plan that certain animals had been left on Earth to benefit mankind. "I shall now cook this deer, and we will celebrate your meal by giving you a new purpose in life."

The Peacemaker spoke, "Today, you have vowed to change from your evil habits, to live in a manner which will better yourself and your Nation. I have brought you a new mind to use. From now on, you will bring Peace to those places where you have done injury." Tekarihoken replied, "Because I have seen your face, the evil that nested in my mind has departed. I am now a new man, and your message is good. What can I do to help further the cause of the good message?" The Peacemaker told Tekarihoken that because he was the first man who accepted the Great Law of Peace, he would make him the first Sachem in the Mohawk Nation. "Because your people have always been afraid of your evil powers, we must now use your new powers in the cause of Peace, Power and Righteousness."

## Hiawatha and Atotarhoh

At the same time the Peacemaker was delivering the message of Peace and Brotherhood to the Mohawk Nation, the same was being done with the Onondaga Nation by a man named Hiawatha.

Hiawatha was having a hard time delivering words of unity to the people. At times, he felt like just dropping everything and not even being bothered. There was no peace at the Onondaga Nation. The people could not even come out of their homes at night without having their lives threatened by evil in the form of warfare, sorcery, and treachery. Hiawatha knew of an evil-minded man who lived south of the Onondaga town. He was so evil that he had snakes coming out of his hair. He ate human flesh. He practiced bad medicine for which he had great powers. Using these powers, he would destroy people. Everyone in the whole village feared him. Anything this man would say, the people would do, fearing that bad medicine would be used on them if they disagreed. This evil man with snakes coming out of his hair had seven crooks in his body and was called Atotarhoh . . .

[The Peacemaker continued his journey to the Oneida, Onondaga, Cayuga, and Seneca Nations, bring the message of peace, power, and righteousness, thus forming the Confederacy.][7]

To assure peace among the nations, the Peacemaker sang and walked before the door of Atotarhoh's house. When he had finished his song, he walked towards Atotarhoh. He rubbed Atotarhoh's body for him to know the strength and life he possessed. When finished, Atotarhoh's seven crooked parts became straight and his hair was free of snakes. With Atotarhoh strong and of good mind, the establishment of the Great Peace could take place. . . .

The Great Peace Law that was devised by the Peacemaker and Hiawatha was then read to the Five Nations assembled and the Confederacy was established.[8]

# 5.6

# The Great Law of Peace

PEACEMAKER, HURON

*The Peacemaker, along with Hiawatha, after working for many years, brought the Great Law of Peace to the Haudenosaunee, or Iroquois Confederacy, on the eastern seaboard. Within this document, women are empowered to make and remove chiefs. The Women's Council also decides when to go to war. They appoint the war chief, who serves only until the end of the war, or until he is removed by their authority. Women own the land; they inherit it from their mothers before them.*

*In 1754, members of the Haudenosaunee, or Iroquois Confederacy, attended a conference in Albany, New York. In discussing the Albany Plan of Union, Benjamin Franklin argued, in racist and demeaning language, that "It would be a very strange thing, if six nations of ignorant savages should be capable of forming a scheme for such a union, and be able to ex-ecute it in such a manner, as that is has subsisted ages, and appears indissoluble, and yet that a like union should be impractical for ten or a dozen English colonies" (Johansen, 1982: 66).[9] Although the issue is hotly debated, many scholars believe that the Great Law of Peace of the Iroquois Confederacy formed the model for the United States Constitution. In fact, in 1987, the U.S. Senate acknowledged the "historical debt" that the United States owed to the Iroquois Confederacy for their example of the "democratic principles of government."[10]*

*In the following selection, one notices that both the U.S. Constitution and the Great Law of Peace provide for a separation of powers, leaders who are selected and removed at the will of the people, through the Clan Mothers and the vote of the people, and that the decision to go to war is not a prerogative of the chief executive. These facets of good government were nowhere in evidence in Europe in the 1500s. Following are some of the words of Degana-wida, the Peacemaker, as published by* Akwesasne Notes *of the Mohawk Nation.*

1. I am Tekanawita [Deganawida]. With the statesmen of the League of Five Nations, I plant the Tree of Great Peace. I plant it in your territory, Atotarho [Tadodaho], and the Onondaga nation: in the territory of you who are Fire-keepers. I name the tree Tsioneratasekowa, the Great White Pine. Under the shade of this Tree of Great Peace, we spread the soft, white feathery down of the Globe Thistle as seats for you, Atotarho, and your cousin statesmen.

We place you upon those seats, spread soft with the feathery down of the Globe Thistle, there beneath the shade of the spreading branches of the Tree of Great Peace. There shall you sit and watch the Fire of the League of Five Nations. All the affairs of the League shall be transacted at this place before you, Atotarho and your cousin statesmen, by the statesmen of the League of Five Nations.

2. Roots have spread out from the Tree of Great Peace, one to the north, one to the east, one to the south, and one to the west. These are the Great White Roots, and their nature is Peace and Strength. If a man or any nation outside the Five Nations shall obey the laws of the Great Peace, the Kaianarekowa, and shall make this known to the statesmen of the League, they may trace back the roots to the Tree. If their minds are clean, and if they are obedient and promise to obey the wishes of the Council of the League, they shall be welcomed to take shelter beneath the Tree of the Long Leaves.

We place at the top of the Tree of Great Peace an eagle, who is able to see far. If he sees in the distance any danger threatening, he will at once warn the people of the League.

7. Whenever the statesmen of the League shall assemble for the purpose of holding a council, the Onondaga statesmen shall open it by expressing their gratitude to their cousin statesmen, and greeting them, and they shall make an address and offer thanks to the earth where men dwell, to the streams of water, the pools and the lakes, to the maize and the fruits, to the medicinal herbs and trees, to the forest trees for their usefulness, and to the animals that serve as food and give their pelts for clothing, to the great winds, the lesser winds, to the Thunderers; to the Sun, the mighty warrior; to the moon, to the messengers of the Creator who reveals his wishes, and to the Great Creator who dwells in the heavens above who gives all the things useful to men, and who is the source and ruler of health and life. Then shall the Onondaga statesmen declare the Council open. The Council shall not sit after darkness has set in.

10. In all cases, the procedure must be as follows: when the Mohawk and Seneca statesmen have unanimously agreed upon a question, they shall report their decision to the Cayuga and Oneida statesmen, who shall deliberate upon the question and report a unanimous decision to the Mohawk statesmen. The Mohawk statesmen will then report the standing of the case to the Firekeepers, who shall render a decision as they see fit in case of a disagreement by the two bodies, or confirm the decisions of the two bodies if they are identical. The Firekeepers shall then report their decision to the Mohawk statesmen who shall announce it to the open Council.[11]

# Matriarchy

## PEACEMAKER, HURON

*Although Benjamin Franklin and other Founding Fathers commented on the civility and democratic government of the Iroquois Confederacy, they neglected the role of women in government, limiting voting rights in the newly forming United States to men of property. In contrast, the Great Law of Peace relies upon the ancestral Clan Mothers to choose and remove chiefs and to decide when to go to war. Inheritance is through the maternal line, with women owning the land "and soil," and with the General Council of Women of the Five Nations determining the conduct and fate of war chiefs. Further, any decision of great importance had to be submitted to the people, with the League Council confirming the "voice of the people."*

17. A bunch of wampum shell strings each two spans in length shall be given to each of the female families in which the chieftain titles are vested. The right of bestowing the titles shall be hereditary in the family of females legally possessing the bunch of shell strings, and the strings shall be the token that the females of the family have the ownership to the chieftainship title for all time to come, subject to certain restrictions mentioned here.

18. If any chief of the League neglects or refuses to attend the Council of the League, the other chiefs of the nation of which he is a member shall require their War Chief to request the female sponsors of the chief so guilty of neglecting his duties to demand his attendance at the Council. If he refuses, the women holding the title shall immediately select another candidate for the title. No chief shall be asked more than once to attend the Council of the League.

19. If at any time it shall be apparent that chief of the League has not in mind the welfare of the people, or disobeys the rules of the Great Law, the men or the women of the League, or both jointly, shall come to the Council and scold the erring chief through his war chief. If the complaint of the people through the war chief is not heeded on the first occasion, it shall be uttered again, and then if no attention is given, a third complaint and a

warning shall be given. If the chief is still disobedient, the matter shall go to the Council of War Chiefs. The War Chiefs shall then take away the title of the erring chief by order of the women in whom the title is vested. When the chief is deposed, the women shall notify the chiefs of the League through their war chief and the chiefs of the League shall sanction the act. The women will then select another of their sons as a candidate and the chiefs shall elect him. Then the chosen one shall be installed by the Installation Ceremony.

When a chief is deposed, his war chief shall address him as follows:

> So you . . . disregard and set at naught the warnings of your women rela-
> tives. You fling the warnings over your shoulder to cast them behind. Be-
> hold the brightness of the Sun, and in the brightness of the Sun's light, I
> depose you of your title and remove the sacred emblem of your chief-
> tainship title. I remove from your brow the deer's antler headdress that
> was the emblem of your position and token of your nobility. I now de-
> pose you, and return the antlers to the women whose heritage they are.

The war chief shall now address the women of the deposed chief and say: "Mothers, as I have deposed your chief, I now return to you the emblem and the title of chieftainship; therefore, repossess them." Again addressing the deposed chief, he shall say:

> As I have deposed and discharged you so you are no longer chief. You
> shall go your way alone. The rest of the people of the League shall not go
> with you, for we know not the kind of mind you possess. As the Creator
> has nothing to do with wrong, so he will not come to rescue you from the
> precipice of destruction in which you have cast yourself. You shall never
> be restored to the position which you once occupied.

Then shall the war chief address himself to the chiefs of the nation to which the deposed chief belongs and say, "Know you, my chiefs, that I have taken the deer's antlers from the brow of . . . , the emblem of his position, and the token of his greatness." The chiefs of the League shall have no alternative then, except to sanction the discharge of the offending chief.

21. Certain physical defects in a statesman of the League make him ineligible to sit in the League council. Such defects are infancy, idiocy, blindness, deafness, dumbness, and impotency. When a statesman of the League is restricted by any of these conditions, a deputy shall be appointed by his sponsors to act for him, but in cases of extreme necessity, the restricted statesman may exercise his rights.

24. The chiefs of the League of Five Nations shall be mentors of the people for all time. The thickness of their skin shall be seven spans, which is to say that they shall be proof against anger, offensive action, and criticism. Their hearts shall be full of peace and good will, and their minds filled with a yearning for

the welfare of the people of the League. With endless patience, they shall carry out their duty. Their firmness shall be tempered with a tenderness for their people. Neither anger nor fury shall find lodging in their minds and all their words and actions shall be marked by calm deliberation.

25. If a chief of the League should seek to establish any authority independent of the jurisdiction of the League of the Great Peace which is the Five Nations, he shall be warned three times in open council, first by the women relatives, second by the men relatives, and finally by the chiefs of the Nation to which he belongs. If the offending chief is still persistent, he shall be dismissed by the war chief of his nation for refusing to conform to the laws of the Great Peace. His Nation shall then install the candidate nominated by the female name holders of his family.

26. It shall be the duty of all the chiefs of the League of Five Nations, from time to time as occasion demands, to act as teachers and spiritual guides of their people, and remind them of their Creator's will and words. They shall say:

> Listen, that peace may continue unto future days!
> Always listen to the words of the Great Creator, for he has spoken.
> United People, let not evil find lodging in your minds.
> For the Great Creator has spoken and the Cause of Peace shall not become old.
> The cause of peace shall not die if you remember the Great Creator.

31. If a chief of the League should become seriously ill and be thought near death, the women who are heirs of his title shall go to his house and lift his crown of deer antlers, the emblem of his chieftainship, and place them at one side. If the Creator spares him and he rises from his bed of sickness, he may rise with the antlers on his brow.

34. If a chief dies and there is no candidate qualified for the office in the family of the women title holders, the chiefs of the nation shall give the title into the hands of a sister family in the clan until such time as the original family produces a candidate, when the title shall be restored to the rightful owners.

No chieftainship title may be carried into the grave. The chiefs of the League may dispossess a dead chief of his title even at the grave.

36. The war chiefs shall be selected from the eligible sons of the female families holding the head chieftainship title.

37. There shall be one war chief from each nation, and their duties shall be to carry messages for their chiefs, and to take up arms in case of emergency.

They shall not participate in the proceedings of the Council of the League, but shall watch its progress and in case of an erroneous action by a chief, they shall receive the complaints of the people and convey the warnings of the women to him. The people who wish to convey messages to the chiefs of the League shall do so through the war chief of their nation. It shall always be his duty to lay the cases, questions, and propositions of the people before the council of the League.

39. If a war chief acts contrary to instructions, or against the provisions of the Laws of the Great Peace, doing so in the capacity of his office, he shall be deposed by his women relatives and by his men relatives. Either the women or the men alone or jointly may act in such a case. The women titleholders shall then choose another candidate.

44. The lineal descent of the people of the Five Nations shall run in the female line. Women shall be considered the progenitors of the nation. They shall own the land, and the soil. Men and women shall follow the status of their mothers.

45. The women heirs of the chieftainship titles of the League shall be called Oianer or Otiianer [Noble] for all time to come.

46. The women of the 48 (now 50) noble families shall be the heirs of the authorized names for all time to come.

47. If the female heirs of a title of a chief of the League become extinct, the title shall be given by the chiefs of the League to a sister family whom they shall elect, and that family shall hold the name and transmit it to their female heirs, but they shall not appoint any of their sons as a candidate for a title until all the eligible men of the former family shall have died, or otherwise have become ineligible.

48. If all the heirs of a chieftainship become extinct, and so all the families in the Clan, then the title shall be given by the chiefs of the League to a family of a sister Clan whom they shall elect.

49. If any of the Otiianer women, heirs of a titleship, shall willfully withhold a chieftainship or other title and refuse to bestow it, or if such heirs abandon, forsake, or despise their heritage, then shall such women be deemed buried, and their family extinct. The titleship shall then revert to a sister family, or Clan, upon application and complaint. The chiefs of the League shall elect the family or Clan which shall in future hold the title.

52. The Otiianer women, heirs of the chieftainship titles, shall, should it be necessary, correct and admonish the holders of the titles. Those only who

attend the Council may do this, and those who do not shall not object to what has been said nor strive to undo the action.

53. When the Otiianer women, holders of a chieftainship title, select one of their sons as a candidate, they shall select one who is trustworthy, of good character, of honest disposition, one who manages his own affairs, and supports his own family, if any, and who has proven a faithful man to his Nation.

54. When a chieftainship title becomes vacant through death or other cause, the Otiianer women of the Clan in which the title is hereditary shall hold a council, and shall choose one of their sons to fill the office made vacant. Such a candidate shall not be the father of any chief of the League. If the choice is unanimous, the name is referred to the men relatives of the Clan. If they should disapprove, it shall be their duty to select a candidate from among their own number. If then the men and women are unable to decide which of the two candidates shall be named, then the matter shall be referred to the chiefs of the League in the Clan. They shall decide which candidate shall be named. If the men and women agree to a candidate, then his name shall be referred to the sister clans for confirmation. If the sister clans confirm the choice, they shall refer their action to the chiefs of the League who shall ratify the choice and present it to their cousin chiefs, and if the cousin chiefs confirm the name, then the candidate shall be installed by the proper ceremony for the conferring of chieftainship titles.

55. A large bunch of shell strings, in the making of which the Five Nations League chiefs have equally contributed, shall symbolize the completeness of the union, and certify the pledge of the nations represented by the chiefs of the League of the Mohawks, the Oneida, the Onondaga, the Cayuga, and the Seneca, that all are united and formed into one body, or union, called the Union of the Great Law which they have established.

A bunch of shell strings is to be the symbol of the Council Fire of the League of Five Nations. And the chief whom the Council of Firekeepers shall appoint to speak for them in opening the Council shall hold the strands of shells in his hands when speaking. When he finishes speaking, he shall place the strings on an elevated place or pole so that all the assembled chiefs and the people may see it and know that the Council is open and in progress.

57. Five arrows shall be bound together very strong and shall represent one nation each. As the Five arrows are strongly bound, this shall symbolize the complete union of the nations. Thus are the Five Nations completely united and enfolded together, united into one head, one body, and one mind. They therefore shall labor, legislate, and council together for the interest of future generations.

The chiefs of the League shall eat together from one bowl the feast of cooked beaver's tail. While they are eating, they are to use no sharp utensils, for if they should, they might accidentally cut one another, and bloodshed would follow. All measures must be taken to prevent the spilling of blood in any way.

59.  A bunch of wampum strings, three spans of the hand in length, the upper half of the bunch being white and the lower half black, and formed from equal contributions of the men of the Five Nations, shall be the token that the men have combined themselves into one head, one body, and one thought, and it shall symbolize their ratification of the peace pact of the League, whereby the chiefs of the Five Nations have established the Great Peace. The white portion of the shell strings represent the women, and the black portion the men. The black portion, furthermore, is a token of power and authority vested in the men of the Five Nations.

This string of wampum vests the people with the right to correct their erring chiefs. In case a part of the chiefs or all of them pursue a course not vouched for by the people and heed not the third warning of their women relatives, then the matter shall be taken to the General Council of the Women of the Five Nations. If the chiefs notified and warned three times fail to heed, then the case falls into the hands of the men of the Five Nations. The War Chiefs shall then, by right of such power and authority, enter the open Council to warn the chief or chiefs to return from their wrong course. If the chiefs heed the warning, they shall say, "We shall reply tomorrow." If then an answer is returned in favor of justice and in accord with this Great Law, then the Chiefs shall individually pledge themselves again, by again furnishing the necessary shells for the pledge. Then shall the War Chief or chiefs exhort the chiefs, urging them to be just and true.

Should it happen that the chiefs refuse to heed the third warning, then two courses are open: either the men may decide in their council to depose the chief or chiefs, or to club them to death with war clubs. Should they in their council decide to take the first course, the War Chief shall address the chief or chiefs, saying,

> Since you the chiefs of the Five Nations have refused to return to the procedure of the Constitution, we now declare your seats vacant, and we take off your horns, the token of your chieftainship, and others shall be chosen and installed in your seats. Therefore, vacate your seats.

Should the men in their council adopt the second course, the War Chief shall order his men to enter the council, to take positions beside the errant chiefs sitting between them wherever possible. When this is accomplished, the war chief holding in his outstretched hand a bunch of black wampum strings shall say to the erring chiefs,

> So now, chiefs of the Five Nations, harken to these last words from your men. You have not heeded the warnings of the General Council of

Women, and you have not heeded the warning of the Men of the Nations, all urging you to the right course of action. Since you are determined to resist and to withhold justice from your people, there is only one course for us to adopt.

At this point, the War Chief shall drop the bunch of black wampum, and the men shall spring to their feet and club the erring chiefs to death. Any erring chief may become submissive before the War Chief lets fall the Black Wampum. Then his execution is withheld.

60. A broad belt of wampum of thirty-eight rows, having a white heart in the center, on either side of which are two white squares all connected with the heart by white rows of beads shall be the emblem of unity of the Five Nations.

The first of the squares on the left represents the Mohawk Nation and its territory, the second square on the left and near the heart represents the Oneida Nation and its territory, and the white heart in the middle represents the Onondaga Nation and its territory. It also means that the heart of the Five Nations is single in its loyalty to the Great Peace, and that the Great Peace is lodged in the heart (meaning with Onondaga League chiefs) and that the Council Fire is to burn there for the Five Nations. Further it means that the authority is given to advance the cause of peace whereby hostile nations out of the League shall cease warfare. The white square to the right of the heart represents the Cayuga Nation and its territory and the fourth and last square represents the Seneca Nation and its territory.

White here symbolizes that no evil nor jealous thought shall creep into the minds of the chiefs while in Council under the Great Peace. White, the emblem of peace, love, charity, and equity surrounds and guards the Five Nations.

65. I, Deganawida, and the United Chiefs, now uproot the tallest tree and into the hole thereby made we cast all weapons of war. Into the depths of the earth, down into the deep underneath currents of water flowing to unknown regions we cast all the weapons of strife. We bury them from sight and we plant again the tree. Thus shall the Great Peace be established and hostilities shall no longer be known between the Five Nations, but peace to the United People.

72. The soil of the earth from one end to the other is the property of the people who inhabit it. By birthright, the Onkwehonwe, the original beings, are the owners of the soil which they own and occupy and none other may hold it. The same law has been held from the oldest times.

73. The Great Creator has made us of one blood, and of the same soil he made us, and as only different tongues constitute different nations, he established different hunting grounds and territories and made boundary lines between them.

93. Whenever an especially important matter or a great emergency is presented before the League Council and the nature of the matter affects the entire body of Five Nations, threatening their utter ruin, then the chiefs of the League must submit the matter to the decision of their people and the decision of the people shall affect the decision of the League Council. This decision shall be a confirmation of the voice of the people.

95. The women of every clan of the Five Nations shall have a Council Fire ever burning in readiness for a council of the Clan. When in their opinion it seems necessary for the interest of the people, they shall hold a council, and their decision and recommendation shall be introduced before the Council of Chiefs by the War Chief for its consideration.

99. The rites and festivals of each nation shall remain undisturbed and shall continue as before, because they were given by the people of old times as useful and necessary for the good of men.[12]

# Did You Hear Wind Sing Your Name?: An Oneida Song of Spring

SANDRA DE COTEAU ORIE, ONEIDA

*In a thirty-two-page booklet, Oneida writer and educator Sandra De Coteau Orie celebrates* An Oneida Song of Spring, *the text's subtitle. Here one can discern echoes of the traditional Oneida opening prayer of thanksgiving, rendered as questions of lyrical sensitivity. The booklet is lushly and beautifully illustrated by Christopher Canyon.*

DID YOU HEAR WIND SING YOUR NAME?
AN ONEIDA SONG OF SPRING
Traveling North
Did you see
Spirit Hawk dancing on the Wind?
Did you feel
morning Sun's warmth upon your face
welcoming you to a new day?
Did you see
the White Birch standing tall among the Darkwoods
and the greening of the Aspen Saplings?
Did you smell
the sweet scent of the sacred Cedar?
Did you see
the fields of the Three Sisters
coming?
Did you see
Sun's face in the Buttercup?
and did you see Sky's blue in the wildwood Violets?
Did you greet
the Four-leggeds
and celebrate the Winged-One's
dances?
Did you trace

Turtle's tracks along the Creek
and know you weren't alone?
Did you hear
Wind sing your name?
Does your memory bring Sweet Grass's fragrance?
Did you taste
the Thunderer's moist sky Waters?
Were you healed by Meadow's wild
Strawberries?
Did your eyes catch Sunset's burgundy?
Did you see Trillium's Stars
lying upon the Forest bed's heaven?
Did you sense
Grandmother Moon guiding you
home again?
Did your heart
bring home the songs of all These living?
Did you, along with These,
travel this sacred circle called
Spring?[13]

# Oneida Counsel Peace between Two Brothers

ONEIDA HEADMEN

*In a speech to Connecticut governor John Trumbull in 1775, the Oneida advised the New Englanders to reconcile with King George III of England since they were "two brothers of one blood." In spite of these efforts and the desire to remain neutral in the American Revolution, the Oneida, urged by the Presbyterian minister Samuel Kirkland, supported the Americans, putting them in opposition to the Iroquois Confederacy, which was allied with the British.[14] The belt that is referred to is a wampum belt, made of shell, which was used within the Haudenosaunee as a diplomatic tool, guaranteeing the legitimacy of the proceeding. Before speaking of the issues between the colonies and Great Britain, the Oneida headmen try to protect the safety of the New England Indians.*

As my younger brothers of the New England Indians, who have settled in our vicinity, are now going down to visit their friends, and to move up parts of their families that were left behind—with this belt by them, I open the road wide, clearing it of all obstacles, that they may visit their friends and return to their settlements here in peace.

We Oneidas are induced to this measure on account of the disagreeable situation of affairs that way; and we hope, by the help of God, they may return in peace. We earnestly recommend them to your charity through their long journey.

Now we more immediately address you, our brother, the Governor, and the chiefs of New England.

Brothers: we have heard of the unhappy differences and great contention between you and Old England. We wonder greatly, and are troubled in our minds.

Brothers: Possess your minds in peace respecting us Indians. We cannot intermeddle in this dispute between two brothers. The quarrel seems to be unnatural. You are two brothers of one blood. We are unwilling to join on either side in such a contest, for we bear an equal affection to both you Old and New England. Should the great king of England apply to us for aid, we shall deny him; if the Colonies apply, we shall refuse. The present situation of you two brothers is new and strange to us. We Indians cannot find, nor recollect in the traditions of our ancestors, the like case, or a similar instance.

Brothers: For these reasons possess your minds in peace, and take no umbrage that we Indians refuse joining in the contest. We are for peace.

Brothers: Was it an alien, a foreign nation, who had struck you, we should look into the matter. We hope, through the wise government and good pleasure of God, your distresses may be soon removed and the dark clouds be dispersed.

Brothers: As we have declared for peace, we desire you will not apply to our Indian brethren in New England for their assistance. Let us Indians be all of one mind, and live with one another; and you white people settle your own disputes between yourselves.

Brothers: We have now declared our minds; please write to us, that we may know yours. We, the sachems and warriors, and female governesses of Oneida, send our love to you, brother governor, and all the other chiefs in New England.[15]

# 5.10

# Oneida Reject Offer of
# Christian Education

### ONEIDA HEADMEN

*Eleazar Wheelock, a Christian minister, invited the Oneida to send their children to his Indian school, which he expanded to become Dartmouth College in 1769. Early in 1772, Wheelock "sent his son Ralph to the Onondaga council in a final effort to get the central Iroquois council to agree to the [English] education of their youth."[16] On June 5, 1772, Oneida chiefs assembled at Mr. Kirkland's house at Kanowalohale, near Vernon, New York, and replied to Wheelock's overture.*

Father, attend, and hear for our father the less [*sic*]. The occasion of our entering your house this morning is to answer the speech delivered us the other day-evening from our great father, which was this (here repeated over the speech verbatim).

Father now attend; hear the result of our council—as you desired us to speak plainly and deal faithfully, so we shall do.

Our minds do not advance with the great minister's proposal: indeed they are at a perfect stand. We see no way open for prosecuting his purposes.

English schools we do not approve of here, as serviceable to our spiritual interest: and almost all those who have been instructed in English are a reproach to us. This we supposed our father was long ago sufficiently appraised of.

And as to our neighboring towns, there is not, at present, the least gleam of light—no appearance at all which embraces such a proposal.

Our father does not know the mind of Indians: their minds are invincible; they are strongly attached to other things. We don't say to what their minds are most strongly inclined, but of this we are confident, that they are not disposed to embrace the Gospel: for here we are upon the spot, with open ears, ready to receive such intelligence.

Moreover, we are despised by our brethren, on account of our christian profession. Time was when we were esteemed as honorable and important in the confederacy, but now we are looked upon as small things, or rather nothing at all. Now may we not well conclude that they don't favor your designs? Or would they not speak well of us, instead of reproaching us for embracing this religion you are endeavoring to publish among us?

As to your expectations of a favorable answer from the Onondagas, we must desire you to cut off your hope, and not protract it to any farther length, for we know by experience that hope deferred is very painful.

Father we must tell you, your former speech there, by your son, made so little impression and left so few marks that we have never been able since to find any traces of it, though we have often discoursed with one and another upon the subject. We never conceived that the least expectation should be at all excited in our great father's mind of their acceptance of his proposal, from what passed there, if he has been rightly informed.

(Then turning to Mr. Kirkland they proceeded—And you, father, well knew, having often heard, the result of that meeting, and we took it for granted you had rightly informed our great father, long ago.)

Our great father the great minister is at great trouble and expense to gospelize us Indians—and must be grieved, even pained in heart, that so many of his designs are frustrated, and so many of his attempts prove utterly abortive! To remedy this, we advise our father to consider well, and take good heed in his future endeavors—yea, let him take very good heed. Let him move slowly, very slowly. Let him examine thoroughly and critically in the minds and state of the Indians, in whatever place he may design any future mission. We pity him on account of his great distance from the Indian country.

How often has he sent, this great distance, with high expectations of success, when there has not been the least encouraging appearance among us! And so his missions have turned out a mere sham, and all in vain! Why, father, we are here upon the spot, within hearing of what passes through the whole house of our confederacy. If we had ever heard anything encouraging, from any quarter of our neighborhood, with respect to the gospel's moving forward, we should have instantly informed you. And here are those who are commissioned more immediately for that purpose.

As to what we understand of your son's mission to Onondaga, and their answer, we lords beg to refer you to those who have attended your son in his journey there, as they undoubtedly may be more perfectly acquainted with the whole transactions, on both sides, and also inform what passed there. Here sits one, Thomas by name, who well knows the whole affair from first to last.

Whenever we hear of any place in our neighborhood, we shall readily inform our father the great minister, that he may not send any more in vain at this great distance.

We would again desire that our father's long deferred expectations from Onondaga may pain him no more—and hope he will take good heed and well digest his future missions. Let him not send again without sufficient information and good encouragement, because some Indians are not wise, and have thought they must too hastily become religious, before they have time to make their choice, and duly considered the nature of the offers made them.

Father, agreeable to your desire we have thus spoken our minds freely and with fidelity.[17]

# 5.11

## Forced from New York in the 1820s

DANIEL BREAD, ONEIDA

*Urged by Samuel Kirkland to fight on the American side in the Revolutionary War, the Oneida served as scouts and "in the winter of 1777 provided bags of corn for George Washington's starving army at Valley Forge even though they themselves did not have enough food."[18]*

*In recognition of their aid, the Continental Congress guaranteed Oneida land in New York, but the State of New York ignored the Treaty of Fort Stanwix (1784) and worked hard at taking the land, moving in settlers, and forcing the Oneida away from their homes and cornfields.*

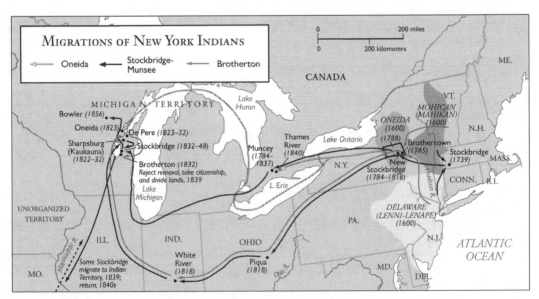

To preserve their nation in the face of U.S. pressure and illegal taking of their land by the State of New York, some New York Indians migrated west to Wisconsin. The Stockbridge-Munsee Band of Mohican and the Brothertown (Brotherton) chose land routes to Wisconsin, while the Oneida traveled mostly by water and secured land west of Green Bay. Map by Zoltan Grossman; reproduced by permission from Wisconsin Cartographers' Guild, *Wisconsin's Past and Present* (Madison: University of Wisconsin Press, 1998), 7.

*Reverend Eleazar Williams, an Episcopalian who was part Mohawk, established a mission in 1816. With the collusion of land speculators (who wanted Oneida land to construct the Erie Canal), war department officials, and church administrators, Williams lobbied to remove the Oneida to Wisconsin. But attempts to assimilate the Oneida into white culture were resisted by most of the Six Nations. Many factors increased divisions within the Iroquois Confederacy, and within the Oneida Nation itself.*

*Despite opposition, Eleazar Williams converted many Oneida to what became known as the First Christian Party, who resided near Oneida Lake where Daniel Bread was born. Another religious influence around the year 1800 was Handsome Lake, a Seneca holy man who preached the Good Word, a message of abstinence from alcohol, accommodation of whites, and maintenance of Haudenosaunee traditions. Daniel Bread of the First Christian Party fought in the War of 1812, was literate in English, and was a well-known orator. As the state of New York and mercantile interests stepped up their desire to take the holdings of the Oneida to build the Erie Canal, Bread expressed his opposition to being forced out of his homeland to Wisconsin.*

It was not originally our situation or desire to emigrate [from New York]. We resisted until overcome by the superior addresses of white men who promised us what has never been fulfilled. We were to have peace and protection. A territory was to be set off for the exclusive occupancy of the remnants of tribes of the State of New York free from the destroying influences and intrusions of strangers. Instead of finding fulfillment of these engagements, we are left exposed to the arts and calumnies of designing white men charged with fraud and extortion and meanness are taken to drive us from the country.[19]

# 5.12

## No! You Will Not Drive Us from Our Lands

ONON-GWAT-GO (OR REVEREND CORNELIUS HILL),
ONEIDA

*After being forced from New York, the Oneidas obtained land from the Menominee at Duck Creek, Wisconsin, and began to settle there. However, when the Americans attempted to remove the Oneida and other Wisconsin Indians to west of the Mississippi, Reverend Cornelius Hill, the first Oneida priest, protested.*

The whites are not willing to give us time to become civilized, but we must remove to some barbarous country as soon as civilization approaches us. The whites claim to be civilized, and from them we must learn the arts and customs of civilized life. The civilization at which I and the greater part of my people aim is one of truth and honor; one that will raise us to a higher state of existence here on earth and fit us for a blessed one in the next world. For this civilization we intend to strive—right here where we are—being sure that we shall find it no sooner in the wilds beyond the Mississippi.

Progress is our motto, and you who labor to deprive us of this small spot of God's footstool will labor in vain. We will not sign your treaty; no amount of money can tempt us to sell our people. You say our answer must be given today. You can't be troubled any longer with these Council Meetings. You shall have your wish—and it is one that you will hear every time you seek to drive us from our lands: NO![20]

# The Way They Used to Get Married

KATIE CORNELIUS, WISCONSIN ONEIDA

*Forced from their more than five million acres in New York, the Oneida arrived in Wisconsin territory. But the General Indian Allotment Act or Dawes Act of 1887 removed land from collective ownership; much of Oneida land in Wisconsin was lost due to failure to understand taxation, combined with ruthless land speculators. The Indian Reorganization Act of 1934 permitted reorganization, but only along lines approved by the federal government.*

*The 1930s was also the period of the Great Depression. As part of the Works Progress Administration, a UW–Madison professor, Morris Swadesh, initiated a project to study the Oneida language. Floyd Lounsbury and others participated in the WPA Federal Writers' Project to collect Oneida-language material. The discovery in 1999 of some green notebooks in the basement of the Anthropology Department at UW–Madison was greeted enthusiastically by Wisconsin Oneida. Carol Cornelius, Green Bay area manager of the Oneida Cultural Heritage Department was delighted with the find: "We're just beside ourselves. Our history has always been written by outsiders. This is our elders writing our history in their own words. It's like living in that time period."[21] This is a wonderful resource for the restoration of the Oneida language. A group of elders, historians, and Oneida-language experts has gathered to read, index, catalog, and translate the 167 notebooks. Here are two selections from the notebooks by Oneida speakers of Wisconsin, as documented by the Oneida Language and Folklore Project, 1938–1941.*

I will tell you a story about how they used to get married. It's about seventy-six years ago [1863]; my mother was married that way. My mother was left an orphan. Both of her parents died at the same time and she was left to live with her grandmother. She was only fifteen years when there was a bundle of clothes left to her grandmother. She was happy now; she thought she would get to dress up. She didn't know that the custom was to buy clothes for the young girl that was about to get married.

One Sunday her grandmother told her to get ready for church and to wear the clothes in the bundle. When they arrived at the church, she was really surprised to see this young man standing there with his parents. Now they told her that he was to be her husband and this was the day she will be married to him. This young girl cried and told her grandmother, "I don't want to get married; I will be good."

The grandmother said, "You will have to go with him, arrangements have already been made. We can't help it. Now go and walk with him." She did, but she cried all the way. [Her grandmother] also told her she was of an age to be getting married. So that is how my mother was married.

But from then on there [weren't] too many marriages like that. Except on a few rare occasions when a young man will tell his folks about which young girl he took a liking to. Well, this is the end of my story.[22]

# 5.14

# Broken Spine and His Wife

SARAH SUMMERS, ONEIDA

*This story also comes from the Oneida Language and Folklore Project.*[23]

It's a long time now since my grandfather (now deceased) and his wife came to Oneida, Wisconsin from Oneida, New York, Oneida Castle. They came here because they didn't want to change their ways to a white man's way of living and his laws. His wife had a small girl child. They got off at DePere; they had come by boat. They walked when they left the boat. There were still large forests and mostly swamps yet at that time, and they had to get through all that to get to Daniel Bread's house to where they were going. They bundled up their baby and covered her face because there were so many mosquitoes. Wild game was plentiful too. Finally, they came to his house. This was in the spring of the year; people around there had already planted, but [the plants] were killed by frost.

Now my grandfather started right in to build them a house. He took logs and split them hurriedly; he used basswood and he stripped the bark and used that for ties to a door. His wife was very unhappy here. She used to cry. There were all kinds of game and partridges and fish were plentiful. Finally, he was able to get two animals; they were oxen. Now he made a sleigh [which] he shared . . . with his neighbors. Now he was ready to go job hunting. He went to Green Bay, where he worked on the boats where he was hired. Then he was able to buy a horse. He cleared the land for planting. He helped his neighbors a lot because he became well off, that he did.[24]

 5·15

# Philadelphia Flowers

ROBERTA J. HILL, ONEIDA

*Roberta J. Hill, an accomplished writer, scholar, and poet, is the author of two collections of poetry:* Star Quilt *and* Philadelphia Flowers. *An enrolled member of the Oneida Nation of Wisconsin, she is a professor of English and American Indian Studies at the University of Wisconsin–Madison. The following poem is the title poem from her collection* Philadelphia Flowers.

### PHILADELPHIA FLOWERS

#### I

In the cubbyhole entrance to Cornell and Son,
a woman in a turquoise sweater
curls up to sleep. Her right arm seeks
a cold spot in the stone to release its worry
and her legs stretch
against the middle hinge.

I want to ask her in for coffee,
to tell her to go sleep in the extra bed upstairs,
but I'm a guest,
unaccustomed to this place
where homeless people drift along the square
bordering Benjamin Franklin Parkway.

From her portrait on the mantel,
Lucretia Mott asks when
will Americans see
how all forms of oppression blight
the possibilities of a people.
The passion for preserving Independence Square

should reach this nameless woman, settling
in the heavy heat of August,

exposed to the glare of every passerby.
What makes property so private? A fence?
No trespassing signs? Militia ready to die for it
and taxes? Lights in the middle stories

of office buildings blaze all night above me.
Newspapers don't explain how wealth
is bound to these broken people.
North of here, things get really rough.
Longshoremen out of work bet on eddies
in the Schuylkill River.

Factories collapse to weed
and ruptured dream. Years ago, Longhouse sachems
rode canoes to Philadelphia,
Entering these red brick halls.
They explained how
the law that kept them unified

required a way to share the wealth.
Inside the hearths of these same halls,
such knowledge was obscured,
and plans were laid to push all Indians
west. This city born of brotherly love
still turns around this conflict.

Deeper in the dusk,
William Penn must weep
from his perch on top of City Hall.
Our leaders left this woman in the lurch.
How can there be democracy
without the means to live?

## II

Every fifteen minutes
a patrol car cruises by. I jolt awake
at four a.m. to sirens screeching
and choppers lugging to the hospital heliport
someone who wants to breathe.

The sultry heat leads me
to the window. What matters? This small
square of night sky and two trees
bound by a wide brick wall.
All around, skyscrapers

are telling their stories
under dwindling stars. The girders
remember where Mohawk ironworkers stayed
that day they sat after work
on a balcony, drinking beer.

Below them, a film crew caught
some commercials. In another room above
a mattress caught fire and someone flung it
down into the frame. A woman in blue
sashayed up the street

while a flaming mattress,
falling at the same speed as a flower,
bloomed over her left shoulder.
Every fifteen minutes
a patrol car cruises by. The men inside

mean business. They understood the scene.
A mattress burning in the street
and business deadlocked. Mohawks
drinking beer above it all.
They radioed insurrection,

drew their guns, then three-stepped
up the stairs. Film crews caught the scene,
but it never played. The Mohawks
didn't guess a swat team had moved in.
When policemen blasted off their door,

the terrified men shoved a table
against the splintered frame.
They fought it out.
One whose name meant Deer got shot
again and again. They let him lie

before they dragged him by his heels
down four flights of stairs. At every step,
he hurdled above his pain
until one final leap
gained him the stars.

The news reported one cop broke his leg.
The film's been banished to a vault. There are

no plaques. But girders whisper at night
in Philadelphia. They know the boarding house,
but will not say. They know as well what lasts
    and what falls down.

### III

Passing Doric colonnades of banks
and walls of dark glass,
passing press-the-button-visitors-please
Liberty Townhouses, I turned
up Broad Street near the Hershey Hotel
and headed toward the doorman
outside the Bellevue. Palms and chandeliers inside.
A woman in mauve silk and pearls stepped into the street.

I was tracking my Mohawk grandmother
through time. She left a trace
of her belief somewhere near Locust and Thirteenth.
I didn't see you, tall, dark, intense,

with three bouquets of flowers in your hand.
On Walnut and Broad, between the Union League
and the Indian Campsite, you stopped me,
shoving flowers toward my arm.

"At least, I'm not begging," you cried.
The desperation in your voice
spiraled through my feet while I fumbled the few bucks
you asked for. I wanted those flowers—

iris, ageratum, goldenrod and lilies—
because in desperation
you thought of beauty. I recognized
the truth and human love you act on,

your despair echoing my own.
Forgive me. I should have bought more
of those Philadelphia flowers, passed hand
to hand so quickly, I was stunned a block away.

You had to keep your pride, as I have done,
selling these bouquets of poems
to anyone who'll take them. After our exchange,
grandmother's tracks grew clearer.

I returned for days, but you were never there.
If you see her—small, dark, intense,
with a bun of black hair and the gaze of an orphan,
leave a petal in my path,
Then I'll know I can go on.

## IV

Some days you get angry enough
to question. There's a plan out east
with a multitude of charts and diagrams.

They planned to take the timber, the good soil.
Even now, they demolish mountains.
Next they'll want the water and the air.

I tell you they're planning to leave our reservations
bare of life. They plan to dump their toxic
wastes on our grandchildren. No one wants to say

how hard they've worked a hundred years.
What of you, learning how this continent's
getting angry? Do you consider what's in store for you?[25]

# The Long Parenthesis

ROBERTA J. HILL, ONEIDA

*In "The Long Parenthesis," Dr. Roberta J. Hill takes another look at the American Dream.*

### THE LONG PARENTHESIS
**For my students at the Wisconsin State Reformatory,**
**Fall 1977**

I didn't want to walk through remote control doors,
the bars, peeling paint, a fifties beige. I didn't hope to save you,
just to teach dashes, colons, the verb you need
for better days outside. My card: "Education."
The Lieutenant warned: "You smile, it's rape
and all your fault. I've filed each armed and dangerous.
Never shut the door." The scar across his left eye
burned brighter than his shirt

I've been here before. My father wore his heart out on you cons,
Twenty-nine years of math, gum on the ass of his second suit,
he served his time. Imprisoned by an ache, he couldn't return,
kept seeing the spoon pierce his student's throat,
the death rattle fill the hall, blood dry on his palm.
The library door was open; the guards were hours away.
He kept saying one of you had drowned.
This mold for a society could make the seas decay.

You live the long parenthesis; each of you a man
who listens to the water drip, sees dust hang in each tier,
whose dash and strut and rebel glare,
ah, rebel that I am, had made you seed for anarchy
or harbingers of war. I'm glad I found you
flesh, sweat, excuses. For weeks your number dropped:
one went home, collared the next day on another warrant,
one anxious in his learning found morning in the hole.

233

Seven of you were left: three races in one room, four billboards
peppered with holes, six windows faced concrete.
What records can they keep of inappropriate looks?
At first you thought, "a woman." I memorized restraint.
When others peered inside, I began to shut the door.
Our classroom needed thunder, a forest lit with moths, the smell
of blooming sweet flag and faces clean of such arrogant despair.
I see you, each writing his escape:

one locked up more inside than bars will ever do;
one sharpened foreign rhetoric like an unforgiving blade;
one puffed up for flight, a comic-loving sparrow;
one craved a mean piano and almost didn't pass;
one smiled at me for weeks and must have worked in secret;
one walked in like a leopard, practiced in his moves;
one, with sleight of hand, planned to reraise himself.
I dragged those early lessons like a red ant does her sand.

Pile one wall there, a peephole here, so each can see the other,
human and alive. My passion's equally vain.
We're out of place in this tyranny of routine,
The suave American Dream where one of every six
guards the thick or dead. Scraping all at once like winter weeds,
we hassled with a future that strong armed us back to now.
We con ourselves: just one chance to snatch a generous pitfall.
Your eyes need time to heal, and healing's hard in there.

We live by more than breath. Behind the all pervading air,
creation quickened seed, flower, fruit and pith. Love's always
changing form. A self that stays divided finds an early grave
or mirrors still more misery in parentheses again. Draw miracles
from yourself. Stumbling in the dark, I'm too vulnerable for answers,
but that delicious morning when you're free, I hope good deeds
take shape behind you, like scarves drawn from a magic hat
one after the other shimmer boldly in the wind.[26]

# 5.17

# Evening at the Warbonnet

BRUCE KING,
HAUDENOSAUNEE-ONEIDA NATION OF WISCONSIN

*Bruce King is a member of the Turtle Clan of the Haudenosaunee-Oneida Nation, of Oneida, Wisconsin, and a noted screenplay writer, producer, and director. Besides the play presented here, he has also written three other plays:* Whispers from the Other Side, Treaty, *and* Dustoff. *He is currently working with the WarDancer Film Group, a production company.* Evening at the Warbonnet, *whose first act is presented here, deals with political issues, particularly those surrounding the American Indian Movement (AIM). In act I, scenes 1 through 7, Artsy, Mable, and Brave Eagle enter a bar that is tended by Ki and Dicky. Scenes 8 and 9 are presented here. In the second act (which is not presented), the various characters, at the instigation of Ki and Ducky, reveal their shortcomings in order to prepare to cross the river separating life and death to meet their Creator. Bruce King gives an author's note to orient us to his play.*

The Warbonnet is an Indian bar. They are located all over Indian country on reservations, reservation borders, in towns, and in the big cities. Most of the time they cater to a rough crowd. The Warbonnet is where those who feel helpless go to "drown their sorrow" and "cry the blues." They look for love, reasons, respect, fights, marks, the whole of the spectrum of humankind that needs to exist in the walled-in world of pretentious comfort.

*Evening at the Warbonnet* is rooted in the belief that the Anishinaabe (Ojibwe) people must cleanse their souls before crossing the river that separates this existence and the afterlife. They do this by dropping their burdens, which can be construed as sins, secrets, and self-punishment. This baggage makes it impossible to make one's way across the river, simply because it weighs heavily on one's soul. The other obstacle, of course, is acknowledging that it exists.

CHARACTERS:
Ki
Ducky
Artsy
Mable
Brave Eagle
Sugar Lin

SETTING:
An Indian bar in any big city

SYNOPSIS OF SCENES:
Act 1 [Scenes 8 and 9 are presented here]
The present—Evening
Act 2 [This act is *not* presented here]
Immediately following

# Scene 8

*(Enter* Sugar Lin, *beautiful, slender, striking red dress showing a lot of leg and cleavage. She moves to the jukebox and plays a song. She begins dancing seductively.)*

KI: See that? That's why I come in here.

(Ki *makes a move to dance with* Sugar Lin, *but she laughs at him and moves to one of the small tables. She gets a cigarette and* Brave Eagle *rushes to light it. She lights up and* Brave Eagle *straddles a chair drinking in her beauty.)*

BRAVE EAGLE: You know, in some mysterious way, I knew you were going to walk into my life tonight. Call it premonition but I have a beer at the bar for you.

(Brave Eagle *attempts to take her hand; she pulls her hand away and fixes a cold look on him.)*

SUGAR LIN: Beer?
BRAVE EAGLE: Or whatever your little heart wants, darlin'. See, my name is Brave Eagle, Lakota warrior, defender of the people. I was named after my great-grandfather who was a chief at the signing of the Fort Laramie treaty. He was also an advisor to Sitting Bull and Crazy Horse. You've heard of them I take it?
SUGAR LIN: Crazy Horse, isn't that a beer?
BRAVE EAGLE: Well . . . anyways, I am the living legacy of the mighty Sioux nation. A Lakota warrior and resistor of the oppressive lifestyles we are forced to live. Though the buffalo may be decimated, and the eagle shackled and chained, their spirits stay alive, here, in my heart, where the white eyes cannot see. They are there with my vision, my gift from the great mystery. My medicine. My power. You know, I had a vision we were going to meet tonight. Destiny has brought us together. In my vision, you couldn't help yourself, you fell madly in love with me.
SUGAR LIN: Visions are like assholes that way, everybody has one. I'm having a vision right now. It's you disappearing. Excuse me.

*(She turns away from him; he stands and moves to the bar.)*

BRAVE EAGLE: *(Under his breath.)* Bull dyke.

KI: Boy, a couple of hours of that and a six pack, I could die a happy man.

MABLE: Oh yi, why do men always react to female beauty like dogs. Geez, you act like you'd really have a chance. You're too old to remember what to do with either one.

KI: Maybe not a six pack, but that, ho ho, like riding a horse. Some things you never get too old for.

ARTSY: What's your make on her, Ducky? Model?

KI: Indian Rodeo Princess!

DUCKY: Naw, she's more glamorous than that. Maybe an actress, movies, top-shelf call girl . . . who knows? See how she moves. The attitude. Used to having her way, I'd say. Used to having dipsticks like him falling all over her . . .

BRAVE EAGLE: Hey, I ain't done yet.

DUCKY: . . . loves the attention, loves to strut her stuff. Seen my share of them in here.

KI: Same. Too bad we can't keep any of them for ourselves, eh Ducky?

MABLE: Would you perverts like a club to hit her over the head with? God, get out of the cave more often, fellas, it's the nineties! Besides, she's just a baby.

(Brave Eagle *straightens himself and approaches* Sugar Lin *once again.)*

ARTSY: Look at that fool kid there, watch him, he's going to do something silly.

*(Note: Chair seat should not be secured, so it will fall off easily.* Brave Eagle *makes a big show of pulling out the chair [rigged] and stylishly placing his foot on it. The seat itself buckles.* Sugar Lin *and the others laugh. She makes her way to the bar.* Brave Eagle *tries to recover, replacing the seat and sitting down nonchalantly.* Ducky *comes over and chases* Brave Eagle *out of the chair and takes it offstage. He returns immediately.)*

SUGAR LIN: Friend of yours?

KI: Used to call me grandfather. Don't know if I want to claim him after that stunt. Who might you be?

SUGAR LIN: Everybody calls me Sugar.

KI: Now there's an Indian name I can live with, but I can see why.

SUGAR LIN: Should I call you grandfather, too?

KI: Oh no, that won't be ness . . .

DUCKY: No, call 'em Ki, as in yippy ki yi-yippy ki yay . . .

KI: We got it, Ducky, all right! Geez . . . uh, heh heh, so, how have you been, Sugar? How's the family?

SUGAR LIN: Fam . . . ? Well, you know. Same ole, same old.

KI AND DUCKY: Yeah, we know.

KI: Well, I want you to meet everyone. Ducky, well, don't worry about him, but this is Mable, the dipstick you know, and this is Artsy. He's Cheyenne but from the look in his eye, ain't nothing shy about him— and that should be it for the night, eh Ducky?

DUCKY: Looks like it.

ARTSY: The pleasure is mine.

SUGAR LIN: Do people call you Art?

KI: Oh, he's a piece of work all right.

ARTSY: You call me whatever you like. Buy you a drink?

(Artsy *stands and offers her his chair.*)

SUGAR LIN: Manners. I like that. Scotch. The good stuff.

MABLE: Great! Scotch for the baby, beer for the old hag.

KI: Give Mable a scotch too, Ducky. Put in on numbnuts' tab. The feds'll cover it.

BRAVE EAGLE: I heard that! I'd have bought her scotch, she just didn't give me a chance is all. Matter of fact, set everybody up again! I'm buying!

DUCKY: Got to see that check or some money there, choker boy.

BRAVE EAGLE: Look, my name is Brave Eagle, you got that? Not numbnuts, sonny, or choker boy. Brave Eagle! I refuse to go by the name the white oppressors forced upon my ancestors.

SUGAR LIN: I happen to like choker boy myself. It's you, honey.

KI: Who gave you your name?

BRAVE EAGLE: You mean Brave Eagle?

KI: Okay, close enough.

BRAVE EAGLE: I did.

EVERYONE EXCEPT BRAVE EAGLE: You did?

BRAVE EAGLE: That's right.

KI: And before you were Brave Eagle, who were you?

BRAVE EAGLE: It doesn't matter. I'm Brave Eagle now.

KI: It matters. That's who you really are. Have you disregarded the name your mother gave you to become someone you don't know?

BRAVE EAGLE: That's not what happened . . .

DUCKY: What does Brave Eagle mean?

BRAVE EAGLE: Well, it kind of speaks for itself, don't you think?

KI: If it speaks for itself, what does it say about you?

BRAVE EAGLE: It says that I am like the eagle, soaring above this earth, brave, cunning and self-reliant.

KI: And you are like that?

BRAVE EAGLE: Well . . . yeah. *(Everyone bursts out laughing.)* Look, my great-grandfather, whose name was Eagleheart, by the way, led one of the last Lakota pony charges against the long knives in a futile attempt to keep his land and people free. When he was captured and imprisoned, they forced another name on him. That is the name my mother lived with. I merely chose the name of my great-grandfather for my own. And one day, when I face the guns of the white devils, when I perish in the burning glory of war . . . all will know my name. Brave Eagle! All will speak my name with honor! Brave Eagle! *(War cry.)* Brave Eagle! *(War cry.)* Hoka Hey! Hoka Hey!

KI: That speaks to me.

DUCKY: Tells me all we need to know.

ARTSY: All right, Junior, settle down, we get the message.

BRAVE EAGLE: No, no you don't. That's the trouble. You don't get the message. We constantly rebel against that which we know is right because we are deluded by options. Options that water down our ancient messages. We forego the life force of our ancestors and live by the examples imposed upon us by the white man. Material wealth, delusions of grandeur, decadence, greed, money, money, money!

SUGAR LIN: What's so terrible about money unless, of course, you don't have any.

BRAVE EAGLE: That's what I mean! We're just as bad, greedy, and one-dimensional as they are, when it comes to money. And this . . . this alcohol, it ruins us. We herd around it like cows because if fortifies us against the trials of life. We turn to it like we used to turn to our amulets, our medicine bundles . . . our messages! But this alcohol ruins us and we let it. We're no longer human beings. We're statistics and consumers. We've relinquished our survival skills, our self-sustaining lifestyles, for what? We're just another faceless entity in the masses of eaters and shitters. We're all lost these days and not just Indians. But we're like the buffalo . . .

ARTSY: Nice speech, Abraham, but we talked about this while you were in the bathroom!

BRAVE EAGLE: Well then, you all should know what these messages are. They may as well be displayed behind that bar. They're not secrets! We all know them in one regional form, if not many!

MABLE: Why do I suddenly feel like I'm in church?

BRAVE EAGLE: The Hopi prophecy. The visions of Wovoka, Black Elk, Chief Seattle, Handsome Lake. The Great Law, the Sacred Hoop. Taken together, they all tell us the same thing. Live by these ways. Impart these messages to the generations to come, keep the words alive. In truth and in telling. This land is alive. When we speak these words, these messages, we replenish its soul. And when we don't man, when we don't the spirit of this land will lash back at us with hell to pay. It's happening already . . . but we sit here, sip our drinks like there's all the time in the world . . . you . . . you . . . you *(he comes to*

Sugar Lin) maybe not you, and you! We don't listen and we don't get
the message!

SUGAR LIN: One message I get, you're sitting here with us.

BRAVE EAGLE: I'm not excluding myself, cutie, I just want to know
what you think?

ARTSY: I'll tell you what I think, I think you're full of shit!

KI: Ah hah hah, this guy's great, inet Ducky?

MABLE: Oh, Artsy, com'on he's just—

ARTSY: I mean it. He's full of himself, Eagles, spirits, messages. I used to
listen to the same kind of raps in the movement. All nicely scented
and devised to appease the yearning we all still feel. I bought it once.
Then I sorted it out. It's not the messages, kid. But I can understand
what they mean about killing the messenger.

BRAVE EAGLE: I'm not trying to pass myself off as . . .

KI: So you, Brave Eagle, I assume you live the way you talk, eh?

MABLE: God, Ki, he's just a kid.

SUGAR LIN: Yeah, look at the way mommy dressed him.

BRAVE EAGLE: To answer your question, yes I try to live within the
parameters set forth by my forefathers.

DUCKY: Oh please! Just ignore him, kid, he only gets worse.

KI: So you, spiritual wonder, you've gained some mystical doorway you
glance into to see how it's all done, is that it?

BRAVE EAGLE: I make allowances. I drink socially. I have to work . . .

KI: Ho ho, hear that, Ducky? He calls it work!

SUGAR LIN: And I suppose you stopped off here on your way to the
sweat lodge, eh?

ARTSY: Just get through burning a little sweetgrass, did we?

*(They start laughing.)*

BRAVE EAGLE: All right, I see your point, but realistically I can't very
well conduct myself in a spiritual manner with the feds on my ass,
now can I?

SUGAR LIN: Feds? The federal police are after you?

MABLE: He tried to tell us that too.

(Sugar Lin *laughs uproariously.*)

BRAVE EAGLE: You go ahead and laugh. Just my being here is a danger
to all of you. As long as I stay, you're safe, but then . . .

SUGAR LIN: What'd you do? To get the federal police after you?

ARTSY: He can't tell you. If he told you, he'd have to kill you afterwards.
(*To* Brave Eagle.) Tell her what you did, sonny.

DUCKY: Tell all of us.

MABLE: It's not awful, is it?

ARTSY: You're not buying this, are you, Mable?

SUGAR LIN: I'll bet I know what it was. *(She begins to approach him.)* It was something daring and electrifying, wasn't it? That's what makes him so mysterious. That's why he has to be so shadowy and protective. Right Brave Eagle or Eagle Brave or whoever you are—that is your name, hmmm?

BRAVE EAGLE: You're right, I can't tell you what went down.

SUGAR LIN: Oh I know that, you don't want to implicate me or us, because we're all brothers and sisters here, right? Wouldn't you like me to be your sister, Mr. Eagle? You could be so noble and courageous, saving me from all those bad, bad FBI men. Why, I would just have to think of some way I could thank you now, hmmm? You could take all the heat yourself, just like a good little warrior poopsi . . . wouldn't you like that? Well, Mr. Eagle, if I'm going to be your little sister and you're going to be my big, strong, brave brother, you're going to have to tell me what you did. Or, we don't have to play brother and sister, you see, we could just be a man and a woman, hmmm? I've always had a thing for guys who live on the edge. Something about outlaws. Expecially Shenabeh outlaws. You are an outlaw, aren't you, Mr. Eagle?

BRAVE EAGLE: I . . . you really like that?

SUGAR LIN: Oh yes! *(She pushes him to a chair at one of the tables. Removing his hat, she becomes enticing.)* Outlaws are like horses, you know, all that motion and speed. But there is a difference between Shenabeh outlaws and run-of-the-mill outlaws. Kind of like mavericks are different from stallions . . . muscle and seed. Then there's the mavericks who are just like Shenabeh outlaws. They run and fight and sweat. You can't catch them. They won't surrender. They barely stand still to mount their females. Then it's raw and passionate and abandoned. Ohhh, the mavericks are the ones I go for. I can pick and choose a stallion anytime I want, but a maverick . . . no one can have them. Because they're unattainable, I want to make one stand still . . . I want one to take me. I want to feel that uncontrollable passion, that lather, that unbridled heat. That's why they just . . . turn . . . me . . . on.

DUCKY: Sugar, you about to set that boy on fire.

SUGAR LIN: So tell me, Mr. Eagle, are you ready to be my maverick? Just what was it that made you a Shenabeh outlaw?

BRAVE EAGLE: I . . . I killed somebody!

*(Everybody starts laughing.* Sugar Lin *pushes him away from herself and struts back to the bar.)*

SUGAR LIN: Ho hum. There you go, Art. Now you know the story.

BRAVE EAGLE: Damn you. Well I did! You know those two feds that got killed at that AIM camp in '75. Leonard Peltier's in Leavenworth for that as we speak. . . .

KI: Ah, yeh yeh yeh, you did that?

DUCKY: How old you say you were, sonny?

KI: From his looks, how old would you say he was when that happened, Duck?

DUCKY: Maybe a year old, give or take a year.

ARTSY: What'd you do Lame Seagull, hit them with a loaded diaper!

*(More laughter.)*

BRAVE EAGLE: I didn't kill them, it was, stop laughing at me. I took out the guy who sent them feds to the Jumping Bull camp in the first place. The snitch who set the AIM bro's up, that's right, he was on the federal payroll as an informer. I found out who he was a couple of years ago. Tracked him down, waited 'til the time was right . . . then I took him out!

KI: For what? Dinner and a movie?

(Brave Eagle *moves to the table and chair angrily.*)

BRAVE EAGLE: Oh look, I got the killer mad . . .

EVERYONE BUT BRAVE EAGLE: Aaaaawwwwwwwww!

BRAVE EAGLE: You know, you all are lucky I have such an understanding nature. I could drop a dime in that phone back there, if the goddamn thing worked, and have warriors come in here and clean this goddamn place out!

KI: What do you think, Ducky?

DUCKY: No way that could happen.

BRAVE EAGLE: DON'T YOU PUSH ME, OLD MAN!!

MABLE: All right, everybody lighten up! Let's all take a deep breath and relax now shall we? (*She moves downstage and sits with* Brave Eagle.) *Listen kid* . . .

BRAVE EAGLE: Don't call me that. Don't call me sonny boy or any of that. I'm a grown man. I know what I'm talking about but they won't take me seriously. I mean, I stuck my neck out telling you guys what's going down and ya'll laughed at me. Everyone thinks it's one big joke. Ha ha, real funny. Well it ain't funny!

MABLE: Okay, okay, Brave Eagle. It's just that you're so young and, well, it's hard to see you as you say. You try to look so mean that it just comes off as sweet. You're not going to strike too many people as a killer with that baby face. I'm old enough to know that that can be deceiving, too, but you're right, we shouldn't be laughing at you that way. But I want you to take a good look at them, all of them. They know life and they've probably known killers and, son, you just don't fit the bill.

BRAVE EAGLE: Little do they know.

MABLE: Fine, but you can't blame them for the way they see you. You're not scaring anybody and I hope you're not here to educate these yo-yos. I'll tell you one thing, I've known those who've killed. You really don't know until they tell you. And most of them don't. Could be anybody. You see that Artsy and Ducky . . . even that Sugar. They might be. Hell, I might be . . . but no one goes barking around the bars about it.

BRAVE EAGLE: Yeah, that is kinda foolish, inet?

MABLE: Hey, you have your own business to deal with and I'll tell you the truth, I don't even want to know. So com'on, give an old lady a thrill. Lighten up and buy me a beer.

DUCKY: All right everybody, listen up! The bar has an open tab! It's on the house from here on in. Thanks to the low number of souls in the house tonight, we can afford to just give this stuff away. So drink all you want, as much as you want, it's on the house.

EVERYBODY: Yaaaaaaayyy!

ARTSY: I've died and gone to heaven!

*(They all flock to the bar.* Ki *strolls over to the jukebox. He plays a number and music fills the air. He dances over to the crowd and gets* Mable *to dance with him.* Sugar Lin *pulls* Artsy *out to dance and* Brave Eagle *joins the threesome. They dance and whoop while* Ducky *circulates giving them bottles of liquor.* Ducky *and* Ki *pull away from the dancers; they raise their arms and the music warps and the dancers go herky-jerky.* Ki *howls, long and mournful, takes his hat from his head, snaps it, and the dancers freeze; the music stops. They are statues.* Ki *and* Ducky *circulate among them. They posture agreement.* Ki *yips. In the background we hear a woman lulu-ing. The dancers drop to the floor, gasping and coughing. They struggle to a chair, the pool table, etc., but what we see is that something has been taken out of them.)*

# Scene 9

MABLE: What? What just happened here! Something happened!

ARTSY: I felt something, like lightheaded or something, like blood rushing.

SUGAR LIN: That wasn't it. It was cold. Like a breeze, blue and lonely, coming over you, passing through you, taking your air—

BRAVE EAGLE: It was more like a dungeon, wet and heavy. Pressing down on you, pressing the breath from you.

(Ducky *circulates with more drinks.*)

DUCKY: Here you go, folks, drink up, drink up . . . as much as you want. You won't get sick and you won't get drunk. Beer, scotch,

whiskey, and rye, it won't screw you up and it won't get you
high.

MABLE: All right, Ki, what's happening here?

KI: Yeh, yeh, yeh, yeh, was a time all you had to do was rinse a
little blood off the ol' hands, rub a little guilt off the ol' self-esteem,
sweep a few dustballs out of the closet . . .

DUCKY: They get the picture, Ki.

KI: Ain't nothing these days compared to the way things used to be,
remember, Ducky? Who do you like?

ARTSY: This is getting weird. What just happened? I'm leaving.

DUCKY: Let's go with that angry one. Get the fire out of the way first.

KI: Anger. That's good, Ducky. Yes, fire, heat, burning anger. What
you so mad about, Artsy?

ARTSY: That's it, I'm out of here!

(Artsy *walks out the door; he immediately turns back in.*)

MABLE: What is it, Artsy?

ARTSY: It's pitch black out there. There's no street, no sidewalk, no cars
or buildings, there's nothing. Nothing—

*(The lights dim; we hear a distant howl, blackout.)*

End of Act 1[27]

# Interview with a Midwife

CAROL CORNELIUS, ONEIDA/MAHICAN;
AND KATSI COOK, MOHAWK

*In her full-length treatment, Carol Cornelius explores the full expression of one aspect of Haudenosaunee culture, that of corn. In* Iroquois Corn in a Culture-Based Curriculum: A Framework for Respectfully Teaching about Cultures, *Dr. Cornelius explores the interaction of corn and culture and presents research and curricula suggestions for teaching about a Native worldview in K–12 classrooms. As an appendix to her articulate and insightful text, she interviews Katsi Cook, a Mohawk and midwife, who discusses the significance of corn in the Haudenosaunee world. The Oneida and Mohawk are original members of the Five Nations Confederacy or Haudenosaunee, also known as the Iroquois Confederacy.*

CAROL: I'd like to talk with you about an article for young people called "Corn in My Kitchen."

KATSI: The best way to present corn to the young people is to have them look at some of the material culture related to the corn. I think, at least for me, I never really understood the corn until I started planting it and growing it and looking for the metaphors and analogies of it in the culture. Even in the corn washing basket making, how the weave is, a basket maker would probably be better at talking about it than I am, the one back home who makes it. The weave is of course to help get the hull off the kernel, but the corn washing basket itself is to me an interesting aspect of corn culture.

I guess as a midwife, I really never had the depth of understanding before about traditional roles of Iroquois women until I grew corn. And I never understood some of the depth of understanding of knowledge of science in traditional societies. That the moment you begin to work with corn, even just in harvesting, everybody picks an ear and pulls back the husk. It's like seeing a brand new baby the way everybody reacts. "Look at this one, here's one red kernel among all white."

It's an interesting education in genetics. I know John Mohawk used to say that the power of the Iroquois women came through their control of agriculture—that the fields came under the domain of the women. When you grow a field of corn you get a sense of that. He said that the women controlled the sexual economy of the village because they decided who would mate, who the couples would be that produced children; even though that may sound a little cold and calculating in a society that's overdosed with notions of romantic love. It was very interesting because when you read the Jesuit journals and early explorers into the continent, they all talk about how healthy Native People were, how strong they were, how resistant to infection. When I went to the Smithsonian to research traditional childbearing, I read stories from all over the continent, and army surgeons who had gone out into the Indian communities were amazed at the resistance to infection that Native women had. There are stories in Northern Canada of a husband and his wife being out in the bush and there being problems with the delivery and a cesarean was performed and the woman survived. I believe this was due to the resistance to infection. When you look at what it would involve, I can see where there would be survival rate[s] from cesarean hundreds of years ago before it ever became part of western medicine.

So the strength of women is an overwhelming theme you read in any history of Native women and I believe it goes back to the corn. Even in looking at midwifery, one of the things we hear in oral stories is that if there was any problem with the baby the Grandmother would take that child home with her. It was up to her to decide that child's future. If the child wasn't able to survive physically in that society the child would be put to death, or allowed to die. An infant will die in a relatively short time if it's not nurtured. It's almost an animalistic thing, and birth is an animalistic thing. I think the women got their sense of how to do this, or their strength to do it because they were in control of the genetics of the community, if in fact they were the ones who controlled the sexual economy. They wouldn't allow marriage for individuals who had obvious deformities, and in the same way the selection of the seed was in choosing characteristics they wanted to reproduce.

I got a lot more sense of our culture in working with corn. The notion of "corn in my kitchen" is a really wonderful one because it brings home to us something that is very complex and in every part of our lives, our spiritual lives, even our emotional lives. One of my favorite teachings about the corn is, that corn is where we learn midwifery. You see corn at birth, at puberty, as a symbol of fertility, reproduction, abundance. So corn has a great deal of meaning. On an emotional and spiritual level corn also has great meaning. We know this because the short-eared corn has kernels covering the nose. The middle one of that is used for the survival of the infant if the mother has died in childbirth. It's ground up in water and fed to the baby to remind the baby even though it's lost its mother, it still has its mother the corn. That babies when they are born, the powder that was used, it wasn't Johnson and Johnson, it was ground up white corn and the baby was cleansed with that after birth. I think that's what they did instead of bathing the child in water although the two are not contradictory.

So corn goes into every facet of our lives once you really begin to look at it. I guess what I realized in getting involved in the cycle of the corn, the blessing of the seed, the preparation of the field, the ceremonies during the corns' gestation, and the harvest and storage and care of the seed is that this is reproduction, this is pregnancy, this is the metaphor, all the ceremonies, all the songs, everything we do is what we're supposed to do at birth. Raising corn is where we learn midwifery. So the same knowledge is applied. The corn's gestation, for example, and Jorge Quintana gives a really good talk about this, the similarities between the gestation of the corn and human gestation. It's a shortened time period for the corn, but some of the same growth factors are there. Instead of a nine-month gestation, it's a three-month growth period. Look at the corn's reproduction; the fallopian tube of the woman or the seminal vesicle is analogous to the corn silk that directs pollen to where the kernel grows. The corn silk is used in pregnancy to help prevent or deal with bladder infections, which happen to be one of those things that plague pregnant women because hormones influence their tubes from the kidney to the bladder. Every part of the corn was used as medicine.

A traditional Mayan priest was the one who gave me a deeper understanding of the relationship of the gestational cycle of the corn to that of women and of a community. He said when you go to plant a field of corn you ask the permission of the insects and all the life in that particular field because you're going to be destroying some of that to make way for corn to grow. In the same way, a couple that wants to have a baby should make that same preparation or plea to the spirit world to assist them in their endeavor to bring a new life from the spirit world to this world and to help them in the growth of that.

The green corn dance, those ceremonies that are done during the corn's growth cycle are also analogous to ceremonies that need to be done during a woman's pregnancy. There are ceremonies that should be done in each trimester, each growth cycle of the fetus. It may differ with each woman, but the themes are the same. To connect her with a nurturing elder, and the corn certainly teaches us nurturing and that's where it becomes even an emotional teaching for us. So the permission is asked to create the field. The relationship between the corn, beans, and squash, the Three Sisters, the companionship, again, a nurturing relationship is what helps the corn to grow. Then the ceremonies during its growth and then at harvest time.

The story of the corn is one of my favorite stories that I think "Corn in My Kitchen" should include and that Roderico told us. He said when a new baby is born the people in the home are supposed to be very happy and people are supposed to talk to each other like you want the baby to talk. Teach the new baby by your actions. In a home where there's a new baby you don't want any loud noises or angry people or bad vibes, the same, he said, is with the corn because people used to hang it in their homes. They didn't have barns like we do now. They would store the corn in caches in different places in nature, but it made sense to keep some of it hanging from the rafters in the kitchen. People in Mexico still do that. They have way of saying, well, three ears of corn a day for each person in the family, and they'll hang that many ears from their rafters. They said when that corn is hanging in your kitchen it's the same as when there's a baby in the house. You have to talk nice to each other. You have to be respectful of one another. You can't use any angry language or bad words because the corn can hear you. If it hears all this negativity it won't grow for you the next year.

I think that kind of metaphor between the corn and the children is very important, [although] certainly in the absence of corn and babies, everyone should strive to have peace in their homes. That's what we all need, to be nurtured. Again that theme of nurturing in pregnancy, in the family, and in the growth of the corn is something that corn teaches us. It teaches us how to take care of each other. No wonder they say return to the arms of mother corn, corn is our mother in the same ways that the earth is our mother, but it's more immediately so our mother because that's what feeds us. We actually take it into our bodies, so corn is a very important thing. I believe in raising a traditional family, a family that has values of closeness, or nurturing each other because through the physical activity of doing something, you learn. You don't learn just by being told to do this. You learn by doing it. Sometimes only the physical experience of something—they say See One, Do One, Teach One, and that's the basis of empirical training. I think corn really does teach us in many ways. Again, the spiritual, emotional, and physical.

So "Corn in My Kitchen"—I'd like to see focus on preparing the corn because it is an involved project, but it gets you out in nature. It makes you have to look for the hardwood ashes that release those amino acids from the hull so it can be used by the body. Corn is a great teacher in just the chemistry of food. You have to know how to use the corn. Luckily for me there are simple ways to use the corn without having to go to all the bother of washing it. It's very time consuming and I don't always get to wash corn. My favorite is corn mush, roasting the corn in the pan and sitting there sorting the corn and the conversations that go on when you are able to do that. To take time out to create the foods that corn provides is a time-consuming thing, but there's much more value in it than opening up a box of pizza, that's for sure. . . .

CAROL: I've heard people complaining about raccoons when they plant only five or six rows.

KATSI: You don't have to worry about raccoons when you've got three or four acres; they can have their share.

CAROL: That's what I thought, if you plant five or six rows, you've planted enough for the raccoons. If you plant twenty rows, you have five rows for them and fifteen rows for your family. I've seen mild-mannered people who would turn into vicious killers if they could get hold of that raccoon! I think it's a loss of that understanding that we have to plant enough so the animals have their share. I learned that from picking corn. If you pick in the first five rows you don't get much, but if you pick in the middle you get a lot of corn, there's good corn in there. That thrill of discovery when you husk an ear. Do you know of anyone who still plants in hills?

KATSI: Because of machinery, if there's a lot of corn, an acre or more, nobody plants in hills, I think the women should keep it up to express that relationship with the corn, beans, and squash, the Three Sisters. Most of us have sisters, if not actual biological sisters, we have women whom we relate to. I think that's a very woman-oriented part of our culture and there should be Three Sisters gardens planted by the women just for that purpose. The squash could have more of a ceremonial purpose, the gourd squash used for rattles; those are part of the Iroquois culture that needs to be revived. I imagine they would use those gourd rattles when they would sing to the women in her menses, in the moon lodge, separate from the village. Different aunties or grandmothers would go sing songs to her and talk with her so that by the time she was ready to become a wife and a mother she already knew about her sexuality and taking care of babies. Not only from her experience as a young woman taking care of children, but the women would instruct her, explaining what you do. There were a lot of instructions necessary because back then abstinence was a traditional part of sexuality. When a woman had a baby or was menstruating, she wasn't around men. You have a real strong sense of women's culture, not like the feminists talk about, it wasn't anti-man, it was very nurturing of the individual woman because by being nurtured you learn how to nurture. That's the biggest lesson Native Women have to share with other women: that we need to nurture one another.

CAROL: I like the way Roderico explained that in his article, that just as the earth rests after harvest, a woman has to rest after giving birth.[28]

6

# Literature of the Stockbridge-Munsee Band of Mohican

# 6.1

# Traditional Teachings

HENDRICK AUPAUMUT, MOHICAN

*A Mohican (Mahican) chief from the Mahicanituk (now called the Hudson River in New York State), Hendrick Aupaumut taught traditional values. When he delivered this teaching, he was Congressional Christian missionary John Sergeant's assistant.*

Our ancestors, before they ever enjoyed Gospel revelation, acknowledged one Supreme Being who dwells above, whom they styled Waun-Theet Mon-nit-toow, or the Great, Good Spirit, the author of all things in heaven and on earth, and [who] governs all events. He is good to all his creatures. They also believed that there is an evil one, called Mton-toow or Wicked Spirit that loves altogether to do mischief, that he excites a person or persons to tell a lie [or to be] angry, fight, hate, steal, to commit murder, and to be envious, malicious, and evil-talking. [The Wicked Spirit] also excites nations to war with one another, to violate their friendship that the Great, Good Spirit [has] given them to maintain for their mutual good, and their children after them.

In order to please the Great, Good Spirit that they acknowledged to be their dependence, and on the other hand to withstand the evil one—therefore, the following custom was observed, which was handed down to them by their forefathers, and communicated to them by Good Spirit.

The head of each family—man or woman—would begin with all tenderness, as soon as daylight, to waken up their children and teach them, as follows:

> My children—you must remember that it is by the goodness of the Great, Good Spirit we are preserved through the night. My children you must listen to my words. If you wish to see many good days and evenings you must love all men, and be kind to all people.
>
> If you see any that are in distress, you must try to help them. Remember that you will also be in distress some time or other. If you see one hungry you must give him something to eat: though you should have but little cake, give him half of it, for you also [are] liable to hunger. If you see one naked, you must cover him with your own raiment. For you must consider that some future time you will also stand in need of such help; but if you will not assist, or have compassion for the poor, you will

displease the Good Spirit; you will be called *uh-wu-theet,* or hard-hearted, and nobody will pity you the time of your distress, but will mock at you.

My little children, if you see an aged man or woman on your way doing something, you must pity them, and help them instantly. In so doing, you will make their hearts glad, and they will speak well of you. And further, if you see your neighbors quarreling, you must try to make them to be good friends again. And you must always listen to the instruction of old folks: thereby you will be wise. And you must not be hasty to speak, when you hear people talking, nor allow yourself too much laughing. And if you find any that will speak evil against you, you must not speak evil words back, but shut your ears and mouth as though you hear nothing, and shun such people. And you must never quarrel with any person for quarreling belongs to evil spirit, and beast. But live in peace with all people: thereby you will please the Great, Good Spirit, and you will be happy.

My little children—you must be very kind to strangers. If you see [a] stranger or strangers come by the side of your fireplace, you must salute them, and take them by the hand, and be friendly to them; because you will be a stranger some time or other. You must never speak any harsh words to strangers, but use them well as you can; thereby they will love you and will speak well of you wherever they be; and if you ever come into a strange country you will meet with such kindness. But if you will not be friendly to such, you will be in danger wherever you go.

My children—again listen. You must be honest in all your ways. You must always speak nothing but the truth wherever you are. But if you should love to tell a lie, everybody will take notice of it; thereby you will bring a bad name to yourself. For instance—whenever people shall see you walking, they will say one to another with scorn, and point at you, "Look at that liar!" and even when you should bring tiding of importance with the truth, they shall not regard what you say.

My children—you must never steal anything from your fellow men, for remember this—you will not be pleased if some of your neighbors should take away your things by way of stealing; and you must also remember that the Great, Good Spirit sees you. But if you will allow yourself to steal, you will hurt your name and disgrace your parents and all relations; and you will be despised by all good people.

My children—you must always avoid bad company. And above all, you must never commit murder, because you wish to see long life. But if you commit murder, the Great, Good Spirit will be angry with you, and your life will be in great danger; also the life of your dear relations.

My children—you must be very industrious. You must always get up early morning to put on your clothes, *muk-sens* [moccasins], and tie your belt about you, that you may be ready to do something; by so doing you will always have something to eat and to put on. But if you will be lazy, you will be always poor. Your eyes shall be on those who are industrious, and perhaps you will be shamefully begging or stealing; and none will give you anything to eat without grudging.

And further, my children—when you are grown up, you must not take wife or husband without the consent of your parents and all relations. But if you will do contrary to this, perhaps you will be joined to one who will bring great darkness to you, and thereby you will be very unhappy. . . ."

Thus they inculcate instruction to their children day after day until they are grown up; and after they are grown, yet they would teach them occasionally. And when young people have children they also teach theirs in like manner. This custom is handed down from generation to another; at the same time it may be observed that there were some that did not take pains to instruct their children, but would set bad examples before them, as well as there are such among civilized nations. But such men were roving about, and could not be contented to stay at one place.[1]

# 6.2

# Mama's Little One

KRISTINA HEATH POTRYKUS,
MOHICAN AND MENOMINEE

*A contemporary storyteller has adapted Hendrick Aupaumut's words to create a beautiful little book appropriate for early grade school students. Originally a term project in a Mohican history course taught by Professor David Wrone of the University of Wisconsin–Stevens Point,* Mama's Little One *is illustrated by the author. Kristina Heath Potrykus is a member of the Woodland Writers, a group of Native writers of children's books. Her family moved to the Mohican Indian Reservation when she was three, and she has lived there ever since. This excerpt from the book begins with the child asking his mother (Guka) a question.*

Why do I have to help Mah ose [Grandfather], Guka?

Mah ose is old and not as strong as he used to be. One day you will be old, too. You will want a young boy to help you.

What if I tell Mah ose that my arm hurts and I cannot help him today?

Then you would not be telling the truth. If you do not always tell the truth, people will not believe you and think that you are lying, even when you do speak the truth. So, Little One, you must always tell the truth.

Guka?

Yes, Little One.

Why must I do so many things today?

Because if you wake up early each morning and work hard, you will have food so you can grow big and strong. You will also have clothes to keep you nice and warm. So, Little One, you must always work hard.

Then I can go play when I'm done?

Yes, you can.

Now listen, Little One. If you see anybody today who needs help, you must help them. For there will come a time when you, too, will need help.

You mean if I helped them, then they would help me?

Yes that's right. Little One, remember that you must not fight with any of your friends today. Be kind to them all. You will please the Great, Good Spirit in this way. Can you do this Little One?

Yes, I think so.

Now get dressed and go join your Noh [father]. He will be pleased to see that you are up so early.

I think that I will enjoy this day, Guka.

You will, Little One. By showing love, compassion, and kindness to all people, you will enjoy many, many days.

I love you, Guka.

And I love you, Little One.[2]

# 6.3

# Ancestral Voices

CATHY J. CALDWELL,
STOCKBRIDGE-MUNSEE BAND OF MOHICAN

*In this poem written in June 1995, Cathy Caldwell meditates on the messages painted and carved on rocks, recognizing them as "ancestral voices." She has taught every grade level from kindergarten to college and is working on her doctoral degree from the University of Wisconsin–Madison.*

### ANCESTRAL VOICES

Only here,
In this world of pigments,
      painting and carvings,
Can the serpent be found
      engraved in smooth rock,
      guarding the waters of Lake Huron;

And the animal spirits
      bristle, leap and stare
      from the boulders,
      frozen against the canyons
      and sacred shorelines of time.

And it is here
      that the *Man-Who-Fell-From-The-Sky*
      lies forever as a shadow
      embedded in stone at the edge of an ocean.

Here a red ochre hunter
      stands poised forever with his bow
      aimed at a multi-tined moose
      in a granite world,

And the warriors ride into battle
      on thin-legged horses

power shields held high,
as fixed figures in combat and courage.

I am intrigued by this rock art,
        these images from the past,
        these signs of life from long ago—
        that challenge our scientists to search
        for answers and explanations . . .

But science has no words to explain
        our woodland spirits,
        our prairie dreams
        our mystic human endurance—
        our painted visions on the stone.[3]

# 6.4

# Historical Overview

DOROTHY W. DAVIDS,
STOCKBRIDGE-MUNSEE BAND OF MOHICAN

*Dorothy W. Davids is chair of the Stockbridge-Munsee Historical Committee. Holding a master's degree from the University of Wisconsin–Milwaukee, she is active in education and, with Dr. Ruth Gudinas, runs Full Circle: Education for a Diverse Society, which hosts retreats for educators and evaluates books for inclusion in their stock of appropriate Native American literature for children and adults.[4] In this selection, Ms. Davids briefly recaps the history of the Mohican Nation, Stockbridge-Munsee Band. They call themselves "Muh-he-con-ne-ok," or "People of the Waters That Are Never Still."*

The history of the Stockbridge-Munsee people is punctuated by repeated migrations and removals. Tradition says that originally a great mass of people moved from the north and west seeking a place where the waters were never still. They established a homeland on both sides of the Mahicanituk (later called Hudson's) River. The earliest known contact between these "Mahican" people and Europeans was with Dutch fur traders in the early seventeenth century. In 1734, the Mahicans agreed to let Protestant missionaries come among them; the missionaries were followed by teachers, farmers, and other colonials. A church and a school were built, and a village named Stockbridge, Massachusetts, grew up around them. The Christian Mahicans who lived there became known as Stockbridge Indians.

Stockbridge Indians fought on the side of the Americans in the Revolutionary War, but by war's end they found that their land titles were not recognized by the new federal government. They were landless. They moved west to lands in New York State provided them by the Oneida tribe, another largely Christian group that had fought against the British. During the following 150 years, the Stockbridge people were forced to move from New York to Indiana and later to several places in Wisconsin, where some Munsee Delaware families joined them. These removals and disruptions created insecurity and tensions that still affect the people today. Resisting removal west of the Mississippi River, the Stockbridge-Munsee moved to a reservation in Shawano County, Wisconsin, in 1856. By 1920, the distribution of their lands dictated

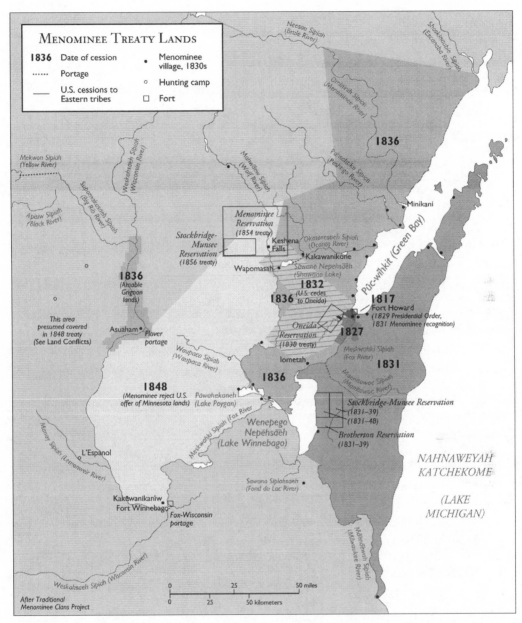

**MENOMINEE TREATY LANDS**

| | | | |
|---|---|---|---|
| **1836** | Date of cession | • | Menominee village, 1830s |
| ...... | Portage | ○ | Hunting camp |
| ⎯⎯ | U.S. cessions to Eastern tribes | □ | Fort |

*Neesow Sipiah (Brûle River)*

*Shahnuhe Sipiah (Escanaba River)*

**1836**

*Orainiah Sipiah (Menominee River)*

*Mahwdowsh Sipiah (Wolf River)*

*Peisehtkin Sipiah (Peshtigo River)*

• Minikani

*Mekwon Sipiah (Yellow River)*

*Weskohseeh Sipiah (Wisconsin River)*

*Saponokocoyoh Sipiah (Big Rib River)*

*Apeiw Sipiah (Black River)*

*Menominee Reservation (1854 treaty)*

○

**1836**
*(Amable Grignon lands)*

*Stockbridge-Munsee Reservation (1856 treaty)*

Keshena Falls •

• Kakawanikone

**1832**
*(U.S. cedes to Oneida)*

**1817**
Fort Howard □
*(1829 Presidential Order, 1831 Menominee recognition)*

*Pûc-wihkit (Green Bay)*

*Okatosesaeh Sipiah (Oconto River)*

*Sawano Nepehsaeh (Shawano Lake)*

Wapomasah •

**1836**
*(U.S. cedes to Oneida)*

○

This area presumed covered in 1848 treaty *(See Land Conflicts)*

Asuaham • Plover portage

*Woupaco Sipiah (Waupaca River)*

○

*Oneida Reservation (1838 treaty)*

**1827**

*Meshwohki Sipiah (Fox River)*

**1831**

Iometah •

**1836**

*Mahnatowoc Sipiah (Manitowoc River)*

**1848**
*(Menominee reject U.S. offer of Minnesota lands)*

*Manoy Sipiah (Lemonwier River)*

L'Espanol •

*Pawahekaneh (Lake Poygan)*

*Stockbridge-Munsee Reservation (1831–39) (1831–48)*

*Wenepego Nepehsaeh (Lake Winnebago)*

*Brothertown Reservation (1831–39)*

*NAHNAWEYAH KATCHEKOME*

*(LAKE MICHIGAN)*

*Meshwohki Sipiah (Fox River)*

*Sawano Sipiohsaeh (Fond du Lac River)*

Kakewanikaniw Fort Winnebago □

Fox-Wisconsin portage

*Mahnedawh Sipiah (Milwaukee River)*

*Weskohsaeh Sipiah (Wisconsin River)*

| 0 | 25 | 50 miles |
|---|---|---|
| 0 | 25 | 50 kilometers |

*After Traditional Menominee Clans Project*

Menominee territory extended for ten million acres from the Escanaba River in Michigan south to Chicago and west to the Wisconsin River. Forced to cede their territory first along the important Green Bay–Fox River trade route, the Menominee's ancestral land rights were terminated in 1848, the year the State of Wisconsin was established. Refusing to move from their homeland, the Menominee were given title to a reservation around the Wolf River that was ¹⁄₃₉th the size of their original territory. Chief Oshkosh's village was established at Keshena Falls. In 1831 the Menominee ceded territory for the Stockbridge-Munsee Reservation. The Brothertown acquired a reservation east of Lake Winnebago in the same year, but lost it in 1839, although some Brothertowners remained in the area. The Brothertown are attempting to regain federal recognition. Map by Zoltan Grossman; reproduced by permission from Wisconsin Cartographers' Guild, *Wisconsin's Past and Present* (Madison: University of Wisconsin Press, 1998), 7.

by the terms of the General Allotment Act again rendered the group landless and destitute.

In 1934 the Indian Reorganization Act gave the Stockbridge-Munsee an opportunity to re-form into a tribal entity. Carl Miller provided the leadership for this tribal rebirth. The new tribe acquired approximately fifteen thousand acres of submarginal timberland and began establishing a tribal presence on the new reservation.[5]

# We Have No More Land

MOHICAN HEADMEN

---

*The forced removal of Mohicans from the eastern seaboard was a policy of the state of New York that violated treaties made during the Revolutionary War. This manipulation is evident in the following exchange between the governor and the Mohican people. Historian Colin Calloway writes: "In late August 1722, William Burnet, governor of New York, met with Mahican [Dutch name for the Mohican] Indians from the Hudson River to renew the Covenant Chain, the metaphor of friendship between the king of England and the Indians. In his opening remarks, the governor admonished the Mahicans for squandering their pelts and corn to buy rum and advised them to be more sober in the future."[6] The polite—but incisive—reply by the Mohicans reveals the underlying dynamic.*

Father, we are sensible that you are much in the right, that rum does a great deal of harm; we approve of all you said on that point. But the matter is this: when our people come from hunting to the town or plantations and acquaint the traders & people that we want powder and shot & clothing, they first give us a large cup of rum. After we get the taste of it, [we] crave for more so that in [time] all the beaver & peltry we have hunted goes for drink, and we are left destitute either of clothing or ammunition. Therefore we desire our father to order the tap or crane to be shut and to prohibit the selling of rum, for as long as the Christians will sell rum, our people will drink it.

Father, we acknowledge that our father is very much in the right to tell us that we squander away our Indian corn that should subsist our wives & children. But one great cause of it is that many of our people are obliged to hire land of the Christians at a very dear rate, to give half the corn for rent, and the other half they are tempted by rum to sell, and so the corn goes [so] that the poor women & children are left to shift as well as they can.

Father, we have no more land. The Christians, when they buy a small spot of land of us, ask us if we have no more land & when we say yes, they inquire the name of the land & take in a greater bounds than was intended to be sold them, [while] the Indians, not understanding what is writ in the deed or bill of sale, sign it and are so deprived of part of their lands.

In former days when the Christians came to settle this country, they came with a ship & desired to fasten their cable to the hills near Hosak above Albany, which we readily granted. And ever since we have lived in friendship and amity together, which we hope will continue so long as sun and moon endure.[7]

# That Our Children Not Be Taken Away from Us for Debt

CHIEF KONKAPOT, MOHICAN

*Their numbers reduced by devastating diseases and responding to intense pressure on their land, the Housatonic tribe of Mohicans met with Governor Jonathan Belcher of Massachusetts in 1735 to request that a Christian missionary be sent to them. Even though many Mohicans were doubtful that Christianity would be beneficial, Chief Konkapot hoped that conversion would save his people from destruction. In the address below, Konkapot expresses fear that his people would be subject to imprisonment or indentured servitude for debt, a colonial practice. His use of relationship terms, such as "father," was standard in Indian diplomacy, indicating that the speaker was entering into kinship with those addressed. However, this custom was misinterpreted by colonialists as submission to their authority.[8]*

We thank your Excellency as our father, that we have received your kindness and love, and we would express our duty and subjection to our rightful sovereign King George whom we pray God long to preserve.

We are desirous to receive the gospel of our Lord Jesus Christ, and hope that our hearts are in what we say, and that we don't speak only out of our lips. And we are thankful that Mr. Williams and other ministers are come to us, and especially that Mr. Sergeant and Mr. Woodbridge have been sent to us, and pray to the great God to keep them and cause they may have health, and live long with us.

And sir, our father, we did not come to you of ourselves and tell you that we wanted any thing, and yet you have taken care of us as your children, and given us learning, &c. No child says to this father, "I would have so and so," but a father when he sees his children in want, is ready to help them. And so we think [of] your Excellency as our father [who] is willing to do to us upon every account.

Sir, our father, our children are afraid of strict laws and of being brought into trouble and put in prison for debt, &c, and we pray that care may be taken by your Excellency as our father and by the General Assembly, that we be not hurt by the severity of the laws, seeing we don't understand how to manage in such affairs, so as that there may not be any danger at any time that our children be taken away from us for debt, &c.

We don't pretend to desire any thing but that if any of our people should commit murder or any other crying wickedness, they should be liable to the law.

Sir, our father, we are concerned for our own children as we think you, as a father, are for us, and therefore we pray that it may be given us in writing (or established by a law) that our children after us be not wronged or injured.[9]

# 6.7

# Watching My Daughter Sleep

CATHY J. CALDWELL,
STOCKBRIDGE-MUNSEE BAND OF MOHICAN

*The concern for children that Konkapot expressed centuries ago is echoed in a mother's calm watchfulness in this poem.*

WATCHING MY DAUGHTER SLEEP
The hour's not lost,
I'm watching it for you.
Each second, each sigh
I count in years
And you do not change;

Except in pictures
gathered through time.

If I could capture the innocence in your breath,
your perfect dreamless quiet,
the softness in your face,
I would not need to sleep myself,
or feel melancholy
for the eyes that will open soon.[10]

# 6.8

# Not Tyrants over Any Nation

HENDRICK AUPAUMUT, MOHICAN

*After describing the Mohican nation as having the "best warriors in the field," Hendrick Au-
paumut, chief sachem of the Stockbridge Mohicans, describes their ability as peacemakers,
who rely on kinship relationships—treating everyone as a relative—as the basis for peace.*

Our forefathers [were] also distinguished in peaceableness, whereby they
had allies, even the remotest nations. According to the ancient custom many
of these nations made renewal covenants with us that their forefathers and
ours had made, with belts and strings of wampum. Some of the belts and
strings are now in our possession. The friendships which our forefathers had
between different nations were denominated after the manner of common
relations.

According to the ancient covenant of our ancestors, the Delaware nation
are our *Grandfathers*. And the Shawnee nation, when they were ready to be de-
voured by their enemies, the different nations, they sent runners to Muh-hu-
con-nuk for help. Then our forefathers went to stand between the Shawnee
and the different tribes, to act as mediators, and to defend them. They res-
cued them from under the jaws of their enemies. The Shawnee nation then
called the Muh-hu-con-nuk nation to be their Elder Brothers, and promised
obedience to them, which they still acknowledged to this day; and they are
our Younger Brothers, or Nkheeth-mon nauk. Our forefathers then removed
the Shawnee nation from their native country, and brought them as far as
Mkhau-wau-muk. There they left them under the care of the Delaware nation, their Grandfather.

Wmau-weew, or Miami nation, formerly had war with our nation, and
when they were conquered they obliged to sue [for] peace. When peace was
established, they entered into a covenant of friendship with our nation, and
kindle fire for them at Kekioke, near the head of the Miami river, which emp-
ties into Lake Erie, and voluntarily given them a large tract of land wherein
they desired them to live, and to be their head.

[The Miami] offered obedience to them as grandchildren ordinarily obey
their grandfathers. But as our forefathers loved not superiority over their fellow

Indians, or using authority as tyrants over any nation, they only accepted the present given to them out of friendship, remembering that it may in time to come, that our children on some occasion or others would come and live there.

From that time on the tract of land has been reserved for our nation to this day, and that covenant had been renewed at different times, and a number of our nation lived on that land these several years past to this day. Therefore the Miami nation are our Grandchildren to this day, and also their allies, to wit, Ottawa nation, Chippewa Nation, Mesquakie, Potawatomi . . . Kickapoo. . . . All these nations ever acknowledged this friendship; whenever they met any of our people they call them Muh-so-mis, or Grandfathers.[11]

# 6.9

# Hunting Now Is Grown Very Scarce

STOCKBRIDGE HEADMEN

*Somehow Mohican land was said to belong to the King of England, even though he had not paid the Stockbridge Indians for it. In clear oratory at the Albany Congress of 1754, the Stockbridge speakers clarify the issue.*

When the white people purchased [land] from time to time of us, they said they only wanted to purchase the low lands. They told us the hilly land was good for nothing, and that it was full of wood and stones. But now we see people living all about the hills and woods, although they have not purchased the lands.

When we enquire of the people who live on the lands what right they have to them, they reply to us that we are not to be regarded, and that these lands belong to the king. But we were the first possessors of them, and when the King has paid us for them, then they may say they are his. Hunting now is grown very scarce, and we are not like[ly] to get our livings that way. Therefore we hope our Fathers will take care that we are paid for our lands, that we may live.[12]

# Return to Me That Land
# That Is Justly Mine

JOHANNIS MTOHKSIN, JACOB NAUNAUPHTAUNK,
AND SOLOMON UHHAUNAUWAUNMUT;
STOCKBRIDGE

*In 1782 a group of Christian Delaware Indians, who had invited the Stockbridge Indians to join them, were massacred by frontiersmen in Gnadenhutten, Ohio. This shocking news added to the injustice the Stockbridge felt after losing their chief, Nimham, and returning from their fighting for the colonists in the American Revolution, to find that their homes and lands had been taken by settlers.*

*On February 8, 1782, the three sons of a tribal chief wrote a letter to the New York General Assembly and Governor George Clinton.*

Brothers, wise men! Attend. When you first came over the great water to this, our Island, you were small; I was great. I then had a fullness of food and clothing. I then was happy and contented. The sands and waters of this river, which you now possess, were mine, that is those on the east side of it. Here I got my food and clothing. You being then smaller, I invited you to sit down with me, and provide for yourself, your women and children. This you did. We were happy in each other, your enemies were my enemies, your friends were my friends. Where you bled by the hatchet of your enemies, there I bled also, for you and your friends. Where your fathers died in battle, my fathers died by their side. The waters of Lake George and Champlain, the hills about Boston and New York bear witness to this. The last time you took up the hatchet against the French King, I went out with you with my hatchet; there I was with all my warriors many years.

The rewards for this service given to your warriors in land were not given to mine. When I returned I found my hunting grounds ruined. You get food and clothing by tilling the earth; I, by killing wild beast on my ancient hunting ground. They can now find no hiding places. You till it all. Some land my fathers told me they had given to you; much they told me they had not given to you. What they gave you not is still mine by the customs and laws of all nations.

The Great Spirit gave my fathers this that he has not taken away by conquest, and I or my fathers have not alienated either by gift or sale, is certainly in the view of that Spirit, mine still.

This I related to my brothers the Bostonians who had also in their possession some of my land. They acknowledge my rights, and gave me full compensation. My claims are from Hudson's River, Wood Creek and Lake Champlain to the mouth of Otter Creek on the north eastward.

Now Brethren; wise men; attend. You once were small, very small. I then was great at that time. I took you under my arm, and helped you. I am now become small, very small. You are become great, very great, you reach into the clouds. You are seen all over the world. I am now not as high as your ankles. I now look to you for help. I am weak through hunger and cold, through want of food and clothing. My women groan and lament, and tears are in the eyes of all my children.

Brother! What I ask is that you resign to me that land, which is justly mine, which I have neither sold or given to you; or give me its value, that I may get food and clothing for myself, my women and children and be happy with you as formerly. Remember too, that by this you will not leave room for lying birds to say that you neglect to do me justice because you are strong. Brothers should you give me anything, let it be given in such a manner that men of evil minds may not deprive me, who am weak, of it unjustly![13]

# 6.11

## Former Concentration Camp and Cemetery: Now a Recreation Area?

### MUHHECONNEUK INTERTRIBAL COMMITTEE ON DEER ISLAND

*After King Philip's War, the New Englanders forced about five hundred Indians into a concentration camp on Deer Island, a peninsula in Boston Harbor. The ghosts of this time still linger in a conflict over this land, which contains a cemetery that was part of the internment camp.*

[We] oppose the adoption of the recently proposed Boston Harbor Island National Park General Management Plan. . . . The proposed park is in violation of federal law, the planning process carried out by the Boston office of the National Park Service was discriminatory and downplays and ignore[s] the uses of these islands as concentration camps for Indians and the legacy of institutional racism that developed out of that history.[14]

# 6.12

# Thanksgiving

DOROTHY W. DAVIDS,
STOCKBRIDGE-MUNSEE BAND OF MOHICAN

*With incisive and ironic wit, Dorothy W. Davids, chair of the Stockbridge-Munsee Historical Committee, describes the Native response to the Puritans aboard the* Mayflower.

A LAST WORD: A COMMEMORATION
It was the Moon of the Long Night
    The Moon of the Popping Trees,
    The Winter Time
        350 years ago.

Off the "stern and rockbound" New England coast
    was moored a ship,
    a miserably small, secondhand vessel,
        a Mayflower, which for weeks and weeks
    had been home to a handful, perhaps a hundred,
        freedom-hungry people.

And Lo! the Wampanoag saw their plight, the Pilgrims' Plight
    —they were tossed about and tired,
    —they lacked housing; they had no jobs,
    —they lacked knowledge and skill
        needed for winter survival;

They obviously needed an expanded nutrition program.
And Massassoit, with great compassion said,
    "Surely they are disadvantaged."

A Grand Council was called.
Samoset, sensing that "Those people" were indeed different,
    cautioned the elders about strangers
    and what their coming would do to the neighborhood.

Another Council member saw other dangers,
    "They will become dependent on our handouts
        and not want to work;
    "We will have to give them food all winter;
        and seed for spring planting."
And indeed they did! The Wampanoag cared for them.

So the winter passed prayerfully
        with housing project progressing
    with hunt providing food and fur.
In the spring, they extended their services
    to provide technical assistance
        —on what to plant how,
        —when, and where
        —how to nurture the plants
        —and discern the harvest time.

The Wampanoag women taught them the proper preparation
    of their food.
        After the planting, the growing, the harvesting,
        WAS THE TIME OF THANKSGIVING!

And then. . . . and later. . . .
    and farther . . . deeper . . . more . . . stronger
Until now, 350 years have passed, and Now,
The Wampanoag, the Pequots, the Narragansetts, the Passamaquoddy,
    The United American Indians of New England
        have declared THANKSGIVING DAY to be
    A NATIONAL DAY OF MOURNING FOR NATIVE AMERICANS!
And the Pilgrims are meeting, discussing, planning
    their Indian programs. And so![15]

6.13

# Mohican Diplomat

### HENDRICK AUPAUMUT, MOHICAN

*Hendrick Aupaumut, chief sachem of the Stockbridge Mohicans, was educated by mission-aries and prevented the Stockbridge from converting to the Handsome Lake religion, which "embodie[d] the most profound tenets of the Longhouse beliefs."[16] Aupaumut was commissioned in the Continental Army and worked to encourage peaceful dialogue rather than war. This selection, written around 1794, comes from* A Short Narration of My Last Journey to the Western Contry, *where Aupaumut has met in council with (among others) the Ottawa, Ojibwe, Potawatomi, and Kickapoo.*

As I propose to mention—The complaints or arguments of these Indians, and my arguments to convince them . . . I will now put down:

First principal thing they argue is this—that the white people are deceitful in their dealings with us the Indians; (says they) The white people have taken all our lands from us, from time to time, until this time, and that they will continue the same way, etc. Then I reply and say it has been too much so, because these white people are governed by one law, the law of the great King of England; and by that law they could hold our lands, in spite of our dissatisfaction; and we were too fond of their liquors. But now they have new laws [that are] their own, and by these laws, Indians cannot be deceived as usual, etc. And they say, but these Big Knives [frontiersmen] have taken away our lands since they have their own way. And then I tell them, for this very reason the United Sachems [U.S. leaders] invite you to treat with them that you may settle these difficulties, for how can these difficulties [be] settled without you [to] treat with them?

Another thing they mention: they say, the Big Knives have used learning to civilize Indians: and after they Christianize a number of them so as to gain their attention, then they would kill them, and have killed of such 96 in one day at Cosuhkeck [Coshocton, Ohio], a few years ago.

Another instance they mention—that one of the chiefs of Shawany [Shawnee] was friendly to the Big Knives and Big Knives gave him a flag, that wherever the chief should come across the Big Knives, he is to hoist up this flag; then they will meet together in peace. But soon after this agreement was made, the Big Knives came in the town of this chief. Some of the Indians could not trust the Big Knives and ran off, but the chief had such confidence in the words of the Big Knives, he hoisted up his flag. But the Big Knives did not [respect this], but killed the chief and a number of his friends.

Another instance they mention—that some of the Delawares were with the Big Knives in the service of Americans, but afterward the Big Knives have fallen upon them and have killed a number of them. And since that, every time the Big Knives get ready to come against us, they would send a message to us for peace—then they come to fight us—and they know how to speak good, but would not do good towards Indians.

Then I tell them I am very sorry to hear these things. If the great men of the United States had a [similar] disposition as the Big Knives had, my nation and other Indians in the East would have been long ago annihilated. But they are not so, especially since they have their liberty—they begin with new things, and now they endeavor to lift up the Indians from the ground, that we may stand up and walk ourselves. Because we the Indians, hitherto have lain flat as it were on the ground, by which we could not see a great way. But if we could stand then we could see some distance. The United States, in seeing our situation, they put their hands on us, and led us in the means of life until we could stand and walk as they are. But on the other hand, the British seeing the Indians in their situation, they would just cover them with a blanket and shirt every fall, and the Indians feel themselves warm, and esteem that usage very highly—therefore they remain as it were on the ground and could not see a great way these many years.

And further I told them, the United Sachems [U.S.] will not speak wrong. Whatever they promise to Indians they will perform. Because out of 30,000 men, they chose one man to attend their great Council Fire—and such men must be very honest and wise, and they will do justice to all people. In this way of conversing with them repeatedly, I make them willing to hear further.

Another thing they urge is that the United States could not govern the hostile Big Knives—and that they, the Big Knives, will always have war with the Indians. If the United States could govern them, then the peace could stand sure. But the Big Knives are independent, and if we have peace with them, they would make slaves of us.

Then I told them, the reason the Big Knives are so bad is because they have run away from their own country of different states, because they were very mischievous, such as thieves and robbers and murderers—and their laws are so strict these people could not live there without being often punished. Therefore they run off in this country and become lawless. They have lived such a distance from the United States, that in these several years the law could not reach them because they would run into the woods, and nobody could find them. But at length the people of the United States settle among them, and the law now binds them. If they would endeavor to run in the woods as usual, you would then have a chance to knock their heads and they know this, therefore they oblige to sit still.

And further says I, we the Indians have such people also; for instance, there are Kuttoohwoh, or Cherokees; they could not live among their own people in their own country, because they have strict laws, so that if any one steals, he must be whipped immediately, and if any commit adultery, his ears will be cut off; and if any one murders, he will be instantly killed, etc. In all my arguments with these Indians, I have (as if I were obliged) to say nothing with regard to the conduct of the New Yorkers, how they cheated my fathers, how they have taken our lands unjustly, and how my fathers were groaning as it were to their graves, in losing their lands for nothing, although they were faithful friends to the whites; and how the white people artfully got their deeds confirmed in their laws, etc. I say, had I mentioned these things to the Indians, it would aggravate their prejudices against all white people.[17]

# Daniel Nimham, Mohican Sachem

DOROTHY W. DAVIDS,
STOCKBRIDGE-MUNSEE BAND OF MOHICAN

*During the 1700s, Europeans and colonists sought to take the land from its inhabitants. The right of ownership through occupation was superceded by pieces of paper. In defending his homeland, Daniel Nimham is remembered by Dorothy Davids, a contemporary historian.*

Between 1700 and 1800, European countries battled for control of the land called America. The French and Indian Wars were really conflicts between England and France over territories they had taken from the native people who were recruited to help them fight. The Revolutionary War and the War of 1812 were fought between the American colonists and England. The "Americanized" colonies no longer wanted to be governed by the Mother country. The Stockbridge Mohicans, as well as the Oneida, Tuscarora and other Native warriors, supported the colonists in their revolution. In one battle, the Battle of Van Cortlandt's Woods, a number of Stockbridge Mohicans lost their lives. When the surviving warriors returned home, they discovered that plans had already been made to remove them from Stockbridge.[18]

# 6.15

# Chief Nimham, Hero of
# Van Cortlandt's Woods

EVA JEAN BOWMAN,
STOCKBRIDGE-MUNSEE BAND OF MOHICAN

*Eva Jean Bowman has worked in the field of education since 1974 and, among other honors, was runner-up for Teacher of the Year, chosen by the Wisconsin Head Start Director's Association. Her forty-four-page book has a map, photos, and eighteen beautiful colored-pencil illustrations made by the students of Bowler Elementary School. This selection begins with the author's preface.*

The reason I wrote this story was because I attended a Stockbridge-Munsee history class, and the teacher, Dr. David Wrone, gave a very good account of Daniel Nimham and his Stockbridge warriors. This made me proud to be part of the Stockbridge-Munsee Tribe.

When our tribe lost their homelands in New York, they were forced to move along many trails, finally settling in the Wisconsin area. My grandfather and my great uncle were among the Stockbridge-Munsee people who settled here.

I want our children, as well as non-Native children, to read about one of our relatives—Daniel Nimham, a war chief who died for what he believed in. He is not a forgotten hero in his homeland of New York. But he was almost forgotten in our trail of history because of the removals of our tribe. Today we, as Native people, gather to celebrate and honor our veterans, both men and women, of the past and future.

I hope that, with this story, I can help our children understand their Mohican history and not forget our native heroes.

## Chief Nimham

Many, many years ago, when native people still owned much of the land here, Chief Daniel Nimham was an important native warrior. He was a very wise Wappinger leader.

The Wappingers were a group of Native people related to the Mohicans who lived north of them. The Wappingers lived on land along the southeastern backs of the Muh-he-kun-ne-tuk. Today this is called the Hudson River.

While Daniel Nimham was growing up, people who had come from Europe were looking for land to live on. They were moving into Wappinger and Mohican lands. They were called "colonists."

When Daniel got older, he was called a chief by his people. The colonists, who could see that he was greatly respected by his own people, called him a king. These are both names of great honor given to respected leaders, and Chief Nimham was respected by everyone.

Chief Nimham tried very hard to keep his people's lands from being taken over by colonists. But after he came home from fighting in a war, he found colonists living on the land he and his people had been living on. Even though he was very angry, Chief Nimham decided to get his people's land back through peaceful means.

First, he wrote a long letter to the colonists' leaders telling them that he and his people had a right to their lands. Then he traveled many miles to New York City to try to keep their lands.

Finally he and three Mohican leaders went all the way across the ocean to London, England, to see the English king. But the king was no help. Chief Nimham had to return to this country knowing that he and the other Wappingers would lose their land.

Soon the colonists' governor and his council said that Daniel's people had no right to keep their land because they did not have a deed. A deed is a piece of paper saying that someone owns a piece of land. The colonists used deeds to prove they owned land.

Daniel said that this was not the Indian people's way. Like other Native people, he believed that Mother Earth cannot be owned, divided up, or sold. The Wappingers and their neighbors, the Mohicans, showed respect for Mother Earth by living from what the seasons gave them. They hunted and fished and planted gardens. They gathered plants for medicines and foods. They used only what they needed from Mother Earth, and they took care of her.

But the colonists who had moved onto the Wappinger land said they had a deed. So Chief Nimham lost the land. By this time he had already moved away to Stockbridge to join his family there. This was a village where some Mohicans lived. It was on land that colonists had not yet taken from the Mohican people.

Daniel Nimham was a strong leader. He fought in legal ways to keep his people's land. We could say he was a peaceful warrior. He never stopped believing that he shared Mother Earth with his family and other Native people.

Chief Nimham was also another kind of warrior, one who fights with weapons. He had learned to hunt when he was a young man. He had learned to fight in earlier battles. He also became known as an Elder because he had learned how to live a good life. But he still believed that we often have to fight for what is right. So, as an Elder, he became a leader of some Mohican warriors from Stockbridge. He and his men were called "excellent marksmen" because they had learned to use their weapons so well.

At that time he got a letter from leaders of the colonists. In the letter they asked him and his Stockbridge warriors to fight in the Revolutionary War. This was the colonists' war against the same king whom chief Nimham had gone to see. The colonists felt that the king, far away in England, was taking away their freedoms.

Chief Nimham wrote back: "You have sent for me to fight. If I do, you must let me fight in my own Indian way. Only point out to me where enemies are and that is all I want to know." Chief Ninham was one of the first Indian men who joined the colonists' in their Revolutionary War. He did this because he felt he was still fighting for his people's land. He believed that a deed did not mean that colonists really owned the Native land. He believed that it still belonged to the Wappingers and the Mohicans, and that it was worth fighting for. He was even willing to die for this land.

There were many English troops fighting against the colonists. They were on foot and on horseback. Chief Nimham, his son Abraham, and the other warriors were few, but they were strong men and good fighters. They finally met the English in a place called Van Cortlandt's Woods. These woods were not far from the same lands that Chief Nimham had tried to save for his people years before. He believed that he and his men were still fighting for their lands.

The English troops attacked Chief Nimham and his warriors on three sides. The Mohicans were on foot. The English troops were on horseback, and there were many, many more than the native warriors. As the fierce battle went on, Chief Nimham knew that he and his warriors were going to lose, even though they were fighting very bravely.

The old chief shouted to his men that they should escape. Then he made his last stand. "My time has come," he shouted to his young warriors. "I am an old tree. I will die here." And he did.

Daniel Nimham was a Wappinger elder, warrior, and leader. He died defending the land that he loved—land near the river called the Muh-he-kun-ne-tuk. Chief Nimham was an old man at the time of his death. He was worthy of the name chief. He was a respected leader of his people.[19]

# 6.16

# Conversion

DOROTHY W. DAVIDS,
STOCKBRIDGE-MUNSEE BAND OF MOHICAN

*With half their warriors killed, those returning home found that whites had moved into their homes and had taken over their gardens and fields. Their service to the American Revolution was repaid with theft of their land. Two chiefs requested that missionaries come to teach them English.*

European Christians with missionary zeal also entered native villages for the purpose of converting the people from their traditional spiritual practices to Christianity. Some native people, noting that the Europeans seemed to be prospering in this new land, felt that perhaps the European's God was more powerful, and agreed to be missionized. . . . The lives of the Mohican people were drastically changed by the fur trade, European missionaries, disease and war. All of these worked together to cause a breakdown in their traditional Mohican life and beliefs. Their spiritual ceremonies were replaced by European customs. Fewer and fewer of the people spoke the Mohican language; thus their thought patterns about the natural world were altered. The ancient arts of basket-and pottery-making continued, but other seasonal occupations were abandoned.[20]

# 6.17

## Matrilineage and Democracy

HENDRICK AUPAUMUT, MOHICAN

*Traditionally, women owned property and passed it on in the female line. Descent was also calculated through the maternal line. If parents separated, Mohican women kept the children and the household goods. This orientation changed due to pressures of the switch from horticulture and subsistence hunting to a commodity market and other forces.*

Our ancestors' government was democratic. They had Wi-gow-wauw or Chief Sachems successively, as well as other nations had; [these were] chosen by the nation, [and] whom they looked upon as conductor and promoter of their general welfare. [They] rendered him obedience as long as he behaved himself agreeably in the office of a Sachem. This office was hereditary by the lineage of a female's offspring, but not on the man's line, but on the woman's part. That is, when Wi-gow-wauw is fallen by death, one of his nephews (if he has any) will be appointed to succeed his uncle as a Sachem, and not any of his sons.

The Sachem always has Who-weet-quau-pe-chee, or Counselors, and one Mo-quau-pauw, or Hero, and one Mkhooh-que-thoth, or Owl, and one Un-nuh-kau-kun, or Messenger or Runner; and the rest of the men are called young men. (But the Six Nations call young men Warriors.) The Sachem is looked upon as a great tree under whose shade the whole nation is to sit. His business is to contemplate the welfare of his people day and night: how to promote their peace and happiness. He also takes pains to maintain and brighten the belt of friendship with all their allies. When he finds any business of a public nature, he is to call his counselors together to consult with them. Then they will determine what is good for the Nation. The Sachem must be a peaceable man—having nothing to do with wars—but he is at times to go from house to house to exhort his people to live in unity and peace.

The Sachem has no stated salary for his services, for it was a disgrace or reproach to any man to ask a reward for any of his public services. But whatever he does for his nation must be done out of friendship and good will. But it was the custom to help their Sachem voluntarily in building a long We-ko-wohm, or wigwam, all complete. And the hunters, when they returned from hunting, each man gives him a skin. The women also at times, some give him Mkith-non, or muk-sens, some belts for the body, others garters, and some other ornament—as wampum to be for his own use. They are also to bring victual to the Sachem to enable him to feed strangers. For whenever strangers arrived at their fireplace they are directed to go to the Sachem's house. There they stay until their business is completed.

The Sachem is allowed to keep Mno-ti, or peaceable bag, or bag of peace, containing about one bushel, some less. This bag is made of Weeth-kuhn-pauk, or bitter sort of hemp that grows on intervals, about three or four feet long, and sometimes made of Wau-pon-nep-pauk, or white hemp, which grows by the side of rivers or edge of marches—amazingly strong and lasting—of which they make strings, and dye part of the strings different colors, then worked and made into a bag of different markings. In this bag they keep various Squau-tho-won, or belts of wampum, also strings, which belts and strings they used to establish peace and friendship with different nations, and to use them on many occasions, and passed as coin. In this bag they keep all belts and strings that they received from their allies of different nations. This bag is, as it were, unmoveable. But it always remains at the Sachem's house, as hereditary with the office of a Sachem. He is to keep the Pipe of Peace made of red hard stone [with] a long stem to it.

Besides this bag, they keep other smaller bags that they called Ne-mau-won-neh Mno-ti or Scrip, which contains nourishment on a journey, which they carry with them when they go out to hold treaties with other fireplaces. In such scrips they occasionally put belts and strings for transacting business aboard. When they find the wampum will fall short, besides what is kept in the bag, the Sachem and his counselors would send their runner to gather or collect wampum from their women, which business they called mauw-peen, or sitting into one place.[21]

# 6.18

# Grandmother Moon

CATHY J. CALDWELL,
STOCKBRIDGE-MUNSEE BAND OF MOHICAN

*Cathy Caldwell's poetry is centered around family, and in this selection, written in 1987, she expresses her intimate relationship with a nonhuman relative.*

### GRANDMOTHER MOON

White moon
of early evening,
Speak to me,
Tell me tales
A grandmother tells,
Show me more
Than your silver light
On crusts of snow.

I am a daughter
Without a dream song—
A silent daughter
Afraid to speak
Until spoken to

I wait for the wind
To remind me of distant voices
in the trees,
But it only chills my face
and brushes snowflakes
from the branches.

White moon
Of early evening,
Swollen with the words of winters past,
I wish to hear your sacred songs

Once again, upon the wind;
I wish to feel the warmth
of a storytime fire;
I wish to lean against your breast
And fall asleep
To the drumming of your heart.[22]

# 6.19

# Eunice Stick

NICOLE HIRTHE AND BRAD PECORE,
STOCKBRIDGE-MUNSEE BAND OF MOHICAN

*In a project in the Stockbridge-Munsee Community, Mohican Nation, a group of youth gathered stories from their elders. Here, two young people write up their interview.*

Eunice came from a very poor family, living with her mother and the rest of her siblings. She and her younger brother attended the Lutheran mission school when she was seven and her brother was six. They both walked to school all the way from Morgan. She laughed as she thought of how they walked all that way, being that young. When Eunice was twelve, she went to the mission to make up two grades in one year because she was behind in her schooling.

Eunice got into a fight or two with one of the students at school who liked to bully around all the kids. Eunice stuck up for everybody. Eunice and this student were kind of related but never got along, so Eunice's mother took her out of school to prevent her from getting into any more trouble. Then she became very sickly, and the mission didn't want to be responsible for her, so she was once again denied school. She stayed home helping her mother with all her younger siblings because she was the oldest, and her mother had all the children close together. But she never forgot about her education.

Being the oldest, she thought she could do what any "growed up person" could do, so she went to work in Neopit at the age of fifteen. Later, at the age of seventeen she and a friend ventured off to Milwaukee seeking employment. For two years Eunice did maid work, then she went to work for an assemblyman. He suggested that she go to government school, and he wrote a letter of recommendation for her to go to the Native American School at Flandreau, South Dakota. She attended that school for a year, but then received a very sad letter from her mother that she was having problems with her sister. So Eunice came back home to help her mother out.

Eunice's grandmother was kind of an old-time Indian and taught her brother the old ways—berry picking, hunting, etc. Her brother was an outdoorsman, and he loved the woods. He hunted gophers because there was a bounty on them and he would give the money to his mother. It was the Depression back then, hard times. Eunice would baby-sit and give her mother the money as well. They ate a lot of fish, but no venison because it was bitter. Eunice made macaroni and tomatoes; the next day was macaroni, tomatoes, and onions. They were that poor, and there wasn't welfare like there is today.

Eunice remembers the time when she went to Milwaukee with her friend. They got a ride into Shawano around 4:00 p.m. Their train wasn't leaving until midnight, so they went to see a movie called *Stowaway* starring Shirley Temple. They were so excited about it all that they just giggled all the way. They didn't sleep at all, and when they arrived in Milwaukee, it was like nothing they had ever seen before. It was dark, and the lights were beautiful. Wherever they looked, there were lights clear around. There they both found jobs and did the best they could.

In 1974, Eunice moved back to the reservation when the Library Museum was just getting started. She got a job working with the elderly. Then Eunice heard about a program that was available to those who wanted their GED. She attended this program once a week in Wausau, finished her GED, and kept on working. Later, Eunice and her friends found out about a college in Stevens Point. Her friends encouraged her to go, so she went there and got her Associate Degree. It was rough because she had received little schooling, but she had education on her mind. She would have gone further if her mother hadn't been sick and her husband very ill. Now she feels that she is too old, and it would be impossible for her to go on.

I had a great experience during this project, considering it was a lot of work and time involved. It gave me a chance to get to know an elder from my tribe. I was nervous because I have only one grandparent left; the rest are deceased, and I don't have much experience speaking with elders. Now, however, I have a better understanding about how to communicate with elders and how to listen with my heart as well as my ears.[23]

# 7

# Literature of the
# Brothertown Nation

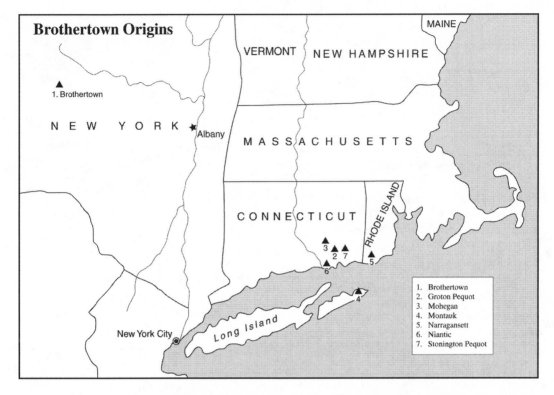

This map shows the seven Christianized Indian settlements that collectively formed the Brothertown Nation before they migrated to Wisconsin. Map adapted from Franz L. Wojciechowksi, "Actors and Actions of the Brothertown Indian Genesis," courtesy of June Ezold, Brothertown Chair Emeritus.

# 7.1

# Brothertown Indian Nation
# of Wisconsin

## BROTHERTOWN INDIAN NATION

*Of Algonquin-speaking origin on the Atlantic coast, members of the Brothertown Nation were forced from their homeland and settled in what became the state of Wisconsin. Their ancestors were from seven tribal communities: Mohegan, Mashantucket, Stonington, Farmington, Charlestown, Niantic, and Montauk. In Algonquin, "Brothertown" is written "Eyamquittoowauconnuck," meaning "Place of Equal Peoples."[1]*

The Brothertown (Brotherton) are descendants of the Pequot and Mohegan (Algonquin-speaking) tribes in southern New England. They became a tribe in 1769 when seven Christian and English-speaking communities organized and moved to land in upstate New York. They cleared the land, planted fields and built houses while under intense pressure to again move west. The Brothertown joined their neighbors, the Oneida and the Stockbridge, and planned a move to Wisconsin. The Brothertown purchased land near Kaukauna that the United States government exchanged for the land called Brothertown Township in Calumet County. Five groups of Brothertown arrived in Wisconsin on ships at the port of Green Bay between 1831 and 1836. Upon arrival, the Brothertown cleared land and began farming after building a church near Jericho. Today, the Brothertown remain a culturally distinct Indian community with the largest concentration residing in the Fond du Lac area.[2]

7.2

# Mission Statement

*The Brothertown Nation of Wisconsin bases its community upon ethical principles and traditional values.*

The mission of the Brothertown Tribe is to continue a stable and dynamic government which will promote and maintain the spiritual, physical, intellectual, social, and economic well being of our citizens; to restore and preserve our unique historical, cultural, and traditional beliefs; to preserve and protect our sovereignty in order to achieve self-determination and self-sufficiency; to promote a positive image of integrity, honesty, respect and fairness when pursuing cultural, economic and social initiatives; to promote peace and harmony for the fulfillment of our vision as community where all people can prosper and grow in mind, body and spirit.

The Brothertown Tribe recognizes and accepts the relationships that must be forged between all who will be affected by our sovereignty.

It is in faith we undertake these tasks and it shall be with a spirit of cooperation and friendship that we reach the goals that we have set apart in this document.[3]

# First of the Mohegans

UNCAS, MOHEGAN

*A character named Uncas appeared in James Fenimore Cooper's novel* Last of the Mohicans, *but this character was a fictional construction, with little relationship to the historic figure. The historic Uncas was a leader or sachem of the Mohegan—not the Mohican— people, culturally distinct groups. The fictional Uncas is portrayed as little more than the (Anglo-American) main character's "sidekick." His inferior status and death in the novel were meant to represent the demise and disappearance of the Indians that Cooper and his contemporaries believed were inevitable. In reality, the historic Uncas was a savvy political leader who, according to historian Michael Leroy Oberg, used the colonists to further the Mohegan community (a community that continues into the present day), even as he was used by them to defend and enlarge colonial interests. Oberg writes that "Uncas deserves much of the credit for the two generations of Anglo-Indian peace that followed the Pequot War, for he dealt effectively not only with English officials in the provincial capitals, but also with frontier settlers on the margins of Puritan New England." Uncas was a powerful sachem who pursued his own agenda, sometimes manipulating the colonists into interfering on his behalf in Native politics. If Uncas had been able to put aside his intense hatred for his competitor in nation building, Miantonomi, when the Narragansett sachem called for a united Indian confederacy to defeat the colonists, Uncas's joining the Narragansett would possibly—even probably—have destroyed the English colonies. Instead, Uncas cast his fate with the English colonists, playing "a critical role in the intercultural politics that shaped New England's development and as significant a part in the region's history as that of any other individual."4*

*Although Uncas's loyalty to both Natives and the colonial governments were questioned during his life and after, Oberg argues that he was a Mohegan patriot who well understood that his "alliance with the English . . . allowed Uncas to break free from the Pequots and to emerge at the head of a regional power. Backed by the threat of English military might, . . . Uncas extended his authority over tributaries of his own, incorporating and adopting them into Mohegan village communities." In incorporating other than Mohegans into his villages through adoption and marriage, Uncas pursued traditional Native politics in his nation building; however, some were in Uncas's villages unhappily, victims of Native and colonial wars. Uncas ruled from a position of power rather than consensus, and demanded tribute in wampum from lesser sachems.5*

*After the Anglo-Indian massacre at Mystic, Uncas appeared before Governor John Winthrop of the Massachusetts Bay Colony to pledge, in the language of Native diplomacy, his loyalty to the fledgling colony. His offer made possible a "peaceful expansion of Puritan settlement in southern New England and the Bay Colony's domination of wampum production in that region." With Uncas as an ally, the "Saints" of the Puritan community gained control of the production of wampum, shell beads used as currency by both Natives and colonialists until the colonists "demonetized wampum in 1663 and 1664." This decree and the importation of English currency devastated the economy of the Mohegan and other Algonquian groups who produced the wampum.[6]*

This heart is not mine, but yours. I have no men; they are all yours. Command me any difficult thing, I will do it. I will not believe any Indians' word against the English, and if any man shall kill an Englishman, I will put him to death, were he never so dear to me.[7]

# To Settle My Posterity to Walk in the Straight Path

UNCAS, MOHEGAN

*Uncas lived a long life that witnessed the once-weak colonists become the regional power that had no further need of his friendship. He hoped that his struggle to protect the Mohegan homeland would not be in vain. In this speech to the Connecticut governor and council in May 1678, Uncas continues to speak the language of friendship and diplomacy.*

The serious consideration [of charges brought by Reverend Fitch] has sometimes put me in mind of what the enemy did sometimes say to my men and the Pequots when we were in pursuit after them, viz.: that we were very zealous in killing our country folk, but said that it will be your own turn next, etc. Therefore, we have fear upon us as you may have jealousies concerning us, which incites me earnestly to desire that all occasions of a distrustful nature may be removed, for I am now grown old and my hearty desire is that friendship and love might be maintained and renewed between us, and that I might leave the same as a legacy to settle my posterity to walk in the straight path, to hold the like correspondence with the English Nation all their days, which is the desire of him who hath been and is your old friend.[8]

# 7·5

# Massacre of Pequot at Mystic in 1637

## MIANTONOMI, NARRAGANSETT

---

*In 1600, some estimate that up to 90,000 people lived "from the Chesapeake Bay to the Appalachian Mountains, once one of the most densely populated regions of all of Native North America," yet by 1700, one hundred years later, "fewer than 3,000 indigenous people remained."⁹ When the Pequot controlled the balance of power between Massachusetts and Connecticut, the colonial governments sent out forces with orders to kill any male Pequot who survived a deliberately induced smallpox epidemic and to capture as many women and children as possible to sell to the West Indian slave markets. A mixed Massachusetts-Connecticut force commanded by Captain John Mason, plus eighty Mohegans under Uncas, and five hundred Narragansetts let by Miantonomi, set out to attack a small Pequot fortified village on the Mystic River. But when the Indians realized that the English intended a massacre, the Narragansetts and Mohegans would not participate. Five survivors took refuge with Uncas's Mohegans—their former enemy. Killing noncombatants was not acceptable to Natives, and the massacre changed allegiances. Five years after the Mystic Massacre, Miantonomi was advocating for a union with the Montauk and other Indian Nations against the English.*

You know our fathers had plenty of deer and skins, our plains were full of deer, as also our woods, and of turkeys, and our coves full of fish and fowl. But these English have gotten our land, they with scythes cut down the grass, and with axes fell the trees. Theirs cows and horses eat the grass and their hogs spoil our clam banks, and we shall all be starved.¹⁰

# Narragansett Act of Submission

CANONICUS, PESSICUS, AND MIXAM;
NARRAGANSETT

*Seeing their growing isolation, their neighboring nations falling to warfare and disease, the Narragansett placed themselves under the protection of "Old England" and King Charles I in 1644. The Puritans resented that they had not submitted to them, but the "Narragansetts astutely asserted their equality with the New England Puritans; they and the colonists were both subjects of the king."[11] Hence, even in submission they asserted in diplomatic language their sovereignty and nation-to-nation status with the British.*

The Act and Deed of the voluntary and free submission of the chief Sachem, and the rest of the Princes, with the whole people of the Narragansetts, unto the Government and protection of that Honorable State of Old-England; set down here, verbatim.

Know all men, colonies, peoples, and nations, unto whom the fame hereof shall come, that we, the chief sachems, princes or governors of the Narragansetts (in that part of American, now called New England), together with the joint and unanimous consent of all our people and subjects, inhabitants thereof, do upon serious consideration, mature and deliberate advice and counsel, great and weighty grounds and reasons moving us thereto, whereof one most effectual unto us is, that noble fame we have heard of the great and mighty prince, Charles, King of Great Britain, in that honorable and princely care he hath of all his servants, and true and loyal subjects, the consideration whereof moves and bends our hearts with one consent, freely, voluntarily, and most humbly to submit, subject, and give over ourselves, people, lands, rights, inheritance, and possessions whatsoever, in our selves and our heirs successively forever, unto the protection, care, and government of that worthy and royal Prince, Charles, King of Great Britain and Ireland, his heirs and successors forever, to be ruled and governed according to the ancient and honorable laws and customs, established in that so renowned realm and kingdom of Old England.

We do, therefore, by these presents, confess, and most willingly and submissively acknowledge ourselves to be the humble, loving and obedient servants and subjects of his Majesty; to be ruled, ordered, and disposed of, in ourselves and ours, according to his princely wisdom, counsel and laws of the honorable State of Old England, *upon condition of His Majesty's royal protection,* and righting us of what wrong is, or may be done unto us, according to his honorable laws and custom, exercised amongst his subjects, in their preservation and safety, and in the defeating and overthrow of his, and their enemies; not that we find ourselves necessitated hereunto in respect of our relation, or occasion we have, or may have, with any of the natives in these parts, knowing ourselves sufficient [in] defense, and able to judge in any matter or cause in that respect; but have just cause of jealousy and suspicion of some of His Majesty's pretended subjects.

Therefore our desire is, to have our matters and causes heard and tried according to his just and equal laws, in that way and order His Highness shall please to appoint: Nor can we yield over ourselves unto any, that are subjects themselves in any case; having ourselves been the chief Sachems, or princes successively, of the country, time out of mind; and for our present and lawful enacting hereof, being so far remote from His Majesty, we have, by joint consent, made choice of four of his loyal and loving subjects, our trusty and well-beloved friends, Samuel Gorton, John Wickes, Randall Houlden and John Warner, whom we have deputed, and made our lawful attorneys or commissioners, not only for the acting and performing of this our deed, in the behalf of his Highness, but also for the safe custody, careful conveyance, and declaration hereof unto his grace: being done upon the lands of the Narragansetts, at a court or general assembly called and assembled together, of purpose for the public enacting and manifestation hereof.[12]

# Our Forefathers Had Everything in Great Plenty

HENRY QUAQUAQUID AND ROBERT ASHPO,
MOHEGAN

*The American revolt against Great Britain had a devastating effect on the Indian Nations of the East, regardless of which side the Indians fought on, or if they didn't fight at all. Even Christian Indians, like those who had been converted by Moravian missionaries, were not immune. Although they were pacifists, more than ninety of them were massacred by American militia at their village of Gnadenhutten, Ohio, in 1782, shortly after the end of the Revolutionary War.[13] After the American Revolution, the Indians of New York were in a new political environment. In a petition to the Connecticut State Assembly, May 1789, they made clear how their situation had changed for the worse.*

We beg leave to lay our concerns and burdens at your excellencies' feet. The times are exceedingly altered, yea the times are turned upside down; or rather we have changed the good times, chiefly by the help of the white people.

For in times past our forefathers lived in peace, love and great harmony, and had every thing in great plenty. When they wanted meat, they would just run into the bush a little way with their weapons, and would soon return, bringing home good venison, raccoon, bear and fowl. If they chose to have fish, they would only go to the river, or along the seashore, and they would presently fill their canoes with [a] variety of fish, both scaled and shellfish. And they had abundance of nuts, wild fruits, ground nuts and ground beans; they planted but little corn and beans. They had no contention about their lands, for they lay in common. They had but one large dish, and could all eat together in peace and love.

But alas! It is not so now; all our hunting and fowling and fishing is entirely gone. And we have begun to work our land, keep horses and cattle and hogs; and we build houses and fence in lots. And now we plainly see that one dish and one fire will not do any longer for us. Some few there are that are stronger than others, and they will keep off the poor, weak, the halt and blind, and will take the dish [for] themselves. Yea, they will rather call the white people and the mulattoes to eat out of our dish, and poor widows and orphans must be pushed aside, and there they must sit, crying and starving, and die.

And so we are now come to our good brethren of the assembly, with hearts full of sorrow and grief, for immediate help. And therefore our most humble and earnest request is that our dish of succotash may be equally divided amongst us, so that every one may have his own little dish by himself, that he may eat quietly and do with his dish as he pleases, that every one may have his own fire.[14]

# A Mohegan Minister's Autobiography

SAMSON OCCUM, MOHEGAN

*Samson Occum, or Occom (1723–1792), was a descendent of Uncas, the Mohegan grand sachem. Occum studied with Reverend Eleazar Wheelock, and preached and raised funds for Wheelock's Indian Charity School. Although Occum raised over 12,000 pounds in a two-year trip to Great Britain, Wheelock did not use the money for Indian education; rather, he used it to establish Dartmouth College.[15] Occum's autobiography was dated September 17, 1768, when he was forty-five.*

I was born a heathen and brought up in heathenism, till I was between 16 & 17 years of age, at a place called Mohegan, in New London, Connecticut, in New England. My parents lived a wandering life, [as] did all the Indians at Mohegan. They chiefly depended upon hunting, fishing, and fowling for their living and had no connection with the English, excepting to traffic with them in their small trifles; and they strictly maintained and followed their heathenish ways, customs, and religion, though there was some preaching among them.

Once a fortnight, in the summer season, a minister from New London used to come up, and the Indians to attend; not that they regarded the Christian religion, but they had blankets given to them every fall of the year and for these things they would attend.

There was a sort of school kept, when I was quite young, but I believe there never was one [student] that ever learned to read anything. When I was about 10 years of age there was a man who went about among the Indian wigwams, and wherever he could find the Indian children, would make them read. But the children used to take care to keep out of his way. And he used to catch me sometimes and make me say over my letters. I believe I learned some of them. But this was soon over too. And all this time there was not one among us that made a profession of Christianity. Neither did we cultivate our land, nor keep any sort of creatures except dogs, which we used in hunting. We dwelt in wigwams. These are a sort of tent, covered with mats, made of flags. And to this time we were unacquainted with the English tongue in general, though there were a few who understood a little of it.

## From the Time of Our Reformation Till I left Mr. Wheelock's

When I was 16 years of age, we heard a strange rumor among the English, that there were extraordinary ministers preaching from place to place and a strange concern among the white people. This was in the spring of the year. But we saw nothing of these things, till some time in the summer, when some ministers began to visit us and preach the word of God. And the common people all came frequently and exhorted us to the things of God, which it pleased the Lord, as I humbly hope, to bless and accompany with divine influence to the conviction and saving conversion of a number of us, amongst whom I was one that was impressed with the things we had heard. These preachers did not only come to us, but we frequently went to their meeting and churches.

After I was awakened and converted, I went to all the meetings I could come at, and continued under trouble of mind about six months, at which time I began to learn the English letters, got me a primer, and used to go to my English neighbors frequently for assistance in reading, but went to no school. . . .

My poor mother was going to Lebanon, and having had some knowledge of Mr. Wheelock and hearing he had a number of English youth under his tuition, I had a great inclination to go to him and be with him a week or a fortnight, and desired my mother to ask Mr. Wheelock whether he would take me a little while to instruct me in reading. Mother did so, and when she came back, she said Mr. Wheelock wanted to see me as soon as possible. So I went up, thinking I should be back again in a few days. When I got up there, he received we with kindness and compassion and instead of staying a fortnight or 3 weeks, I spent 4 years with him.

After I had been with him some time, he began to acquaint his friends of my being with him, and of his intentions of educating me, and my circumstance. And the good people began to give some assistance to Mr. Wheelock, and gave me some old and some new clothes. Then he represented the case to the honorable commissioners at Boston, who were commissioned by the honorable society in London for propagating the gospel among the Indians in New England and parts adjacent, and they allowed him 60 pounds in old tender, which was about 6 pounds sterling and they continued it 2 or 3 years; I can't tell exactly.

While I was at Mr. Wheelock's, I was very weakly and my health much impaired, and at the end of 4 years, I overstrained my eyes to such a degree, I could not pursue my studies any longer. And out of these 4 years I lost just about one year, and was obliged to quit my studies.

## From the Time I Left Mr. Wheelock Till I went to Europe

As soon as I left Mr. Wheelock, I endeavored to find some employ among the Indians; went to Nahantuck, thinking they may want a school master, but

they had one; then went to Narragansett, and they were indifferent about a
school, and went back to Mohegan, and heard a number of our Indians were
going to Montauk, on Long Island, and I went with them, and the Indians
there were very desirous to have me keep a school amongst them. I consented, and went back a while to Mohegan.

Sometime in November I went on the island. I think it is 17 years ago last
November. I agreed to keep school with them half a year, and left it with them
to give me what they pleased. They took turns to provide food for me. I had
near 30 scholars this winter. I had an evening school too for those that could
not attend the day school—and began to carry on their meetings. They had a
minister, one Mr. Horton, the Scotch Society's missionary. But he spent I
think two-thirds of his time at Sheenecock, 30 miles from Montauk.

We met together 3 times for divine worship every Sabbath and once on
every Wednesday evening. I used to read the scriptures to them and used to
expound upon some particular passages in my own tongue. Visited the sick
and attended their burials.

When the half-year expired, they desired me to continue with them, which
I complied with, for another half year. When I had fulfilled that, they were ur-
gent to have me stay longer, so I continued amongst them till I was married,
which was about 2 years after I went there. And continued to instruct them in
the same manner as I did before. After I was married a while, I found there
was need of a support more than I needed while I was single, and made my
case known to Mr. Buell and to Mr. Wheelock, and also the needy circumstances and the desires of these Indians of my continuing among them, and
the commissioners were so good as to grant 15 pounds a year sterling.

I kept on in my service as usual, yea I had additional service. I kept school
as I did before and carried on the religious meetings as often as ever, and attended the sick and their funerals, and did what writings they wanted, and
often sat as judge to reconcile and decide their matters between them, and
had visitors of Indians from all quarters, and, as our custom is, we freely entertain all visitors. . . .

In the whole I lost 5 horses. All these losses helped to pull me down, and by
this time I got greatly in debt, and acquainted my circumstances to some of
my friends, and they represented my case to the commissioners of Boston,
and interceded with them for me, and they were pleased to vote 15 pounds for
my help, and soon after sent a letter to my good friend at New London, ac-
quainting him that they had superseded their vote. My friends were so good
as to represent my needy circumstance still to them, and they were so good at
last, as to vote 15 pounds and sent it, for which I am very thankful.

The Reverend Mr. Buell was so kind as to write in my behalf to the gentlemen of Boston. He told me they were much displeased with him, and heard
also once again that they blamed me for being extravagant. I can't conceive
how these gentlemen would have me live. I am ready to forgive their ignorance, and I would wish they had changed circumstances with me but one

month, that they may know by experience what my case really was. But I am now fully convinced that it was not ignorance, for I believe it can be proved to the world that these same gentlemen gave a young missionary, a single man one hundred pounds for one year, and fifty pounds for an interpreter, and thirty pounds for an introducer, so it cost them one hundred and eight pounds in one single year, and they sent too where there was no need of a missionary.

Now you see what difference they made between me and other missionaries. They gave me 180 pounds for 12 years service, which they gave for one year's service in another mission. In my service (I speak like a fool, but I am constrained) I was my own interpreter. I was both a schoolmaster and minister to the Indians, yea I was their ear, eye and hand, as well as mouth. I leave it with the world, as wicked as it is, to judge whether I ought not to have had half as much as they gave a young man just mentioned, which would have been but 50 pounds a year. And if they ought to have given me that, I am not under obligations to them; I owe them nothing at all.

What can be the reason that they used me after this manner? I can't think of anything but this: as a poor Indian boy said, who was bound out to an English family, and he used to drive plow for a young man, and he whipped and beat him almost every day, and the young man found fault with him, and complained of him to his master and the poor boy was called to answer for himself before his master, and he was asked, what it was he did, that he was so complained of and beat[en] almost every day. He said, he did not know, but he supposed it was because he could not drive any better. But says he, I drive as well as I know how; and at other times he beats me, because he is of a mind to beat me, but says he believes he beats me for most of the time "because I am an Indian."

So I am ready to say, they have used me thus because I can't influence the Indians so well as other missionaries. But I can assure them I have endeavored to teach them as well as I know how. But I must say, "I believe it is because I am a poor Indian." I can't help that God has made me so, I did not make myself so.[16]

# The Diary of Samson Occum

JIM OTTERY, BROTHERTOWN

*A member of the Brothertown Indians of Wisconsin, Jim Ottery is an assistant professor in the Department of English at the University of Illinois at Springfield. As part of a February 2000 talk titled "Samson Occum's Diary and the Brothertown Indians: The Problem of Life Stories in the Other's Tongue," Dr. Ottery began his presentation with the following poem based on Occum's autobiography and material from* A Man Called Sampson *by Will and Rudy Ottery.*

### THE DIARY OF SAMSON OCCUM

He put his life into words: his life
as a Presbyterian preacher, his life
as a preacher and teacher before that
in the society for Propagating
the Gospel in New England,
two years of that life devoted
to raising of funds in old England
for an Indian Charity School in Connecticut,
"funds misdirected" toward the foundation
of a white Dartmouth College instead.

He put his life into words, in the language
that was not his mother tongue, the language
not learned until he was 16—
in the language that was not his
until he almost reached manhood,
he wrote of his life until that time
in very few words of the language that was not
his mother tongue—

*I was born a Heathen*
*and Brought up in Heathenism*
*until I was between 16 & 17 Years of age,*
*at a place called Mohegan . . .*

He put his life into the language
that wasn't his mother tongue,
the English learned first when he was 16,
(then reading Hebrew at 21),
until "after a year of study" he stopped
because ("his eyes would fail him").
In the language that was not his mother tongue
he would write (so the transcribed diary
with "erasures" goes):

*Having Seen and heard*
*Several Representations,*
*In England and Scotland*
[two words crossed out]
*by . . .*
*Some gentlemen . . .*
*Concerning me,*
*and finding many*
[crossed out: misrepresentations]
*gross Mistakes*
*in their account, -*
*I thought it my Duty to Give*
*a Short, Plain, and Honest*
*Account of my Self*
*whilst I am still alive,*
*. . . to doe Justice to myself*
*and to those*
*who may desire*
[two words crossed out]
*to know something concerning*
[word crossed out]
*me . . .*

Samson Occum put his life into words
and we read it in another's words
another who read enough of his life
to write of Mohegan
"at the center of the most fervent
religious awakening" there,
"and how two converted were
Sarah Occum" and Samson her son,
how Sarah convinced a "good" reverend
(who years later "misdirects" the Indian Charity School funds)
to teach her son the white man's language,

how she had no money to pay his lessons,
how she "contributed some labor" to the Rev. Wheelock
and perhaps other members of the Wheelock family.

Samson Occum put his life into the words of the white man
because he "*believed* in order to be saved
the Indian had to conform to white ways"
conform to the ways of the white man
who slaughtered his mother's people at Mystic River,
conform to the ways of the white man
who would crowd out the Mohegans
and the rest of the New England tribes,
conform to ways of the white man
who brought "intemperance, licentiousness and disease,"
conform to the ways of the white man
because his ways, Samson Occum could see,
were to be the ways of the New World,
conform to the ways of the white man and hope
that white men someday would be
better men for it.

Samson Occum put his life into the words of the white man
because he believed it was what he had to do.
But not his entire life.
In the language that's not his mother tongue:
he doesn't write much of his wife,
he doesn't write much of daughters and sons
he does not write much of his personal "life" —
how poverty, depression may have led to alcohol.
He does not write of these things in the white man's words:
Sometimes there aren't words for your life
in a language that's not your mother tongue.[17]

# 7.10

# An Execution Sermon

SAMSON OCCUM, MOHEGAN

*When drunk, a Christian Mohegan, Moses Paul, murdered a prominent Anglo-American. Moses Paul requested that Samson Occum deliver the sermon at his execution. On September 2, 1771, Occum spoke passionately about the evils of alcohol and the virtue of temperance. This tract was reprinted nineteen times.*

*La Vonne Brown Ruoff comments that this sermon "derives its theology from the Great Awakening, [but] derives its form from the execution sermon, a genre which originated in Old England and achieved great popularity in New England. Its popularity is based on its relationship to the religious practices of the early colonial period, when . . . confessing one's sins [was] part of private and church ritual. These confessions became an essential part of American conversion literature that flourished in the eighteenth and early nineteenth centuries."[18]*

Death is called the king of terrors, and it ought to be the subject of every man and woman's thoughts daily, because it is that unto which they are liable every moment of their lives. Therefore it cannot be unreasonable to think, speak and hear of it at any time, and especially on this mournful occasion. For we must all come to it, how soon we cannot tell. Whether we are prepared or not prepared, ready or not ready, whether death is welcome or not welcome, we must feel the force of it: Whether we concern ourselves with death or not, it will concern itself with us. Seeing that this is the case with every one of us, what manner of persons ought we to be in all holy conversation and godliness; how ought men to exert themselves in preparation for death, continually; for they know not what a day or an hour may bring forth, with respect to them.

But alas! According to the appearance of mankind in general, death is the least thought of. They go on from day to day as if they were to live here forever, as if this was the only life. They contrive, rack their inventions, disturb their rest, and even hazard their lives in all manner of dangers, both by sea and land. Yea, they leave no stone unturned that they may live in the world, and at the same time have little or no contrivance to die well. God and their souls are neglect, and heaven and eternal happiness are disregarded. Christ and his religion are despised—yet most of these very men intend to be happy when they come to die, not considering that there must be great preparation in order to die well.

Yea there is none so fit to live as those that are fit to die; those that are not fit to die are not fit to live. Life and death are nearly connected; we generally own that it is a great and solemn thing to die. If this be true, then it is a great and solemn thing to live, for as we live so we shall die. But I say again, how does mankind realize these things? They are busy about the things of the world as if there was no death before them. . . .

But on the other hand, life is the most precious thing, and ought to be the most desired by all rational creatures. It ought to be prized above all things, yet there is nothing so abused and despised as life, and nothing so neglected: I mean eternal life is shamefully disregarded by men in general, and eternal death is chosen rather than life. This is the general complaint of the Bible from the beginning to the end. As long as Christ is neglected, life is refused, as long as sin is cherished, death is chosen. And this seems to be the woeful case of mankind of all nations, according to their appearance in these days. For it is too plain to be denied, that vice and immorality, and floods of iniquity are abounding everywhere amongst all nations, and all orders and ranks of men, and in every sect of people. Yea there is a great agreement and harmony among all nations, and from the highest to the lowest to practice sin and iniquity, and the pure religion of Jesus Christ is turned out of doors, and is dying without. Or, in order words, the Lord Jesus Christ is turned out of doors by men in general, and even by his professed people. "He came to his own, and his own received him not." But the devil is admitted, he has free access to the houses and hearts of the children of men: Thus life is refused and death is chosen. . . .

My poor kindred, you see the woeful consequences of sin, by seeing this our poor miserable countryman now before us, who is to die this day for his sins and great wickedness. And it was the sin of drunkenness that has brought this destruction and untimely death upon him. There is a dreadful woe denounced from the Almighty against drunkards; and it is this sin, this abominable, this beastly and accursed sin of drunkenness that has stript us of every desirable comfort in this life. By this we are poor, miserable and wretched; by this sin we have no name nor credit in the world among polite nations; for this sin we are despised in the world, and it is all right and just, for we despise ourselves more; and if we don't regard ourselves, who will regard us? And it is for our sins and especially for that accursed, that most devilish sin of drunkenness that we suffer every day. For the love of strong drink we spend all that we have, and every thing we can get. By this sin we can't have comfortable houses, nor any thing comfortable in our house; neither food nor raiment, nor decent utensils. We are obliged to put up with any sort of shelter just to screen us from the severity of the weather, and we go about with very mean, ragged and dirty clothes, almost naked. And we are half-starved, for the most of the time obliged to pick up any thing to eat. And our poor children are suffering every day for want of the necessaries of life. They are very often crying for want of food, and we have nothing to give them. And in the cold weather they are shivering and crying, being pinched with cold. All this for the love of strong drink. And this is not all the misery and evil we bring on ourselves in this world, but when we are intoxicated with strong drink we drown our rational powers, by which we are distinguished from the brutal creation; we unman ourselves, and bring ourselves not only level with the beast of the field, but seven degrees beneath them. Yea we bring ourselves level with the devils; I don't know but we make ourselves worse than devils, for I never heard of drunken devils.

My poor kindred, do consider what a dreadful abominable sin drunkenness is. God made us men, and we choose to be beasts and devils. God made us rational creatures, and we choose to be fools. Do consider further, and behold a drunkard and see how he looks when he has drowned his reason; how deformed and shameful does he appear? He disfigures every part of him, both soul and body, which was made after the image of God. He appears with awful deformity, and his whole visage is disfigured; if he attempts to speak he cannot bring out his words distinctly, so as to be understood. If he walks he reels and staggers to and fro, and tumbles down. And see how he behaves: he is now laughing, and then he is crying, he is singing, and the next minute he is mourning, and is all love with every one, and anon he is raging and for fighting, and killing all before him even the nearest and dearest relations and friends. Yea, nothing is too bad for a drunken man to do. He will do that which he would not do for the world, in his right mind; he may lie with his own sister or daughter as Lot did. . . .

Again, a man in drunkenness is in all manner of dangers, he may be killed by his fellow men, by wild beasts, and tame beasts; he may fall into the fire, into the water, or into a ditch; or he may fall down as he walks along, and break his bones or his neck; and he may cut himself with edge-tools. Further, if he has any money or any thing valuable, he may lose it all, or may be robbed, or he may make a foolish bargain and be cheated out of all he has. . . .

And to conclude, consider my poor kindred, you that are drunkards, into what a miserable condition you have brought yourselves. There is a dreadful woe thundering against you every day, and the Lord says that drunkards shall not inherit the kingdom of heaven.[19]

# 7.11

# Nation Building and Cultural Adaptation

## JOSEPH JOHNSON, MOHEGAN

*Another student of Eleazar Wheelock's Charity School for Indians, Joseph Johnson, was influenced by fellow Mohegans Samson Occum and David and Jacob Fowler and committed to the idea of forming a separate community of Christian Indians.[20] Johnson asked the Oneida of the Six Nations Confederacy to cede a part of their territory to a group of Christian converts from seven different localities in New England. He delivered this speech to the Oneida council on January 20, 1774.*

A Speech to the Oneida Indians, by Joseph Johnson, an Indian of the Mohegan Tribe, chosen to act on the behalf of the New England Indians.

Our dear and well beloved Brethren: It is with much pleasure that we see so many of you assembled together at this time and upon this occasion. We give you our great respects, and sincere love. We look upon you at present as upon an elder brother as a nation, and beloved brethren, we pray you to consider of us, and harken to us, as to a younger brother. Not only consider of us as two persons, but view us to be speaking, or acting for all our brethren in New England, or at least for seven towns. We pray you to consider seriously of our words, you old men who are wise, and you warriors, and stouthearted young men. Listen unto us, yea let children harken, that what we say may not soon be forgotten.

Brethren, in the first place we will acquaint you of the state and circumstances of our New England brethren, and also we will inform you of our proceedings hitherto. Brethren, we in New England, or at least many of us are very poor, by reason of the ignorance of our forefathers who are now dead. Brethren, you know that the English are a very wise people, and can see great ways. But some say that the Indians can see but little ways, and we believe that our forefathers could not see but very little ways. Brethren, you also know that some of the English love to take the advantage of poor, ignorant, and blind Indians. Well, so it was in the days of our forefathers in New England. But not to expose the unjust acts of our English brethren, I shall not

313

say much more about them, lest I cast a prejudice in your hearts against the English brethren. Notwithstanding there are so many wicked, or unjust men among the English, yet there are a great many good and just men amongst the English, who love the poor Indians from the bottom of their hearts, and wishes us all a well being in this world, and the world to come, life everlasting. But all I have to say about the English at present is this: whilst our forefathers were blind, and ignorant, yea drowned in spirituous liquors, the English stripped them yea, they as it were cut off their right hands, and now we, their children, just opening our eyes, and having knowledge grafted and growing in our hearts and just reviving or coming to our senses, like one that has been drunk—I say that now we begin to look around and consider, and we perceive that we are stripped indeed, having nothing to help ourselves. Thus our English brethren leave us, and laugh. So now Brethren, we leave the English, those who have acted unjustly towards us in New England; I say we leave them all in the hands of that God who knoweth all things, and will reward every one according to their deeds, whether good or evil.

Brethren, we seeing ourselves in such circumstances, began last spring to talk, and to consider together. A meeting was appointed at Mohegan, that being nigh the center, and was attended the 13th day of last March AD 1773, and there was a vast number of people: men, women, and children. There we met, and there we consulted together. There was present at this meeting Indians of seven towns, and it was proposed that certain men out of every town should go out and seek a place somewhere, for us seven towns to settle down together in peace. Some were of a mind to go southward as far as to Ohio, and some not so far that way. Some said we could purchase land higher and it would not do to live so far from the English. At last it came into our minds to try to purchase some land from some of the Six Nations. So a time was appointed by our great men, councilors and teachers, that those chosen men should go forth out of every town to seek a place for us to settle on, and as our spring work was coming on our headmen thought proper that those chosen men should not go till the hurrying work was over, that is, after mowing and reaping. And as it pleases the tribes to choose me for one that should come into these parts to try to get some land upon some terms, I thought proper to send to his Honor, Sir William Johnson for advice in this affair; and I wrote a letter to his Honor Sir William, and acquainted him of all our circumstances, desires, and purposes, and it pleased his Honor in his great condescension to take notice of us, and sent back a word of encouragement which made many of our hearts glad. . . . Yea here is in my hand the writing drawn from the records of his Honor Sir William, which if you please, you may hear, so as things past may be fresh in your memories again.

This paper, or writing I carried myself through six towns of Indians in New England, and at every town I called the people together both small and great, male and female, and they received the good news with great joy. I did not go to the seventh town, by reason of the inconveniency of going by water, and also my business called me to be at home, so I made as much haste as possible. However they have heard of your good will. . . .

But God who is good—and doeth good continually, gave us health and strength, and prospered us by the way, and now in his own due time hath brought us safe to this place, and is allowing us an opportunity to [ . . . ] your faces in comfort, and to converse with you in peace at this time. So to God we give our sincere thanks at this time, in the presence of you all, for all his goodness towards us. We rejoice that God gave us favor in the eyes of his Honor Sir William Johnson, and we rejoice that God gave us favor in your eyes. And we were glad to hear that you found it in your hearts to pity us, or our brethren in New England when you heard of our circumstances; and not only we thank you, but all our brethren in New England gave you their hearty thanks. Yea, we have abundant reason to rejoice. We thought to try to purchase land of you, but we are exceedingly glad that it is in your hearts to give us land, yea, we thank you that you have given us so much already.

Brethren, this silver pipe was sent to me, and this tobacco pouch with it, to dispose of them according to the advice of his Honor Sir William Johnson. . . . His Honor was pleased to fill the pouch and sent it by me to you chiefs, that this day you might smoke out of this silver pipe. So now I deliver this pipe unto you, as a sure token from our several tribes in New England that we are one and sincere in what we say and do.[21]

# 7.12

## Second Speech to the Oneidas

JOSEPH JOHNSON, MOHEGAN

*The Oneida response to Johnson's request was favorable, accepting the Brothertowners into the League of Six Nations. In this speech given four days after his first one, Johnson thanks the Oneidas for the land, but requests a larger parcel. However, because of the instability on the eastern seaboard due to the soon-to-begin American Revolutionary War, the new community could not settle on the Oneida reservation until 1783. This they did without Johnson, who died around the beginning of the Revolutionary War in 1776.*

Brethren, we ought all to adore God for his goodness to us from day to day and we ought to bless him that he is allowing us this opportunity to assemble ourselves together this once more, in this house, to consult together a little about the affairs of this world. Brethren, what we have further for your consideration is this, our purposes, or designs, if God [is] willing. This I know my elder brothers, that we may consult together, and agree to do so and so, yet if it is not the will of God, all our councils and purposes will come to nought, or all will be in vain. But if it please God, and He opens your hearts to pity us, and to receive us as a younger brother, and help us in very deed, then will we come up and settle together in peace, when you shall think fit, and where it will be most agreeable for us. All we desire is to live in peace and to have things convenient.

Brethren, I am very glad that my ears have heard those things which I have heard from you, in your consultations since we have been in your town. And as perhaps this is the last opportunity that I shall speak unto you, my elder brothers at this time, be so kind as to harken to the words of your younger brother, who would speak this once more in the name of seven towns in New England.

And I rejoice that you find in your hearts love still remaining there, and pity towards your younger brothers in New England. I thank you that you have so deliberately considered of those few words which I desired you to consider, and we thank you for your kind answer which you gave to us, and to our brethren in New England. We thank you that you have taken us to be your younger brothers; we thank you that you look upon us to be of the same blood as yourselves, and we thank you that you have received us into your body, so that now we may say we have one head, one heart, and one blood. And may God keep us united together in very deed until we both grow white-headed, and may God grant, that we may set down together, in his own due time in peace.[22]

# 7.13

# Eulogy on King Philip

WILLIAM APESS, PEQUOT

*During King Philip's War (1675–76) of resistance to expanding English settlement, the Narragansett of Rhode Island were massacred by an English assault on their main village. Surviving Narragansett joined Metacomet (King Philip) in his resistance, but when King Philip was captured, his body was quartered, and his head was displayed as a trophy on Plymouths' Fort Hill watchtower "for decades."²³*

*In a Boston theater speech given in January of 1836, William Apess, a Pequot Christian minister, delivered a fierce speech that eulogized King Philip. Apess was "unsparing about the falsity of 'Christian' missionaries to the Indians who shamed and humiliated those to whom they had supposedly come in the name of Christ, a savior . . . who was himself not white and whose salvation was for all, no matter their color, class, gender, or nationality. He condemned not only the most egregious behavior of those ministers who assisted or directly joined in land deals at the expense of Native Americans but also the mistaking of Christianity as an instrument of Euro-American notions of what constituted civilization," writes Barry O'Connell, who published Apess's complete writings.²⁴*

*In "Eulogy on William Apess," Robert Warrior celebrates the "pinnacle of Apess's intellectual career, his* Eulogy on King Philip," *which Warrior describes as "a stunning revision of American history in which Apess condemns the historical and contemporary practices by which Natives lost and were losing their lands to invading Euroamerican[s]."²⁵*

I do not arise to spread before you the fame of a noted warrior, whose natural abilities shone like those of the great and mighty Philip of Greece, or of Alexander the Great, or like those of Washington—whose virtues and patriotism are engraven on the hearts of my audience. Neither do I approve of war as being the best method of bowing to the haughty tyrant, Man, and civilizing the world. No, far from me be such a thought. But it is to bring before you beings made by the God of Nature, and in whose hearts and heads he has planted sympathies that shall live forever in the memory of the world, whose brilliant talents shone in the display of natural things, so that the most cultivated, whose powers shown with equal luster, were not able to prepare mantles to cover the burning elements of an uncivilized world. What, then? Shall we cease to mention the mighty of the earth, the noble work of God?

Yet those purer virtues remain untold. Those noble traits that marked the wild man's course lie buried in the shades of night; and who shall stand? I appeal to the lovers of liberty. But those few remaining descendants who now remain as the monument of the cruelty of those who came to improve our race and correct our errors—and as the immortal Washington lives endeared and engraven on the hearts of every white in America, never to be forgotten in time—even such is the immortal Philip honored, as held in memory by the degraded but yet grateful descendants who appreciate his character; so will every patriot, especially in this enlightened age, respect the rude yet all-accomplished son of the forest, that died a martyr to his cause, though unsuccessful, yet as glorious as the *American* Revolution. Where, then, shall we place the hero of the wilderness?

Justice and humanity for the remaining few prompt me to vindicate the character of him who yet lives in their hearts and, if possible, melt the prejudice that exists in the hearts of those who are in the possession of his soil, and only by the right of conquest—is the aim of him who proudly tells you, the blood of a denominated savage runs in his veins. It is, however, true that there are many who are said to be honorable warriors, who, in the wisdom of their civilized legislation, think it no crime to wreak their vengeance upon whole nations and communities, until the fields are covered with blood and the rivers turned into purple fountains, while groans, like distant thunder, are heard from the wounded and the tens of thousands of the dying, leaving helpless families depending on their cares and sympathies for life; while a loud response is heard floating through the air from the ten thousand Indian children and orphans, who are left to mourn the honorable acts of a few civilized men.

Now, if we have common sense and ability to allow difference between the civilized and the uncivilized, we cannot but see that one mode of the warfare is as just as the other; for while one is sanctioned by authority of the enlightened and cultivated men, the other is an agreement according to the pure laws of nature, growing out of natural consequences; for nature always has her defense for every beast of the field; even the reptiles of the earth and the fishes of the sea have their weapons of war. But though frail man was made for a nobler purpose—to live, to love, and adore his God, and do good to his brother—for this reason, and this alone, the God of heaven prepared ways and means to blast anger, man's destroyer, and cause the Prince of Peace to rule, that man might swell those blessed notes. My image is of God; I am not a beast.

But as all men are governed by animal passions who are void of the true principles of God, whether cultivated or uncultivated, we shall now lay before you the true character of Philip, in relation to those hostilities between himself and the whites; and in so doing, permit me to be plain and candid.

The first inquiry is: Who is Philip? He was the descendant of one of the most celebrated chiefs in the known world, for peace and universal benevolence toward all men; for injuries upon injuries, and the most daring robberies and barbarous deeds of death that were ever committed by the

American Pilgrims, were with patience and resignation borne, in a manner that would do justice to any Christian nation or being in the world—especially when we realize that it was voluntary suffering on the part of the good old chief. His country extensive, his men numerous, so as the wilderness was enlivened by them, say, a thousand to one of the white men, and they also sick and feeble—where, then, shall we find one nation submitting so tamely to another, with such a host at their command? For injuries of much less magnitude have the people called Christians slain their brethren, till they could sing, like Samson: With a jawbone of an ass have we slain our thousands and laid them in heaps. It will be well for us to lay those deeds and depredations committed by whites upon Indians before the civilized world, and then they can judge for themselves.

It appears from history that, in 1614, "There came one Henry Harly unto me, bringing with him a native of the Island of Capawick [Chappaquiddick], a place at the south of Cape Cod, whose name was Epenuel. This man was taken upon the main by force, with some twenty-nine others," very probably good old Massasoit's men (see Harlow's Voyage, 1611), "by a ship, and carried to London, and from thence to be sold for slaves among the Spaniards; but the Indians being too shrewd, or, as they say, unapt for their use, they refused to traffic in Indians' blood and bones." This inhuman act of the whites caused the Indians to be jealous forever afterward, which the white man acknowledges upon the first pages of the history of his country. (See Drake's *History of the Indians*, 7.)[26]

How inhuman it was in those wretches, to come into a country where nature shone in beauty, spreading her wings over the vast continent, sheltering beneath her shades those natural sons of an Almighty Being, that shone in grandeur and luster like the stars of the first magnitude in the heavenly world; whose virtues far surpassed their more enlightened foes, notwithstanding their pretended zeal for religion and virtue. How they could go to work to enslave a free people and call it religion is beyond the power of my imagination and outstrips the revelation of God's word. O thou pretended hypocritical Christian, whoever thou art, to say it was the design of God that we should murder and slay one another because we have the power. Power was not given us to abuse each other, but a mere power delegated to us by the King of heaven, a weapon of defense against error and evil; and when abused, it will turn to our destruction. Mark, then, the history of nations throughout the world.

But notwithstanding the transgression of this power to destroy the Indians at their first discovery, yet it does appear that the Indians had a wish to be friendly. When the Pilgrims came among them (Iyanough's men), there appeared an old woman, breaking out in solemn lamentations, declaring one Captain Hunt had carried off three of her children, and they would never return here. The Pilgrims replied that they were bad and wicked men, but they were going to do better and would never injure them at all. And, to pay the poor mother, gave her a few brass trinkets, to atone for her three sons and appease her present feelings, a woman nearly one hundred years of age. O white woman! What would you think if some foreign nation, unknown to you, should come and carry away from you three lovely children, whom you had dandled on the knee, and at some future time you should behold them and break forth in sorrow, with your heart broken and merely ask, "Sirs, where are my little ones?" and some one should reply: "It was passion, great passion." What would you think of them? Should you not think they were beings made more like rocks than men? Yet these same men came to these Indians for support and acknowledge themselves that no people could be used better than they were; that their treatment would do honor to any nation; that their provisions were in abundance; that they gave them venison and sold them many hogsheads of corn to fill their stores, besides beans. This was in the year 1622. Had it not been for this humane act of the Indians, every white man would have been swept from the New England colonies. In their sickness, too, the Indians were as tender to them as to their own children; and for all this, they were denounced as savages by those who had received all the acts of kindness they possibly could show them. After these social acts of the Indians toward those who were suffering, and those of their countrymen, who well knew the care their brethren had received by them—how were the Indians treated before that? Oh, hear! In the following manner, and their own words, we presume, they will not deny.

December (O[ld]. S[tyle].) 1620, the Pilgrims landed at Plymouth, and without asking liberty from anyone they possessed themselves of a portion of the country, and built themselves houses, and then made a treaty, and commanded them to accede to it. This, if now done, it would be called an insult, and every white man would be called to go out and act the part of a patriot, to defend their country's rights; and if every intruder were butchered, it would be sung up every hilltop in the Union that victory and patriotism was the order of the day. And yet the Indians (though many were dissatisfied), without the shedding of blood or imprisoning anyone, bore it. And yet for their kindness and resignation toward the whites, they were called savages and made by God on purpose for them to destroy. We might say, God understood his work better than this. But to proceed: It appears that a treaty was made by the Pilgrims and the Indians, which treaty was kept during forty years; the young chiefs during this time [were] showing the Pilgrims how to live in their country and find support for their wives and little ones; and for all this, they were receiving the applause of being savages. The two gentleman chiefs were Squanto and Samoset, that were so good to the Pilgrims.

The next time we present before you are things very appalling. We turn our attention to the dates 1623, January and March, when Mr. Weston's colony came very near starving to death; some of them were obliged to hire themselves to the Indians, to become their servants, in order that they might live. Their principal work was to bring wood and water; but, not being contented with this, many of the whites sought to steal the Indians' corn; and because the Indians complained of it, and through their complaint, some one of their number being punished, as they say, to appease the savages. Now let us see who the greatest savages were; the person that stole the corn was a stout athletic man, and because of this they wished to spare him and take an old man who was lame and sickly and that used to get his living by weaving, and because they thought he would not be of so much use to them, he was, although innocent of any crime, hung in his stead. O savage, where art thou, to weep over the Christian's crimes? Another act of humanity for Christians, as they call themselves, that one Captain Standish, gathering some fruit and provisions, goes forward with a black and hypocritical heart and pretends to prepare a feast for the Indians; and when they sit down to eat, they seize the Indians' knives hanging about their necks, and stab them to the heart. The white people call this stabbing, feasting the savages. We suppose it might well mean themselves, their conduct being more like savages than Christians. They took one Wittumumet, the chief's head, and put it upon a pole in their fort and, for aught we know, gave praise to their God for success in murdering a poor Indian; for we know it was their usual course to give praise to God for this kind of victory, believing it was God's will and command for them to do so. We wonder if these same Christians do not think it the command of God that they should lie, steal, and get drunk, commit fornication and adultery. The one is as consistent as the other. What say you, judges, is it not so, and was it not according as they did? Indians think it is.

But we will proceed to show another inhuman act. The whites robbed the Indian graves, and their corn, about the year 1632, which caused Chicataubut to be displeased, who was chief, and also a son to the woman that was dead. And according to the Indian custom, it was a righteous act to be avenged of the dead. Accordingly, he called all his men together and addressed them thus: "When last the glorious light of the sky was underneath this globe, and birds grew silent, I began to settle, as is my custom, to take repose. Before my eyes were fast closed, methought I saw a vision, at which my spirit was much troubled. A spirit cried aloud, 'Behold, my son, whom I have cherished, see the paps that gave thee suck, the hands that clasped thee warm, and fed thee oft. Can thou forget to take revenge of those wild people that have my monument in a despiteful manner, disdaining our ancient antiquities and honorable customs? See, now, the sachem's grave lies, like unto the common people of the ignoble race, defaced. Thy mother doth complain and implores thy aid against these thievish people, now come hither. If this be suffered, I shall not rest quiet within my everlasting habitation.'" War was the result. And where is there a people in the world that would see their friends robbed of their common property, their nearest and dearest friends; robbed, after their last respects to them? I appeal to you, who value your friends and affectionate mothers, if you would have robbed them of their fine marble, and your storehouses broken open, without calling those to account who did it. I trust not; and if another nation should come to these regions and begin to rob and plunder all that came in their way, would not the orators of the day be called to address the people and arouse them to war for such insults? And, for all this would they not be called Christians and patriots? Yes, it would be rung from Georgia to Maine, from the ocean to the lakes, what fine men and Christians there were in the land. But when a few red children attempt to defend their rights, they are condemned as savages by those, if possible, who have indulged in wrongs more cruel than the Indians.

But there is still more. In 1619 a number of Indians went on board of a ship, by order of their chief, and the whites set upon them and murdered them without mercy; says Mr. Dermer, "without the Indians giving them the least provocation whatever." Is this insult to be borne, and not a word to be said? Truly, Christians would never bear it; why, then, think it strange that the denominated savages do not? O thou white Christians, look at acts that honored your countrymen, to the destruction of thousands, for much less insults than that. And who, my dear sirs, were wanting of the name of savages—whites, or Indians? Let justice answer.

But we have more to present; and that is the violation of a treaty that the Pilgrims proposed for the Indians to subscribe to, and they the first to break it. The Pilgrims promised to deliver up every transgressor of the Indian treaty to them, to be punished according to their laws, and the Indians were to do likewise. Now it appears that an Indian had committed treason by conspiring against the king's life, which is punishable with death; and Massasoit makes demand for the transgressor, and the Pilgrims refuse to give him up, although by their oath of alliance they had promised to do so. Their reasons were, he was beneficial to them. This shows how grateful they were to their former safeguard and ancient protector. Now, who would have blamed this venerable old chief if he had declared war once and swept the whole colonies away? It was certainly in his power to do it, if he pleased; but no, he forbore and forgave the whites. But where is there a people, called civilized, that would do it? We presume, none; and we doubt not but the Pilgrims would have exerted all their powers to be avenged and to appease their ungodly passions. But it will be seen that this good old chief exercised more Christian forbearance than any of the governors of that age or since. It might well be said he was a pattern for the Christians themselves; but by the Pilgrims he is denounced, as being a savage.

It does not appear that Massasoit or his sons were respected because they were human beings but because they feared him; and we are led to believe that, if it had been in the power of the Pilgrims, they would have butchered them out and out, notwithstanding all the piety they professed.

Only look for a few moments at the abuses the son of Massasoit received. Alexander being sent for with armed men, and while he and his men were breaking their fast in the morning, they were taken immediately away, by the order of the governor, without the least provocation but merely through suspicion. Alexander and his men saw them and might have prevented it but did not, saying the governor had no occasion to treat him in this manner; and the heartless wretch informed him that he would murder him upon the spot if he did not go with him, presenting a sword at his breast; and had it not been for one of his men he would have yielded himself up upon the spot. Alexander was a man of strong passion and of a firm mind; and this insulting treatment of him caused him to fall sick of a fever, so that he never recovered. Some of the Indians were suspicious that he was poisoned to death. He died in the year 1662. "After him," says that eminent divine, Dr. Mather, "there rose up one Philip, of cursed memory." Perhaps if the Doctor was present, he would find that the memory of Philip was as far before his, in the view of sound, judicious men, as the sun is before the star at noonday. But we might suppose that men like Dr. Mather, so well versed in Scripture, would have known his work better than to have spoken evil of anyone, or have cursed any of God's works. He ought to have known that God did not make his red children for him to curse; but if he wanted them cursed, he could have done it himself. But, on the contrary, his suffering Master commanded him to love his enemies and to pray for his persecutors, and to do unto others as he would that men should do unto him. Now, we wonder if the sons of the Pilgrims would like to have us, poor Indians, come out and curse the Doctor, and all their sons, as we have been by many of them. And suppose that, in some future day, our children should repay all these wrongs, would it not be doing as we, poor Indians, have been done to? But we sincerely hope there is more humanity in us than that.

In the history of Massasoit we find that his own head men were not satisfied with the Pilgrims, that they looked upon them to be intruders and had a wish to expel those intruders out of their coast; and no wonder that from the least reports the Pilgrims were ready to take it up. A false report was made respecting one Tisquantum, that he was murdered by an Indian, one of Coubanant's men. Upon this news, one Standish, a vile and malicious fellow, took fourteen of his lewd Pilgrims with him, and at midnight, when a deathless silence reigned throughout the wilderness; not even a bird is heard to send forth her sweet songs to charm and comfort those children of the woods; but all had taken their rest, to commence anew on the rising of the glorious sun. But to their sad surprise there was no rest for them, but they were surrounded by ruffians and assassins; yes, assassins, what better name can be given them? At that late hour of the night, meeting a house in the wilderness, whose inmates were nothing but a few helpless females and children; soon a voice was heard—"Move not, upon the peril of your life." I appeal to this audience if there was any righteousness in their proceedings. Justice would say no. At the same time some of the females were so frightened that some of them undertook to make their escape, upon which they were fired upon. Now, it is doubtless the case that these females never saw a white man before, or ever heard a gun fired. It must have sounded to them like the rumbling of thunder, and terror must certainly have filled all their hearts. And can it be supposed that these innocent Indians could have looked upon them as good and trusty men? Do you look upon the midnight robber and assassin as being a Christian and trusty man? These Indians had not done one single wrong act to the white but were as innocent of any crime as any beings in the world. And do you believe that Indians cannot feel and see, as well as white people? If you think so, you are mistaken. Their power of feeling and knowing is as quick as yours. Now this is to be borne, as the Pilgrims did as their Master told them to; but what color he was I leave it. But if the real sufferers say one word, they are denounced as being wild and savage beasts.

But let us look a little further. It appears that in 1630 a benevolent chief bid the Pilgrims welcome to his shores and, in June 28, 1630, ceded his land to them for the small sum of eighty dollars, now Ipswich, Rowley, and a part of Essex. The following year, at the July term, 1631, these Pilgrims of the New World passed an act in court, that the friendly chief should not come into their houses short of paying fifty dollars or an equivalent, that is, ten beaver skins. Who could have supposed that the meek and lowly followers of virtue would have taken such methods to rob honest men of the woods? But, for this insult, the Pilgrims had well-nigh lost the lives and their all, had it not been prevented by Robbin, an Indian, who apprised them of their danger. And now let it be understood, notwithstanding all the bitter feelings the whites have generally shown toward Indians, yet they have been the only instrument in preserving their lives.

The history of New England writers say that our tribes were large and respectable. How, then, could it be otherwise, but their safety be rested in the hands of friendly Indians? In 1647, the Pilgrims speak of large and respectable tribes. But let us trace them for a few moments. How have they been destroyed? Is it by fair means? No. How then? By hypocritical proceedings, by being duped and flattered; flattered by informing the Indians that their God was going to speak to them, and then place them before the cannon's mouth in a line, and then putting the match to it and kill thousands of them. We might suppose that meek Christians had better gods and weapons than cannon; weapons that were not carnal, but mighty through God, to the pulling down of strongholds. These are the weapons that modern Christians profess to have; and if the Pilgrims did not have them, they ought not to be honored as such. But let us again review their weapons to civilize the nations of this soil. What were they? Rum and powder and ball, together with all the diseases, such as smallpox and every other disease imaginable, and in this way sweep off thousands and ten of thousands. And then it has been said that these men who were free from these things, that they could not live among civilized people. We wonder how virtuous people could live in a sink of diseases, a people who had never been used to them.

And who is to account for those destructions upon innocent families and helpless children? It was said by some of the New England writers that living babes were found at the breast of their dead mothers. What an awful sight! And to think, too, that these diseases were carried among them on purpose to destroy them. Let the children of the Pilgrims blush, while the son of the forest drops a tear and groans over the fate of his murdered and departed fathers. He would say to the sons of the Pilgrims (as Job said about his birthday), let the day be dark, the 22nd day of December 1622; let it be forgotten in your celebration, in your speeches, and by the burying of the rock that your fathers first put their foot upon. For be it remembered, although the Gospel is said to be glad tidings to all people, yet we poor Indians never have found those who brought it as messengers of mercy, but countrawise. We say, therefore, let every man of color wrap himself in mourning, for the 22nd of December and the 4th of July are days of mourning and not of joy. (I would here say, there is an error in my book; it speaks of the 25th of December, but it should be the 22nd. See *Indian Nullification*.) Let them rather fast and pray to the great Spirit, the Indian's God, who deals out mercy to his red children, and not destruction.

O Christians, can you answer for those beings that have been destroyed by your hostilities, and beings too that lie endeared to God as yourselves, his Son being their Savior as well as yours, and alike to all men? And will you presume to say that you are executing the judgments of God by so doing, or as many really are approving the works of their fathers to be genuine, as it is certain that every time they celebrate the day of the Pilgrims they do? Although in words they deny it, yet in the works they approve of the iniquities of their fathers. And as the seed of iniquity and prejudice was sown on that day, so it still remains; and there is a deep-rooted popular opinion in the hearts of many that Indians are made, etc., on purpose for destruction, to be driven out by white Christians, and they to take their places; and that God had decreed it from all eternity. If such theologians would only study the works of nature more, they would understand the purposes of good better than they do: that the favor of the Almighty was good and holy, and all his nobler works were made to adorn his image, by being his grateful servants and admiring each other as angels, and not, as they say, to drive and devour each other. And that you may know the spirit of the Pilgrims yet remains, we will present before you the words of a humble divine of the Far West. He says, "The desert becomes an Eden." Rev. Nahum Gold, of Union Grove, Putnam, writes under that date June 12, 1835, says he, "Let any man look at this settlement, and reflect what it was three years ago, and his heart can but kindle up while he exclaims, 'what God has wrought!' The savage has left the ground for civilized man; the rich prairie, from bringing forth all its strengths to be burned, is now receiving numerous enclosures, and brings a harvest of corn and wheat to feed the church. Yes, sir, this is now God's vineyard; he has gathered the vine, the choice vine, and brought it from a far country, and has planted it on a goodly soil. He expects fruit now. He gathered out the stones thereof, and drove the red Canaanites from trampling it down, or in any way hindering its increase" (*New York Evangelist*, August 1).

But what next should we hear from this very pious man? Why, my brethren, the poor missionaries want money to go and convert the poor heathen, as if God could not convert them where they were but must first drive them out.

If God wants the red men converted, we should think that he could do it as well in one place as in another. But must I say, and shall I say it, that missionaries have injured us more than they have done us good, by degrading us as a people, in breaking up our governments and leaving us without any suffrages whatever, or a legal right among men? Oh, what cursed doctrine is this! It most certainly is not fit to civilize men with, much more to save their souls; and we poor Indians want no such missionaries around us. But I would suggest one thing, and that is, let the ministers and people use the colored people they have already around them like human beings, before they go to convert any more; and let them show it in their churches; and let them proclaim it upon the housetops; and I would say to the benevolent, withhold your hard earnings from them, unless they do do it, until they can stop laying their own wickedness to God, which is blasphemy.

But if God was like his subjects, we should all have been swept off before now; for we find that, of late, Pilgrims' children have got to killing and mobbing each other, as they have got rid of most all the Indians. This is worse than my countrymen ever did, for they never mobbed one another; and I was in hopes that the sons of the Pilgrims had improved a little. But the more honorable may thank their fathers for such a spirit in this age. And remember that their walls of prejudice [were] built with untempered mortar, contrary to God's command; and be assured it will fall upon their children, though I sincerely hope they will not be seriously injured by it—although I myself now and then feel a little of its pressure, as though I should not be able to sustain the shock. But I trust the Great Spirit will stand by me, as also good and honorable men will, being as it were the last, still lingering upon the shores of time, standing as it were upon the graves of his much injured race, to plead their cause and speak for the rights of the remaining few. Although it is said by many that the Indians had no rights, neither do they regard their rights; nor can they look a white man in the face and ask him for them. If the white man did but know it, the Indian knows it would do no good to spend his breath for naught. But if we can trust Roger Williams's word in regard to Indian rights: He says, no people were more so; that the cause of all their wars [was] about their hunting grounds. And it is certain their boundaries were set to their respective tribes; so that each one knew his own range. The poet speaks thus of Canonicus, in 1803:

> Almighty Prince, of venerable age,
> A fearless warrior, but of peace the friend;
> His breast a treasury of maxims sage,
> His arm a host, to punish or defend.

It was said he was eighty-four years of age when he died, an able defender of his rights. Thus it does appear that Indians had rights, and those rights were near and dear to them, as your stores and farms and firesides are to the whites, and their wives and children also. And how the Pilgrims could rejoice at their distresses, I know not; what divinity men were made of in those days rather puzzles me now and then. Now, for example, we will lay before you the conduct of an Indian and the whites and leave you, dear sirs, to judge.

History informs us that in Kennebunk there lived an Indian, remarkable for his good conduct, and who received a grant of land from the state and fixed himself in a new township, where a number of white families were settled. Though not ill-treated, yet the common prejudices against Indians prevented any sympathy with him, though he himself did all that lay in his power to comfort his white neighbors, in case of sickness and death. But now let us see the scene reversed. This poor Indian, that had nourished and waited to aid the Pilgrims in their trouble, now vainly looks for help, when sickness and death comes into his family. Hear his own words. He speaks to the inhabitants thus: "When white man's child die, Indian man he sorry; he help bury him. When my child die, no one speak to me; I make his grave alone. I bury can no live here." He gave up his farm, dug up the body of his child, and carried it 200 miles, though the wilderness, to join the Canadian Indians. What dignity there was in this man; and we do not wonder that he felt so indignant at the proceedings of the then called Christians. But this was as they were taught by their haughty divines and orators of the day. But, nevertheless, the people were to blame, for they might have read for themselves; and they doubtless would have found that we were not made to be vessels of wrath, as they say we were. And had the whites found it out, perhaps they would not have rejoiced at a poor Indian's death or, when they were swept off, would not have called it the Lord killing the Indians to make room for them upon their lands. This is something like many people wishing for their friends to die, that they might get their property. I am astonished when I look at people's absurd blindness—when all are liable to die, and all subject to all kinds of diseases. For example, why is it that epidemics have raged so much among the more civilized? In London, in 1660, the plague; and in 1830 and 1831, the cholera, in the Old and New World, when the inhabitants were lain in heaps by that epidemic. Should I hear of an Indian rejoicing over the inhabitants, I would no longer own him as a brother. But, dear friends, you know that no Indian knew by the Bible it was wrong to kill, because he knew not the Bible and its sacred laws. But it is certain the Pilgrims knew better than to break the commands of their Lord and Master; they knew that it was written, "Thou shalt not kill."

But having laid a mass of history and exposition before you, the purpose of which is to show that Philip and all the Indians generally felt indignantly toward whites, whereby they were more easily allied together by Philip, their king and emperor, we come to notice more particularly his history. As to his Majesty, King Philip, it was certain that his honor was put to the test, and it was certainly to be tried, even at the loss of his life and country. It is a matter of uncertainty about his age; but his birthplace was at Mount Hope, Rhode Island, where Massasoit, his father, lived till 1656, and died, as also his brother, Alexander, by the governor's ill-treating him (that is Winthrop), which caused his death, as before mentioned, in 1662; after which, the kingdom fell into the hands of Philip, the greatest man that ever lived upon the American shores. Soon after his coming to the throne, it appears he began to be noticed, though, prior to this, it appears that he was not forward in the councils of war and peace. When he came into office it appears that he knew there was great responsibility resting upon himself and country, that it was likely to be ruined by those rude intruders around him, though he appears friendly and willing to sell them lands for almost nothing, as we shall learn from dates of the Plymouth colony, which commence June 23, 1664. William Benton of Rhode Island, a merchant, buys Mattapoisett of Philip and wife, but no sum is set which he gave for it. To this deed, his counselors, and wife, and two of the Pilgrims were witnesses. In 1665 he sold New Bedford and Compton for forty dollars. In 1667 he sells to Constant Southworth and others all the meadowlands from Dartmouth to Mattapoisett, for which he received sixty dollars. The same year he sells to Thomas Willet a tract of land two miles in length and perhaps the same in width, for which he received forty dollars. In 1668 he sold a tract of some square miles, now called Swansea. The next year he sells five hundred acres in Swansea, for which he received eighty dollars. His counselors and interpreters, with the Pilgrims, were witnesses to these deeds.

Osamequan, for valuable considerations, in the year 1641 sold to John Brown and Edward Winslow a tract of land eight miles square, situated on both sides of the Palmer's River. Philip, in 1668, was required to sign a quit claim of the same, which we understand he did in the presence of his counselors. In the same year Philip laid claim to a portion of land called New Meadows, alleging that it was not intended to be conveyed in a former deed, for which Mr. Brown paid him forty-four dollars, in goods; so it was settled without difficulty. Also, in 1669, for forty dollars, he sold to one John Cook a whole island called Nokatay, near Dartmouth. The same year Philip sells a tract of land in Middleborough for forty-two dollars. In 1671 he sold to Hugh Cole a large tract of land lying near Swansea, for sixteen dollars. In 1672 he sold sixteen square miles to William Breton and others, of Taunton, for which he and his chief received five hundred and seventy-two dollars. This contract, signed by himself and chiefs, ends the sales of lands with Philip, for all [of] which he received nine hundred and seventy-four dollars, as far as we can learn by the records.

Here Philip meets with a most bitter insult, in 1673, from one Peter Talmon of Rhode Island, who complained to the Plymouth court against Philip, of Mount Hope, predecessor, heir, and administrator of his brother Alexander, deceased, in an action on the case, to the damage of three-thousand and two hundred dollars, for which the court gave verdict in favor of Talmon, the young Pilgrim; for which Philip had to make good to the said Talmon a large tract of land at Sapamet and other places adjacent. And for the want thereof,

that is, more land that was not taken up, the complainant is greatly dam-
nified. This is the language in the Pilgrims' court. Now let us review this a little.
The man who bought this land made the contract, as he says, with Alexander,
ten or twelve years before; then why did he not bring forward his contract
before the court? It is easy to understand why he did not. Their object was
to cheat, or get the whole back again in this way. Only look at the sum demanded, and it is enough to satisfy the critical observer. This course of proceedings caused the chief and his people to entertain strong jealousies of the
whites.

In the year 1668 Philip made a complaint against one Weston, who had
wronged one of his men of a gun and some swine; and we have no account
that he got any justice for this injured brethren. And, indeed, it would be a
strange thing for poor unfortunate Indians to find justice in those courts of
the pretended pious in those days, or even since; and for a proof of my asser-
tion I will refer the reader or hearer to the records of legislatures and courts
throughout New England, and also to my book, *Indian Nullification*.

We would remark still further: Who stood up in those days, and since, to
plead Indian rights? Was it the friend of the Indian? No, it was his enemies
who rose—his enemies, to judge and pass sentence. And we know that such
kind of characters as the Pilgrims were, in regard to the Indians' rights, who,
as they say, had none, must certainly always give verdict against them, as,
generally speaking, they always have. Prior to this insult, it appears that Philip
had met with great difficulty with the Pilgrims, that they appeared to be suspicious of him in 1671; and the Pilgrims sent for him, but he did not appear to
move as though he cared much for their messenger, which caused them to be
still more suspicious. What grounds the Pilgrims had is not ascertained, unless
it is attributed to a guilty conscience for wrongs done to Indians. It appears
that Philip, when he got ready, goes near to them and sends messengers to
Taunton, to invite the Pilgrims to come and treat with him; but the governor,
being either too proud or afraid, sends messengers to him to come to their
residence in Taunton, to which he complied. Among these messengers was
the Honorable Roger Williams, a Christian and a patriot and a friend to the
Indians, for which we rejoice. Philip, not liking to trust the Pilgrims, left some
of the whites in his stead to warrant his safe return. When Philip and his men
had come near the place, some of the Plymouth people were ready to attack
him; this rashness was, however, prevented by the commissioner of Massachusetts, who met there with the governor to treat with Philip; and it was
agreed upon to meet in the meetinghouse. Philip's complaint was that the Pilgrims had injured the planting grounds of his people. The Pilgrims, acting as
umpires, say the charges against them were not sustained; and because it was
not, to their satisfaction, the whites wanted that Philip should order all his
men to bring in his arms and ammunition; and the court was to dispose of
them as they pleased. The next thing was that Philip must pay the cost of the
treaty, which was four hundred dollars. The pious Dr. Mather says that Philip

was appointed to pay a sum of money to defray the charges that his insolent clamors had put the colony to. We wonder if the Pilgrims were as ready to pay the Indians for the trouble they put them to. If they were, it was with the instruments of death. It appears that Philip did not wish to make war with them but compromised with them; and in order to appease the Pilgrims he actually did order his men, whom he could not trust, to deliver them up; but his own men withheld, with the exception of a very few.

Now, what an unrighteous act this was in the people who professed to be friendly and humane and peaceable to all men. It could not be that they were so devoid of sense as to think these illiberal acts would produce peace but, contrawise, continual broils. And, in fact, it does appear that they courted war instead of peace, as it appears from a second council that was held by order of the governor at Plymouth, September 13, 1671. It appears that they sent again for Philip; but he did not attend but went himself and made a complaint to the governor, which made him write to the council and ordered them to desist, to be more mild, and not to take such rash measures. But it appears that on the 24th the scene changed, that they held another council; and the disturbers of the peace, the intruders upon a peaceable people, say they find Philip guilty of the following charges:

1. That he had neglected to bring in his arms, although competent time had been given him.

2. That he had carried insolently and proudly toward us on several occasions, in refusing to come down to our courts (when sent for), to procure a right understanding betwixt us.

What an insult this was to His Majesty; an independent chief of a powerful nation should come at the beck and call of his neighbors whenever they pleased to have him do it. Besides, did not Philip do as he agreed, at Taunton? That is, in case there was more difficulty they were to leave it to Massachusetts, to be settled there in the high council, and both parties were to abide by their decision—but did the Pilgrims wait? No. But being infallible, of course, they could not err.

The third charge was: harboring divers Indians, not his own men but the vagabond Indians.

Now, what a charge this was to bring against a king, calling his company vagabonds, because it did not happen to please them; and what right had they to find fault with his company? I do not believe that Philip ever troubled himself about the white people's company and prefer charges against them for keeping company with whom they pleased. Neither do I believe he called their company vagabonds, for he was more noble than that.

The fourth charge is that he went to Massachusetts with his council and complained against them and turned their brethren against them.

This was more a complaint against themselves than Philip, inasmuch as it represents that Philip's story was so correct that they were blamable.

5. That he had not been quite so civil as they wished him to be.

We presume that Philip felt himself much troubled by these intruders and of course put them off from time to time, or did not take much notice of their proposals. Now, such charges as those, we think, are to no credit of the Pilgrims. However, this council ended much as the other did, in regard to disarming the Indians, which they never were able to do. Thus ended the events of 1671.

But it appears that the Pilgrims could not be contented with what they had done, but they must send an Indian, and a traitor, to preach to Philip and his men, in order to convert him and his people to Christianity. The preacher's name was Sassamon. I would appeal to this audience: Is it not certain that the Plymouth people strove to pick a quarrel with Philip and his men? What could have been more insulting than to send a man to them who was false, and looked upon as such? For it is most certain that a traitor was, above all others, the more to be detested than any other. And not only so; it was the laws of the Indians that such a man must die, that he had forfeited his life; and when he made his appearance among them, Philip would have killed him upon the spot if his council had not persuaded him not to. But it appears that in March 1674 one of Philip's men killed him and placed him beneath the ice in a certain pond near Plymouth doubtless by the order of Philip. After this, search was made for him, and they found there a certain Indian, by the name of Patuckson; Tobias, also, his son, were apprehended and tried. Tobias was one of Philip's counselors, as it appears from the records that the trial did not end here, that it was put over, and that two of the Indians entered into bonds for $400, for the appearance of Tobias at the June term, for which a mortgage of land was taken to that amount for his safe return. June having arrived, three instead of one are arraigned. There was no one but Tobias suspected at the previous court. Now two others are arraigned, tried, condemned, and executed (making three in all) [on] June the 8th, 1675, by hanging and shooting. It does not appear that any more than one was guilty, and it was said that he was known to acknowledge it; but the other two persisted in their innocence to the last.

This murder of the preacher brought on the war a year sooner than it was anticipated by Philip. But this so exasperated King Philip that from that day he studied to be revenged of the Pilgrims, judging that his white intruders had nothing to do in punishing his people for any crime and that it was in violation of treaties of ancient date. But when we look at this, how bold and how daring it was to Philip as though they would bid defiance to him, and all his authority; we do not wonder at his exasperation. When the governor finds that His Majesty was displeased, he then sends messengers to him and wishes to know why he would make war upon him (as if he had done right), and wished to enter into a new treaty with him. The king answered them thus: "Your governor is but a subject of King Charles of England; I shall not treat with a subject; I shall treat of peace only with a king, my brother; when he comes, I am ready."

The answer of Philip's to the messengers is worthy of note throughout the world. And never could a prince answer with more dignity in regard to his official authority than he did—distaining the idea of placing himself upon a par of the minor subjects of a king; letting them know, at the same time, that he felt his independence more than they thought he did. And indeed it was time for him to wake up, for now the subjects of King Charles had taken one of his counselors and killed him, and he could no longer trust them. Until the execution of these three Indians, supposed to be the murders of Sassamon, no hostility was committed by Philip or his warriors. About the time of their trial, he was said to be marching his men up and down the country in arms; but when it was known, he could no longer restrain his young men, who, upon the 24th of June [1675], provoked the people of Swansea by killing their cattle and other injuries, which was a signal to commence war, and what they had desired, as a superstitious notion prevailed among the Indians that whoever fired the first gun of either party would be conquered, doubtless a notion they had received from the Pilgrims. It was upon a fast day, too, when the first gun was fired; and as the people were returning from church, they were fired upon by the Indians, when several of them were killed. It is not supposed that Philip directed this attack but was opposed to it. Though it is not doubted that he meant to be revenged upon his enemies; for during some time he had been cementing his countrymen together, as it appears that he had sent to all the disaffected tribes, who also had watched the movements of the comers of the New World and were as dissatisfied as Philip himself was with the proceedings.

Now around the council fires they met,
The young nobles for to greet;
Their tales of woe and sorrows to relate,
About the Pilgrims, their wretched foes.

And while their fires were blazing high,
Their king and Emperor to greet;
His voice like lightning fires their hearts,
To stand the test or die.

See those Pilgrims from the world unknown,
No love for Indians do know:
Although our fathers fed them well
With venison rich, of precious kinds.

No gratitude to Indians now is shown,
From people saved by them alone;
All gratitude that poor Indian do know,
Is, we are robbed of all our rights.

At this council it appears that Philip made the following speech to his chiefs, counselors, and warriors:

> Brothers, you see this vast country before us, which the Great Spirit gave to our fathers and us; you see the buffalo and deer that now are our support. Brothers, you see these little ones, our wives and children, who are looking to us for food and raiment; and you now see the foe before you, that they have grown insolent and bold; that all our ancient customs are disregarded; the treaties made by our fathers and us are broken, and all of us insulted; our council fires disregarded, and all the ancient customs of our fathers; our brothers murdered before our eyes, and their spirits cry to us for revenge. Brothers, these people from the unknown world will cut down our groves, spoil our hunting and planting grounds, and drive us and our children from the graves of our fathers, and our council fires, and enslave our women and children.

This famous speech of Philip was calculated to arouse them to arms, to do the best they could in protecting and defending their rights. The blow had now been struck, the die was cast, and nothing but blood and carnage was before them. And we find Philip as active as the wind, as dexterous as a giant, firm as the pillows of heaven, and fierce as a lion, a powerful foe to contend with indeed, and as swift as an eagle, gathering together his forces to prepare them for the battle. And as it would swell our address too full to mention all the tribes in Philip's train of warriors, suffice it to say that from six to seven were with him at different times. When he begins the war, he goes forward and musters about 500 of his men and arms them complete, and about 900 of the other, making in all about fourteen hundred warriors when he commenced. It must be recollected that this war was legally declared by Philip, so that the colonies had a fair warning. It was no savage war of surprise, as some suppose, but one sorely provoked by the Pilgrims themselves. But when Philip and his men fought as they were accustomed to do and according to their mode of war, it was more than what could be expected. But we hear no particular acts of cruelty committed by Philip during the siege. But we find more manly nobility in him than we do in all the head Pilgrims put together, as we shall see during this quarrel between them. Philip's young men were eager to do exploits and to lead captive their haughty lords. It does appear that every Indian heart had been lighted up at the council fires, at Philip's speech, and that the forest was literally alive with this injured race. And now town after town fell before them. The Pilgrims with their force were marching in one direction, while Philip and his forces were marching in another, burning all before them, until Middleborough, Taunton, and Dartmouth were laid in ruins and forsaken by its inhabitants.

At the great fight at Pocasset, Philip commanded in person, where he also was discovered with his host in the dismal swamp. He had retired here with his army to secure a safe retreat from the Pilgrims, who were in close pursuit of him, and their numbers were so powerful they thought the fate of Philip was sealed. They surrounded the edge of the swamp, in hopes to destroy him and his army. At the edge of the swamp Philip had secreted a few of his men to draw them to ambush, upon which the Pilgrims showed fight, Philip's men retreating and the whites pursuing them till they were surrounded by Philip and nearly all cut off. This was a sorry time to them; the Pilgrims, however, reinforced but ordered a retreat, supposing it impossible for Philip to escape; and knowing his forces to be great, it was conjectured by some to build a fort to starve him out, as he had lost but few men in the fight. The situation of Philip was rather peculiar, as there was but one outlet to the swamp and a river before him nearly seven miles to descend. The Pilgrims placed a guard around the swamp for 13 days, which gave Philip and his men time to prepare canoes to make good his retreat, in which he did, to the Connecticut River, and in his retreat lost but fourteen men. We may look upon this move of Philip's to be equal, if not superior, to that of Washington crossing the Delaware. For while Washington was assisted by all the knowledge that art and science could give, together with all the instruments of defense and edged tools to prepare rafts and the like helps for safety across the river, Philip was naked as to any of these things, possessing only what nature, his mother, had bestowed upon him; and yet makes his escape with equal praise. But he would not even [have] lost a man had it not been for Indians who were hired to fight against Indians, with promise of their enjoying equal rights with their white brethren; but not one of those promises have as yet been fulfilled by the Pilgrims or their children, though they must acknowledge that without the aid of Indians and their guides they must inevitably been swept off. It was only, then, by deception that the Pilgrims gained the country, as their word has never been fulfilled in regard to Indian rights.

Philip having now taken possession of the back settlements of Massachusetts, one town after another was swept off. A garrison being established at Northfield by the Pilgrims, and while endeavoring to reinforce it with thirty-six armed, twenty out of their number was killed and one taken prisoner. At the same time Philip so managed it as to cut off their retreat and take their ammunition from them.

About the month of August, they took a young lad about fourteen years of age, whom they intended to make merry with the next day; but the Pilgrims said God touched the Indians' heart, and they let him go. About the same time, the whites took an old man of Philip's, whom they found alone; and because he would not turn traitor and inform them where Philip was, they pronounced him worthy of death and by them was executed, cutting off first his arms and then his head. We wonder why God did not touch the Pilgrims' heart and save them from cruelty, as well as the Indians.

We would now notice an act in King Philip that outweighs all the princes and emperors in the world. That is, when his men began to be in want of money, having a coat neatly wrought with mampampeag (i.e., Indian money), he cut it to pieces and distributed it among all his chiefs and warriors, it being better than the old continental money of the Revolution in Washington's day, as not one Indian soldier found fault with it, as we could ever learn; so that it cheered their hearts still to persevere to maintain their rights and expel their enemies.

On the 18th of September, the Pilgrims made a tour from Hadley to Deerfield, with about eighty men, to bring their valuable articles of clothing and provisions. Having loaded their teams and returning, Philip and his men attacked them, and nearly slew them all. The attack was made near Sugarloaf Hill. It was said that in this fight the Pilgrims lost their best men of Essex and all their goods—upon which there were many made widows and orphans in one day. Philip now having done what he could upon the western frontiers of Massachusetts and believing his presence was wanted among his allies, the Narragansetts, to keep them from being duped by the Pilgrims, he is next known to be in their country.

The Pilgrims determined to break down Philip's power, if possible, with the Narragansetts: Thus they raised an army of 1,500 strong, to go against them and destroy them if possible. In this, Massachusetts, Plymouth, and Connecticut all join in severally, to crush Philip. Accordingly, in December, in 1675, the Pilgrims set forward to destroy them. Preceding their march, Philip had made all the arrangements for the winter and had fortified himself beyond what common for his countrymen to do, upon a small island near Kingston, R.I. Here he intended to pass the winter with his warriors and their wives and children. About 500 Indian houses [were] erected of a superior kind, in which was deposited all their stores, tubs of corn, and other things, piled up to a great height, which rendered it bulletproof. It was supposed that 3,000 persons had taken up their residence in it. (I would remark that Indians took better care of themselves in those days than they have been able to since.) Accordingly, on the 19th day of December, after the Pilgrims had been out in the extreme cold for nearly one month, lodging in tents, and their provisions being short, and the air full of snow, they had no other alternative than to attack Philip in the fort. Treachery, however, hastened his ruin; one of his men, by hope of reward from the deceptive Pilgrims, betrayed his country into their hands. The traitor's name was Peter. No white man was acquainted with the way, and it would have been almost impossible for them to have found it, much less to have captured it. There was but one point where it could have been entered or assailed with any success, and this was fortified much like a blockhouse, directly in front of the entrance, and also flankers to cover the crossfire—besides the high palisades, an immense hedge of fallen trees of nearly a rod of thickness. Thus surrounded by trees and water, there was but one place that the Pilgrims could pass. Nevertheless, they made the attempt. Philip now had directed his men to fire, and every platoon of the Indians swept every white man from the path one after another, until six captains, with a great many of the men, had fallen. In the meantime, one Captain Moseley with some of his men had somehow or other gotten into the fort in another way and surprised them, by which the Pilgrims were enabled to capture the fort, at the same time setting fire to it and hewing down men, women, and children indiscriminately. Philip, however, was enabled to escape with many of his warriors. It is said at this battle eighty whites were killed and one hundred and fifty wounded, many of whom died of their wounds afterward, not being able to dress them till they marched 18 miles, also leaving many of their dead in the fort. It is said that 700 of the Narragansetts perished, the greater part of them being women and children.

It appears that God did not prosper them much, after all. It is believed that the sufferings of the Pilgrims were without a parallel in history; and it is supposed that the horrors and burning elements of Moscow will bear but a faint resemblance of that scene. The thousands and ten thousands assembled there with their well-disciplined forces bear but little comparison to that of modern Europe, when the inhabitants, science, manners, and customs are taken into consideration. We might as well admit the above fact and say the like was never known among any heathen nation in the world; for none by those worse than heathens would have suffered so much, for the sake of being revenged upon those of their enemies. Philip had repaired to his quarters to take care of his people and not to have them exposed. We should not have wondered quite so much if Philip had gone forward and acted thus. But when a people calling themselves Christians conduct in this manner, we think they are censurable, and no pity at all ought to be had for them.

It appears that one of the whites had married one of Philip's countrymen; and they, the Pilgrims, said he was a traitor, and therefore they said he must die. So they quartered him; and as history informs us, they said, he being a heathen, but a few tears were shed at his funeral. Here, then, because a man would not turn and fight against his own wife and family, or leave them, he was condemned as a heathen. We presume that no honest men will commend those ancient fathers for such absurd conduct. Soon after this, Philip and his men left that part of the country and retired farther back, near the Mohawks, where in July 1676, some of his men were slain by Mohawks. Notwithstanding this, he strove to get them to join him; and here it is said that Philip did not do that which was right, that he killed some of the Mohawks and laid it to the whites in order that he might get them to join him. If so, we cannot consistently believe that he did right. But he was so exasperated that nothing but revenge would satisfy him. All this act was worse than our political men do in our days, of their strife to wrong each other, who profess to be enlightened; and all for the sake of carrying their points. Heathenlike, either by sword, calumny, or deception of every kind; and the late duels among the [so-]called high men of honor is sufficient to warrant my statements. But while we pursue our history in regard to Philip, we find that he made many successful attempts against the Pilgrims, in surprising and driving them from their posts, during the year 1676, in February and through till August, in which time many Christian Indians joined him. It is thought by many that all would have joined him, if they had been to their choice, as it appears they did not like their white brethren very well. It appears that Philip treated his prisoners with a great deal more Christian-like spirit than the Pilgrims did; even Mrs. Rowlandson, although speaking with bitterness sometimes of the Indians, yet in her journal she speaks not a word against him. Philip even hires her to work for him, and pays her for her work, and then invites her to dine with him and smoke with him. And we have many testimonies that he was kind to his prisoners; and when the English wanted to redeem Philip's prisoners, they had the privilege.

Now, did Governor Winthrop or any of those ancient divines use any of his men so? No. Was it known that they received any of their female captives into their houses and fed them? No, it cannot be found upon history. Were not the females completely safe, and none of them were violated, as they acknowledge themselves? But was it so when the Indian women fell into the hands of the Pilgrims? No. Did the Indians get a chance to redeem their prisoners? No. But when they were taken they were either compelled to turn traitors and join their enemies or be butchered upon the spot. And this is the dishonest method that the famous Captain Church used in doing his great exploits; and in no other way could he ever gained one battle. So, after all, Church only owes his exploits to the honesty of the Indians, who told the truth, and to his own deceptive heart in duping them. Here it is to be understood that the whites have always imposed upon the credulity of the Indians. It is with shame, I acknowledge, that I have to notice so much corruption of a people calling themselves Christians. If they were like my people, professing no purity at all, then their crimes would not appear to have such magnitude. But while they appear to be by profession more virtuous, their crimes still blacken. It makes them truly appear to be like mountains filled with smoke, and thick darkness covering them all around.

But we have another dark and corrupt deed for the sons of the Pilgrims to look at, and that is the fight and capture of Philip's son and wife and many of his warriors, in which Philip lost about 130 men killed and wounded; this was in August 1676. But the most horrid act was taking Philip's son, about ten years of age, and selling him to be a slave away from his father and mother. While I am writing, I can hardly restrain my feelings, to think a people calling themselves Christians should conduct so scandalous, so outrageous, making themselves appear so despicable in the eyes of the Indians; and even now, in this audience, I doubt but there is men honorable enough to despise the conduct of those pretended Christians. And surely none but such as believe they did right will ever go and undertake to celebrate that day of their landing, the 22nd of December. Only look at it; then stop and pause: My fathers came here for liberty themselves, and then they must go and chain that mind, that image they professed to serve, not content to rob and cheat the poor ignorant Indians but must take one of the king's sons and make a slave of him. Gentlemen and ladies, I blush at these tales, if you do not, especially when they professed to be a free and humane people. Yes, they did; they took a part of my tribe and sold them to the Spaniards in Bermuda, and many others; and then on the Sabbath day, these people would gather themselves together and say that God is no respecter of persons; while the divines would pour forth, "He says that he loves God and hates his brother is a liar, and the truth is not in him"—and at the same time they hating and selling their fellow men in bondage. And there is no manner of doubt but that all my countrymen would have been enslaved if they had tamely submitted. But no sooner would they butcher every white man that come in their way, and even put an end to their own wives and children, and that was all that prevented them from being slaves; yes, *all*. It was not the good will of those holy Pilgrims that prevented. No. But I would speak, and I could wish it might be like the voice of thunder, that it might be heard afar off, even to the ends of the earth. He that will advocate slavery is worse than a beast, is a being devoid of shame, and has gathered around him the most corrupt and debasing principles in the world; and I care not whether he be a minister or member of any church in the world—no, not excepting the head men of the nation. And he that will not set his face against its corrupt principles is a coward and not worthy of being numbered among men and Christians—and conduct, too, that libels the laws of the country, and the word of God, that men profess to believe in.

After Philip had his wife and son taken, sorrow filled his heart, but notwithstanding, as determined as ever to be revenged, though [he] was pursued by the duped Indians and Church into a swamp, one of the men proposing to Philip that he had better make peace with the enemy, upon which he slew him upon the spot. And the Pilgrims, being also repulsed by Philip, were forced to retreat with the loss of one man in particular, whose name was Thomas Lucas, of Plymouth. We rather suspect that he was some related to Lucas and Hedge, who made their famous speeches against the poor Marshpees, in 1834, in the Legislature, in Boston, against freeing them from slavery that their fathers, the Pilgrims, had made of them for years.

Philip's forces had now become very small, so many having been duped away by the whites and killed that it was now easy surrounding him. Therefore, upon the 12th of August, Captain Church surrounded the swamp where Philip and his men had encamped, early in the morning, before they had risen, doubtless led on by an Indian who was either compelled or hired to turn traitor. Church had now placed his guard so that it was impossible for Philip to escape without being shot. It is doubtful, however, whether they would have taken him if he had not been surprised. Suffice it to say, however, this was the case. A sorrowful morning to the poor Indians, to lose such a valuable man. When coming out of the swamp, he was fired upon by an Indian and killed dead upon the spot.

I rejoice that it was even so, that the Pilgrims did not have the pleasure of tormenting him. The white man's gun, missing fire, lost the honor of killing the truly great man, Philip. The place where Philip fell was very muddy.

Upon this news, the Pilgrims gave three cheers; then Church ordering his body to be pulled out of the mud, while one of those tenderhearted Christians exclaims, "What a dirty creature he looks like." And we have also Church's speech upon that subject, as follows: "For as much as he has caused many a Pilgrim to lie above ground unburied, to rot, not one of his bones shall be buried." With him fell five of his best and most trusty men, one the son of a chief, who fired the first gun in the war.

Captain Church now orders him to be cut up. Accordingly, he was quartered and hung up upon four trees, his head and one hand given to the Indian who shot him, to carry about to show, at which sight it so overjoyed the Pilgrims that they would give him money for it, and in this way [he] obtained a considerable sum. After which his head was sent to Plymouth and exposed upon a gibbet for twenty years, and his hand to Boston, where it was exhibited in savage triumph; and his mangled body denied a resting place in the tomb, and thus adds the poet,

> Cold with the beast he slew, he sleeps,
> O'er him no filial spirit weeps.

I think that, as a matter of honor, I can rejoice that no such evil conduct is recorded of the Indians, that they never hung up any of the white warriors who were head men. And we add the famous speech of Dr. Increase Mather; he says, during the bloody contest the pious fathers wrestled hard and long with their God, in prayer, that he would prosper their arms and deliver their enemies into their hands. And when upon stated days of prayer the Indians got the advantage, it was considered as a rebuke of divine providence (we suppose the Indian prayed best then), which stimulated them to more ardor. And on the contrary, when they prevailed they considered it as an immediate interposition in their favor. The Doctor closes thus: "Nor could they, the Pilgrims, cease crying to the lord against Philip, until they had prayed the bullet through his heart." And in speaking of the slaughter of Philip's people at Narragansett, he says, "We have heard of two and twenty Indian captains slain, all of them, and brought down to hell in one day." . . .

But not to forget Philip and his lady, and his prophecy: It is (that is, 1671), when Philip went to Boston, his clothing was worth nearly one hundred dollars. It is said by some of the writers in those days that their money being so curiously wrought, that neither Jew nor devil could counterfeit it—a high encomium upon Indian arts; and with it they used to adorn their sagamores in a curious manner. It was said that Philip's wife was neatly attired in the Indian style; some of the white females used to call her a proud woman because she would not bow down to them and was so particular in adorning herself. Perhaps, while these ladies were so careful to review the queen, they had forgot that she was truly one of the greatest women there was among them, although not quite so white. But while we censure others for their faults in spending so much time to view their fair and handsome features, whether colored or white, we would remind all the fair sex it is what they all love, that is, jewels and feathers. It was what the Indian women used to love, and still love—and customs, we presume, that the whites brought from their original savage fathers, 1,000 years ago. Every white that knows their own history knows there was not a whit of difference between them and the Indians of their days. . . .

How deep, then, was the thought of Philip, when he could look from Maine to Georgia, and from the ocean to the lakes, and view with one look all his brethren withering before the more enlightened to come; and how true his prophecy, that the white people would not only cut down their groves but would enslave them. Had the inspiration of Isaiah been there, he could not have been more correct. Our groves and hunting grounds are gone, our dead are dug up, our council fires are put out, and a foundation was laid in the first Legislature to enslave our people, by taking from them all rights, which has been strictly adhered to ever since. Look at the disgraceful laws, dis[en]franchising us as citizens. Look at the treaties made by Congress, all broken. Look at the deep-rooted plans laid, when a territory becomes a state, that after so many years the laws shall be extended over the Indians that live within their boundaries. Yea, every charter that has been given was given with the view of driving the Indians out of the states, or dooming them to become chained under desperate laws, that would make them drag out a miserable life as one chained to the galley; and this is the course that has been pursued for nearly two hundred years. A fire, a canker, created by the Pilgrims from across the Atlantic, to burn and destroy my poor unfortunate brethren, and it cannot be denied. What, then, shall we do? Shall we cease crying and say it is all wrong, or shall we bury the hatchet and those unjust laws and Plymouth Rock together and become friends? And will the sons of the Pilgrims aid in putting out the fire and destroying the canker that will ruin all that their fathers left behind them to destroy? (By this we see how true Philip spoke.) If so, we hope we shall not hear it said from ministers and church members that we are so good no other people can live with us, as you know it is a common thing for them to say Indians cannot live among Christian people; no, even the president of the United States tells the Indians they cannot live among civilized people, and we want your lands and must have them and will have them. As if he had said to them, "We want your land for our use to speculate upon; it aids us in paying off our national debt and supporting us in Congress to drive you off.

"You see, my red children, that our fathers carried on this scheme of getting your land for our use, and we have now become rich and powerful; and we have a right to do with you just as we please; we claim to be your fathers. And we think we shall do you a great favor, my dear sons and daughters, to drive you out, to get you away out of the reach of our civilized people, who are cheating you, for we have no law to reach them, we cannot protect you although you be our children. So it is no use, you need not cry, you must go, even if the lions devour you, for we promised the land you have to somebody else long ago, perhaps twenty or thirty years; and we did it without your consent, it is true. But this has been the way our fathers first brought us up, and it is hard to depart from it; therefore, you shall have no protection from us." Now while we sum up this subject, does it not appear that the cause of all wars from beginning to end was and is for the want of good usage? That the white have always been the aggressors, and the wars, cruelties, and bloodshed is a job of their own seeking, and not the Indians? Did you ever know of Indians hurting those who [were] kind to them? No. We have a thousand witnesses to the contrary. Yea, every male and female declares it to be the fact. We often hear of the wars breaking out upon the frontiers, and it is because the same spirit reigns there that reigned here in New England; and wherever there are any Indians, that spirit still reigns; and at present, there is no law to stop it. What, then, is to be done? Let every friend of the Indians now seize the mantle of Liberty and throw it over those burning elements that have spread with such fearful rapidity, and at once extinguish them forever. It is true that now and then a feeble voice has been raised in our favor. Yes, we might speak of distinguished men, but they fall so far short in the minority that it is heard but at a small distance. We want trumpets that sound like thunder, and men to act as though they were going at war with those corrupt and degrading principles that robs one of all rights merely because he is ignorant and of a little different color. Let us have principles that will give everyone his due; and then shall wars cease, and the weary find rest. Give the Indians his rights, and you may be assured war will cease . . .

And so all of my people have been treated, whether Christians or not. I say, then, a different course must be pursued, and different laws must be enacted, and all men must operate under one general law. And while you ask yourselves, "What do they, the Indians, want?" you have only to look at the unjust laws made for them and say, "They want what I want," in order to make men of them, good and wholesome citizens.[27]

# 7.14

# Protectors of Mary Rowlandson

SAM SACHEM, KUTQUEN, QUASSOHIT, AND
PETER JETHRO; ALGONQUIANS

*According to Hilary E. Wyss, "Christian Indians played an important role in one of the most famous events of King Philip's War, Mary Rowlandson's captivity and release. Invisible but crucial as couriers, spies, informants, and scribes, Christian Indians, existing only in the margins of Rowlandson's captivity narrative, played central roles in both her captivity and her release. The wife of a minister, Rowlandson has been seen as having produced 'the archetype of a kind of official mythology in which the colonial experience was symbolized by the peril of a white Christian woman in the Indian-haunted wilderness.'" Christian Indians were in a precarious position with both non-Christian Natives and the colonists, but they were crucial intermediaries. The Massachusetts colony sent "at least five messages to Metacomet (King Philip) by way of Christian Indians. Tom Nepanet and Peter Conway were given permission to leave Deer Island to risk their lives carrying messages for the English, while Peter Jethro and James Printer wrote the messages sent by King Philip's men. . . . Christian Indians [were] crucial and often overlooked mediators in the process of intercultural negotiation."[28] In the following letter, King Philip's allies respond to Governor John Leverett's proposed negotiations for Pequot captives, including Mary Rowlandson.*

To Governor and Council in Boston, and people that are in war with us:

We now give answer by this one man, but if you like my answer, send one more man besides this one, Tom Napanet, and send with all true heart and with all your mind by two men. Because you know and we know that your heart [is] great sorrowful with crying for your los[s of] many many hundred men and all your house[s] and all your land and women, child[ren] and cattle, as all your thing[s] that you have lost, and on your backside stand.

Signed by Sam Sachem; Kutquen and Quassohit, Sagamous; Peter Jethro Scribe.

Mr. Rowlandson, you[r] wife and all your child[ren are] well, but one died. Your sister is well and her three child[ren]. John Kittell, your wife and all your child[ren are] well, and all them prisoners taken at Nashaway [are] all well.

Mr. Rowlandson, see your loving sister, [her] hand C Hanah, and old Kettel wife, [her] hand. + Brother Rowlandson, pray send three pound of tobacco for me.

This writing by your enemies—Samuel Ushattuhgun and Gunrshit, two Indian Sagamores.[29]

# Out-Skating the Devil

CAROLINE K. ANDLER, BROTHERTOWN

*The legend of John Onion has been told for many years among the Brothertowners, according to Caroline K. Andler, who credits the* Narragansett Dawn *as her source. She is the Brothertown genealogist.*

Old John Onion lived in the Charlestown woods near the old Narragansett Indian school house located about a mile back of the Indian church, on what is now called School House Pond. He came down to the pond to skate one bright cold night, feeling mighty frisky. He out-skated all the other lads, and vowed he could out-skate the devil. The other lads left him to his task. It wasn't long before he realized he wasn't skating alone. The faster and fancier he skated, this figure followed. He shouted but no reply. Soon he recalled his vow of the early evening, and John asked no more questions. Breathlessly he skated to make the shore, but the dusky figure skated by him and disappeared. John did not stop to remove his skates but skated right up the banks of the pond, right through the woods, as fast as his legs could carry him, and on right into the house. He never after tried out-skating the devil.[30]

# 7.16

## Makia'wisag, or "Little People"

FIDELIA FIELDING, MOHEGAN

*A traditional Mohegan story displayed the central social rule of "generosity and reciprocity," a value seen in this story recorded "early in the twentieth century."[31] It was translated by Gladys Tantaquidgeon, Fielding's niece, and Jerome Roscoe Skeesuck. Fielding was the last speaker of the Mohegan-Pequot language; she would not teach the language to younger Mohegans, fearing they "would be punished for speaking it."[32] J. R. Skeesuck had many descendents, including Caroline K. Andler, Brothertown genealogist.*

The *makia'wisag* were dwarfs who lived in the woods. They were the ones who made the pictures and scratchings on the rock that stood on Fort Hill. The old glass bottles, which are plowed out of the ground here and there, were left by them, as were also the brass kettles found in graves.

The last of them to be seen around here were some whom Martha Uncas told about. It must have been before 1800. She was then a child coming down the Yantic River in a canoe with her parents. They saw some *makia'wisag* running along the shore. A pine forest grew near the water, and they could be seen through the trees. Her mother saw them and said, "Don't look at the dwarfs, they will point their fingers at you, and then you cannot see them." She turned her head away. There did not seem to be many of them.

The dwarfs came to people's houses, asking for something to eat. According to the old Indians, one must always give the dwarfs what was wanted; for if they were refused, they would point their fingers at one, so that one could not see them, and the dwarfs would take whatever they chose.

There was an Indian and his wife who lived near here long ago. They saw some *makia'wisag*. It was this way: One stormy night there was a rap on their door. When the woman opened the door, the wind blew very hard. Some one was standing outside, but she did not know who it was. When she found out what the person wanted, she told her husband that someone wanted her to go and take care of a sick woman a long way off. She decided to go, and packed up her things to leave. The person was a dwarf, but she thought he was a boy. He led her far away through the storm. After a while they reached a small underground house. The dwarf led the Indian woman inside, and there lay a dwarf woman ill on a bed of skins. The Indian woman then recognized them as *makia'wisag*. She stayed with them some time and cared for the sick one until she got well. When she was ready to return home the dwarf gave the Indian woman a lot of presents, blindfolded her, and led her back to her home.

The Indians often tried to find these dwarfs, but they never succeeded. They were never heard of afterwards. I believe these were the last. They generally kept away from the Indians, but never molested them. People used to think that the mounds in this part of the Thames Valley were made by the dwarfs.[33]

# 7·17

# A Son of the Forest

WILLIAM APESS, PEQUOT

---

*William Apess, Pequot and Christian minister, wrote one of the earliest autobiographies by a Native American. He was also the publisher in 1829 of his autobiography, which is titled, in full,* A Son of the Forest: The Experience of William Apess, a Native of the Forest. *All his writings are collected in* On Our Own Ground: The Complete Writings of William Apess, a Pequot, *edited by Barry O'Connell.[34]*

William Apess, the author of the following narrative, was born in the town of Colrain, Massachusetts, on the thirty-first of January, in the year of our Lord seventeen hundred and ninety-eight. My grandfather was a white man and married a female attached to the royal family of Philip, king of the Pequot tribe of Indians, so well known in that part of American history which relates to the wars between the whites and the natives. My grandmother was, if I am not misinformed, the king's granddaughter and a fair and beautiful woman. This statement is given not with a view of appearing great in the estimation of others—what, I would ask, is *royal* blood?—the blood of a king is no better that that of the subject. We are in fact but one family; we are all the descendants of one great progenitor—Adam. I would not boast of my extraction, as I consider myself nothing more than a worm of the earth.

I have given the above account of my origin with the simple view of narrating the truth as I have received it, and under the settled conviction that I must render an account at the last day, to the sovereign Judge of all men, for every word contained in this little book.

As the story of King Philip is perhaps generally known, and consequently the history of the Pequot tribe, over whom he reigned, it will suffice to say that he was overcome by treachery, and the goodly heritage occupied by this once happy, powerful, yet peaceful people was possessed in the process of time by their avowed enemies, the whites, who had been welcomed to their land in that spirit of kindness so peculiar to the red men of the woods. But the violation of their inherent rights, by those to whom they had extended the hand of friendship, was not the only act of injustice which this oppressed and afflicted nation was called to suffer at the hands of their white neighbors—alas! They were subject to a more intense and heart-corroding affliction, that of having their daughters claimed by the conquerors, and however much subsequent efforts were made to soothe their sorrow, in this particular, they considered the glory of their nation as having departed.

From what I have already stated, it will appear that my father was of mixed blood, his father being a white man and his mother a native or, in other words, a red woman. On attaining a sufficient age to act for himself, he joined the Pequot tribe, to which he was maternally connected. He was well received, and in a short time afterward married a female of the tribe, in whose veins a single drop of white man's blood had never flowed. Not long after his marriage, he removed to what was then called the back settlements, directing his course first to the west and afterward to the northeast, where he pitched his tent in the woods of a town called Colrain, near the Connecticut River, in the state of Massachusetts. In this, the place of my birth, he continued some time and afterward removed to Colchester, New London County, Connecticut. At the latter place, our little family lived for nearly three years in comparative comfort.

Circumstances, however, changed with us, as with many other people, in consequence of which I was taken together with my two brothers and sisters into my grandfather's family. One of my uncles dwelt in the same hut. Now my grandparents were not the best people in the world—like all others who are wedded to the beastly vice of intemperance, they would drink to excess whenever they could procure rum, and as usual in such cases, when under the influence of liquor, they would not only quarrel and fight with each other but would at times turn upon their unoffending grandchildren and beat them in a most cruel manner. It makes me shudder, even at this time, to think how frequent and how great have been our sufferings in consequence of the introduction of this "cursed stuff" into our family—and I could wish, in the sincerity of my soul, that it were banished from our land.

Our fare was of the poorest kind, and even of this we had not enough. Our clothing also was of the worst description: Literally speaking, we were clothed with rags, so far only as rags would suffice to cover our nakedness. We were always contented and happy to get a cold potato for our dinners—of this at times we were denied, and many a night have we gone supperless to rest, if stretching our limbs on a bundle of straw, without any covering against the weather, may be called rest. Truly, we were in a most deplorable condition—too young to obtain subsistence for ourselves, by the labor of our hands, and our wants almost totally disregarded by those who should have made every exertion to supply them. Some of our white neighbors, however, took pity on us and measurably administered to our wants, by bringing us frozen milk, with which we were glad to satisfy the calls of hunger. We lived this way for some time, suffering both from cold and hunger. Once in particular, I remember that when it rained very hard my grandmother put us all down cellar, and when we complained of cold and hunger, she unfeelingly bid us dance and thereby warm ourselves—but we had no food of any kind; and one of my sisters almost died of hunger. Poor dear girl, she was quite overcome. Young as I was, my very heart bled for her. I merely relate this circumstance, without any embellishment or exaggeration, to show the reader how we were treated. The intensity of our sufferings I cannot tell. Happily, we did not continue in this very deplorable condition for a great length of time. Providence smiled on us, but in a particular manner.

Our parents quarreled, parted, and went off to a great distance, leaving their helpless children to the care of their grandparents. We lived at this time in an old house, divided into two apartments—one of which was occupied by my uncle. Shortly after my father left us, my grandmother, who had been out among the whites, returned in a state of intoxication and, without any provocation whatever on my part, began to belabor me most unmercifully with a club; she asked me if I hated her, and I very innocently answered in the affirmative as I did not then know what the word meant and thought all the while that I was answering aright; and so she continued asking me the same question, and I as often answered her in the same way, whereupon she continued beating me, by which means one of my arms was broken in three different places. I was then only four years of age and consequently could not take care of or defend myself—and I was equally unable to seek safety in flight. But my uncle who lived in the other part of the house, being alarmed for my safety, came down to take me away, when my grandfather made toward him with a firebrand, but very fortunately he succeeded in rescuing me and thus saved my life, for had he not come at the time he did, I would most certainly have been killed. My grandparents who acted in this unfeeling and cruel manner were by my mother's side—those by my father's side were Christians, lived and died happy in the love of God; and if I continue faithful in improving that measure of grace with which God hath blessed me, I expect to meet them in a world of unmingled and ceaseless joys. But to return:

The next morning, when it was discovered that I had been most dangerously injured, my uncle determined to make the whites acquainted with my condition. He accordingly went to a Mr. Furman, the person who had occasionally furnished us with milk, and the good man came immediately to see me. He found me dreadfully beaten, and the other children in a state of absolute suffering; and as he was extremely anxious that something should be done for our relief, he applied to the selectmen of the town on our behalf, who after duly considering the application adjudged that we should be severally taken and bound out. Being entirely disabled in consequence of the wounds I had received, I was supported at the expense of the town for about twelve months.

When the selectmen were called in, they ordered me to be carried to Mr. Furman's—where I received the attention of two surgeons. Some considerable time elapsed before my arm was set, which was consequently very sore, and during this painful operation I scarcely murmured. Now this dear man and family were sad on my account. Mrs. Furman was a kind, benevolent, and tenderhearted lady—from her I received the best possible care: Had it been otherwise I believe that I could not have lived. It pleased God, however, to support me. The great patience that I manifested I attribute mainly to my improved situation. Before, I was almost always naked, or cold, or hungry—now, I was comfortable, with the exception of my wounds.

In view of this treatment, I presume that the reader will exclaim, "What savages your grandparents were to treat unoffending, helpless children in this cruel manner." But this cruel and unnatural conduct was the effect of some cause. I attribute it in a great measure to the whites, inasmuch as they introduced among my countrymen that bane of comfort and happiness, ardent spirits—seduced them into a love of it and, when under its unhappy influence, wronged them out of their lawful possession—that land, where reposed the ashes of their sires; and not only so, but they committed violence of the most revolting kind upon the persons of the female portion of the tribe who, previous to the introduction among them of the arts, and vices, and debaucheries of the white, were as unoffending and happy as they roamed over their goodly possessions as any people on whom the sun of heaven ever shone. The consequence was that they were scattered abroad. Now many of them were seen reeling about intoxicated with liquor, neglecting to provide for themselves and families, who before were assiduously engaged in supplying the necessities of those depending on them for support. I do not make this statement in order to justify those who had treated me so unkindly, but simply to show that, inasmuch as I was thus treated only when they were under the influence of spirituous liquor, that the whites were justly chargeable with at least some portion of my sufferings.

After I had been nursed for about twelve months, I had so far recovered that it was deemed expedient to bind me out, until I should attain the age of twenty-one years. Mr. Furman . . . was a poor man, a cooper by trade, and obtained his living by the labor of his hands. As I was only five years old, . . . it would be some considerable time before I could render him much service. But such was the attachment of the family toward me that he came to the conclusion to keep me until I was of age, and he further agreed to give me so much instruction as would enable me to read and write. When I attained my sixth year, I was sent to school, and continued for six successive winters. During this time I learned to read and write, though not so well as I could have wished. This was all the instruction of the kind I ever received. Small and imperfect was the amount of knowledge I obtained, yet in view of the advantages I have thus derived, I bless God for it. . . .

I believe that it is assumed as a fact among divines that the Spirit of Divine Truth, in the boundless diversity of its operations, visits the mind of every intelligent being born into the world—but the time when is only fully known to the Almighty and the soul which is the object of the Holy Spirit's enlightening influence. It is also conceded on all hands that the Spirit of Truth operates on different minds in a variety of ways—but always with the design of convincing man of sin and of judgment to come. And, oh, that men would regard their real interests and yield to the illuminating influences of the Spirit of God—then wretchedness and misery would abound no longer, but everything of the kind give place to the pure principles of peace, godliness, brotherly kindness, meekness, charity, and love. These graces are spontaneously produced in the human heart and are exemplified in the Christian deportment of every soul under the mellowing and sanctifying influences of the Spirit of God. They are the peaceable fruits of a meek and quiet spirit.

The perverseness of man in this respect is one of the great and conclusive proofs of his apostasy, and of the rebellious inclination of his unsanctified heart to the will and wisdom of his Creator and his Judge.

I have heard a great deal said respecting infants feeling, as it were, the operations of the Holy Spirit on their minds, impressing them with a sense of their wickedness and the necessity of a preparation for a future state. Children at a very early age manifest in a strong degree two of the evil passions of our nature—*anger* and *pride*. We need not wonder, therefore, that persons in early life feel good impressions; indeed, it is a fact, too well established to admit of doubt or controversy, that many children have manifested a strength of intellect far above their years and have given ample evidence of good work of grace manifest by the influence of the Spirit of God in their young and tender minds. But this is perhaps attributable to the care and attention bestowed upon them.

If constant and judicious means are used to impress upon their young and susceptible minds sentiments of truth, virtue, morality, and religion, and these efforts are sustained by a corresponding practice on the part of parents or those who strive to make these early impressions, we may rationally trust that as their young minds expand they will be led to act upon the wholesome principles they have received—and that at a very early period these good impressions will be more indelibly engraved on their hearts by the cooperating influences of that Spirit, who in the days of his glorious incarnation said, "Suffer little children to come unto me, and forbid them not, for of such is the kingdom of heaven."

But to my experience—and the reader knows full well that experience is the best school master, for what we have experienced, that we know, and all the world cannot possibly beat it out of us. I well remember the conversation that took place between Mrs. Furman and myself when I was about six years of age; she was attached to the Baptist church and was esteemed as a very pious woman. Of this I have not the shadow of doubt, as her whole course of conduct was upright and exemplary. On this occasion, she spoke to me respecting a future state of existence and told me that I might die and enter upon it, to which I replied that I was too young—that old people only died. But she assured me that I was not too young, and in order to convince me of the truth of the observation, she referred me to the graveyard, where many

younger and smaller persons than myself were laid to molder in the earth. I
had of course nothing to say—but, notwithstanding, I could not fully com-
prehend the nature of death and the meaning of a future state. Yet I felt an
indescribable sensation pass through my frame; I trembled and was sore
afraid and for some time endeavored to hide myself from the destroying mon-
ster, but I could find no place of refuge. The conversation and pious admoni-
tions of this good lady made a lasting impression upon my mind. At times,
however, his impression appeared to be wearing away—then again I would
become thoughtful, make serious inquiries, and seem anxious to know something more certain respecting myself and that stare of existence beyond the
grave, in which I was instructed to believe. About this time I was taken to
meeting in order to hear the word of God and receive instruction in divine
things. This was the first time I had ever entered a house of worship, and instead of attending to what the minister said, I was employed in gazing about
the house or playing with the unruly boys with whom I was seated in the gal-
lery. On my return home, Mr. Furman, who had been apprised of my conduct, told me that I had acted very wrong. He did not, however, stop here. He
went on to tell me how I ought to behave in church, and to this very day I
bless God for such wholesome and timely instruction. In this particular I was
not slow to learn, as I do not remember that I have from that day to this mis-
behaved in the house of God.

It may not be improper to remark, in this place, that a vast proportion of
the misconduct of young people in church is chargeable to their parents and
guardians. It is to be feared that there are too many professing Christians who
feel sanctified if their children or those under their care enter on the Sabbath
day within the walls of the sanctuary, without reference to their conduct while
there. I would have such persons seriously ask themselves whether they think
they discharge the duties obligatory on them by the relation in which they
stand to their Maker, as well as those committed to their care, by so much
negligence on their part. The Christian feels it a duty imposed on him to conduct his children to the house of God. But he rests not there. He must have an
eye over them and, if they act well, approve and encourage them; if otherwise, point out to them their error and persuade them to observe a discreet
and exemplary course of conduct while in church.

After a while, I became very fond of attending on the word of God—then
again I would meet the enemy of my soul, who would strive to lead me away,
and in many instances he was but too successful, and to this day I remember
that nothing scarcely grieved me so much, when my mind has been thus
petted, than to be called by a nickname. If I was spoken to in the spirit of kindness, I would be instantly disarmed of my stubbornness and ready to perform
anything required of me. I know nothing so trying to a child as to be repeatedly called be an improper name. I thought it disgraceful to be called an Indian; it was considered as a slur upon an oppressed and scattered nation, and
I have often been led to inquire where the whites received this word, which

they so often threw as an opprobrious epithet at the sons of the forest. I could not find it in the Bible and therefore concluded that it was a word imported for the special purpose of degrading us. At other times I thought it was derived from the term *in-gen-uity*. But the proper term which ought to be applied to our nation, to distinguish it from the rest of the human family is that of *"Natives"*—and I humbly conceive that the natives of this country are the only people under heaven who have a just title to the name, inasmuch as we are the only people who retain the original complexion of our father Adam. Notwithstanding my thoughts on this matter, so completely was I weaned from the interests and affections of my brethren that a mere threat of being sent away among the Indians into the dreary woods had much better effect in making me obedient to the commands of my superiors than any corporal punishment that they ever inflicted. I had received a lesson in the unnatural treatment of my own relations, which could not be effaced, and I thought that, if those who should have loved and protected me treated me with such unkindness, surely I had not reason to expect mercy or favor at the hands of those who knew me in no other relation than that of a cast-off member of the tribe. A threat, of the kind alluded to, invariably produced obedience on my part, so far as I understood the nature of the command.

I cannot perhaps give a better idea of the dread which pervaded my mind on seeing any of my brethren of the forest than by relating the following occurrence. One day several of the family went into the woods to gather berries, taking me with them. We had not been out long before we fell in with a company of white females, on the same errand—their complexion was, to say the least, as *dark* as that of the natives. This circumstance filled my mind with terror, and I broke from the party with my utmost speed, and I could not muster courage enough to look behind until I had reached home. By this time my imagination had pictured out a tale of blood, and as soon as I regained breath sufficient to answer the questions which my master asked, I informed him that we had met a body of the natives in the woods, but what had become of the party I could not tell. Notwithstanding the manifest incredibility of my tale of terror, Mr. Furman was agitated; my very appearance was sufficient to convince him that I had been terrified by something, and summoning the remainder of the family, he sallied out in the quest of the absent party, whom he found searching for me among the bushes. The whole mystery was soon unraveled. It may be proper for me here to remark that the great fear I entertained of my brethren was occasioned by the many stories I had heard of their cruelty toward the whites—how they were in the habit of killing and scalping men, women, and children. But the whites did not tell me that they were in a great majority of instances the aggressors–that they had imbrued their hands in the lifeblood of my brethren, driven them from their once peaceful and happy homes—that they had introduced among them the fatal and exterminating diseases of civilized life. If the whites had told me how cruel they had been to the "poor Indian," I should have apprehended as much harm from them.[35]

# 7.18

# Sketch of the Brothertown Indians

THOMAS COMMUCK, BROTHERTOWN

*In 1859 Thomas Commuck wrote a letter to Lyman Draper, secretary for the State Historical Society of Wisconsin, briefly summarizing the Brothertown journey from the east coast to Wisconsin.*

It is a well-known fact in American history that at the time of the landing of the Pilgrim Fathers at Plymouth Rock, there were several powerful Indian tribes inhabiting the Atlantic coast in the States of Massachusetts, Rhode Island, Connecticut, and New York. It is equally well known that fierce and bloody wars were waged and carried on between the whites and said tribes, until the latter became nearly extinct, and those who survived were so crushed in spirit as to excite no fear, and as little notice or interest in the public mind at that time. And as the country grew up and increased in the number, wealth and enterprise of their civilized and christianized conquerors, the small and scattered remnants of those once powerful tribes sank in a corresponding degree into insignificance, and scarce received a passing notice amidst the mighty rush and bustle consequent upon the planting and consolidating a mighty Republic; and even at the present time, it is perhaps thought by thousands of American born citizens, that some, if not all, of the aforesaid tribes have become now entirely extinct—if not, they ask, Where are they? The answer to this question forms the subject of this letter.

Some time in the year 17—, I am unable to give the precise date, but it was many years after the tribes above spoken of were conquered and dispersed, some here and some there, an Indian by the name of David Fowler, of the Montauk tribe, who lived on the east end of Long Island, having acquired a tolerable English education, took a tour into the interior of the State of New York. Fortunately, he fell in with a large and powerful tribe of his "red brethren" called the Oneidas, the principal chief of whom, finding that Fowler possessed a good degree of the "book learning," and other useful knowledge of the "pale faces," kindly invited him to set up his lodge, and rest among them awhile; and in the meantime to open a school for educating the children of the nation. To this proposition, Fowler consented, and remained among

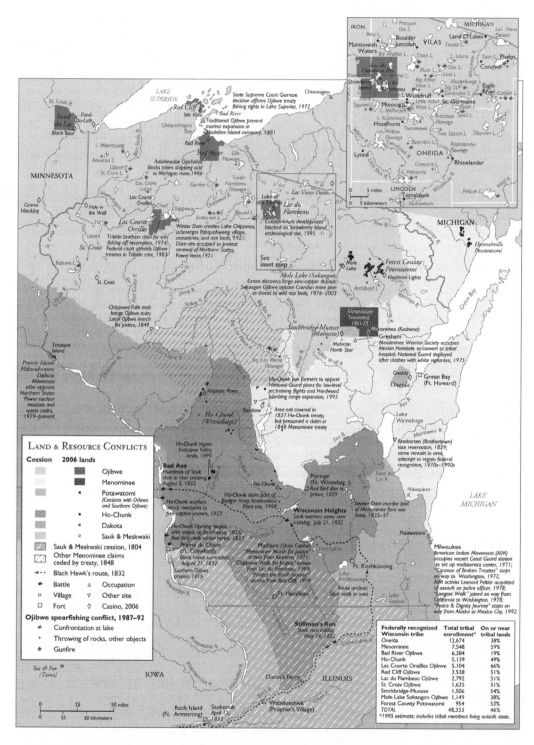

Map by Zoltan Grossman; reproduced by permission from Wisconsin Cartographers' Guild, *Wisconsin's Past and Present* (Madison: University of Wisconsin Press, 1998), 15.

them a year or eighteen months. During this time the chief made many in-quiries relative to his red brethren in the East, particularly of the following tribes: Narragansetts, Pequots, Montauks, Mohegans, Nahanticks, and an-other tribe who were called Farmington Indians; what their Indian name was is unknown.

Fowler gave a true statement of the fallen and degraded condition of those tribes, and ended by intimating that unless they soon emigrated to some more friendly clime, where they would be more free from the contaminating influence and evil example, etc., of their white brethren, and be farther re-moved from that great destroyer, worst of all, "fire-water," they would be-come wholly extinct. The Oneida chief listened with deep emotion to the pitiful, yet truthful tale, of the many wrongs and oppressions, insults and stratagems, that had, from time to time, been unsparingly practiced upon them and saw at once, that not a glimmering beam of hope shone along their pathway, to cheer their gloomy condition, and beckon them onwards to a prospect of a brighter future. And at the close of the narrative, very gener-ously gave to Mr. Fowler, for the benefit of his eastern brethren, a very valu-able tract of land, about twelve miles square, situated fourteen miles south of where the city of Utica, N.Y., now stands. At the time instructing him to re-turn without a moment's delay, to his own tribe, and spread the glad news among the other tribes, and endeavor to prevail on as many as possible from each tribe, to emigrate as soon as convenient, and take possession of the same. These instructions Mr. Fowler carried out and in due course of time, a few from each of said tribes emigrated and took possession of the tract, and commenced a settlement. And in consequence of the good wishes, and kind and brotherly feelings that actuated and bound them together, they unani-mously concluded to call the new settlement by the name of Brothertown, and thus a new Nation sprang into existence, phoenix-like, from the ashes (if I may so call it) of six different tribes, and they were ever after, while they re-mained in the state of New York, known as the Brothertown tribe of Indians.

Here, sir, I might leave them, and let it be again supposed that they had become extinct, but the fact that the writer hereof (who is a Narragansett) united with them in 1825, and has continued with them until the present time, he trusts will be deemed a sufficient apology, if he feels inclined to continue their history to the present times, after their settlement in their new home as aforesaid. Their pale-faced brethren began, after a while, to settle among them worked some of their land on shares, some leased the lands for a term of years, and in some instances, for the extraordinary term of ninety-nine years, and at their own risk, commenced making valuable improvements, both in clearing the lands and erecting buildings. It will readily be perceived that such a procedure would in process of time lead to difficulties and perplexities. As might have been expected, the white men refused to leave the soil until they had received ample, and in some instances, extortionate sums of money as in-demnity for their improvements.

Finally such strife and contention grew out of this state of affairs that the parties found it necessary to apply to the government of the State of New York to adjust their difficulties. On examination, the Legislature found the case so complex and the claims of each party such that equal justice could not be meted out to each in any other manner than to divide the whole tract of land into two equal parts. The Indians were then allowed to choose one part, and all the whites who were found residing on such part were forthwith required to leave and settle on the other half of the town or tract, and all the Indians who were found residing on the last-mentioned half were required to remove onto the first-chosen part.

The part on which the whites now found themselves was then thrown into market, and the money arising from the sale thereof was deposited in the treasury of the State of New York, for the benefit of the Brothertown Indians. It will be borne in mind, however, that the whites were first indemnified for their improvements out of said money, when the Brothertowns drew the interest on the remainder, annually, until the year 1841, when they petitioned and drew out the principal, about $30,000.

After their difficulties were adjusted by the legislature, as aforesaid, the whites and Brothertowns lived as neighbors, and trafficked together in peace and harmony for several years. And the legislature passed several acts which were intended as a safeguard to their rights and property. This code had its desired effect for awhile, but at length the genius of the ever-restless pale-face discovered flaws in said code, of which they took advantage, and immediately commenced trespassing, by cutting and carrying away much valuable timber. This of course led to much litigation, which in the end was almost sure to prove disastrous to the poor Indian. For the white man could carry away fifty or a hundred dollars worth of timber, and when sued, the Indian would obtain a sixpenny judgment against him. And even if anything like a righteous judgment was obtained, the trespasser would carry the suit up, and thus again the Indian would in the end make a losing business in the shape of lawyers' fees. Added to all of these discouragements, intemperance began to prevail, to an alarming extent among the Nation.

What was to be done? Annihilation began again to stare them in the face, as it had formerly done on the Atlantic coast. Once more the subject of seeking out a new home in the Far West was agitated and fairly discussed, and after the most mature deliberation, the Brothertowns concluded to send delegates to treat with some of their red brethren of the West, for a portion of their lands. An attempt was first made in Indiana, which failed though two or three individuals succeeded in obtaining a half section of land each, by a clause in the treaty with the Delawares in 1818. These individual tracts were sold by the parties by consent of the president of the United States, but unfortunately for the purchasers, and their successors, the heirs of said Indiana who obtained and sold, said half sections discovered a few years ago that there was some want of legality in the purchase by the whites and the said heir-at-law set up a claim to the said lands, and the question is now at issue between them and the whites who are in possession, and who will probably finally triumph.

About the same time above spoken of, the Stockbridge, Munsee, Seneca, Tuscarora, and Oneida tribes were negotiating a treaty by consent of the President of the United States with the Menominee, Winnebago, and other tribes who owned the country at and around Green Bay. They succeeded in making a purchase of a large tract of land, and partly paid for it, but unfortunately they were likely to fail in being able to pay up the last installment, and at this critical juncture, the Brothertown, who had also sent delegates to Green Bay to obtain lands, were told by the Stockbridges, Munsees, etc., that if they would advance money to pay up the last installment, they should become equal owners in the whole purchase. This the Brothertowns did, and once more fondly began to anticipate an end to all their difficulties and perplexities. This I believe was in 1827.

This treaty was ratified by the President and Senate of the United States, but by the interference of certain prominent and self-interested individuals who resided at Green Bay and . . . aided by the influence of certain government officials, the several tribes concerned came very near being cheated out of their purchase. It would be tedious to go into all the particulars of this nefarious and scandalous attempt. Suffice it to say that after the most strenuous exertions of the tribes from year to year, which was necessarily accompanied with the expenditure of large sums of money during a course of some ten or twelve years, they at last succeeded in securing, each, a small reservation. By this final adjustment, the Brothertowns obtained one township of land, eight miles long by four miles wide on the east side of Winnebago Lake, and this in lieu of a tract thirty by twelve miles square, which they in justice and equity ought to have had.

As early as 1831, four families of the Brothertowns emigrated from the State of New York, and took possession of what they justly considered their lands, and remained there until the final settlement of their difficulties. The whole tribe then emigrated in a very few years, and commenced clearing up farms in the dense forest, which covered their whole township.[36]

# 7.19

# Rhetorical Sovereignty

JIM OTTERY, BROTHERTOWN

*For Dr. Jim Ottery, an English professor at the University of Illinois at Springfield and a Brothertown Indian, the difficulty of teaching across cultures is compounded by issues of students' and teachers' ethnicity, the privileging of Edited American English (Standard Written English), and the central issue of who has control in a colonized classroom. This selection is excerpted from his speech "Samson Occum's Diary and the Brothertown Indians: The Problem of Life Stories in the Other's Tongue." When he delivered this speech, he was teaching at the Columbia College of Chicago, an open-admissions college.*

I teach mostly basic writing and reading courses to freshmen students at an open admissions institution. The issues raised by teaching English to the often academically under-prepared native speakers or to non-native speakers for whom English is a second language provides another perspective from which to view this problem of one's life story being told in the Other's tongue. While educators at the time of Samson Occum had no ethical qualms about the lethal side effects of acculturation, the same is not true today. In the 1970s the issue was viewed as a matter of linguistic ethics as the [Conference on College] Composition and Communication published its declaration of "Students' Right to Their Own Language."[37] This controversial affirmation declares that for a teacher to privilege what we now call Edited American English over a student's mother tongue is committing a "violent" act, an act of violating that student and her or his "mother culture."

The issue of students' right to their own language is one that I encounter every day as I help students from diverse backgrounds learn how to write [E]dited American English. In "Decolonizing the Classroom: Freshman Composition in a Multicultural Setting," Esha Niyogi De and Donna Uthus Gregory highlight the idea that "westernization [in Westernization I read 'valorizing Edited American English'] seems inevitably to erase individual histories and with them the capacity to imagine a future in non-Western terms."[38] I can't help but think of all of that from the standpoint of composition rhetoric theory, since I am a writing teacher. But even more so, I can't help but contemplate that point when I think of my ancestor, Samson Occum

and his diary. The problem of a life written in the Other's tongue is high-
lighted by critical commentary about the diary. . . .

How best to do a presentation on "Samson Occum's Diary and the Brothertown Indians: The Problem of Life Stories in the Other's Tongue"? The
issue becomes, I think, that which Scott Richard Lyons, a scholar of Ojibwe
ancestry writes of as being one of "Rhetorical Sovereignty." The long battle
Brothertown Indians have been fighting for sovereignty is familiar to me in
the terms in which Lyons frames it: "Our claims to sovereignty entail much
more than arguments for tax-exempt status or the right to build and operate
casinos [land reclamation]; they are nothing less than the attempt to survive
and flourish as a people." Such sovereignty is doubly important for a people
who gave it up in the first place, as Samson Occum did, in an attempt to survive the precepts of a supposedly Christian people.[39]

# 7.20

## Petition for Federal Acknowledgment as an American Indian Tribe

BROTHERTOWN INDIAN NATION OF WISCONSIN

*On October 21, 1995, the Brothertown Indians filed this petition asking for federal recognition. After centuries of supporting the fledgling English colonies, including military service in the American Revolutionary War, the Brothertown have demonstrated their cultural integrity and historic significance to the founding of the United States. It is only appropriate that the United States finally recognize their status. Caroline K. Andler, tribal genealogist for the Brothertown Nation, supplied the following piece.*

For 150 years the Brothertown Indian Nation has maintained itself in spite of overwhelming economic, social and political pressures. We have been forced to move repeatedly in order to preserve our way of life. We have received guarantees from the United States, only to find the same government acting to strip us of our land. In our forefathers' final effort to preserve our land base, they accepted land in severalty and citizenship, but instead of keeping the tribe together, the Act hastened our land loss. Despite the interference and failure of the federal government to protect the tribe, we, the Brothertown Indian Nation, have survived. It is our desire to continue the community of Brothertown Indians for our children and children's children and on and on for perpetuity. Let it be known, for all to hear, the Brothertown Indian Nation has made this historical step of petitioning for federal Acknowledgement as the beginning of a new chapter in the life of the Brothertown Indians.[40]

# NOTES

## Foreword

1. Malea Powell, "Blood and Scholarship: One Mixed-Blood's Story," in *Race, Rhetoric, and Composition,* ed. Keith Gilyard (Portsmouth, NH: Boynton/Cook Heinemann, 1999), 2.

2. Powell, "Rhetorics of Survivance: How American Indians *Use* Writing," *College Composition and Communication* 53, no. 3 (2002): 396. An example of unconscious hostility is found in the biography of Samson Occum, who was Mohegan/Pequod and one of the founders of the Brothertown Indian tribe before it moved from New York to Wisconsin. The book's author, William DeLoss Love, a Congregationalist minister and Ph.D. historian, writes in the first chapter:

> The *civilization* of American Indians, to whom our land from sea to sea once belonged is an endeavor nearly three centuries old. At no time since the forefathers came to New England have they or their descendants been wholly unmindful of this obligation. Heroic lives have been devoted to evangelizing the Indians, teachers have sought to educate them, laws have been enacted in their behalf, and a paternal government has expended vast sums in their maintenance. Although the results of all wisely ordered efforts have been better than is generally supposed, *the ultimate issue is still undetermined....*
>
> *... The main inquiry has been whether the Indian is capable of being permanently established in the ways of civilized life;* and, if so, what conditions will best accomplish this end. He has been known in our literature chiefly as a *savage.* What may he become if he is Christianized, brought into church estate, educated in industrial pursuits, invested with the rights in the land which supports him, and trusted with the responsibilities of government? (*Samson Occom and the Christian Indians of New England* [Syracuse, NY: Syracuse University Press, 2000], 1–2, my emphasis)

To his dubious credit, Love held Samson Occum up as an example of an Indian who had traversed "the distance from heathenism to American citizenship" (2).

3. Qtd. in Powell, "Blood and Scholarship," 6.

4. Craig S. Womack, *Red on Red: Native American Literary Separatism* (Minneapolis: University of Minnesota Press, 1999), 3.

5. Dexter Fisher, foreword to *American Indian Stories* by Zitkala-Ša (Lincoln: University of Nebraska Press, 1985), vii.

6. Qtd. in Dorothea M. Susag, "Zitkala-Ša (Gertrude Simmons Bonnin): A Power(full) Literary Voice," *SAIL: Studies in American Indian Literatures* 5, no. 4 (1993). http://oncampus.richmond.edu/faculty/ASAIL/SAIL2/54.html.

7. Scott Lyons, "Rhetorical Sovereignty: What Do American Indians Want from Writing?" *College Composition and Communication* 51, no. 3 (2000): 449.

8. N. Scott. Momaday, "The Man Made of Words," in *Native American Literature*, ed. Lawana Trout (Lincolnwood, IL: NTC Publishing Group, 1999), 636.

9. James Berlin's *Writing Instruction in Nineteenth-Century American Colleges* and *Rhetoric and Reality: Writing Instruction in American Colleges, 1900–1985* are seminal works in the movement to redefine rhetoric. He begins the former with the question of how we know things: "Why do we think the way that we do?" (ix). Malea Powell cites his influence on her: "In positioning myself as a scholar who does American Indian rhetorics, I want consciously to mark both portions of that figuration. The *rhetoric* part emerges from Jim Berlin's 'social epistemic rhetoric' [*Rhetoric and Reality*, 107] in that it attempts to mediate and negotiate the material contradictions of multiply positioned and constructed subjects; the *American Indian* part is linked to my often perplexing experience as a mixed-blood" ("Blood and Scholarship," 2).

10. Womack, *Red on Red*, 16–17.

11. Momaday, *The Man Made of Words* (New York: St. Martin's, 1997), 3.

12. Powell, "Rhetorics of Survivance," 405, my emphasis.

## Introduction

1. Susan Martin, *Wonderful Power: The Story of Ancient Copper Working in the Lake Superior Basin* (Detroit: Wayne State University Press, 1999).

2. Robert J. Salzer and Grace Rajnovich, *The Gottschall Rockshelter* (St. Paul: Prairie Smoke Press, 2001), 4–5.

3. Salzer and Rajnovich, *Gottschall Rockshelter*, 31.

4. Truman Lowe, interview by Tigerman, Effigy Mounds National Monument, Harpers Ferry, IA, October 2, 2004.

5. Charlie O. Rasmussen, *Where the River Is Wide: Pahquahwong and the Chippewa Flowage* (Odanah, WI: Great Lakes Indian Fish and Wildlife Commission Press, 1998), 31–33.

## Part 1. Literature of the Menominee Nation

1. Virgil J. Vogel, *Indian Names on Wisconsin's Map* (Madison: University of Wisconsin Press, 1991), 4.

2. Robert E. Ritzenthaler, ed., "The Old Copper Culture of Wisconsin," *Wisconsin Archeologist* 38, no. 4 (1957): 185–329; Susan Martin, *Wonderful Power: The Story of Ancient Copper Working in the Lake Superior Basin* (Detroit: Wayne State University Press, 1999).

3. S. Verna Fowler, "Menominee," in *Encyclopedia of North American Indians*, ed. Frederick E. Hoxie (New York: Houghton Mifflin, 1996), reprinted by permission of Houghton Mifflin Company. All rights reserved. Fowler, *The Menominee* (Austin, TX: Raintree Steck-Vaughn, 2001).

4. J. W. Powell, *Indian Linguistic Families of America North of Mexico* (Lincoln: University of Nebraska Press, 1991). See Boas 1991.

5. Fowler, "Menominee."

6. Walter James Hoffman, "The Menominee Indians," 14th annual report, pt. 1 (Washington, DC: Smithsonian Institution Bureau of American Ethnology, 1896).

7. Frances Densmore, "Menominee Music," Bulletin 102 (Washington, DC: Smithsonian Institution Bureau of American Ethnology, 1932), 146–49. Reprinted by permission of the Bureau of American Ethnology.

8. Alanson Skinner and John V. Satterlee, *Folklore of the Menomini Indians,* Anthropological Papers of the American Museum of Natural History 13, pt. 3 (New York: American Museum of Natural History, 1915), 239–41.

9. Skinner and Satterlee, *Folklore of the Menomini,* 255.

10. Leonard Bloomfield, *Menomini Texts,* American Ethnological Society, vol. 2 (New York: G. E. Stechert, 1928), 133–59.

11. Alanson Skinner, *Social Life and Ceremonial Bundles of the Menomini Indians,* Anthropological Papers 13, pt. 1 (New York: American Museum of Natural History, 1913).

12. Fowler, "Menominee," 371–73.

13. David R. M. Beck, *Siege and Survival: History of the Menominee Indians, 1634–1856* (Lincoln: University of Nebraska Press, 2002), 113–14.

14. Grizzly Bear to Gov. Porter, 26 October 1832, "Journal," in Documents Relating to the Negotiation of Ratified and Unratified Treaties with Various Indian Tribes, 1801–1969 (National Archives). Reprinted by permission.

15. Neopit, *Shawano County Advocate,* March 16, 1882.

16. Fowler, "Menominee," 371–73.

17. Jane B. Katz, ed., *I Am the Fire of Time: The Voices of Native American Women* (New York: Dutton, 1977), 148–51. Reprinted by permission.

18. Fowler, Verna, personal communication with Tigerman, July 23, 2005.

19. "American Indian and Alaska Native Policy," Committee on Interior Affairs, *Senate Concurrent Resolution 26,* 92nd Cong., 1st sess. (July 21, 1971).

20. Al Gedicks, *Resource Rebels: Native Challenges to Mining and Oil Corporations* (Cambridge, MA: South End Press, 2001), 127–55.

21. Gedicks, *Resource Rebels,* 140. Reprinted by permission of South End Press.

22. Robin Kirk, *More Terrible Than Death: Massacres, Drugs, and America's War in Colombia* (New York: Public Affairs, 2003), 227; "Colombian Rebel to Face Charges," *News from Indian Country,* May 7, 2003, 1A.

23. Jane B. Katz, ed., *Messengers of the Wind: Native American Women Tell Their Life Stories* (New York: Ballantine, 1995). Reprinted by permission of Ballantine Books, a division of Random House, Inc.

## Part 2. Literature of the Ho-Chunk Nation

1. James L. Theler and Robert F. Boszhardt, *Twelve Millennia: Archaeology of the Upper Mississippi River Valley* (Iowa City: University of Iowa Press, 2003), 59, 61.

2. Katherine Stevenson, "The Woodland Tradition," *Wisconsin Archeologist* 78, nos. 1–2 (January–December 1997): 140–201.

3. Robert A. Birmingham and Leslie E. Eisenberg, *Indian Mounds of Wisconsin* (Madison: University of Wisconsin Press, 2000).

4. Once known as Winnebago, the Ho-Chunk or Hochunkgra reclaimed their original name in 1994 via constitutional reform. Susette LaMere-Arentz, manager, Division of Cultural Resources, letter to Tigerman, August 16, 2004.

5. Robert A. Birmingham and Amy Rosebrough, "On the Meaning of Effigy Mounds," *Wisconsin Archeologist* 84, nos. 1–2 (2003): 24.

6. Dave Erickson, *Gather Like the Waters* (Lone Rock, WI: Ootek Productions, 1994). Reprinted by permission. Available from Ootek Productions, E3177 Flowage Road, Lone Rock, WI 53556.

7. I. A. Lapham, *The Antiquities of Wisconsin* (Madison: University of Wisconsin Press, 2001).

8. Paul Radin, *The Winnebago Tribe* (Lincoln: University of Nebraska Press, 1970); Birmingham and Eisenberg, *Indian Mounds of Wisconsin;* Dennis Lenzendorf, *Effigy Mounds: A Guide to Effigy Mounds National Monument* (Fort Washington, PA: Eastern National, 2000).

9. Theodore H. Lewis, unpublished manuscript of effigy mounds survey, supplied by Robert Boszhardt, Wisconsin regional archaeologist, Mississippi Valley Archaeology Center, La Crosse, WI.

10. LaMere-Arentz, letter to Tigerman.

11. Radin, *Winnebago Tribe;* Birmingham and Eisenberg, *Indian Mounds of Wisconsin.*

12. Jan Vansina, *Oral Tradition as History* (Madison: University of Wisconsin Press, 1985).

13. Erickson, *Gather Like the Waters.* Reprinted by permission.

14. Robert Salzer, "Preliminary Report on the Gottschall Site," *Wisconsin Archeologist* 68, no. 4 (December 1987): 419–72; Robert J. Salzer and Grace Rajnovich, *The Gottschall Rockshelter* (St. Paul: Prairie Smoke Press, 2001).

15. Patty Loew, *Indian Nations of Wisconsin: Histories of Endurance and Renewal* (Madison: Wisconsin Historical Society Press, 2001), 1.

16. Salzer and Rajnovich, *Gottschall Rockshelter.*

17. Truman Lowe, interview with Tigerman, Effigy Mounds National Monument, Harpers Ferry, IA, October 2, 2004.

18. Salzer and Rajnovich, *Gottschall Rockshelter,* 71.

19. Paul Radin, *The Road of Life and Death: A Ritual Drama of the American Indians* (Princeton, NJ: Princeton University Press, 1973).

20. Salzer and Rajnovich, *Gottschall Rockshelter,* 3, 69.

21. Paul Radin, "The Thunderbird Warclub: A Winnebago Tale," *Journal of American Folklore* 44 (1973): 143–65. Stylistic edits have been made by the editor.

22. David Lee Smith, *Folklore of the Winnebago Tribe* (Norman: University of Oklahoma Press, 1997), 25.

23. Smith, *Folklore of the Winnebago Tribe,* 25. Reprinted by permission of the publisher.

24. David Lee Smith, "The History of the Winnebago People," unpublished manuscript supplied by Dennis Lenzendorf, Effigy Mounds National Monument, Harpers Ferry, IA, 1994. Reprinted by permission of the author.

25. Radin, *Winnebago Tribe,* 19–21. Reprinted by permission of the University of Nebraska Press.

26. David R. M. Beck, *Siege and Survival: History of the Menominee Indians, 1634–1856* (Lincoln: University of Nebraska Press, 2002), 98.

27. Speech of Four Legs, August 7, 1827, in "Journal of Treaty at Butte Des Morts," Documents Relating to Negotiation of Ratified and Unratified Treaties, reel 2, frame 15, qtd. in Beck, *Siege and Survival,* 100–101. Reprinted by permission of the University of Nebraska Press.

28. August Derleth, *The Wisconsin: River of a Thousand Isles* (Madison: University of Wisconsin Press, 1985), 65. Reprinted by permission of the publisher.

29. Mark Diedrich, *Winnebago Oratory: Great Moments in the Recorded Speech of the Hochungra, 1742–1887* (Rochester, MN: Coyote Books, 1991), 24. Reprinted by permission of the author.

30. For a docudrama of the theft of the mining district, see *The Rush for Grey Gold* (Lone Rock, WI: Ootek Productions, 1998).

31. Derleth, *Wisconsin,* 65–67. Reprinted by permission of the University of Wisconsin Press.

32. Treaty Council, July 1829, Office of Indian Affairs, Record Group 75, National Archives, Prairie du Chien Agency, Letters Received, rolls 696–702, cited in Diedrich, *Winnebago Oratory,* 33. Reprinted by permission of the author.

33. Caleb Atwater, 1831, cited in Diedrich, *Winnebago Oratory,* 34. Reprinted by permission of the author.

34. Diedrich, *Winnebago Oratory,* cites Treaty Journal, July 1829, 35. Reprinted by permission of the author.

35. Donald Jackson, ed., *Black Hawk: An Autobiography* (Urbana: University of Illinois Press, 1955),

36. Memo of talk, November 8, 1832, Office of Indian Affairs, Record Group 75, Prairie du Chien Agency, roll 696, cited in Diedrich, *Winnebago Oratory,* 46. Reprinted by permission of the author.

37. Diedrich, *Winnebago Oratory,* 58.

38. Council with Henry Dodge, September 16, 1838, Office of Indian Affairs, Prairie Du Chien Agency, roll 698; *Wisconsin Territorial Gazette* (Burlington), October 20, 1836; both cited in Diedrich, *Winnebago Oratory,* 58. Reprinted by permission of Coyote Books.

39. Nancy Oestreich Lurie, "Winnebago," in *Handbook of North American Indians,* vol. 15, ed. Bruce G. Trigger (Washington, DC: Smithsonian, 1978), 700, 690.

40. Lurie, "Winnebago," 690.

41. Smith, "History," 682–83.

42. Winnebago Petition, March 10, 1874, Office of Indian Affairs, Winnebago Agency, roll 945, cited in Diedrich, *Winnebago Oratory,* 99. Reprinted by permission of the author.

43. Arnold Krupat, *Native American Autobiography: An Anthology* (Madison: University of Wisconsin Press, 1994), 219.

44. Nancy Oestreich Lurie, ed., *Mountain Wolf Woman, Sister of Crashing Thunder: The Autobiography of a Winnebago Indian* (Ann Arbor: University of Michigan Press, 1961), 1–7. Reprinted by permission of the publisher.

45. Michelle Burnham, "'I Lied All the Time': Trickster Discourse and Ethnographic Authority in Crashing Thunder," *American Indian Quarterly* 22, no. 4 (Fall 1998): 469–84.

46. Nancy O. Lurie, personal communication with Tigerman, July 7, 2003.

47. Paul Radin, *Crashing Thunder: The Autobiography of a Winnebago Indian* (Lincoln: University of Nebraska Press, 1983), 11–12.

48. Smith, *Folklore of the Winnebago Tribe,* 33–34. Reprinted by permission of the University of Oklahoma Press.

49. Smith, *Folklore of the Winnebago Tribe,* 40–41. Reprinted by permission of the University of Oklahoma Press.

50. Erickson, *Gather Like the Waters.* Reprinted by permission.

## Part 3. Literature of the Ojibwe Nation

1. Patty Loew, *Indian Nations of Wisconsin: Histories of Endurance and Renewal* (Madison: Wisconsin Historical Society Press, 2001) 54. Reprinted by permission of the publisher.

2. Edward Benton-Banai, *The Mishomis Book: The Voice of the Ojibway* (St. Paul: Indian Country Press, 1979), 95–102. Reprinted by permission of the author.

3. Loew, *Indian Nations*, 54–57. Reprinted by permission of Wisconsin Historical Society Press.

4. Anton Treuer, ed., *Living Our Language: Ojibwe Tales and Oral Histories* (St. Paul: Minnesota Historical Society Press, 2001), 18.

5. Treuer, *Living Our Language*, 41–45. Reprinted by permission of Minnesota Historical Society Press.

6. Benton-Banai, *Mishomis Book*, 2–3. Reprinted by permission of the author.

7. Rick Whaley with Walter Bresette, *Walleye Warriors: An Effective Alliance against Racism and for the Earth* (Philadelphia: New Society, 1994), 6–8.

8. Whaley, *Walleye Warriors*, 86–89. Reprinted by permission of New Society.

9. Whaley, *Walleye Warriors*, 28. Reprinted by permission of New Society.

10. William Wolf, Lac Courte Oreille Council Minutes, May 17, 1921.

11. Charlie O. Rasmussen, *Where the River Is Wide: Pahquahwong and the Chippewa Flowage* (Odanah, WI: Great Lakes Indian Fish and Wildlife Commission Press, 1998), 25. Reprinted by permission of the author.

12. Rasmussen, *Where the River Is Wide*, 28.

13. Loew, *Indian Nations*, 68–69. Reprinted by permission of Wisconsin Historical Society Press.

14. Rasmussen, *Where the River Is Wide*, 38.

15. Rasmussen, *Where the River Is Wide*, 50. Reprinted by permission of the author.

16. James W. Oberly, "Tribal Sovereignty and Natural Resources: The Lac Courte Oreilles Experience," in *Buried Roots and Indestructible Seeds: The Survival of American Indian Life in Story, History, and Spirit*, ed. Mark A. Lindquist and Martin Zanger (Madison: University of Wisconsin Press, 1994), 148.

17. Rasmussen, *Where the River Is Wide*, 150.

18. Oberly, "Tribal Sovereignty," 143.

19. Rasmussen, *Where the River Is Wide*, 49.

20. Al Gedicks, *Resource Rebels: Native Challenges to Mining and Oil Corporations* (Cambridge, MA: South End Press, 2001), 127–28. Reprinted by permission of the publisher.

21. Gedicks, *Resource Rebels*, 128.

22. Kimberly Blaeser, "From Aboard the Night Train," in *Earth Song, Sky Spirit: Short Stories of the Contemporary Native American Experience*, ed. Clifford Trafzer (New York: Doubleday, 1993), 25–36. Reprinted by permission of the author.

23. Andrew Connors, "Avian Messiah and Mistress Media," in Trafzer, *Earth Song*, 355–81. Reprinted by permission of the author.

24. Denise Sweet, "My Mother and I Had a Discussion One Day," in *Songs for Discharming* (Greenfield Center, NY: Greenfield Review Press, 1997), 40–41. Reprinted by permission of the publisher.

25. Danielle M. Hornett, *Sage Dreams, Eagle Visions* (East Lansing: Michigan State University Press, 2004). Reprinted by permission of the author.

26. William Whipple Warren, *History of the Ojibways, Based upon Traditions and Oral Statements* (St. Paul: Minnesota Historical Society Press, 1984), 78–79.

## Part 4. Literature of the Potawatomi Nation

1. James A. Clifton, "Potawatomi," in *Handbook of North American Indians*, vol. 15, ed. Bruce G. Trigger (Washington, DC: Smithsonian, 1978), 725–42.

2. Alanson Skinner, "The Mascoutens or Prairie Potawatomi Indians, Part III: Mythology and Folklore," *Milwaukee Public Museum Bulletin* 6, no. 3 (1924/1927): 332–33. Reprinted by permission of The Milwaukee Public Museum, Inc.

3. Clifton, "Potawatomi," 732.

4. Skinner, "Mascoutens, Part I: Social Life and Ceremonies," 177. Reprinted by permission of The Milwaukee Public Museum, Inc.

5. Skinner, "Mascoutens, Part I," 177. Reprinted by permission of The Milwaukee Public Museum, Inc.

6. Susan Campbell, e-mail to Tigerman, February 15, 2004.

7. Susan Campbell, "Cage NokmIsen," Potawatomi Web, www.kansasheritage .org/PBP/books/poetry/nokmesen.html (accessed 22 November 2005). Reprinted by permission of the author.

8. Chief Menominee to Lewis Cass, U. S. secretary of war, November 15, 1836, National Archives, microfilm M234, roll 355; frames 715–16.

9. R. David Edmunds, *The Potawatomis: Keepers of the Fire* (Norman: University of Oklahoma Press, 1978) 266–67.

10. Speech by Menominee, August 6, 1838, in Senator Tipton letter to Governor Wallace, September 18, 1838, *Indiana Historical Collections* 26:713–18.

11. Skinner, "Mascoutens, Part II: Notes on the Material Culture," 393–94. Reprinted by permission of The Milwaukee Public Museum, Inc.

12. Lee White, *How Mko Lost His Tail* (Crandon, WI: Indian Country Educational Supplies, 1999). Reprinted by permission of the author.

13. Skinner, "Mascoutens, Part I," 177. Reprinted by permission of The Milwaukee Public Museum, Inc.

14. Skinner, "Mascoutens, Part I," 178. Reprinted by permission of The Milwaukee Public Museum, Inc.

15. Harry H. Anderson, ed., "Myths and Legends of Wisconsin Indians," *Milwaukee History* 15, no. 1 (Spring 1992): 2–36. Reprinted by permission of Milwaukee County Historical Society.

16. Skinner, "Mascoutens, Part II," 368–71. Reprinted by permission of The Milwaukee Public Museum, Inc.

17. Loew, *Indian Nations,* 92.

18. Skinner, "Mascoutens, Part III," 366–67. Reprinted by permission of The Milwaukee Public Museum, Inc.

19. Collected by Jeremiah Curtin in 1883; Anderson, "Myths and Legends," 5–6. Reprinted by permission.

20. James A. Clifton, *The Prairie People: Continuity and Change in Potawatomi Indian Culture, 1665–1965* (Iowa City: University of Iowa Press, 1998), 312.

21. Simon Pokagon, *Queen of the Woods* [*O-Gi-Maw-Kwe Mit-I-Gwa-Ki*] (Hartford, MI: C. H. Engle, 1899).

## Part 5. Literature of the Oneida Nation

1. Carol Cornelius, *Iroquois Corn in a Culture-Based Curriculum: A Framework for Respectfully Teaching about Cultures* (Albany: State University of New York Press, 1999), 69.

2. Oneida Cultural Heritage Department, courtesy of Carol Cornelius. Also available online in both English and the original language through the official Web site of the Oneida Nation: http://www.oneidanation.org/?page_id=62&parent_page_id=18.

3. Demus Elm and Harvey Antone, *The Oneida Creation Story* (Lincoln: University of Nebraska Press, 2000) 30–39. Reprinted by permission of the publisher.

4. Thelma Cornelius McLester, "Oneida," in *Encyclopedia of North American Indians,* ed. Frederick E. Hoxie (New York: Houghton Mifflin, 1996) 441–43. Reprinted by permission of Houghton Mifflin Company. All rights reserved.

5. Cornelius, *Iroquois Corn,* 165.

6. John C. Mohawk, "Iroquois Confederacy," in Hoxie, *Encyclopedia of North American Indians,* 298–302. Reprinted by permission of Houghton Mifflin Company. All rights reserved.

7. Oneida Cultural Heritage Department, January 10, 2005.

8. Mohawk Nation, *Our Traditional Teachings* (Cornwall Island, Ontario: North American Indian Traveling College, 1984). Reprinted by permission of the publisher.

9. The citation in the original text refers to Bruce E. Johansen, *Forgotten Founders: Benjamin Franklin, the Iroquois and the Rationale for the American Revolution* (Ipswich, MA: Gambit, 1982), 66.

10. Colin G. Calloway, *First Peoples: A Documentary Survey of American Indian History* (Boston: Bedford/St. Martin's, 2004), 47.

11. Mohawk Nation, *The Great Law of Peace of the Longhouse People* [*Kaianerekowa Hotinonsionne*], *Akwesasne Notes* Magazine, 1977. Reprinted by permission.

12. Mohawk Nation, *Great Law of Peace.* Reprinted by permission.

13. Sandra De Coteau Orie, *Did You Hear Wind Sing Your Name?: An Oneida Song of Spring* (New York: Walker, 1995). Reprinted by permission of the publisher. The booklet is available from Full Circle, N9136 Big Lake Road, Gresham, WI 54128.

14. Colin G. Calloway, ed., *The World Turned Upside Down: Indian Voices from Early America* (Boston: Bedford/St. Martin's, 1994), 148.

15. Oneida Headmen, Speech to Governor Trumbull, *American Archives,* 4th ser., vol. 2 (1775): 116–17.

16. Calloway, *World Turned Upside Down,* 66.

17. James Dow McCallum, ed., *The Letters of Eleazar Wheelock's Indians* (Hanover, NH: Dartmouth College Publications, 1932) 281–88.

18. Thelma Cornelius McLester, "Oneida," 442.

19. Daniel Bread et al. to Enos Troop, April 13, 1831, Petition of New York Tribes, Thomas Dean MSS, State Historical Society of Wisconsin, Madison.

20. Cornelius Hill, qtd. in *Ta luh Ya Wa Gu* (Oneida: Holy Apostles Church Mission to the Oneidas, 1822–1972), 7–8.

21. Carol Cornelius, qtd. in Susan Lampert Smith, "Oneidas Find Their Past in a Pile of Green Notebooks," *Wisconsin State Journal* (Madison), October 17, 1999, 1C+.

22. Katie Cornelius, "The Way They Used to Get Married," in *The Oneida Indian Journey: From New York to Wisconsin, 1784–1860,* ed. Laurence M. Hauptman and L. Gordon McLester III (Madison: University of Wisconsin Press, 1999), 116. Reprinted by permission of the publisher. Originally published in *A Collection of Oneida Stories,* transcribed by Maria Hinton (Oneida: Oneida Nation of Wisconsin, 1996). Available from Oneida Nation Elementary School, P.O. Box 365, N7125 Seminary Road, Oneida, WI 54155.

23. Hinton, *Collection of Oneida Stories;* Hauptman and McLester, *Oneida Indian Journey.*

24. Sarah Summers, "Broken Spine and His Wife," in *Collection of Oneida Stories*

and *Oneida Indian Journey*, 118. Reprinted by permission of the University of Wisconsin Press.

25. Roberta Hill Whiteman, "Philadelphia Flowers," *Philadelphia Flowers* (Duluth: Holy Cow! Press, 1996), 59–64. Reprinted by permission of Holy Cow! Press.

26. Roberta Hill Whiteman, "The Long Parenthesis," in Rayna Green, ed. *That's What She Said: Contemporary Poetry and Fiction by Native American Women* (Bloomington: Indiana University Press, 1984), 283–84. Reprinted by permission of the author.

27. Bruce King, "Evening at the Warbonnet," in *Stories of Our Way: An Anthology of American Indian Plays*, ed. Hanay Geiogamah and Jaye T. Darby (Los Angeles: UCLA American Indian Studies Center, 1999), 357–406. Reprinted by permission of the author.

28. Carol Cornelius, "Interview of Katsi Cook, Akwesasne Mohawk Midwife," in Cornelius, *Iroquois Corn*, 253–62.

## Part 6. Literature of the Stockbridge-Munsee Band of Mohican

1. Electa F. Jones, *Stockbridge, Past and Present; or, Records of an Old Mission Station* (Springfield, MA: Samuel Bowles, 1854), 18–20.

2. Kristina Heath, *Mama's Little One* (Gresham, WI: Muh-He-Con-Neew Press, 1998). Reprinted by permission of the author.

3. Cathy J. Caldwell, personal communication with Tigerman, September 9, 2003. Reprinted by permission.

4. The mailing address is Full Circle, N9136 Big Lake Road, Gresham, WI 54128.

5. Dorothy W. Davids, "Stockbridge-Munsee (Mohican)," in *Encyclopedia of North American Indians*, ed. Frederick E. Hoxie (New York: Houghton Mifflin, 1996), 6ll. Reprinted by permission of Houghton Mifflin Company. All rights reserved.

6. Colin G. Calloway, ed., *The World Turned Upside Down: Indian Voices from Early America* (Boston: Bedford/St. Martin's Press, 1994) 88.

7. E. B. O'Callaghan, ed., *Documents Relative to the Colonial History of the State of New York*, 15 vols. (Albany: Weed, Parson, 1855), 5:662–63.

8. Patrick Frazier, *The Mohicans of Stockbridge* (Lincoln: University of Nebraska Press, 1992) 1–33.

9. Frederic Kidder, "Indian Treaties," *Maine Historical Society Collections* 4 (1856): 119–67; qtd. in Frazier, *The Mohicans of Stockbridge*, 33–34.

10. Cathy J. Caldwell, personal communication with Tigerman, September 9, 2003. Reprinted by permission.

11. Hendrick Aupaumut, qtd. in Jones, *Stockbridge, Past and Present*, 16–17.

12. *Documents Relative to the Colonial History of the State of New York* 6:881–82; *Documentary History of the State of Maine* 12:289; qtd. in Frazier, *Mohicans of Stockbridge*, 146.

13. "Petition," *Papers of the Continental Congress*, February 8, 1782 (National Archives, M247, roll 73, item 59, vol. 3, p. 211); qtd. in Frazier, *Mohicans of Stockbridge*, 234–35.

14. Jim Adams, "Ghost of King Philip's War Haunts Boston Harbor Park," *Indian Country Today*, January 21, 2004, B1+.

15. Originally published as "A Thanksgiving Mourning" in *Great Plains Observer*, November 1971, p. 3. Reprinted by permission of the author.

16. Ted Montour, "Handsome Lake," in *Encyclopedia of North American Indians*, ed. Frederick E. Hoxie (New York: Houghton Mifflin, 1996), 231. Reprinted by permission of Houghton Mifflin Company. All rights reserved.

17. Hendrick Aupaumut, *A Short Narration of My Last Journey to the Western Contry*, Memoirs of the Pennsylvania Historical Society, vol. 2 (Philadelphia: Pennsylvania Historical Society, 1827).

18. Dorothy W. Davids, *Brief History of the Mohican Nation, Stockbridge-Munsee Band* (Bowler, WI: Stockbridge-Munsee Historical Committee, 2001), 3. Reprinted by permission of the author.

19. Eva Jean Bowman, *Chief Ninham, Forgotten Hero* (Bowler, WI: Muh-He-Con-Neew Press, 1999). Reprinted by permission of the publisher. Bowman's spelling, "Ninham," has been silently changed to "Nimham" in the excerpt.

20. Davids, *Brief History*, 3.

21. Aupaumut, qtd. in Jones, *Stockbridge, Past and Present*, 20–21.

22. Cathy J. Caldwell, personal communication with Tigerman, September 10, 2003. Reprinted by permission.

23. Nicole Hirthe and Brad Pecore, "Eunice Stick," in Mohican Nation Youth, *Stories of Our Elders* (Bowler, WI: Muh-He-Con-Neew Press, 1999), 17–19.

## Part 7. Literature of the Brothertown Nation

1. Guillermo Delgado-P. and John Brown Childs, "First Peoples/African American Connections," in *Sovereignty Matters: Locations of Contestation and Possibility in Indigenous Struggles for Self-determination*, ed. Joanne Barker (Lincoln: University of Nebraska Press, 2005), 71.

2. Brothertown Indian Nation, www.brothertownindians.org (accessed November 28, 2005). Reprinted by permission.

3. Brothertown Indian Nation Mission Statement, www.brothertownindians.org/Mission.htm (accessed November 28, 2005). Reprinted by permission.

4. Michael Leroy Oberg, *Uncas: First of the Mohegans* (Ithaca, NY: Cornell University Press, 2003), 2–3, 13, 14.

5. Oberg, *Uncas*, 213–14.

6. Oberg, *Uncas*, 79, 158.

7. Richard S. Dunn, James Savage, and Laetitia Yeandle, eds., *The Journal of John Winthrop, 1630–1649* (Cambridge, MA: Harvard University Press, 1996), 258, qtd. in Oberg, *Uncas*, 79.

8. Uncas, speech to the Connecticut governor and council, May 1678, Indian Affairs, Series 1:37, Connecticut Archives, Connecticut State Library, Hartford.

9. Ward Churchill, *A Little Matter of Genocide: Holocaust and Denial in the Americas* (San Francisco: City Lights, 1997), 168.

10. Miantonomi, in *Collections of the Massachusetts Historical Society*, 3rd ser. (Boston, 1833), 3:154. Also qtd. in Colin G. Calloway, ed., *The World Turned Upside Down: Indian Voices from Early America* (Boston: Bedford/St. Martin's, 1994), 80.

11. Calloway, *World Turned Upside Down*, 80.

12. Narragansett Sachems, *Records of the Colony of Rhode Island* (Providence: A. C. Greene, 1856), 1:134–36. Also qtd. in Calloway, *World Turned Upside Down*, 81.

13. Calloway, *World Turned Upside Down*, 147.

14. John W. De Forest, *History of the Indians of Connecticut from the Earliest Known Period to 1850* (Hartford, 1852). Also qtd. in Calloway, *World Turned Upside Down*, 178.

15. Will Ottery and Rudi Ottery, "The Brothertown Tribe," in *A Man Called Sampson* (Camden, ME: Penobscot Press, 1989).

16. Papers of Eleazar Wheelock, Collection 126, microfilm, September 17, 1768, Dartmouth College, Hanover, NH.

17. Jim Ottery, "Samson Occum's Diary and the Brothertown Indians: The Problem of Life Stories in the Other's Tongue," McNickle Center Colloquium, Newberry Library, 2000. Reprinted by permission of the author.

18. A. LaVonne Brown Ruoff, introduction to "Samson Occom (Mohegan), 1723–1792," in *The Heath Anthology of American Literature*, vol. 1, ed. Paul Lauter (Lexington, MA: D. C. Heath, 1990), 730.

19. Samson Occum, *A Sermon Preached by Samson Occum* (New Haven, CT: Thomas and Samuel Green, 1772).

20. Hilary E. Wyss, *Writing Indians: Literacy, Christianity, and Native Community in Early America* (Amherst: University of Massachusetts Press, 2000), 124.

21. Joseph Johnson's speech to the Oneidas, January 20, 1774, Wheelock Papers, Dartmouth College, 774120.

22. Joseph Johnson's second speech to the Oneidas, January 24, 1774, Wheelock Papers, Dartmouth College, 774122.

23. Churchill, *A Little Matter of Genocide*, 177.

24. William Apess, *On Our Own Ground: The Complete Writings of William Apess, a Pequot*, ed. Barry O'Connell (Amherst: University of Massachusetts Press, 1992), 275.

25. Robert Warrior, "Eulogy on William Apess: Speculations on His New York Death," *Studies in American Indian Literature* 16, no. 2 (2004): 1–13.

26. The two citations are in the original work.

27. William Apess, *Eulogy on King Philip: As Pronounced at the Odeon, in Federal Street, Boston* (Boston, 1836). Also qtd. in Apess, *On Our Own Ground*, 277–310.

28. Wyss, *Writing Indians*, 18, 38.

29. Samuel Drake, *The Book of the Indians*, 11th ed., Boston, 1851. Also qtd. in Wyss, *Writing Indians*, 39.

30. Caroline K. Andler, e-mail message to Tigerman, August 19, 2004. Reprinted by permission.

31. Frank G. Speck, "Native Tribes and Dialects of Connecticut: A Mohegan-Pequot Diary," in Forty-third Annual Report of the Bureau of American Ethnology to the Secretary of the Smithsonian Institution, 1925–*1926* (Washington, DC: Smithsonian, 1928), 207.

32. Oberg, *Uncas*, 224 n.

33. Speck, "Native Tribes and Dialects," 261.

34. William Apess, *A Son of the Forest and Other Writings*, ed. Barry O'Connell (Amherst: University of Massachusetts Press, 1997), 3–11.

35. William Apess, *A Son of the Forest: The Experience of William Apess, a Native of the Forest* (New York, 1829).

36. Thomas Commuck, "Sketch of the Brothertown Indians," *Wisconsin Historical Collections* 4 (1859): 291–98.

37. "Students' Right to Their Own Language," *College Composition and Communication* 25, no. 3 (Fall 1974): 1–32.

38. Esha Niyogi De and Donna Uthus Gregory, "Decolonizing the Classroom: Freshman Composition in a Multicultural Setting," in *Writing in Multicultural Settings*, ed. Carol Severino, Juan C. Guerra, and Johnnella E. Butler (New York: Modern Language Association, 1997).

39. Ottery, "Samson Occum's Diary and the Brothertown Indians."

40. Brothertown Indian Nation of Wisconsin, "Petition for Federal Acknowledgment as an American Indian Tribe," 1995. Reprinted by permission. As this book went to press, the Brothertown Indian Nation had not yet received a response to their request for federal recognition as an American Indian tribe.

# BIBLIOGRAPHY

Adams, Jim. "Ghost of King Philip's War Haunts Boston Harbor Park." *Indian Country Today,* January 21, 2004, B1+.

"American Indian and Alaska Native Policy." Committee on Interior Affairs, *Senate Concurrent Resolution 26,* 92nd Congress, 1st sess. July 21, 1971.

Anderson, Harry, H., ed. "Myths and Legends of Wisconsin Indians." *Milwaukee History* 15, no. 1 (Spring 1992): 2–36.

Apess, William. *Eulogy on King Philip: As Pronounced at the Odeon, in Federal Street, Boston.* Boston: author, 1836.

———. *On Our Own Ground: The Complete Writings of William Apess, A Pequot.* Edited by Barry O'Connell. Amherst: University of Massachusetts Press, 1992.

———. *A Son of the Forest: The Experience of William Apes, a Native of the Forest: Comprising a Notice of the Pequod Tribe of Indians.* New York: author, 1829.

———. *A Son of the Forest and Other Writings.* Edited by Barry O'Connell. Amherst: University of Massachusetts Press, 1997.

Atwater, Caleb. *Remarks Made on a Tour to Prairie du Chien, Thence to Washington City, in 1829.* Columbus: Isaac N. Whiting, 1831.

Aupaumut, Hendrick. *A Short Narration of My Last Journey to the Western Contry.* Memoirs of the Pennsylvania Historical Society, vol. 2. Philadelphia: Pennsylvania Historical Society, 1827.

Baraga, Frederic. *A Dictionary of the Ojibway Language.* St. Paul: Minnesota Historical Society Press, 1992.

Barker, Joanne, ed. *Sovereignty Matters: Locations of Contestation and Possibility in Indigenous Struggles for Self-determination.* Lincoln: University of Nebraska Press, 2005.

Barnouw, Victor. *Wisconsin Chippewa Myths and Tales and Their Relation to Chippewa Life.* Madison: University of Wisconsin Press, 1977.

Barreca, Elaine. "The Secret of EB3/47." *Beloit Magazine,* December 1992, 6–7.

Barreiro, Jose, ed. "Indian Corn of the Americas: Gift to the World." Special issue, *Northeast Indian Quarterly* 6 (Spring/Summer 1989).

Bataille, Gretchen M., ed. *Native American Representations: First Encounters, Distorted Images, and Literary Appropriations.* Lincoln: University of Nebraska Press, 2001.

Bataille, Gretchen M., and Kathleen M. Sands. *American Indian Women, Telling Their Lives.* Lincoln: University of Nebraska Press, 1984.

Benton-Banai, Edward. *The Mishomis Book: The Voice of the Ojibway.* St Paul: Indian Country Press, 1979.

Beck, David R. M. *Siege and Survival: History of the Menominee Indians, 1634–1856.* Lincoln: University of Nebraska Press, 2002.

Berlin, James. *Rhetoric and Reality: Writing Instruction in American Colleges, 1900–1985.* Carbondale: Southern Illinois University Press, 1987.

——. *Writing Instruction in Nineteenth-Century American Colleges.* Carbondale: Southern Illinois University Press, 1984.

Bieder, Robert. "'In the Old Language': A Glossary of Ojibwe Words, Phrases, and Sentences in Louise Erdrich's Novels." *American Indian Culture and Research Journal* 27, no. 3 (2003): 53–70.

——. *Native American Communities in Wisconsin, 1600–1960: A Study of Tradition and Change.* Madison: University of Wisconsin Press, 1995.

Bierhorst, John. *The Red Swan: Myths and Tales of the American Indians.* New York: Farrar, Straus and Giroux, 1976.

——, ed. *The Sacred Path: Spells, Prayers, and Power Songs of the American Indians.* New York: William Morrow, 1983.

Birmingham, Robert A. "The Last Millennium: Wisconsin's First Farmers." *Wisconsin Academy Review* 46 (Winter 1999–2000): 4–8.

——. "Uncovering the Story of Fort Blue Mounds." *Wisconsin Magazine of History* 86 (Summer 2003): 46–57.

Birmingham, Robert A., Carol Mason, and James B. Stoltman, eds. "Wisconsin Archaeology." *Wisconsin Archeologist* 78, nos. 1–2 (1997), 223–49.

Birmingham, Robert A., and Leslie E. Eisenberg. *Indian Mounds of Wisconsin.* Madison: University of Wisconsin Press, 2000.

Birmingham, Robert A., and Amy Rosebrough. "On the Meaning of Effigy Mounds." *Wisconsin Archeologist* 84, nos. 1–2 (2003).

Blaeser, Kimberly. "From Aboard the Night Train." In Trafzer, *Earth Song,* 23–36.

——, ed. *Stories Migrating Home: A Collection of Anishinaabe Prose.* Bemidji: Loonfeather Press, 1999.

——. *Trailing You: Poems.* Greenfield Center, NY: Greenfield Review Press, 1995.

Blair, Emma Helen. *The Indian Tribes of the Upper Mississippi Valley and Region of the Great Lakes.* Lincoln: University of Nebraska Press, 1996.

Bloomfield, Leonard. *Menomini Texts.* New York: G. E. Stechert, 1928.

Boas, Franz, and J. W. Powell. *Introduction to Handbook of American Indian Languages and Indian Linguistic Families of America North of Mexico.* Edited by Preston Holder. Lincoln: University of Nebraska Press, 1991 [1966].

Bogue, Margaret Beattie. "As She Knew Them: Juliette Kinzie and the Ho-Chunk, 1830–1833." *Wisconsin Magazine of History* 85, no. 2 (Winter 2001–2002): 44–57.

Bonvillain, Nancy. *The Sac and Fox.* New York: Chelsea House, 1995.

Borich, Michael. *The Black Hawk Songs.* Urbana: University of Illinois Press, 1975.

Boszhardt, Robert F. *Deep Cave Rock Art in the Upper Mississippi Valley.* St. Paul: Prairie Smoke Press, 2003.

Bowman, Eva Jean. *Chief Ninham, Forgotten Hero.* Gresham, WI: Muh-He-Con-Neew Press, 1999.

Bowman, Nicole R. "Cultural Differences of Teaching and Learning: A Native American Perspective of Participating in Educational Systems and Organizations." *American Indian Quarterly* 27, nos. 1 and 2 (Winter/Spring 2003): 91–102.

Bread, Daniel, et al., to Enos Troop. Petition of New York Tribes. April 13, 1831. Thomas Dean MSS. State Historical Society of Wisconsin, Madison.

Broker, Ignatia. *Night Flying Woman: An Ojibway Narrative.* St. Paul: Minnesota Historical Society Press, 1983.

Brothertown Indian Nation. "Mission Statement." www.brothertownindians.org/Mission.htm (accessed June 30, 2006).

Brothertown Indian Nation of Wisconsin. "Petition for Federal Acknowledgement as an American Indian Tribe." 1995. Supplied courtesy of Caroline K. Andler, Brothertown genealogist.

Burnham, Michelle. "'I Lied All the Time': Trickster Discourse and Ethnographic Authority in Crashing Thunder." *American Indian Quarterly* 22, no. 4 (Fall 1998): 469–84.

Callahan, Kevin L. *The Jeffers Petroglyphs: Native American Rock Art on the Midwestern Plains*. St. Paul: Prairie Smoke Press, 2001.

Calloway, Colin G. *First Peoples: A Documentary Survey of American Indian History*. 2nd ed. Boston: Bedford/St. Martin's, 2004.

——, ed. *The World Turned Upside Down: Indian Voices from Early America*. Boston: Bedford/St. Martin's, 1994.

Campbell, Susan. "Cage NokmIsen." Potawatomi Web. http://www.kansasheritage .org/PBP/books/poetry/nokmesen.html (accessed June 30, 2006).

Campisi, Jack. "The Brothertown Indian Nation of Wisconsin: A Brief History." Fond du Lac, WI: Brothertown Indian Nation, 1991.

——. "Oneida." In Trigger, *Handbook of North American Indians*, 481–90.

Campisi, Jack, and Laurence Hauptman, eds. *The Oneida Indian Experience: Two Perspectives*. Syracuse: Syracuse University Press, 1988.

Champagne, Duane, ed. *Native America: Portrait of the Peoples*. Detroit: Visible Ink, 1994.

Churchill, Ward. *A Little Matter of Genocide: Holocaust and Denial in the Americas, 1492 to the Present*. San Francisco: City Lights, 1997.

Clifton, James A. "Potawatomi." In Trigger, *Handbook of North American Indians*, 725–42.

——. *The Prairie People: Continuity and Change in Potawatomi Indian Culture, 1665–1965*. Iowa City: University of Iowa Press, 1998.

"Colombian Rebel Appears in U.S. Court." *News From Indian Country* [Hayward, WI], June 16, 2003, 1.

"Colombian Rebel to Face Charges." *News From Indian Country* [Hayward, WI], May 7, 2003, 1A.

Coltelli, Laura. *Winged Words: American Indian Writers Speak*. Lincoln: University of Nebraska Press, 1990.

Commuck, Thomas. "Sketch of the Brothertown Indians." *Wisconsin Historical Collections* 4 (1859). State Historical Society of Wisconsin, Madison.

Conners, Andrew. "Avian Messiah and Mistress Media." In Trafzer, *Earth Song*, 353–82.

Conway, Thor. *Painted Dreams: Native American Rock Art*. Minocqua, WI: NorthWord Press, 1993.

Conway, Thor, and Julie Conway. *Spirits on Stone: The Agawa Pictographs*. San Luis Obispo, CA: Heritage Discoveries, 1990.

Cornelius, Carol. "Activities to Accompany 'The Corn Spirit.'" In Barreiro, "Indian Corn of the Americas."

——. *Iroquois Corn in a Culture-Based Curriculum: A Framework for Respectfully Teaching about Cultures*. Albany: State University of New York Press, 1999.

——. "The Thanksgiving Address: An Expression of Haudenosaunee Worldview." *Akwe:kon Journal* 9, no. 3 (1992): 14–25.

Cornelius, Katie. "The Way They Used to Get Married." In Hauptman and McLester, *The Oneida Indian Journey*, 114–16.

Council with Henry Dodge. September 16, 1838. Roll 698. Office of Indian Affairs, Prairie du Chien Agency, National Archives.

Curtin, Jeremiah. "Interview with Shawequet." *Milwaukee History* 15, no. 1 (Spring 1992): 27–32.

Cutler, Charles L. *O Brave New Words!: Native American Loanwords in Current English.* Norman: University of Oklahoma Press, 1994.

Danforth, Cristina. "A Message from the Chairwoman." Oneida Nation of Wisconsin. Oneida, WI: n.d.

Davids, Dorothy W. *Anüshiik.* Gresham, WI: Muh-He-Con-Neew Press, 2002.

———. *Brief History of the Mohican Nation, Stockbridge-Munsee Band.* Bowler, WI: Stockbridge-Munsee Historical Committee, 2001.

———. "Stockbridge-Munsee (Mohican)." In Hoxie, *Encyclopedia of North American Indians,* 611.

Davis, Mary B., ed. *Native America in the Twentieth Century: An Encyclopedia.* New York: Garland, 1996.

Day, A. Grove. *The Sky Clears: Poetry of the American Indians.* New York: Macmillan, 1951.

De Forest, John W. *History of the Indians of Connecticut from the Earliest Known Period to 1850.* Hartford, 1852.

Delgado-P., Guillermo, and John Brown Childs. "First Peoples/African American Connections." In Barker, *Sovereignty Matters,* 67–86.

Deloria, Vine, Jr. *God Is Red: A Native View of Religion.* 3rd ed. Golden, CO: Fulcrum, 2003.

———. *Red Earth, White Lies: Native Americans and the Myth of Scientific Fact.* Golden, CO: Fulcrum, 1997.

Densmore, Frances. *How Indians Use Wild Plants for Food, Medicine and Crafts.* New York: Dover, 1974.

———. "Menominee Music." Bulletin 102. Washington, DC: Smithsonian Institution Bureau of American Ethnology, 1931.

Derleth, August. *The Wisconsin: River of a Thousand Isles.* Madison: University of Wisconsin Press, 1985.

Dewdney, Selwyn. *The Sacred Scrolls of the Southern Ojibway.* Toronto: University of Toronto Press, 1975.

Diedrich, Mark. *Winnebago Oratory: Great Moments in the Recorded Speech of the Hochungra, 1742–1887.* Rochester, MN: Coyote Books, 1991.

———. *The Chiefs Hole-In-The-Day of the Mississippi Chippewa.* Minneapolis: Coyote Books, 1986.

———. *Ojibway Oratory: Great Moments in the Recorded Speech of the Chippewa, 1695–1889.* Rochester, MN: Coyote Books, 1990.

Documents Relating to the Negotiation of Ratified and Unratified Treaties with Various Indian Tribes, 1801–1969. Washington, DC: National Archives.

Donovan, Kathleen M. *Feminist Readings of Native American Literature: Coming to Voice.* Tucson: University of Arizona Press, 1998.

Dooling, D. M. and Paul Jordan-Smith, eds. *I Become Part of It: Sacred Dimensions in Native American Life.* San Francisco: HarperCollins, 1992.

Drake, Samuel G. *The Book of the Indians; or, Biography and History of the Indians of North America, from Its First Discovery to the Year 1841.* 11th ed. Boston: B. B. Mussey, 1851.

Dunn, Anne M. *When Beaver Was Very Great: Stories to Live By.* Mt. Horeb, WI: Midwest Traditions, 1995.

Eastman, Charles A. *Indian Heroes and Great Chieftains.* New York: Dover, 1997.

Edmunds, R. David. "Main Poc: Potawatomi Wabeno." *American Indian Quarterly* 9, no. 3 (Summer 1985): 259–72.

———. "Potawatomi." In Hoxie, *Encyclopedia of North American Indians,* 506–8.

———. *The Potawatomis: Keepers of the Fire.* Norman: University of Oklahoma Press, 1978.

Edmunds, R. David, and Joseph Peyser. *The Fox Wars: The Mesquakie Challenge to New France.* Norman: University of Oklahoma Press, 1993.

Elm, Demus, and Harvey Antone. *The Oneida Creation Story.* Translated and edited by Floyd G. Lounsbury and Bryan Gick. Lincoln: University of Nebraska Press, 2000.

Emerson, Thomas, et al., eds. *Late Woodland Societies: Tradition and Transformation across the Midcontinent.* Lincoln: University of Nebraska Press, 2000.

Erdoes, Richard, and Alfonso Ortiz, eds. *American Indian Myths and Legends.* New York: Pantheon, 1984.

———, eds. *American Indian Trickster Tales.* New York: Viking, 1998.

Erickson, Dave. *Gather Like the Waters.* Lone Rock, WI: Ootek Productions, 1994.

Fagan, Brian. *Ancient North America: The Archaeology of a Continent.* New York: Thames and Hudson, 1991.

Fawcett, Melissa Jayne. *Medicine Trail: The Life and Lessons of Gladys Tantaquidgeon.* Tucson: University of Arizona Press, 2000.

Fisher, Dexter. Foreword to *American Indian Stories,* by Zitkala-Ša. Lincoln: University of Nebraska Press, 1985.

Four Legs. Speech. August 7, 1827. In "Journal of Treaty at Butte Des Morts." Documents Relating to Negotiation, reel 2, frame 15.

Fowler, Verna. *The Menominee.* Austin, TX: Raintree Steck-Vaughn, 2001.

———. "Menominee." In Hoxie, *Encyclopedia of North American Indians,* 371–73.

Frazier, Patrick. *The Mohicans of Stockbridge.* Lincoln: University of Nebraska Press, 1992.

Gartner, William G. *The Geoarchaeology of Sediment Renewal Ceremonies at Gottschall Rockshelter, Wisconsin.* Madison: University of Wisconsin–Madison MS thesis, 1993.

Gedicks, Al. *Resource Rebels: Native Challenges to Mining and Oil Corporations.* Cambridge, MA: South End Press, 2001.

Geiogamah, Hanay, and Jaye T. Darby, eds. *Stories of Our Way: An Anthology of American Indian Plays.* Los Angeles: UCLA American Indian Studies Center, 1999.

Gibson, A. M. *The Kickapoos: Lords of the Middle Border.* Norman: University of Oklahoma Press, 1963.

Gill, Sam D., and Irene F. Sullivan. *Dictionary of Native American Mythology.* Santa Barbara, CA: ABC-CLIO, 1992.

Goc, Michael J., and Ben Guthrie, eds. *Reflections of Lac du Flambeau: An Illustrated History of Lac Du Flambeau, Wisconsin, 1745–1995.* Friendship, WI: New Past Press, 1995.

Green, Rayna, ed. *That's What She Said: Contemporary Poetry and Fiction by Native American Women.* Bloomington: Indian University Press, 1984.

Gresczyk, Rick, and Margaret Sayers. *Everyday Ojibwe.* Minneapolis: Eagle Works, n.d.

———. *Ojibwe Word Lists.* Minneapolis: Eagle Works, n.d.

Grizzly Bear [Kaushkannaniew]. Speech to Governor Porter. October 26, 1832. In Documents Relating to the Negotiation, reel 2.

Gross, Lawrence W. "Bimaadiziwin, or the 'Good Life,' as a Unifying Concept of Anishinaabe Religion." *American Indian Culture and Research Journal* 26, no. 1 (2002): 15–32.

Grossman, Zoltan. "The Ho-Chunk and Dakota Nations." In Wisconsin Cartographers' Guild, *Wisconsin's Past and Present*.

———. "Native Nations of Eastern Wisconsin." In Wisconsin Cartographers' Guild, *Wisconsin's Past and Present*.

Hall, Robert L. "Red Banks, Oneota, and the Winnebago: Views from a Distant Rock." *Wisconsin Archeologist* 74, nos. 1–4 (1993): 10–79.

Hampton, Carol. "Native American Church." In Hoxie, *Encyclopedia of North American Indians*, 418–20.

Harjo, Joy, and Gloria Bird, eds. *Reinventing the Enemy's Language:* Contemporary Native Women's Writing of North America. New York: Norton, 1997.

Hauptman, Laurence, and L. Gordon McLester III. *Chief Daniel Bread and the Oneida Nation of Indians of Wisconsin.* Norman: University of Oklahoma Press, 2002.

———, eds. *The Oneida Indian Journey: From New York to Wisconsin, 1784–1860.* Madison: University of Wisconsin Press, 1999.

Heath, Kristina. *Mama's Little One.* Gresham, WI: Muh-He-Con-Neew Press, 1998.

Henry, Gordon, Jr. *The Light People: A Novel.* Norman: University of Oklahoma Press, 1994.

Herring, Joseph. "Kenekuk, The Kickapoo Prophet: Acculturation Without Assimilation." *American Indian Quarterly* 9, no. 3 (Summer 1985): 295–307.

Highsmith, Hugh. *The Mounds of Koshkonong and Rock River: A History of Ancient Indian Earthworks in Wisconsin.* Fort Atkinson, WI: Fort Atkinson Historical Society and Highsmith Press, 1997.

Hill, Cornelius. *Ta Luh Ya Wa Gu.* Oneida: Holy Apostles Church Mission to the Oneidas, 1822–1972.

Hill, Roberta J. *See* Whiteman, Roberta Hill.

Hinton, Maria, ed. *A Collection of Oneida Stories.* Oneida, WI: Oneida Nation of Wisconsin, 1996.

Hirschfelder, Arlene, ed. *Native Heritage: Personal Accounts by American Indians, 1790 to the Present.* New York: Macmillan, 1995.

Hirthe, Nicole, and Brad Pecore. "Eunice Stick." In Mohican Nation Youth, *Stories of Our Elders*.

Hobson, Geary, ed. *The Remembered Earth: An Anthology of Contemporary Native American Literature.* Albuquerque: University of New Mexico Press, 1981.

Hoffman, W. J. "The Menominee Indians." 14th Annual Report, pt. 1. Washington, DC: Smithsonian Institution Bureau of American Ethnology, 1896.

Holiday, Diane, and Bobbie Malone. *Digging and Discovery: Wisconsin Archaeology.* Madison: State Historical Society of Wisconsin, 1997.

Holzhueter, John. *Madeline Island and the Chequamegon Region.* Madison: State Historical Society of Wisconsin, 1974.

Hornett, Danielle M. *Sage Dreams, Eagle Visions.* East Lansing: Michigan State University Press, 2004.

Hoxie, Frederick E., ed. *Encyclopedia of North American Indians: Native American History, Culture, and Life from Paleo-Indians to the Present.* New York: Houghton Mifflin, 1996.

Indian Country Wisconsin. "Potawatomi Oral Tradition." http://www.mpm.edu/wirp/ICW-137.html (accessed June 30, 2006).

Jackson, Donald, ed. *Black Hawk: An Autobiography.* Urbana: University of Illinois Press, 1955.

Johnston, Basil. *Ojibway Ceremonies.* Lincoln: University of Nebraska Press, 1990.

———. *Ojibway Heritage.* Lincoln: University of Nebraska Press, 1990.

———. *Ojibway Tales.* Lincoln: University of Nebraska Press, 1993.

Jones, Electa F. *Stockbridge, Past and Present; or, Records of an Old Mission Station.* Springfield, MA: Samuel Bowles, 1854.

Jones, William. "Episodes in the Culture-Hero Myth of the Sauks and Foxes." *Journal of American Folklore* 14 (October–December 1901): 225–39.

Joseph Johnson's speech to the Oneidas. January 20, 1774. Wheelock Papers. 774120. Dartmouth College.

Joseph Johnson's second speech to the Oneidas. January 24, 1774. Wheelock Papers. 774122. Dartmouth College.

Kapler, Joseph, Jr. "Austin Quinney." In "Beyond Face Value: Investigating Wisconsin's Painted Past." *Wisconsin Magazine of History* 87, no. 2 (Winter 2003/2004): 44–45.

Katz, Jane, ed. *I Am the Fire of Time: The Voices of Native American Women.* New York: Dutton, 1977.

———, ed. *Messengers of the Wind: Native American Women Tell Their Life Stories.* New York: Ballantine, 1995.

Keesing, Felix M. *The Menomini Indians of Wisconsin: A Study of Three Centuries of Cultural Contact and Change.* Madison: University of Wisconsin Press, 1987.

Kegg, Maude. *Portage Lake: Memories of an Ojibwe Childhood.* Edited by John D. Nichols. Minneapolis: University of Minnesota Press, 1993.

Kidder, Frederic. "Indian Treaties." *Maine Historical Society Collections* 4 (1856): 119–67.

King, Bruce. "Evening at the Warbonnet." In Geiogamah and Darby, *Stories of Our Way,* 357–406.

Kinietz, W. Vernon. *The Indians of the Western Great Lakes, 1615–1760.* Ann Arbor: University of Michigan Press, 1940.

Kinzie, Juliette M. *Wau-Bun: The "Early Day" in the Northwest.* Urbana: University of Illinois Press, 1992 [1856].

Kirk, Robin. *More Terrible Than Death: Massacres, Drugs, and America's War in Columbia.* New York: Public Affairs, 2003.

Klein, Laura F., and Lillian A. Ackerman, eds. *Women and Power in Native North America.* Norman: University of Oklahoma Press, 1995.

Koehler, Lyle. A Rock Art Survey in Western Jackson and Trempealeau Counties, Wisconsin, 1995–1996. La Crosse, WI: Mississippi Valley Archaeology Center, 1996.

Kohl, Johann Georg. *Kitchi-Gami: Life among the Lake Superior Ojibway.* St. Paul: Minnesota Historical Society Press, 1985 [1860].

Kroeber, Karl, ed. *Traditional Literatures of the American Indian: Texts and Interpretations.* 2nd ed. Lincoln: University of Nebraska Press, 1997.

Krupat, Arnold. *Ethnocriticism: Ethnography, History, Literature.* Berkeley: University of California Press, 1992.

———. *For Those Who Come After: A Study of Native American Autobiography.* Berkeley: University of California Press, 1985.

———. *Native American Autobiography: An Anthology.* Madison: University of Wisconsin Press, 1994.

Landes, Ruth. *The Mystic Lake Sioux: Sociology of the Mdewakantonwan Santee.* Madison: University of Wisconsin Press, 1968.

———. *Ojibwa Religion and the Midéwiwin.* Madison: University of Wisconsin Press, 1968.

———. *The Ojibwa Woman.* Lincoln: University of Nebraska Press, 1997.

Lapham, I. A. *Antiquities of Wisconsin, as Surveyed and Described.* Madison: University of Wisconsin Press, 2001.

Lauter, Paul, et al., eds. *The Heath Anthology of American Literature.* Lexington, MA: D.C. Heath, 1990.

Leeming, David, and Jake Page. *The Mythology of Native North America.* Norman: University of Oklahoma Press, 1998.

Lenzendorf, Dennis. *Effigy Mounds: A Guide to Effigy Mounds National Monument.* Fort Washington, PA: Eastern National, 2000.

Lesley, Craig, ed. *Talking Leaves: Contemporary Native American Short Stories.* New York: Dell, 1991.

Lewis, Theodore H. "Effigy Mounds Survey." Unpublished manuscript supplied courtesy of Robert Boszhardt, Mississippi Valley Archaeology Center, La Crosse, WI.

———. *Lewis Notebook Number 32. Northwestern Archeological Survey.* St. Paul: Minnesota Historical Society, 1891–92.

Lindquist, Mark, and Martin Zanger, eds. *Buried Roots and Indestructible Seeds: The Survival of American Indian Life in Story, History, and Spirit.* Madison: University of Wisconsin Press, 1994.

Lobo-Cobb, Angela, ed. *A Confluence of Colors: The First Anthology of Wisconsin Minority Poets.* Madison, WI: Blue Reed Arts, 1984.

———, ed. *Winter Nest: A Poetry Anthology of Midwestern Women Poets of Color.* Madison, WI: Blue Reed Arts, 1987.

Loew, Patty. *Indian Nations of Wisconsin: Histories of Endurance and Renewal.* Madison: Wisconsin Historical Society Press, 2001.

———. *Native People of Wisconsin.* Madison: Wisconsin Historical Society Press, 2003.

Love, W. DeLoss. *Samson Occom and the Christian Indians of New England.* Syracuse: Syracuse University Press, 2000 [1899].

Lowe, David. "Rock Art Survey of the Blue Mounds Creek and Mill Creek Drainages in Iowa and Dane Counties, Wisconsin." *Wisconsin Archeologist* 68, no. 4 (1987): 341–75.

Lurie, Nancy Oestreich, ed. *Mountain Wolf Woman, Sister of Crashing Thunder: The Autobiography of a Winnebago Indian.* Ann Arbor: University of Michigan Press, 1961.

———. "Winnebago." In Trigger, *Handbook of North American Indians,* 690–707.

———. *Wisconsin Indians.* Madison: State Historical Society of Wisconsin, 1980.

Lyons, Scott. "Rhetorical Sovereignty: What Do American Indians Want from Writing?" *College Composition and Communication* 51, no. 3 (2000): 447–68.

Makes Strong Move, Dawn. "Wak'djunk'aga and the Car." In David L. Smith, *Folklore of the Winnebago Tribe,* 40–41.

Marple, Eldon. *The Visitor Who Came to Stay: Legacy of the Hayward Area.* Hayward, WI: Country Print Shop, 1971.

Martin, Susan R. *Wonderful Power: The Story of Ancient Copper Working in the Lake Superior Basin.* Detroit: Wayne State University Press, 1999.

Mason, Carol I. *Introduction to Wisconsin Indians: Prehistory to Statehood.* Salem, WI: Sheffield Publishing, 1988.

Mason, Ronald J. "Oneota and Winnebago Ethnogenesis: An Overview." *Wisconsin Archeologist* 74, nos. 1–4 (1993): 400–21.

McBride, Elizabeth. "Written in Stone." *Wisconsin Trails*, August 1995, 20–25.

McCallum, James Dow, ed. *The Letters of Eleazar Wheelock's Indians.* Hanover, NH: Dartmouth College Publications, 1932.

McDonnell, Janet A. *The Dispossession of the American Indian, 1887–1934.* Bloomington: Indiana University Press, 1991.

McLester, Thelma Cornelius. "Oneida." In Hoxie, *Encyclopedia of North American Indians,* 441–43.

McLuhan, T. C. *Touch the Earth: A Self-Portrait of Indian Existence.* New York: Dutton, 1971.

Menominee. Speech. August 6, 1838. In Senator Tipton letter to Governor Wallace, September 18, 1838. *Indiana Historical Collections* 26:713–18.

Menominee, Chief. Menominee's Petition. November 15, 1836. In letter to Lewis Cass, U. S. secretary of war. National Archives, microfilm M234, roll 355, frames 715–16.

Meserve, Walter T. "English Works of Seventeenth-Century Indians." *American Indian Quarterly* 8, no. 3 (1956): 264–76.

Miantonomi. *Collections of the Massachusetts Historical Society* 3. Boston, 1833.

Miller, Jay. "Delaware." In Hoxie, *Encyclopedia of North American Indians,* 157–59.

Minutes of Indian Council, Michilimakinac County. *Historical Collections of Cofrin Library* 23: 453–54.

Mohawk, John C. "Iroquois Confederacy." In Hoxie, *Encyclopedia of North American Indians,* 298–302.

Mohawk Nation. *The Great Law of Peace of the Longhouse People [Kaianerekowa Hotinonsionne].* Akwesasne Notes Magazine, 1977.

———. *Our Traditional Teachings.* Cornwall Island, Ontario: North American Indian Traveling College, 1984.

Mohican Nation Youth. *Stories of Our Elders.* Gresham, WI: Muh-He-Con-Neew Press, 1999.

Momaday, N. Scott. *The Man Made of Words: Essays, Stories, Passages.* New York: St. Martin's, 1997.

———. "The Man Made of Words." In Trout, *Native American Literature.*

Montaur, Ted. "Handsome Lake." In Hoxie, *Encyclopedia of North American Indians,* 231.

Morrison, Eliza. *A Little History of My Forest Life: An Indian-White Autobiography.* Edited by Victoria Brehm. Tustin, MI: Ladyslipper Press, 2002.

Murphy, Lucy E. *A Gathering of Rivers: Indians, Métis, and Mining in the Western Great Lakes, 1737–1832.* Lincoln: University of Nebraska Press, 2000.

Nabokov, Peter, ed. *Native American Testimony: A Chronicle of Indian-White Relations from Prophecy to the Present, 1492–2000.* Rev. ed. New York: Penguin, 1999.

Narragansett Sachems. "Act of Submission." *Records of the Colony of Rhode Island.* Providence: A. C. Greene, 1856.

Neopit. *Shawano County Advocate,* March 16, 1882.

Nesper, Larry. *The Walleye War: The Struggle for Ojibwe Spearfishing and Treaty Rights.* Lincoln: University of Nebraska Press, 2002.

Niatum, Duane, ed. *Harper's Anthology of 20th Century Native American Poetry.* San Francisco: Harper & Row, 1988.

Nies, Judith. *Native American History: A Chronology of the Vast Achievements of a Culture and Their Links to World Events.* New York: Ballantine, 1996.

Nichols, John D., and Earl Nyholm. *A Concise Dictionary of Minnesota Ojibwe*. Minneapolis: University of Minnesota Press, 1995.

Northrup, Jim. *The Rez Road Follies: Canoes, Casinos, Computers, and Birch Bark Baskets*. Minneapolis: University of Minnesota Press, 1999.

———. *Walking the Rez Road*. Stillwater, MN: Voyageur Press, 1993.

Northrup, Jim, Denise Sweet, Marcie Rendon, and Linda Grover. *Nitaawichige: Selected Poetry and Prose by Four Anishinaabe Writers*. Duluth: Poetry Harbor, 2002.

Nute, Grace Lee. *The Voyageur*. St. Paul: Minnesota Historical Society Press, 1987 [1931].

Oberg, Michael Leroy. *Uncas: First of the Mohegans*. Ithaca, NY: Cornell University Press, 2003.

Oberly, James. "Decision on Duck Creek: Two Green Bay Reservations and Their Boundaries, 1816–1966." *American Indian Culture and Research Journal* 24, no. 3 (2000): 39–76.

———. "Tribal Sovereignty and Natural Resources: The Lac Courte Oreilles Experience." In Lindquist and Zanger, *Buried Roots*, 127–53.

O'Callaghan, E. B., ed. *Documents Relative to the Colonial History of the State of New York*. 15 vols. Albany: Weed, Parson, 1853–1887.

Occum, Samson. *A Sermon Preached by Samson Occum*. New Haven, CT: Thomas & Samuel Green, 1772.

Oneida Headman. Speech to Governor Trumbull. *American Archives*, 4th ser., vol. 2 (1775): 116–17.

Orie, Sandra De Coteau. *Did You Hear Wind Sing Your Name?: An Oneida Song of Spring*. New York: Walker, 1995.

Ortel, Jo. *Woodland Reflections: The Art of Truman Lowe*. Madison: University of Wisconsin Press, 2003.

Ottery, James. "Samson Occum's Diary and the Brothertown Indians: The Problem of Life Stories in the Other's Tongue." McNickle Center Collegium, Newberry Library, 2000. http://members.xoom.com/_XMCM/Brothertown/Brothertown/SamsonOccumbyJO.htm (accessed March 23, 2000).

———. "Samson Occum's Diary and Darcy McNickel's 'Train Time.'" *Studies in American Indian Literature* 13, no. 4 (Winter 2001).

Ottery, Will, and Rudi Ottery. *A Man Called Sampson*. Camden, ME: Penobscot Press, 1989.

Otto, Simon. *Ah-Soo-Can-Nah-Nah: Storyteller*. Indian River, MI: Talking Leaves, 1997.

Parkman, Francis. *The Conspiracy of Pontiac and the Indian War after the Conquest of Canada*. 2 vols. Reprint ed. Lincoln: University of Nebraska Press, 1994.

Pokagon, Simon. *Queen of the Woods [O-Gi-Maw-Kwe Mit-I-Gwa-Ki]*. Hartford, MI: C. H. Engle, 1899.

Potawatomi Web. "Menominee's Letters." http://www.kansasheritage.org/PBP/history/menomine.html (accessed June 30, 2006).

Potrykus, Kristina Heath. *See* Heath, Kristina.

Powell, Malea. "Blood and Scholarship: One Mixed-Blood's Story." In *Race, Rhetoric, and Composition*, edited by Keith Gilyard. Portsmouth, NH: Boynton/Cook Heinemann, 1999.

———. "Rhetorics of Survivance: How American Indians *Use* Writing." *College Composition and Communication* 53, no. 3 (2002): 396–434.

Powell, Suzanne. *The Potawatomi*. New York: F. Watts, 1997.

Prucha, Francis P, ed. *Documents of United States Indian Policy.* 2nd ed. Lincoln: University of Nebraska Press, 1990.

Radin, Paul. *Crashing Thunder: The Autobiography of a Winnebago Indian.* Lincoln: University of Nebraska Press, 1983.

———. *The Road of Life and Death: A Ritual Drama of the American Indians.* Princeton, NJ: Princeton University Press, 1973.

———. "The Thunderbird Warclub: A Winnebago Tale." *Journal of American Folklore* 44 (1973): 143–65.

———. *The Trickster: A Study in American Indian Mythology.* New York: Schocken, 1972.

———. *The Winnebago Tribe.* Lincoln: University of Nebraska Press, 1970.

Rasmussen, Charlie O. *Ojibwe Journeys: Treaties, Sandy Lake and the Waaabanong Run.* Odanah, WI: Great Lakes Indian Fish & Wildlife Commission Press, 2003.

———. *Where the River Is Wide: Pahquahwong and the Chippewa Flowage.* Odanah, WI: Great Lakes Indian Fish & Wildlife Commission Press, 1998.

Red Bird, David. "Little Brother Snares the Sun." In Erdoes and Ortiz, *American Indian Myths and Legends,* 164–66.

Ritzenthaler, Robert E., ed. "The Old Copper Culture of Wisconsin." *Wisconsin Archeologist* 38, no. 4 (1957): 185–329.

Ritzenthaler, Robert E., and Pat Ritzenthaler. *The Woodland Indians of the Western Great Lakes.* Milwaukee, WI: Milwaukee Public Museum, 1983.

Rosebrough, Amy, and Bobbie Malone. *Water Panthers, Bears, and Thunderbirds: Exploring Wisconsin's Effigy Mounds.* Madison: Wisconsin Historical Society Press, 2003.

Ross, Hamilton Nelson. *La Pointe: Village Outpost on Madeline Island.* Madison: State Historical Society of Wisconsin, 2000.

Ruoff, A. LaVonne Brown. Introduction to "Samson Occom (Mohegan), 1723–1792." In Lauter, *Heath Anthology of American Literature.*

Salzer, Robert. "Bear-Walking: A Shamanistic Phenomenon among the Potawatomi Indians in Wisconsin." *Wisconsin Archeologist* 53, no. 3 (1972): 110–411.

———. "Preliminary Report on the Gottschall Site." *Wisconsin Archeologist* 68, no. 4 (December 1987): 419–72.

———. "A Wisconsin Rock Art Site." *Wisconsin Academy Review* 33, vol. 2 (March 1987): 67–71.

———. "Wisconsin Rock Art." *Wisconsin Archeologist* 78, nos. 1–2 (1997): 48–76.

Salzer, Robert J., and Grace Rajnovich. *The Gottschall Rockshelter: An Archaeological Mystery.* St. Paul: Prairie Smoke Press, 2001.

Satz, Ronald. *Chippewa Treaty Rights: The Reserved Rights of Wisconsin's Chippewa Indians in Historical Perspective.* Madison: Wisconsin Academy of Sciences, Arts, and Letters, 1991.

Scherz, James P. "New Surveys of Indian Mound Layout." *Wisconsin Academy Review* 33, no. 2 (March 1987): 63–66.

Schoolcraft, Henry Rowe. *Algic Researches: North American Indian Folktales and Legends.* Mineola, NY: Dover, 1999 [1839].

———. *Historical and Statistical Information Respecting the History, Condition and Prospects of the Indian Tribes of the United States.* 6 vols. Philadelphia: Lippincott, Grambo, 1851–1857.

Severino, Carol, Juan C. Guerra, and Johnnella E. Butler, eds. *Writing in Multicultural Settings.* New York: Modern Language Association, 1997.

Silvern, Steven. "Reclaiming the Reservation: The Geopolitics of Wisconsin Anishi-naabe Resource Rights." *American Indian Culture and Research Journal* 24, no. 3 (2000): 131–83.

Simmons, William S. The Spirit of the New England Tribes: Indian History and Folklore, 1620–1984. Hanover, NH: University Press of New England, 1986.

Skinner, Alanson. "The Mascoutens or Prairie Potawatomi Indians, Part I: Social Life and Ceremonies." Bulletin of the Public Museum of the City of Milwaukee 6, no. 1 (1924): 1–260.

———. "The Mascoutens or Prairie Potawatomi Indians, Part II: Notes on the Material Culture." Milwaukee: Bulletin of the Public Museum of the City of Milwaukee 6, no. 2 (1924): 261–326.

———. "The Mascoutens or Prairie Potawatomi Indians, Part III: Mythology and Folklore." Bulletin of the Public Museum of the City of Milwaukee 6, no. 3 (1924/1927): 327–411.

———. *Social Life and Ceremonial Bundles of the Menomini Indians.* Anthropological Papers of the American Museum of Natural History 13, pt. 1. New York: American Museum of Natural History, 1913.

Skinner, Alanson, and John v. Satterlee, *Folklore of the Menomini Indians.* Anthropological Papers of the American Museum of Natural History 13, pt. 3. New York: American Museum of Natural History, 1915.

Slotkin, Richard, and James K. Folsom, eds. *"So Dreadfull a Judgment": Puritan Responses to King Philip's War, 1676–1677.* Middletown, CT: Wesleyan University Press, 1978.

Smith, David Lee, ed. *Folklore of the Winnebago Tribe.* Norman: University of Oklahoma Press, 1997.

———. "The History of the Winnebago People." Unpublished manuscript supplied courtesy of Dennis Lenzendorf, Effigy Mounds National Monument, Harpers Ferry, IA, 1994.

Smith, Susan Lampert. "Climbing the Education Mountain." *Wisconsin State Journal,* July 21, 2002, A1+.

———. "Oneidas Find Their Past in a Pile of Green Notebooks." *Wisconsin State Journal,* October 17, 1999, 1C+.

Smith, Waukon G. "Wak'djunk'aga and the Eagle." In David L. Smith, *Folklore of the Winnebago Tribe,* 33–34.

Soens, A. L., ed. *I, the Song: Classical Poetry of Native North America.* Salt Lake City: University of Utah Press, 1999.

Speck, Frank G. "Native Tribes and Dialects of Connecticut: A Mohegan-Pequot Diary." Forty-third Annual Report of the Bureau of American Ethnology to the Secretary of the Smithsonian Institution, 1925–1926. Washington, DC: Smithsonian, 1928.

Spindler, George, and Louise Spindler. *Dreamers without Power: The Menominee Indians.* New York: Holt, Rinehart, & Winston, 1971.

Spindler, Louise S. "Menominee." In Trigger, *Handbook of North America Indians,* 708–24.

Stevenson, Katherine. "The Woodland Tradition." *Wisconsin Archeologist* 78, nos. 1–2 (January–December 1997): 140–201.

"Stockbridge-Munsee Buy New York Land." *News From Indian Country* [Hayward, WI], November 2002, 2A.

Stoltman, James. "Prehistoric Mound Builders of the Mississippi Valley." Davenport, IA: Putnam Museum, 1985.

"Students' Right to Their Own Language." *College Composition and Communication* 25, no. 3 (Fall 1974): 1–32.

Sultzman, Lee. "Potawatomi History." The Citizen Potawatomi Nation. http://www.dickshovel.com/pota.html (accessed June 30, 2006).

Summers, Sarah. "Broken Spine and His Wife." In Hauptman and McLester, *Oneida Indian Journey*, 117–18.

Susag, Dorothea M. "Zitkala-Ša (Gertrude Simmons Bonnin): A Power(full) Literary Voice." *SAIL: Studies in American Indian Literatures* 5, no. 4 (Winter 1993): 3–24. http://oncampus.richmond.edu/faculty/ASAIL/SAIL2/54.html (accessed June 30, 2006).

Sweet, Denise. *Days of Obsidian, Days of Grace: Selected Poetry and Prose by Four Native American Writers.* Duluth: Poetry Harbor, 1994.

———. *Songs for Discharming: Poems.* Greenfield Center, NY: Greenfield Review Press, 1997.

Tanner, Helen Hornbeck, ed. *Atlas of Great Lakes Indian History.* Norman: University of Oklahoma Press, 1987.

———. *The Ojibwa.* New York: Chelsea House, 1992.

Tanner, John. *The Falcon: A Narrative of the Captivity and Adventures of John Tanner.* New York: Penguin, 1994 [1830].

Thayer, Crawford B., ed. *Massacre at Bad Axe: An Eye-Witness Account of the Black Hawk War of 1832.* [S.I.: s.n.,] 1984.

Theler, James L. "Animal Remains Recovered at Native American Archaeological Sites in the Upper Mississippi River Valley." Unpublished manuscript supplied courtesy of James Theler, University of Wisconsin–LaCrosse.

Theler, James L., and Robert F. Boszhardt. *Twelve Millennia: Archaeology of the Upper Mississippi River Valley.* Iowa City: University of Iowa Press, 2003.

Thompson, Stith, ed. *Tales of the North American Indians.* New York: Dover, 2000.

Tooker, Elisabeth, ed. *Native North American Spirituality of the Eastern Woodlands: Sacred Myths, Dreams, Visions, Speeches, Healing Formulas, Rituals, and Ceremonials.* New York: Paulist Press, 1979.

Trafzer, Clifford E., ed. *Blue Dawn, Red Earth.* New York: Doubleday, 1996.

———, ed. *Earth Song, Sky Spirit: Short Stories of the Contemporary Native American Experience.* New York: Doubleday, 1993.

Treaty Council. July 1829. Record Group 75, letters received, reels 696–702. Office of Indian Affairs, Prairie du Chien Agency, National Archives.

Treuer, Anton, ed. *Living Our Language: Ojibwe Tales and Oral Histories.* St. Paul: Minnesota Historical Society Press, 2001.

Treuer, David. *The Hiawatha.* New York: Picador, 1999.

———. *Little.* St. Paul: Graywolf Press, 1995.

Trigger, Bruce G., ed. *Handbook of North American Indians: Northeast*, vol. 15. Washington, DC: Smithsonian, 1978.

Trout, Lawana, ed. *Native American Literature: An Anthology.* Lincolnwood, IL: NTC Publishing, 1998.

Turner, Frederick W., ed. *The Portable North American Indian Reader.* New York: Penguin, 1977.

Two-Rivers, E. Donald. *Survivor's Medicine: Short Stories.* Norman: University of Oklahoma Press, 1998.

Vansina, Jan. *Oral Tradition as History.* Madison: University of Wisconsin Press, 1985.

Velie, Alan R., ed. *American Indian Literature: An Anthology.* Rev. ed. Norman: University of Oklahoma Press, 1991.

——, ed. *The Lightning Within: An Anthology of Contemporary American Indian Fiction.* Lincoln: University of Nebraska Press, 1991.

——, ed. *Native American Perspectives on Literature and History.* Norman: University of Oklahoma Press, 1995.

Vennum, Thomas, Jr. *Wild Rice and the Ojibway People.* St. Paul: Minnesota Historical Society Press, 1988.

Vizenor, Gerald. *The Everlasting Sky: Voices of the Anishinabe People.* St. Paul: Minnesota Historical Society Press, 2000.

——, ed. *Summer in the Spring: Anishinaabe Lyric Poems and Stories.* New ed. Norman: University of Oklahoma Press, 1993 [1965].

——, ed. *Touchwood: A Collection of Ojibway Prose.* St. Paul: New Rivers Press, 1987.

——. "Trickster Discourse: Comic Holotropes and Language Games." In *Narrative Chance: Postmodern Discourse on Native American Indian Literatures,* edited by Gerald Vizenor. Albuquerque: University of New Mexico Press, 1989.

Vogel, Virgil J. *American Indian Medicine.* Norman: University of Oklahoma Press, 1970.

——. *Indian Names on Wisconsin's Map.* Madison: University of Wisconsin Press, 1991.

Wallace, Paul A. W. *White Roots of Peace: The Iroquois Book of Life.* Santa Fe, NM: Clear Light, 1994 [1946].

Warhus, Mark. *Another America: Native American Maps and the History of Our Land.* New York: St. Martin's, 1997.

Warren, William W. *History of the Ojibway People* [reprint of *History of the Ojibways, Based upon Traditions and Oral Statements*]. St. Paul: Minnesota Historical Society Press, 1984 [1885].

Warrior, Robert Allen. "Eulogy on William Apess: Speculations on His New York Death." *Studies in American Indian Literature* 16, no. 2 (2004): 1–13.

——. *Tribal Secrets: Recovering American Indian Intellectual Traditions.* Minneapolis: University of Minnesota Press, 1994.

Weatherford, Jack. *Indian Givers: How the Indians of the Americas Transformed the World.* New York: Crown, 1988.

Whaley, Rick, and Walter Bresette. *Walleye Warriors: An Effective Alliance against Racism and for the Earth.* Philadelphia: New Society Publishers, 1994.

Wheelock, Eleazar, Papers. Collection 126, microfilm. Dartmouth College, Hanover, NH.

White, Lee. *How Mko Lost His Tail.* Crandon, WI: Indian Country Educational Supplies, 1999.

White, Richard. *The Middle Ground: Indians, Empires, and Republics in the Great Lakes Region, 1650–1815.* Cambridge: Cambridge University Press, 1991.

Whiteman, Roberta Hill. "The Long Parenthesis." In Green, *That's What She Said.*

——. *Philadelphia Flowers.* Duluth, MN: Holy Cow! Press, 1996.

——. *Star Quilt.* Duluth, MN: Holy Cow! Press, 2001.

——. "Under These Viaducts." *Northeast Indian Quarterly* 6, no. 4 (Winter 1989).

Wilson, James. *The Earth Shall Weep: A History of Native America.* New York: Atlantic Monthly Press, 1999.

Winnebago Petition. March 10, 1874. Roll 945. Office of Indian Affairs, Winnebago Agency, National Archives.

Wisconsin Cartographers' Guild. *Wisconsin's Past and Present: A Historical Atlas.* Madison: University of Wisconsin Press, 1998.

Wisconsin Cartographers' Guild, and Bobbie Malone. *Mapping Wisconsin History.* Madison: State Historical Society of Wisconsin, 2000.

Wolf, William. Lac Courte Oreille Council Minutes. May 17, 1921.

Womack, Craig S. *Red on Red: Native American Literary Separatism.* Minneapolis: University of Minnesota Press, 1999.

Wyatt, Sarah. "A Day in the Life of Wisconsin on January 1 of the Year 1000." *Wisconsin State Journal,* December 31, 1999.

Wyss, Hilary E. *Writing Indians: Literacy, Christianity, and Native Community in Early America.* Amherst: University of Massachusetts Press, 2000.